CHARLES EVANS HUGHES

THE MACMILLAN COMPANY
NEW YORK · BOSTON · CHICAGO
DALLAS · ATLANTA · SAN FRANCISCO

MACMILLAN AND CO., LIMITED
LONDON · BOMBAY · CALCUTTA
MADRAS · MELBOURNE

**THE MACMILLAN COMPANY
OF CANADA, LIMITED**
TORONTO

Charles E. Hughes

BY MERLO J. PUSEY

Charles Evans Hughes

IN TWO VOLUMES

Volume One

THE MACMILLAN COMPANY

New York · 1951

To
my wife and co-worker,
DOROTHY RICHARDS PUSEY

PREFACE

CHARLES EVANS HUGHES himself contributed more to this volume than any other individual. In declining many requests that he write his own story, he used to say that personal memoirs had a way of turning into apologia and therefore did not interest him. Knowing, however, that others would write about him, he wished them to have the facts. Through thirty-five years of public life he carefully preserved important documents and letters, and after his retirement as Chief Justice of the United States he wrote several hundred pages of biographical notes. These have been my primary sources of information.

Even more fruitful in some respects were my interviews with Mr. Hughes in the latter years of his retirement. During the spring and fall months that he spent in Washington, I visited him once or twice a week over a period of two and a half years. Seated at his desk in a reminiscent mood, he would often answer my questions for three hours without a break, speaking with candor and clarity—drawing upon his amazing memory of events over fourscore years. In this manner we reviewed his experiences as a youth and as a young lawyer and discussed all the momentous events of his public career.

Through the six years required to complete this biography, I had exclusive access to Mr. Hughes' voluminous papers in the Library of Congress and the Supreme Court and to part of his private correspondence. Among the former are extensive memoranda prepared in 1933 and 1934 by Henry C. Beerits with the aid and supervision of Mr. Hughes. These too proved to be an excellent source of background material. Mr. Beerits had also arranged and classified the Hughes Papers—those now in the Library of Congress—so as to make them more readily accessible.

Several interviews with Charles Evans Hughes, Jr., gave me new insight into his father's personality and an array of facts about their joint practice of law. In one of the busiest years of his career, the younger Mr. Hughes read my earlier chapters and offered many constructive suggestions. His untimely death in 1950 robbed his profession of one of its ablest and most eminent practitioners and deprived me of counsel that had proved of the utmost value.

Other members of the Hughes family have been most cooperative. I am especially indebted to Catherine Hughes Waddell and Elizabeth Hughes Gossett for permission to use many of the personal letters written by their father, mother, and grandparents—letters discovered on a closet shelf during the last illness of Chief Justice Hughes. Mrs. Waddell and her husband, Chauncey L. Waddell, and Mrs. Gossett and her husband, William T. Gossett, also read the entire manuscript and suggested corrections and additions. In no instance, however, did they request me to alter any conclusion. Responsibility for the tone of the work, for its imperfections, and for its appraisal of Charles Evans Hughes as a man and a public figure is entirely mine. It is an authorized but not an official biography.

Many of Mr. Hughes' friends and former associates gave invaluable help by way of interviews, letters, and criticism of different parts of the manuscript. Especially outstanding in this group are former Justice Owen J. Roberts, Chief Justice D. Lawrence Groner of the United States Court of Appeals (retired), and Edwin McElwain, Mr. Hughes' last law clerk, all of whom read the chapters on the Chief Justiceship; also Justices Felix Frankfurter, Robert H. Jackson, and Hugo Black of the United States Supreme Court; Chief Judge John J. Parker of the United States Court of Appeals, Fourth Circuit; Henry P. Chandler, Director of the Administrative Office of the United States Courts; Charles Elmore Cropley, clerk of the Supreme Court; Thomas E. Waggaman, marshal of the court; also former President Herbert Hoover; William D. Mitchell, former Attorney General; Sumner Welles, Joseph C. Grew, and Henry P. Fletcher, all former Undersecretaries of State; J. V. A. MacMurray, William R. Castle, Charles Cheney Hyde, A. W. Dulles, and William H. Beck.

I am heavily indebted to John Lord O'Brian for his advice and criticism of the governorship chapters; to Herbert Elliston and Francis White for similar aid in regard to some of the State Department chapters; to Joseph M. Lalley for his comments on the early chapters; to Dr. Anna Youngman for reading several chapters on economic policy; to Dr. Frederick M. Davenport for his help with the chapters on 1916; to Judge Meier Steinbrink for his stories and counsel, chiefly in connection with the aircraft investigation; to Henry M. Wriston for criticism of the chapter on Brown University; and to Allan Nevins and Charles E. Cuningham for many suggestions regarding the entire manuscript.

I wish also to thank Milo R. Maltbie, Grenville Clark, Roscoe Pound, Francis V. Keesling, Laurence H. Green, former Ambassador Edwin C. Wilson, Harvey D. Hinman, Senator Joseph C. O'Mahoney, former Senator Burton K. Wheeler, J. Reuben Clark, Jr., Edward M. Bassett, Mrs. J. Butler Wright, Mrs. Ruth B. Shipley, Michael J. McDermott, former Congressman James W. Wadsworth, William F. Unger, Ambassador David Bruce, Randolph Paul, John W. Davis, Fred K. Nielsen, G. Howland Shaw, Roy Vallance, Oscar R. Ewing, Harold L. Ickes, Mark DeWolfe Howe, E. Kimball MacColl,

Judge William H. Wadhams, and Charles Warren, historian of the Supreme Court; also Mrs. Franzetta DeGooyer, who typed the manuscript.

Finally I wish to thank Eugene Meyer, chairman of the board of the *Washington Post,* and Mrs. Meyer for their generous aid and encouragement, and Philip L. Graham, president and publisher of the *Washington Post,* for many helpful suggestions.

MERLO J. PUSEY

CONTENTS

Volume One.

ILLUSTRATIONS

Volume One

Volume Two

CHARLES EVANS HUGHES

Chapter 1

HOUR OF TRAVAIL

THE HOT wave of rebellion sweeping up from the South aroused Glens Falls to fighting fury. The townsfolk marched with torches—a "veritable river of fire" —for Abraham Lincoln. They recruited the stoutest of their sons for the Union Army. Patriotism mounted to a high pitch, but it did not save the picturesque paper-mill town on the Hudson River from the repercussions of the catastrophe that was shaking the nation.

Greenbacks drove hard money out of circulation, and the local authorities were forced to issue "shinplasters" to keep the economy functioning. Copperheads held clandestine meetings and openly raided the first drafting booths set up in the town. From New York City came news of a secession movement led by Mayor Fernando Wood himself, and the election of Horatio Seymour as governor of New York in 1862 was soon to add fears of revolution in the North to the perils of the war. Worst of all was the news of disaster following disaster that came from the battle fronts. As the stagecoach completed its run from Fort Edward, a flag would go up and the people would gather on the porch of the Glens Falls Hotel to hear the war news. Not infrequently some pair of these stern Hudson Valley folk went away sobbing over the loss of a soldier son.

In the cold spring of 1862, however, a temporary wave of cheering news reached the upper Hudson. The *Monitor* had met the *Merrimac* and forced that menacing raider to withdraw to Norfolk. Pensacola had been captured, and Grant was pounding his way through Tennessee. McClellan had begun his Peninsular Campaign. The North had found renewed hope, even though the war was making a heavy drain upon its resources and the peril overhanging the great American experiment was still keenly felt. It was in this hour of the nation's exertion to redeem itself from calamity that Charles Evans Hughes was born on April 11, 1862.

Outside of the Hughes household the event caused no stir. It had no announcement in the local press. The child's parents, the Reverend Mr. David Charles Hughes and Mary Catherine Connelly Hughes, had lived in Glens Falls only a year and a half—since the young pastor had accepted a call from the First Baptist Church in the autumn of 1860. Only five years before he had

1

landed on the shores of America from the Old World, alone and friendless. Fervent, energetic, and adventurous, he was one of the millions of poor immigrants who looked upon the United States as a land of promise.

In a brief period the young pastor had been absorbed into the New World ferment, becoming an evangelist for unity and freedom as well as Christian doctrine. Two months after his ordination at Glens Falls, he had been employed to fill a second pulpit—that of the First Baptist Church of near-by Sandy Hill (now Hudson Falls). This added $300 a year to his meager income and gave an additional outlet for his untiring efforts. In both churches he labored "with great acceptance," [1] preached the doctrine of abolition and pounded the pulpit in indignation over the activities of the Copperheads.

Through this exciting period the Hughes family lived humbly in a small one-story frame house, with the living-room door and two windows opening on quiet Maple Street a short distance from the church. Incidentally, this house was to be moved in the seventies from 135 Maple Street to its present location at 16 Center Street, and this would later give rise to a controversy as to whether it was actually the birthplace of Charles E. Hughes. At one time the State of New York would accept the claim that Governor Hughes came into this world within the house at 47 Maple Street.[2] But that claim would be undermined by eyewitnesses of the moving previously referred to [3] and by the recollections of old-timers in Glens Falls, including Mrs. Celia Gould Ames who took care of Mary Hughes during her confinement and gave the infant Charlie his first bath.[4]

David Charles Hughes was a product of the Wesleyan movement that had claimed the devotion of his forebears in the middle of the eighteenth century.[5] Of Welsh descent, he had been born in Monmouthshire, England, migrating in 1855 because he had been favorably impressed by Franklin's *Autobiography* and because he thought he had a "providential call" to preach in America. We first hear of him in the United States when he presented his credentials to the New York Conference of the Methodist Church.

"Well, young man," said the presiding elder, "I see that you are from Hingland."

"No, sir," David Charles replied, "I am from England."

"You'll do," was the presiding elder's abrupt decision.[6]

In three days the young Welshman who wished to become an American was sent to a little parish at Vails Gate on the slope of Storm King on the Hudson. His good English had given him a favorable introduction to America, and his

[1] A. W. Holden, *A History of the Town of Queensbury*, p. 203.
[2] *State Service* (New York State publication), November, 1919.
[3] Author's interview with Dr. Frederick G. Streeter, July 30, 1946.
[4] Author's interview with Mrs. William H. Barber, July 30, 1946.
[5] For details of David Charles Hughes' ancestry, see Appendix I.
[6] CEH, Biographical Notes, p. 9.

fluency and clear enunciation would further contribute to his early success in the ministry.

As a member of the New York Conference "on trial," he was appointed to the New Windsor Circuit, Newburgh District, and there he served until December, 1856. A letter of commendation from the presiding elder indicates that he gave up this work "to enter school & prepare for College." A private school in Maryland afforded him the opportunity of supporting himself by teaching some subjects while he studied others. About a year and a half later, however, he was in charge of a Methodist parish at Eddyville on Rondout Creek, New York, and it was there that he met and fell in love with Mary Catherine Connelly, whose parents' home was then at New Salem on the opposite side of the creek. By dint of preaching and teaching, he earned enough to carry him through a year at Wesleyan University in 1858–1859. At the end of that precious year he went cheerfully back to preaching and continued his scholastic efforts in his spare time. Having become proficient in Latin and Greek, he studied Hebrew during his thirties, aided at first by the instruction of a rabbi.

Mary Connelly became a great influence in his life from the moment he met her. Her father, William Connelly, Jr., invited the young preacher to go with him to the station at Rhinebeck to meet his daughter who was apparently returning from a year of schooling at Fort Edward Institute. David Charles saw her smile; he admired her golden hair and light blue eyes; he noted that she was delicate and reserved. When she spoke, he felt an intellectual kinship between them. Before he left her at this first meeting, he realized that he was in love.

His affection struck a responsive chord in Mary Connelly. They were drawn together by a common zeal for study, by the depth of religious feeling which they shared, and by their evangelical conceptions of Christian truth. There were sharp contrasts between them—between her fair complexion and his typically Welsh black hair, snapping black eyes, and swarthy skin. While she was cautious and reflective and of strong will, he was emotional, impulsive, generous, and sociable, with a flair for adventure. But these differences were complementary rather than antagonistic. The only real threat to their happiness was her mother's deep suspicion of this "foreigner" who had the audacity to fall in love with her daughter.

Margaret Ann Terpenning Connelly was a positive character who dominated her entire household, including her mild-mannered, blue-eyed husband. She viewed the courtship of her daughter by a young immigrant as many another clannish American mother has done. "Who was this upstart, this dark-hued Welshman? Who knew but that he had left a wife in Wales? Who really knew anything about him?" [7] Considering the fact that David Charles Hughes was a

7 *Ibid.*, p. 20.

stranger in a strange land and that Mary Connelly was a reserved and cautious young lady, his courtship could not be an easy one.

But Mary Connelly, despite her quiet nature, had a mind of her own.[8] She had escaped the limitations of her environment in the little Dutch community where she lived by attending two of the leading institutions of learning then open to young women. First, at Ford Edward Institute, she had delved into history, logic, the United States Constitution, Evidences of Christianity, Kames' *Elements of Criticism*, Cicero, French, and German. The following year she had spent at the Hudson River Institute at Claverack, where she specialized in French. Then she had taught in the little district school in Esopus and later established her own school for girls at Kingston.

It was soon evident that she loved the dark Welshman who persisted in courting her in spite of her mother's hostility. As to their religious differences, it was her influence that proved decisive. She had been brought up a Baptist. Her faith was "like that of the Christian martyrs," and those who knew her best felt that, notwithstanding her natural timidity, "she would have gone to the stake rather than be untrue to her religious convictions." [9] Through her persuasion the young Methodist preacher who had fallen in love with her became a Baptist. A certificate from Pastor William S. Mikels shows that David Charles Hughes joined the Sixteenth Baptist Church in New York on October 5, 1860. He married Mary Connelly in Kingston on November 20 of the same year.

The only child of this marriage has written of his parents: "They were brought together in a spiritual union which held them in the closest companionship as they pursued the same aims and cherished the same hopes. . . . Their love for each other, which at the outset had surmounted the obstacles raised by the differences in their early environment and in temperament, grew in strength throughout the forty-nine years of their union, as they labored together in unity of spirit for a common cause and with a profound faith. I have never known any persons more sincere in what they professed or more constantly dominated by a sense of religious duty." [10]

When their son was born, they looked upon him as a precious soul entrusted to their care, and, in spite of poverty, war, and political ferment, they bent every effort toward dedication of his life to the church.

[8] For details of Mary Connelly's ancestry, see Appendix II.
[9] CEH, Notes, p. 20.   [10] *Ibid.*, pp. 2, 20.

Chapter 2

HOTHOUSE ENVIRONMENT

CONSCIOUSNESS of the world about him had scarcely dawned for young Charlie Hughes when his parents moved to Sandy Hill. Like Glens Falls, Sandy Hill was a thriving paper-mill town. Its Baptist congregation raised the salary of the Reverend Mr. Hughes to $500 with a donation, or $600 without a donation, and he decided to devote himself exclusively to that parish. His family was received into the Sandy Hill church on May 15, 1863.[1]

Young Charlie learned to go to Church while he was still a toddler. For a time his mother's cousin, Kate van Nostrand, had been his nurse, but after a year or two his mother managed the household without assistance. Going to church thus became a necessity, for his father conducted the services and his mother sang in the choir. The strain of sitting through religious services was relieved in some measure when a close friend of his parents, Mrs. Charles Stone, gave him a little rocking chair that could be placed beside his mother in the choir gallery. He became very fond of that chair, and it has been handed down through the Hughes family as a relic.

At Sandy Hill, too, he made an impressionable acquaintance with Nellie, the family's cream-colored mare. Nellie was accustomed to both saddle and harness. On her back, or behind her in buggy or sleigh, Pastor Hughes made the rounds of his parish. Sometimes Nellie hauled the whole family on excursions to Fort Edward or Glens Falls. The exciting trip behind Nellie to the Stones' residence where he was given the little chair was Charlie Hughes' earliest recollection.[2] From these days he also retained dim memories of the martial music that was frequently heard in Sandy Hill—of his father giving words of encouragement to the men who were ready to march away in defense of the Union. Still more memorable was "the awful strain, the cry of anguish, when the news came of the death of our martyred President." [3] Young Charlie had good reason to remember the assassination of Lincoln. When his father came bursting into the house with the tragic news from Washington, he was in a state of grief that the child had never before witnessed. "Mary," cried the distracted pastor to his wife, "I could not feel worse if you had been killed." [4]

The reputation of the Reverend Mr. Hughes for enthusiastic preaching and

---

[1] *The First Baptist Church of Hudson Falls, N.Y.: A Brief History.*
[2] CEH, Notes, p. 43.   [3] Governor Hughes' speech at Sandy Hill, August 27, 1907.
[4] CEH, Notes, p. 21.

devotion to his parish spread to other New York towns in spite of the meager communications of the day. On February 14, 1866, Deacon Harmon, speaking for the pulpit committee of the West Baptist Church at Oswego, suggested that the congregation extend a call to "Rev. Mr. Hews of Sandy Hill to become our pastor." [5] Brother Thomas Kingsford, who had made starch big business in Oswego even in the sixties, moved to offer "Rev. Mr. Hews" $1,200 annually. To this the congregation added a "donation." The Sandy Hill Baptists were reluctant to let their pastor go and did not accept his resignation when he first tendered it. Nor did he accept the new call immediately, but went to Oswego for four weeks "that he might become acquainted with the church and they with him." [6] The tryout brought mutual satisfaction, and the new pastor plunged into the work of building up the parish and getting its $70,000 meeting-house completed.

The Hugheses' new home at 40 West Oneida Street was a two-story white frame house with green shutters and front porch set back a respectable distance behind an ornamental picket fence. Here Charlie found new playmates, including Ginny (Virginia) Kingsford, who was about his own age, and Florence Sprague, who was somewhat older than he. Charlie was a delicate little fellow. Although a vigorous infant at birth, he had suffered, at the age of two, an attack of what was called "inflammation of the lungs," which left him an easy prey to several maladies. The winter winds off Lake Ontario seemed to cut through him, producing chronic catarrh. He suffered much from tonsilitis; no one in those days suggested the removal of tonsils. Nearly all the usual diseases of childhood came his way, including a serious case of scarlet fever, but that was not until he was ten. Contributing further to his lack of robustness was a very whimsical appetite. "For years," he tells us in his Biographical Notes, "I did my best to resist the efforts to persuade me to eat meat and vegetables. My diet was chiefly milk, graham bread, griddle cakes and maple syrup, 'johnny-cake' and honey."

But for the devotion and intelligent care of his mother, a born nurse, Charlie probably would not have lived to maturity. As he was an only child, his mother could give most of her attention to his physical well-being and his spiritual and mental training. He was taught to read at the age of three and a half. Memorizing was easy for him, and he soon had a fairly large repertoire of biblical lore. Weakness of the eyes—a handicap which persisted in some degree throughout his youth but which he fully overcame in later life—threatened to impede his progress. When he was five, his mother gave him a *New Testament and Psalms* with large type so that he could take his turn in reading the verses at family prayers, and when even that help proved insufficient he would recite verses from memory.

[5] West Baptist Church Record Book No. 1.   [6] *Ibid.*

Religious zeal and moral fervor infused all his early education. His precocity encouraged his mother to believe that he would have a great career in the ministry, and she redoubled her efforts to prepare him for it even before he reached school age. The youngster had scarcely a waking moment in his mother's presence without being instructed in one way or another. As an experienced teacher, she was elated by practicing her pedagogical art on so receptive a pupil. And for him the absorption of information was a fascinating experience.

Strict discipline accompanied her teaching. While Charlie was encouraged to pursue the studies he especially liked, he was not permitted to neglect any subject that his mother regarded as essential. As he advanced in the "three R's," he was started in Fasquelle's *Lessons*, which gave him at least a foundation in French. His mother also took him through a German primer. She was strong in mathematics, and her exercises in "mental arithmetic" gave Charlie the most useful training he ever had.[7] She would have him toe a mark on the floor and, without changing his position, "do in his head" the various sums she gave him. He was urged to think quickly and accurately without recourse to paper or pencil—a faculty that would add greatly to his prowess as investigator, advocate, and public speaker.

At six Charlie was sent to school in Oswego and acquired an acute dislike for it. School meant for him unnecessary confinement and an incredible waste of time. He listened with increasing boredom to the teacher's repetition of morsels of learning that were already familiar to him. In later years he denied that he had been in any sense a prodigy, and insisted that some descriptions of his early performances were overdrawn.[8] But he had certainly experienced a hothouse intellectual growth that left him quite out of place in the Oswego school.

After three or four weeks he begged for the privilege of resuming his studies at home. Having planned his campaign carefully, he walked into his father's study and handed him a neat little document entitled "Charles E. Hughes' Plan of Study." With initiative, order, and foresight that are certainly rare in a youngster of six years, he had listed in separate columns each subject that he wished to study at home and the hour that he would give to it. Of course, this does not mean that he had no interests beyond books, study, and religion. Years later, when his father, with understandable parental pride, had informed the press of the "Plan," Hughes dismissed it as solely a means of giving him more time to play "when the studying was done." [9]

The "Plan" was accepted, and Charlie made a practice of beginning his lessons early in the morning, before his parents were up. He sat by the great stove in the living room—the "Morning Glory," very high and imposing, sending out its heat to the room above as well as to the main living quarters. The

[7] CEH, Notes, p. 26.   [8] *Ibid.*   [9] *Outlook,* Oct. 20, 1906, p. 405.

memory of its red coals shining through the isinglass became inseparably associated in his mind with the studies he pursued under his "Plan." [10]

Charlie's father sought to guide the boy's reading, which soon became extensive. The elder Hughes had an unquenchable desire for books, and this had led him to extravagances in accumulating a large library. Mrs. Hughes' thrift and caution saved the household from debt in spite of these outlays. But the family experienced many privations, and its treasures (such as were not laid up in Heaven) were very largely contained between the covers of books.

When Charlie was five, his father gave him a copy of Miss Corner's *England and Wales*—a history "adapted for youth, schools and families." Fact and not fiction was what the elder Hughes prescribed. One day he found his son engrossed in a story book from the Sunday School library, his cheeks flushed with pleasure and excitement. The lad was invited to walk with his father along the shore of Lake Ontario.

"Charlie, do you know why these stones are of different colors?" the father asked as he gathered up a handful of pebbles.

"No, sir, I don't."

"Do you know why they are smooth and round?"

"No, sir."

"Would you like to know?"

"Yes, sir." [11]

The elder Hughes then said that it is much more important to know why pebbles are round and smooth than to have the most intimate acquaintance with Jack the Giant Killer or the Forty Thieves. On his sixth birthday, Charlie received *The Wonders of Science, or Young Humphry Davy*—the boy "who taught himself Natural Philosophy." A complete set of *Chambers's Miscellany* was also put into his hands, and he spent many hours browsing over its carefully digested information and selected literature.

Charlie's father tutored him in Greek, and on his eighth birthday presented him with a Greek *New Testament with Lexicon*. The lad could not do much with this, but he learned the alphabet and he liked to look up words in the lexicon. "I remember," he wrote in his old age, "that I was able, to the amusement of the family and others, to rattle off the genealogy of the first chapter of Matthew. My efforts were aided by another Greek *Testament* with the English version in a parallel column and in a childish way I liked to compare the Greek and English words." [12]

Meanwhile the Reverend Mr. Hughes had greatly enriched the spiritual life of Oswego. In appreciation the congregation raised his salary to $1,800 a year in 1867 and agreed to give him an additional $200 at the end of the year

[10] CEH, Notes, p. 27.
[11] Burton J. Hendrick, in *McClure's Magazine*, March, 1908, p. 521.
[12] CEH, Notes, p. 28.

"provided there be money in the church treasury not otherwise appropriated." In January, 1869, the pastor conducted a week of prayer meetings, "and such a week," the clerk recorded, "has not before in years been enjoyed by our church." [13] So rich was the manifestation of the spirit that the congregation voted to continue the meetings for two more weeks. In three years the pastor's untiring zeal had brought 106 souls into the church.[14]

Nevertheless, dissension arose. The warmhearted and impetuous pastor had endeared himself to the rank and file, but he had also antagonized a few powerful members. In a meeting on March 25, 1869, Brother Kingsford reported a prospective indebtedness of $700. It was a sign of discontent. The pastor summoned Brother Harmon to the chair, reviewed "in a few feeling words" his three years spent with the congregation, and tendered his resignation.

Young Charlie, aged seven, sat alone in the minister's pew, listening to these strange proceedings with increasing apprehension. Should he stay, he asked himself, when the other nonmembers filed out at the conclusion of the religious services? His father had asked all *members* to remain, and he was not yet a member. In spite of this, he decided to sit tight because his father was still there. When his father offered his resignation and withdrew to the study, however, the lad was frightened and followed his father into retreat.[15]

A flood of protests then broke loose against acceptance of the pastor's resignation. "Remarks expressive of the highest esteem for Bro. Hughes were indulged in by Brethren William H. Harmon, Burt, Rope, Colby, Selden Clark, Thompson, and Sister Smith." [16] The congregation unanimously resolved not to accept the resignation, and the Reverend Mr. Hughes withdrew it. A few weeks later, however, after he had attended the "anniversarys" at Boston, he again resigned, with the explanation that two or three influential brethren were trying to prejudice the people against him. Since the Lord had opened another field of labor to him, he said, his resignation would have to be considered irrevocable. "This was very unexpected," the faithful clerk wrote into his minutes, "and many were there that wept like children in fact the whole assembly did save a few, it was to [sic] much for them to bear, to think that they have got to part with a Bro. and Pastor whom they so much loved." [17]

Emotion was also at a high pitch on the last Sunday that the Hugheses spent at the Oswego church, on June 6, 1869. The members expressed their "affectionate esteem" and resolved that "in the labors of Bro. Hughes and his devoted wife, we have discovered the power of an earnest Christian life. We

[13] West Baptist Church Record Book No. 1, Jan. 9, 1869.
[14] *History of West Baptist Church, Oswego, N.Y., 1853–1897*, p. 41.
[15] Author's interview with CEH, Oct. 15, 1946.
[16] Church Record Book No. 1, March 25, 1869.
[17] *Ibid.*, May 30, 1869.

beg to assure them that their unselfish labors among us will never be forgotten and that our prayers . . . will follow them." [18]

With the memory of this friendly farewell warming their hearts, the Hugheses moved to Newark and were soon settled in the parsonage of the Fifth Baptist Church. Being an evangelist at heart, David Charles Hughes rejoiced in the enlarged opportunity which Newark offered. Here he was close to the throbbing pulse of the new America that was in the making. Here was greater need for his unflagging industry, for his ministrations to the afflicted and the unfortunate, and for his spirited sermons. In financial reward, too, he had probably made some gain, for free use of the parsonage at Newark supplemented his $1,500 a year. The Hugheses thanked God for all these blessings and entered upon a new chapter in their ministry with intensified devotion to the Christian ideal.

[18] *Ibid.*, June 6, 1869.

Chapter 3

SCHOOL AT LAST

MRS. HUGHES, as well as her son, was "delicate" in health. When she was a child, the family doctor had once brusquely remarked, "Mary, you will never make old bones." In her mature years that prognosis gave her husband many anxious hours, and one day he communicated his uneasiness to his son. Charlie, with the budding self-assertion of a nine-year-old, had spoken rudely to his mother. "My boy," his father rebuked him in private, "you must never speak to your mother in that way. She will not be with us very long." From that time on, Hughes tells us, "I always regarded my mother with a certain anxiety, but she well understood the care of the body and had her little remedies for temporary ailments. She bore all the burdens of a pastor's wife with unfailing regularity and with a constant joy in the performance of duty." [1]

Charlie continued to be afflicted with various ailments. The parsonage at 164 Elm Street was near what were then unreclaimed marshes, and fever and ague (*malaria*) were prevalent. But he was wiry and took great pains to develop his physical strength with the aid of a horizontal bar and two flying rings that his father had erected in the yard back of the parsonage.

Adjoining the parsonage was a vacant lot where he played baseball with the boys of the neighborhood. "One old cat" and "two old cat" were their favorite forms of the national game, and over the fence was "out." When Charles E. Hughes, candidate for the Presidency of the United States, revisited this spot in 1916, he recalled that one day while he was playing there as a youngster a friend aimed a chestnut burr with unfortunate accuracy at the head of a passer-by. The friend disappeared with lightning speed, while Charlie stood in his tracks, laughing. The man with the stinging cheek came over and knocked him down, and he rolled all the way to the foot of a high bank on which he had been standing. [2]

Charlie Hughes and his friends had no television, no motion pictures, no comic strips, no radio. But they did not know what they missed. Interspersed among their glorious days of baseball were happy hours given to "cops and robbers," "red lion," and other games. In winter the Chief Justice-to-be had great fun with his sled "hooking rides" behind passing carts.

For the days when Charlie could not play outdoors, he had other diversions.

[1] CEH, Notes, p. 21.　　[2] Author's interview with CEH; *New York Times*, Oct. 7, 1916.

As he had no brother or sister, he learned to play alone. At one time his parents thought of adopting a child to give him companionship, but Charlie, overhearing the discussion and knowing the family's meager resources, marched into the room and said he thought it would be a mistake. It was more important, he said, to give him an education than companionship at home.

"One of my favorite sports was 'travel,'" he tells us. "In the attic in the Newark parsonage, I had a large playroom. One of my father's parishioners gave me an enormous hobby-horse, about as big as a small pony, and I rigged up a shoe-box, with a driver's seat and whipsocket, and with trunk straps for reins I set forth on my journeys which were very extensive. I loved to get hold of a travel book and pretend, with the book before me, to go with my stout steed from place to place. Especially helpful in these excursions was Thomson's *Land and the Book*, descriptive of Palestine with inset pictures, and I traveled up and down that land, reading the descriptions to aid my imagination, as they seemed very familiar in view of my Bible lessons." [3]

In this period, too, Charlie became more familiar with his father's library. It consisted mainly of theological works, commentaries, histories, biographies, and works of reference—a formidable mental diet for a youngster. But he learned to know each book at least from its cover, and he catalogued a "good part of them." While he completed his "required reading" willingly, his real delight came from browsing through the library for interesting stories. These he seized upon with the zest of an explorer entering a choice but unknown land.

When he discovered *The Pilgrim's Progress*, he read it several times. This led him to Bunyan's *The Holy War*. At the age of eight a large volume of Shakespeare's plays piqued his curiosity, and he struck up a fascinated acquaintance with the Bard. "Of course I could not appreciate Shakespeare at so early an age," he wrote from the viewpoint of mature reflection, "but I loved the stories. *The Tempest, Twelfth Night* and *The Merry Wives of Windsor* were my favorites." [4] In the same manner he discovered Byron, Tom Moore, and a book of anecdotes for ministers. On his ninth birthday his father gave him a copy of Coffin's *The Seat of Empire* which he had obtained in Minneapolis while attending a religious meeting there. Charlie was so thrilled by this description of the Northwest that he resolved that he would make his home in Minneapolis when he grew up. His choicest possession, however, was a profusely illustrated copy of *Robinson Crusoe* which had been brought from England and given to him by James Clare.

This young Englishman, James Clare, who lived with the Hughes family in Newark for some time and taught Charlie in Sunday school, described his pupil as being "wrapped up in his books" and as a proficient Bible student. But he never regarded Charlie Hughes as a bookworm. "Withal he was a regu-

3 CEH, Notes, pp. 28, 29.   4 *Ibid.*, pp. 29, 30.

lar boy," Clare once told the press, "delighting in boyish pranks, even if his father or his Sunday school were the victims." [5] Fun of every sort had a strong attraction for Charlie, although his bent toward mischief was restrained by the keen sense of discipline implanted in him by his parents.

Charlie made a "second experiment in attending school" at the age of eight and again gave it up. The following year, however, he attended the Tenth Ward Public School in Oliver Street, entering one grade below the graduating class. "My chief interest in the school work," he wrote of this experience, "was in the course in American History, taught by Mrs. [J. A.] Hallock, the wife of the Principal. She was one of the best teachers I ever had. She seemed to give me special attention and I loved her dearly." [6] His scholastic record hovered close to the perfection mark. In 1873, the year of his graduation, his report card bore seven marks of one hundred, two of ninety-nine, one of ninety-eight, and two of ninety-seven.

The happiest times of Charlie Hughes' early youth came in the long summer days that he spent on Grandfather Connelly's fruit farm at Port Ewen. The place had a restful and enticing atmosphere, with stately fir trees on each side of the walk leading to the house and other fine trees shading the front lawn. More important to a youngster of Charlie's fertile imagination was its enchanting view of the Hudson River.

"My outing began," he recalled, "with a trip on the 'Mary Powell,' the fastest and most graceful steamer on the Hudson River, leaving New York in the afternoon and reaching her berth at Rondout between eight and nine in the evening. I generally went on Saturday with my Uncle 'Simmie' [7] (whose family made their home with my grandfather). I sat on the deck with him and a number of his cronies from the Custom House (who also had their families up the river) and I heard endless discussion on New York politics which seemed to me a world of extraordinary cunning. Then, there were the good playtimes with my cousins. I took my part in berry-picking, but when I was nine or ten, being overcome by the heat, I was made paymaster, receiving the berries and paying the berry-pickers. Then there was the gathering of apples, a chore I never liked. But it was fun to drive with my grandfather in the late afternoon to Rondout Creek where the fruit was put on the steamer for New York. I recall that my father, who had been much on horseback in his first parishes, and prided himself on his horsemanship, wished me to learn to ride and sent the saddle he had used to my grandfather's place. So I saddled 'Billy'—the trusted family horse— and galloped about on the dusty country roads. Best of all, there was a rustic seat under an apple tree at the far end of the orchard which lay on the crest of a knoll commanding an extensive view up the river. I never tired of that

[5] Newark *Sunday Call*, Feb. 9, 1930.
[6] CEH, Notes, p. 30.   [7] Carey Simpson Connelly.

charming scene. Immediately below was the mouth of Rondout Creek with its busy boats, the most of which I learned to know as well as the larger steamers which called across the river at Rhinebeck. The river teemed with life, always interesting, but I loved the river itself, with its broad sweep and majestic serenity, and the view of the rolling upland toward the Berkshires on the East and of the Catskills to the North,—the wonderful heights, as they then seemed to me, full of mystery and legend. On the warm summer days, whenever I had a chance, I would sit and watch the river in a sort of enchantment." [8]

On June 14, 1875, Charlie wrote to his parents from Port Ewen the first letter of his that has survived:

I again have the pleasure of writing from this little Paradise. The country air surrounds me while the sun shines forth in its brilliancy and Grandpa's well welcoming the thirsty to draw and drink. Such is my situation, and now I guess I am beginning to see the loveliness, beauty and glory of nature. . . .

This morning I rode "Billy" very long, first with the sheepskin, and I got him so he can run as fast as you please and don't hurt me. He does not canter a bit. I put the saddle on him afterward and it went just as well. I can harness, unharness, put saddle on and off and tend to him, clean him, etc.

I hope you have a pleasant time on the excursion. Please excuse my absence and give my love to all who inquire after me. Write as soon as you receive this. Grandma and Grandpa are well and send their love to you—so are Aunt Hattie, Charlie, Henry, Mamie, Maggie. Charlie is as cunning as he can be. He is our pet and it has been very curious to me to see the different phases of character—first, in Charlie, 16 months old—then, in Henry, a boy of 4—then, in Maggie, of 8 and then, Mamie, 10. And, then, myself, 13 . . .

But I must draw to a close. I hope that you will pray earnestly for me. That, if it be possible, I may regain some of the spiritual power I once possessed and more completely obey the sentiments expressed in Ephesians 6:1. [The citation reads: "Children, obey your parents in the Lord: for this is right."]

Here is the first intimation that the intense religious zeal that Charlie's parents had instilled into him was beginning to wane. The lad was starting to think for himself, and while his budding sense of differing with his parents disturbed him at first, it did not seem to interfere with his enjoyment of life.

In the summer of 1873 came an entirely new thrill. The Hugheses decided to treat themselves to the almost incredible luxury of a trip to Europe. The journey they had often dreamed of became feasible when Leonard W. Cronkhite of Sandy Hill, a friend at whose home the Hughes family frequently visited during their August vacations, advanced the necessary funds on easy terms. The trip was planned primarily in the interests of Mary Hughes' health, but her husband was eager to visit his relatives in England and Wales, and their son was panting for adventure. They sailed in June on the *City of Antwerp*,

8 CEH, Notes, pp. 31–32.

landed at Liverpool, and went directly to Abertillery, Monmouthshire, where Mr. Hughes' sister lived.

Charlie was keenly disappointed in his Aunt Jane. She was postmistress of Abertillery and obviously a woman of ability. Since the death of her husband, Edward Jones, she had also continued his business—a general store. But she had opposed her brother's migration to the United States, and now, after eighteen years, it was apparent that she had never forgiven him for becoming an American and marrying an American woman. One night in a London lodginghouse Charlie was awakened by his father's sobbing because of the icy reception his sister had accorded him. The lad pretended to remain asleep and overheard his mother's efforts to soothe his father's grief. The incident widened the gulf that already existed in his mind between himself and his Aunt Jane.

David Charles Hughes had become thoroughly Americanized by early naturalization as well as by habit and turn of mind. Young Charles' upbringing had been completely dominated by American thought and custom; he never acquired any feeling of identification with his father's kin abroad. On the steamer he had fought over the American Revolution with an English boy, and when he got to Wales his relatives there seemed entirely foreign to him. In later years, when his name had become well known in Europe, the Welsh effusively claimed him as their own, and the University of Wales twice offered him an honorary degree. He accepted neither the adoption nor the degree. While he greatly admired the character of the Welsh, he refused to forget the Dutch, Scotch-Irish, English, and German strains in his ancestry; and his feeling of oneness with a people was reserved for his own American countrymen.

Charlie was much more favorably impressed by his uncles. His father's brother Jabez, whom they visited in South Wales, proved to be "a kindly man, full of humor." His uncle John Richard Hughes was an eminent preacher of the Calvinistic Methodist denomination at Anglesey, North Wales. Charlie went to hear his Uncle John preach in Welsh and was deeply affected even though he could not understand a word of it. Uncle John had what the Welsh call *hwyl*— that mysterious power which seems to give a Celtic orator unexplained eloquence and excites his listeners without their knowing why they are excited.

Taking leave of relatives, the Hugheses were lured by the scenes that have drawn many thousands of Americans to the Old World. Charlie found Warwick Castle so fascinating that he wrote a theme on the subject when he returned to school. The armor, jewels, and ancient furniture held his interest, but most curious of all was the "famous iron porridge pot, which holds 102 gallons, and which he [Sir Guy, the giant, Earl of Warwick in the tenth century] had filled every morning for his breakfast." In London they took a room in a King Street lodginghouse with only one bed for three, but spent two exciting weeks sightseeing. Religion was not forgotten. Twice they went to hear Charles Spurgeon, and father and son made notes on his sermons. After London, came the thrill of exploring Paris. Charlie's enjoyment of the journey was "beyond words." He devoured the guidebooks with unflagging enthusiasm and became so well informed on London and Paris that his parents permitted him to plan many of their excursions. His mind registered so faithfully what he saw that when he again visited Europe as a young man these two cities seemed very familiar.

Returning to Wales from Paris, they took passage for New York on the *City of Richmond*. It was the first trip for this steamer, and she was trying to undercut the record of a sister ship which was said to have crossed the Atlantic in seven days. Engine trouble developed, however, and, as the vessel approached Nantucket Shoals in a dense fog, a shrill feminine scream of terror turned the anxiety of the passengers into panic. Frightened men and women in their night attire filled the passageways. Rumors of a terrible accident ran through the disheveled crowds. Charlie Hughes thought the ship might be going down, and he never forgot the excitement of that scene. Not until the next morning did they learn the reason for the commotion. A young actress who had imbibed too much at a gay champagne supper had gotten into the wrong stateroom. After disrobing in the dark, so as not to disturb her companion, she had aimed at the top berth and happened to grasp its occupant by the beard. Her screams as she ran from the room had been given an absurd misinterpretation because of the prevailing anxiety.[9]

At the age of eleven Charlie entered the Newark High School. It was an excellent school, and he looked forward to preparing for college by the fall of 1877. Especially to his liking was the Latin course taught by John L. Heffron, a tall, handsome young graduate of Madison (now Colgate) University. But high-school days for Charlie Hughes were to be very brief. During the recess one day in January, 1874, he joined in a game of "red lion," as he had often done before. A group of boys with their hands linked together chased and caught him. In accord with the rules of the game, he joined the line and the chase continued, the line growing ever longer. With all the heedlessness of adolescents acting in unison, the line whipped its center link into a stone pillar. That center link was Charlie. He lost his two upper front teeth and was badly hurt. Before he recuperated from this experience, his father resigned his pastorate in Newark and the family moved to New York.

[9] CEH, Notes, p. 33.

Chapter 4

SIDEWALKS OF NEW YORK

CHARLES E. HUGHES was to become the most conspicuous figure in New York, and, later on, its foremost lawyer. His name and his doings were to fill many thousands of columns in the city's leading newspapers. In 1874, however, his introduction to the great metropolis was very humble. His father accepted a secretaryship in the American Bible Union, and the family found lodgings in the four-story brownstone house at 32 Great Jones Street in which the Union had its headquarters. The remainder of the house was rented to other lodgers, with Mrs. Hughes acting as landlady.

The boy's schooling became a baffling problem. New York had no public high school that he could attend. Graduates of the public schools entered the College of the City of New York, which offered a five-year course. But the college would take no student under the age of fourteen, and Charlie was not yet twelve. His only chance of getting back into school was to join the graduating class of a New York public school, and even for this he would have to wait until the following September. Circumstances thus conspired to give him more than six months of freedom in a city that held unlimited fascination for him.

Up to this time Charlie had visited New York only occasionally in the company of his father when he attended the Ministers' Conference on Mondays. He had been much excited by the crush of traffic on lower Broadway, with irate policemen and swearing drivers trying to extricate the stalled buses and trucks. Now he was free to explore all the city's wonders, and in spite of the inferiority complex he had acquired because of his missing front teeth, he lost no time in getting his excursions under way.

Being near the center of the city, Great Jones Street was an ideal base for the young explorer's operations. That oddly named thoroughfare was really the part of Third Street which lay between Broadway and the Bowery. "The neighborhood to a considerable extent was still residential," Hughes recalled in his later years. "Lafayette Street had not been cut through, and from Astor Place to Great Jones Street was known as Lafayette Place and had a number of commodious homes as well as the Astor Library. On the corner of Lafayette Place and Great Jones Street, next to our house, was the church building which had recently been St. Thomas's, then removed to Fifth Avenue. This building bore an enormous sign with the words 'Moral Amusements.' Across Lafayette Place and on the western corner of Great Jones Street was a large mansion occupied by the Columbia Law School. Many a time I climbed up the iron fence which surrounded it to see Professor Dwight, with the white pitcher of water on his table, lecturing to the law school students." [1] Several years were to elapse, however, before any thought of growing up to be a lawyer himself ever entered Charlie Hughes' mind.

His expeditions took him as far as the Battery on the south and Central Park on the north. No one interfered with his wanderings, and that undoubtedly added to the sheer joy he found in them. Equipped with a little street directory and a willing pair of legs, he commanded the entire town. For New York in the 1870's consisted of Manhattan; a break at Central Park separated the metropolis from Harlem, Bloomingdale, and the other communities beyond. Down in the Wall Street area the Trinity Church steeple dominated the skyline, and the old Equitable Building was the chief mecca for sight-seers.

Sometimes Charlie indulged in the luxury of a ride in one of the quaint old buses that came to typify "little old New York." And there were other means of getting about. When he was tired of walking, he would jump on the tail-end of an empty horse-drawn truck and "ride joyously with dangling legs."

Bustling, skyscraperless New York was in the throes of its last fight with Boss Tweed. Corruption and crime were a part of its nature, and this too held an interest for young Hughes. On one of his later excursions he saw political workers near the polling places with greenbacks in their hands, marshaling the voters, and never forgot that experience. In his Notes he tells us:

Any part of New York that had a bad reputation was particularly interesting. I wandered about Chatham Street, the Five Points, Cherry Hill and various places that were notorious. The Bowery was a fascinating place and little escaped my curious eye. On Broadway, around the corner from Great Jones Street, stood the Grand Central Hotel, one of the leading hotels of the City, where but a short time before Stokes had shot Jim Fisk. I regarded it with awe. The stretches of the lower East Side, then predominantly Irish, became very familiar. I went to Sunday School at an old Baptist Church on Stanton Street, east of the Bowery, an institution which already seemed sadly out of touch with the neighborhood. I loved to sit in the small parks. Union Square was a beautiful park with fountain and trees. Madison Square was also a delightful spot, but best of all to my mind was Stuyvesant Square and broad Second Avenue with its spacious residences and shade trees. Central Park, then a sylvan retreat of the "horse and buggy" age, was a dream of beauty, and when I had a visiting cousin we would make a day of it, investigating its by-paths. I have known New York through all the transformations of the past sixty-eight years but the memory of the old town as I first became intimately acquainted with it stands out most vividly.[2]

[1] CEH, Notes, pp. 36–37.   [2] Ibid., pp. 37–38.

In September, 1874, Charlie took the entrance examination of Public School No. 35 on Thirteenth Street and was admitted to the graduating class, A First. No. 35 was at that time the most famous of the New York public schools for boys, having won great distinction under the principalship of Thomas Hunter. That eminent teacher had left the school to head the Normal College for Girls (now Hunter College) before young Hughes arrived, but the fame of No. 35 for scholarship and discipline was maintained under his successors. The school attracted students from all parts of the city and boasted that its graduates became leaders in many walks of life.

Despite the fact that he was in the highest of four units of the graduating class, Charlie found himself covering a great deal of familiar ground. No Latin was offered. The teacher of "A First" was middle-aged Charles Gates, who was later to become principal of No. 35. He was an able instructor, but the students were most impressed when he asked them to put aside their books and talked about his philosophy of life or the great world outside. Specialists came in once or twice a week—a French teacher with purple hair, who amused the students but taught them virtually nothing, and a lecturer in chemistry, who was almost toothless and not easily understood. The one terrifying hour of the week was that given to drawing, for which young Hughes had not the slightest talent. He toiled longer over the required sketches than over anything else, but to no purpose. So futile were his efforts that his father had him excused from that course.[3]

Charlie had been at No. 35 only a few weeks when his parents moved to Greenpoint, Brooklyn. Although it was a long journey from Greenpoint to No. 35, he would not hear of shifting to another school. Usually he took the Twenty-third Street ferry and walked (except in bad weather) from Avenue A to the school at Thirteenth Street and Sixth Avenue, carrying his books and lunch box. Ice in the ferry slips frequently caused delay in winter, but Charlie did not object so long as he could continue on at No. 35.

Whenever possible, he also sought his recreation among his school friends in New York. Skating became his favorite sport, and Central Park offered many opportunities to indulge in it. No palatial apartment houses then obstructed the sweep of wintry winds across the park. Eighth Avenue west of the park was a haven for squatters living in little shanties and tending their chickens, goats, and pigs. On the Fifth Avenue side of the park, according to the recollections of the enthusiastic skater from Greenpoint, there were only two houses —on the corners of Sixty-second and Sixty-fourth streets.

The most notable burgeoning of young Hughes' talents at No. 35 came in writing. Early in the term Mr. Gates called for an essay on "Bones." That was

[3] *Ibid.*, p. 40.

a stumper, but Charlie laboriously produced a paper which met the test. Then came an invitation to put in voluntary essays. At the suggestion of his father, Charlie wrote expansively on "The Elements of Success." Three such elements held his attention: "Knowledge, Determination and Industry." Knowledge, he thought, "also involves thoughtfulness and clear headedness." Determination could be exemplified by Grant's decision to "fight it out on this line if it took all summer." Industry? "The well known Latin proverb, 'Perseverance conquers all things' should be stamped on the memory of every person who wishes to succeed. Without industry no man can succeed."

This effort pleased the authorities so much that the young essayist was asked to read his paper in chapel. With such encouragement, he produced a series of essays,[4] making an ambitious choice of subjects. "Happiness and Its Constituents" was a ringing youthful appeal for virtue: "Happiness is that state of mind produced by the enjoyment of good . . . and an untroubled conscience. . . . For as soon as evil is committed, its loud and thunderous notes peal and echo through the regions of the soul. . . . Whenever we turn aside from following Duty's beckoning finger, that moment happiness ceases." This paper was marked "Excellent," and another straight dose of moralizing entitled "True Manhood" brought a similar reward.

The most controversial essay of the series was "Light Reading and Its Consequences." Written language was a great blessing, Charlie pontificated, "but like all other human inventions this has been put to base uses and to one of these corruptions has been assigned the name of light reading." The gist of his complaint was that "light reading will not educate our moral sense, but will blind, pervert and weaken it. . . . Light reading is fanciful," he continued, "and its chief power consists in working up the imagination to such a degree, that we will either go off in ecstasy of delight or sink into tears on account of the good or bad luck of our fictitious hero . . . if one were never to see a book nor learn a letter he would be in a more hopeful condition for true progress than one who confines himself wholly to light reading."

This boyish rehashing of countless admonitions he had received from his parents and Mr. Gates is the source of various absurd stories to the effect that Hughes grew up in ignorance of fictional literature. Actually, he was devoted to Shakespeare, Byron, and Moore long before this essay was written; he never thought of their works as "light reading." A year later he was to discover a volume of Smollett in his father's library and become absorbed in the adventures of Peregrine Pickle and Roderick Random, and he was soon to be reveling in many works of the great novelists. The target of this essay was the drivel to be found in the *New York Weekly* and similar sensa-

---

[4] All these essays have been preserved among CEH's personal papers.

tional publications of the time, which some of the boys devoured during their lunch period.[5]

In any event, these preachments reflected but a temporary phase of his intellectual development. An impressionable boy of twelve, Charlie got a regular diet of moralizing at the family table. Visiting grownups, usually preachers, added quantity but seldom variety to the wisdom offered him. Accompanying his parents to church gatherings, he heard innumerable discourses on moral and religious subjects. Occasionally, too, his father took him to hear an eminent lecturer. Henry Ward Beecher and Wendell Phillips held the boy spellbound. His extensive notes on these lectures and sermons were a natural source of material for his essays. When No. 35 offered "merits" for such papers plus the distinction of reading each of them in chapel, he reproduced, almost as faithfully as a dictaphone, the platitudes that had been dinned into him.

Charlie's chief competitor, R. Floyd Clarke, won his "merits" by declamations. At chapel, Clarke recited "The Battle of Ivry" and other pieces with fine effect. Another classmate, Harry G. S. Noble, was to become president of the New York Stock Exchange. It was a less conspicuous lad, Harry G. Tobey (later of Charleston, South Carolina), who became Charlie's seatmate and best friend at No. 35.

Their commencement in June, 1875, was an affair of distinction. The well drilled graduating class, with its four divisions, marched from the school to the old Academy of Music at Fourteenth Street and Irving Place and was seated in tiers on the stage. The boys' parents and friends filled the boxes and orchestra seats and the general public the balconies. Charlie Hughes delivered the "salutatory" on the subject of "Self-Help," inspired by his reading of Samuel Smiles. In addition to that signal honor, the school gave him a silver medal inscribed "For Composition."

Young Hughes thus found himself graduated from a public school for the second time, but he was still a year short of the minimum age for admittance to college. Rebelling against the arbitrary rules that held him back, he resolved that he would graduate from some college in 1880 when his classmates at No. 35 would be getting their A.B. degrees. With that determination goading him —determination which was one of "The Elements of Success"—he once more took up a course of study at home.

Greenpoint in the 1870's was an attractive village. It was the seventeenth ward of Brooklyn, but a stretch of undeveloped land separated it from other built-up sections; it was connected with Williamsburg by only a one-horse car line using queer little vehicles with a single door at the rear. "Filled with

[5] CEH, Notes, p. 41.

people who were always friendly and neighborly in the true sense of the word," [6] it was a community of self-respecting families of moderate income. For a few months the Hugheses occupied part of a three-story shingled rowhouse at 109 Oak Street. Then for nine years they lived in a modest red brick rowhouse at 127 Milton Street. Directly opposite their house lived Ralph Albert Blakelock, celebrated painter of Brooklyn. A few houses down the street lived Herbert Baker, future oil magnate, and, up the street, Thomas C. Smith, who built the Little Church Around the Corner in Manhattan.

Charlie Hughes played baseball with the boys of the neighborhood on Paddy Flood's lots. He had a velocipede on which he used to scoot along the otherwise quiet and uncongested residential streets. Swimming in the East River was a favorite sport for the Greenpoint lads. They left their clothes on the docks and swam sans trunks without being molested. Charlie looked on enviously without joining in this fun; he did not know how to swim.

To the rural charm of Greenpoint was added the glamour of the shipbuilding industry extending along the shores of Newtown and Bushwick creeks. Of still greater interest were the Greenpoint churches, which were thronged every Sunday. During the Reverend Mr. Hughes' pastorate at the Union Baptist Church, more than four hundred new members were added to his congregation. His parish boasted that its Sunday school, with approximately a thousand members, was one of the largest, if not the largest, in the state. Brooklyn was a paradise for Protestant ministers.

The Sunday-school May Walk, which brought together the children and young people of most of the Protestant denominations, was a leading event of the year. Each class marched as a unit under its own banner, the little girls dressed in their best finery, the boys in their Sunday clothes. Reverend Hughes, grave and erect, led his own special division. The procession moved slowly through lines of spectators on Manhattan Avenue to the ringing of firehouse bells. At the end of the Walk came "union services"—inspirational but in a lighter vein. Then the serving of ice cream and strawberries in the cool groves of what had been the Meserole farm gave the day a happy climax.

Even more enjoyable were the annual midsummer excursions. Two barges were lashed together to accommodate Pastor Hughes' Sunday school on such occasions, with a gangway providing easy access from one to the other. A tugboat would pull the barges up the Hudson to Iona Island (or down to Long Branch or some pleasant resort on Long Island Sound) while bands played and a holiday atmosphere prevailed. The young people were inclined to dance in spite of lifted eyebrows. At the picnic grounds the boys went swimming, played games, and devoured incredible quantities of food.

The Reverend Mr. Hughes once more made his influence strongly felt, as

[6] Granville F. Sturgis in the *Brooklyn Eagle*, June 9, 1940.

he had done at Glens Falls, Sandy Hill, Oswego, and Newark. Liquor and tobacco took the place of the Copperheads as the chief objects of his reforming zeal.[7] His parishioners thought of him as a lovable character who stimulated them to the attainment of new self-respect, a balanced budget, and a new house of worship. His salary of $2,000 a year without a parsonage, a maximum that he was never to exceed, was often in arrears,[8] but not his fidelity to what he believed to be the work of God.

[7] Brooklyn *Daily Eagle,* Feb. 9, 1930.   [8] CEH, Notes, p. 22.

Chapter 5

EMANCIPATION

IN HIS rambles about the city, young Hughes had often visited Washington Square and observed the dignified buildings of New York University with profound respect. The idea of entering there made his heart tingle with excitement. In the summer of 1875, however, chance suddenly shifted his interest to an even bolder venture.

The Hugheses visited their friends, the Cronkhites, at Sandy Hill, and Charlie was thrown into the company of Mr. Cronkhite's nephew and namesake, who had just finished his sophomore year at Madison (now Colgate) University. Young Hughes was flattered by the companionship of this college man several years his senior and thrilled by the stories he heard of college life on the hill at Hamilton. Up to this time schooling outside of New York had seemed utterly beyond his reach. Now the idea of going away to college was suddenly made to appear feasible. He began a whirlwind campaign to win his parents' consent.

In concept as well as in results this campaign may be regarded as Charles E. Hughes' second big case. The first, of course, was when, at the age of six, he won the privilege of studying at home instead of going to school. In neither instance was he attempting to imitate a lawyer's methods. Courts and law were utterly foreign to his experience. Nevertheless, his logical young mind formulated a set of convincing arguments, and his fervor gave them a real impact. Obtaining a Madison catalogue from his friend, he studied it with the object of proving that he could prepare at home during the following year for the entrance examinations. The expenses would be light, he argued, especially in view of the reductions in room rent and tuition granted to ministers' sons. His friend Cronkhite, without that advantage, got along on an allowance from his uncle of $300 a year. Then came the clincher: "Was not Madison University a Baptist institution, with many studying for the ministry? Was not Hamilton a safe and wholesome place, and did I not need the invigoration of life in the country, among the hills? I would be so careful, so obedient!" [1]

Remembering his college life at Wesleyan, Charlie's father soon capitulated. His mother was more hesitant. She could not bear to think of her "little boy" (for he was not only young but also slight and small for his age) being away

[1] CEH, Notes, p. 47.

24

from her constant care. But Charlie was determined and did not relax his efforts until he had "carried the day."

Behind his adolescent enthusiasm for a rural college was another powerful motive that he diplomatically concealed from his parents. He was eager to get away from home.[2] The strict regimen to which he had been subjected since his infancy had created in him a distaste for religious formalities and a longing for freedom to follow his own inclinations. As a minister's son, he had been expected to be a little angel—to attend all the church gatherings, to be an example to the other boys, to neglect nothing. Anything resembling sports or even pleasure on Sunday was tabooed. While his mind was receptive to religious teachings, his parents overgorged him, with the effect of defeating the very purpose to which they were so conscientiously devoting themselves.

In later life Hughes discussed this experience with candor that could not have been attained at the time:

It was the fondest hope of my parents that I should enter the ministry and I was early "dedicated." Their chief concern was that as soon as possible I should apprehend religious truth as they understood it, and whatever precocity I had was utilized for that purpose. My childish peccadilloes were evidence of the sinful nature of which I partook with the rest of humanity, and I was constantly warned of the necessity of subduing my evil inclinations, lest they "grow with my growth and strengthen with my strength," as my mother was wont to say. It was natural that when I was caught in a grievous fault I should have a conviction of sin. I readily absorbed the doctrines I was taught, and when at the age of nine I was admitted to membership in the Church, the Deacons who examined me were amazed—as I was later informed—at the "mastery" I displayed of the tenets of the denomination. As I look back upon that training at home, in the light of subsequent views and experiences, I realize that what interested me most was the dialectic rather than the premises. In that period, as soon as it was practicable, I also assumed certain duties of leadership. At Newark, I organized a boys' club which for about a year met regularly at the parsonage and I addressed the club from time to time. I took an interest in my father's classes for the Sunday school teachers and prepared references for his syllabi.

But with all this unusual sort of activity for a small boy, I retained a healthy love of play and frolic . . . and I was always eager for new experiences. A year or more before I left home for college, my spirit had begun to flutter in its cage. I recognized my parents' sincerity—I responded to their warm affection—I would not wound them for the world—but I became restive at required attendance at so many meetings and wished greater freedom. Then I began to question my father about the problem of evil and I wanted to know how what I observed in the ways of nature and of men could be reconciled with the goodness, the omniscience and the omnipotence of the Creator. Despite these disturbing thoughts I still had a deep religious feeling and I was more inquiring than rebellious. I also became increasingly conscious of internal difficulties in the church administration, due as I imagined to the shortcomings of church trustees which were fully discussed at the family table.

[2] Author's interview with CEH, Dec. 4, 1945.

Tiring of the routine of services and observing my father's pastoral troubles, I concluded that I would not enter the ministry. My parents hoped that I would have a different, and in their eyes a truer, vision of opportunity and duty as I matured. But in this they were destined to be disappointed.[3]

The Hughes family returned home about the end of August, and Charlie took up his preparatory studies with unbounded enthusiasm. His father now took him in charge, directing his study and occasionally holding recitations. This supervision was an inadequate substitute for the drill of a preparatory school, but it enabled young Hughes to set his own pace, and he lost no time in school exercises. At first he found it "very hard going," but he was soon advancing rapidly. In a period of nine months he did his lessons regularly in Latin and Greek grammar and prose composition, brushed up on Caesar's *Commentaries,* read six books of the *Aeneid,* four orations of Cicero, and three books of the *Anabasis.* In English and mathematics he had comparatively little to do to complete his preparation. His "emancipation" was now definitely in sight.

Charlie's father took him to Hamilton for the entrance examination in June, 1876. "With one exception," he wrote of this experience, "I took the regular written examinations which I passed without difficulty. The exception was in Greek, in which I had, for some reason unknown to me, a separate and private examination. By appointment, I went to the home of Dr. N. Lloyd Andrews, professor of Greek, and to my surprise he took me into his library, handed me an *Anabasis* and pointed out various passages. He left me for a few minutes and then put me through an oral examination, which satisfied him. Perhaps, because of my extreme youth, he sought to try me out in order to see whether it was worth while to let me enter. Anyway, I was duly matriculated, selected my room in old West College (I believe it was No. 39), observed with wonder and admiration the Commencement exercises and returned home the happiest of boys.

"In the following September, I went back to Hamilton to enter the freshman class and a new life began. As my mother often said—her 'little boy left home and never came back.' It was a different youth, with a broadened outlook, who visited his parents in the later vacation periods." [4]

Young Hughes' morale was at a low ebb, however, in his first hours alone at Madison. After his father had left him, he watched the students arrive in the stages from the railroad station. They clustered about the dormitory steps cheering and singing lustily "The Bull-Dog on the Bank" and "The Son of a Gambolier." The uninitiated little freshman felt lonely and unprotected. What would these gay and boisterous youths do to a newcomer so completely at their mercy when they discovered him? But these fears soon melted away; he

---

[3] CEH, Notes, pp. 44–46.   [4] *Ibid.,* p. 48.

found that he was well received and quickly entered into all the joys of their common campus life.

What was then Madison University was beautifully located on a hill overlooking the lovely, picture-book village of Hamilton. In the 1870's the university had three main buildings—East and West College (the dormitories) and Alumni Hall, which contained the classrooms, library, chapel, and a large hall at the top for commencements. Some distance beyond was the building which housed the Theological Seminary. Below the hill, across what was then a treeless meadow, was the preparatory school known as Colgate Academy. Dr. James Morford Taylor had not yet begun his transformation of the campus, which was to make the bog into a lake mirroring lacy willow trees and the rough meadow into lawns with charming roads and paths. Indeed, the editor of the *Madisonensis,* biweekly publication of the senior class, was so unimpressed by the rustic charm of the campus in 1876 that he likened it to "a vast wilderness unfrequented by man, inhabited only by wild beasts and such things." [5]

The college's accommodations and physical equipment were primitive. The dormitories lacked central heating, lighting, running water, and, of course, bathtubs. The unfurnished rooms were in suites of two, a small study, with one large window and window seat, and an adjoining cubicle. Most of the students had small cylindrical stoves in one corner of their study. On these they heated whatever water they used for bathing or washing—water carried from an outside pump which, in cold weather, was surrounded by ice several inches thick. Coal purchased by the students for their stoves was kept in bins lining the halls. Their toilet was a little stone outhouse at the far end of the campus, with the rudest accommodations. As there were no servants, the boys took care of their own rooms—after a fashion.

Charlie Hughes took furniture from home for his "suite." In his study he had a round deal table with a black oilcloth cover, which served as a desk; a lounge, two straight-backed chairs, one camp chair, and a small bookcase. Certainly it was a modest abode. But he was filled with pride and happiness as master of his little domain, "unconscious of lacking anything which a collegeman could rightly expect." [6]

All the students took their meals in the town, walking down the hill, across the swamp, and back again, three times a day. This was exercise enough for even a lively, undersized freshman determined to build up his physique, and the barnlike structure called a gymnasium was little used. At first Charlie boarded with the mother of one of his Greenpoint friends, Ralph W. Thomas, who had entered the academy; but he was soon to be drawn more closely into the bosom of the college.

[5] Nov. 18, 1876.   [6] CEH, Notes, p. 50.

Madison had a faculty of about ten professors, including the president, Ebenezer Dodge, a Baptist preacher and professor of metaphysics. Charlie's favorites were N. Lloyd Andrews, professor of Greek, the students' beloved "Kaì yàp"; and James M. Taylor, professor of mathematics. Professor "Jim," as he was affectionately called, was an ideal teacher, helpful, precise, and thorough—a man who made mathematics a "window to the universe."

The young freshman from Greenpoint concluded that the number of good students was relatively large, and some were of outstanding ability. In his own class of 1880 were George A. Williams, who became a professor of Greek at Kalamazoo College, and Edward F. Waite, for thirty years an eminent judge in Minneapolis. Heading the sophomore class was Albert Perry Brigham, who was to leave the ministry and become professor of geology at Colgate, winning high distinction as an author of standard works on physical geography. The leader of the junior class was Benjamin S. Terry, later professor of English history at the University of Chicago. Foremost among all the young men at Madison that year was David Call, valedictorian of the class of 1877, who was soon to be president of Des Moines University, although his career was to be cut short by death.

Lonesome and uneasy over their son's absence, the Reverend and Mrs. Hughes continued by letter the intensive training and character-molding efforts in which they had been engaged since his birth. On September 4, 1876, his mother wrote to him:

My dear Charlie,

Your letter of Monday morning gave us much pleasure and I can assure you we praise God for his loving care over you. . . . We are in usual health, though somewhat pressed with care in consequence of the backwardness of ———— in meeting your Pa's salary. We had hoped to send you the money for your board today (we fear that Mrs. Thomas may be burdened also). But, as yet, the money is not received. Pray that God will give our people a liberal spirit. . . .

Charlie, I fear you don't sleep enough. I think you get up too early. Remember, you will be able to do more and better work in the same time if your brain is *thoroughly rested*. Don't commit the blunder in the beginning of your college course of *overdoing*. You will never amount to anything in the world of letters, etc., if you *overwork now*. Do be guided by us in this respect as well as in other respects.

Now a word in regard to your washing. Don't wear your clothes too long—especially, your flannels.

I do wish to know whether you have been troubled at all with sore throats since you have been in Hamilton. Be frank, my dear boy, about the state of your health, mind and experiences. . . .

We miss you, O, so much. Still, the Lord helps us to bear your absence, knowing it is for your good. . . .

Well, goodbye. May the Lord bless you, my boy, in all your efforts is the constant prayer of your loving,

Mother

On September 18 Charlie's father gave expression to his feelings:

It was an unspeakable relief to receive from the hand of the letter carrier this Monday morning your anxiously expected and thrice-welcome letter. And when I read its contents . . . and found how good the Lord had been to our dear, dear child, I need not assure you that our hearts were uplifted to God in praise and thanksgiving—warmed with an unusual inspiration of gratitude.

When I arose this morning, I remarked to your dear Ma that I had had not the remotest conception of the place that you filled in my heart. From the moment I bid you adieu on Thursday morning until your letter came, your form was constantly before my mind's eye. It is most emphatically proved that—"where our treasure is, there our heart is also." Don't misunderstand me in what I have said. I was not *anxious* about you. I felt perfectly free from any solicitude about you. I had perfect confidence that that covenant keeping God, to whom we have ever commended you, and who has so wonderfully cared for and guided you up to the present time, will not forsake you now. We were very thankful that you could commend yourself to God in believing prayer; and that you were so signally heard and that the God of peace had filled you with all peace and joy in believing. And our prayer is that your life will always be characterized by prayerfulness, trustfulness, purity of heart, sincerity of motive, unreserved consecration to God in your relations to God; and industry, thoroughness in your studies, undeviating courtesy to all around you, and an honest, manly, frank, generous and gentlemanly treatment of everybody without exception—however others may treat you. . . .

Ma joins me in tenderest love and interest. She will answer your next letter. Write soon and believe me,

As ever your loving
FATHER

A week later Charlie received these questions and instructions from his father:

MY DEAR CHARLIE,

Your thrice welcome letter reached us on Saturday afternoon. To say that we were glad to receive it, is speaking very moderately. . . . And, that you could say that, "in spiritual matters," the Lord is blessing you, filled our hearts with joy and thankfulness. Our prayers constantly ascend, our dear boy, for your *spiritual* as well as your *temporal* good. Indeed, we know if you are faithful to your obligations; if, in all things, you have an eye to the glory of God; living in fellowship with the Father and His Son, Jesus Christ; habitually walking in the light as He is in the light; and daily equipped in the armor of God; we will have no solicitude in respect to your college, social or other personal duties.

There are a few things which you have not yet mentioned, which we should like to know.

1. Your management of your stove.
2. Does your stove kettle work as you expected?
3. Do you air your bedding and bedroom every morning?
4. Are you careful to keep your neck and ears and wrists and nails perfectly clean every morning?

5. How about table manners? (I noticed when I took tea at Mrs. Thomas's that you sat with your elbows on the table: see to it that you refrain from any such breach of good manners.) Be gentlemanly at table. "Familiarity," remember, "breeds contempt."

6. At what temperature do you keep your room?

7. Do you practice on the piano?

8. What is your hour for retiring?

9. *Be sure you do not for once overdo in the gymnasium.*

10. What is the result of the Dodge Prize Exam?

11. Do you find it difficult to keep up with your class without over-much studying?

12. How many hours do you give to your respective studies?

13. Have you yet recited: if so, how did you get along?

In regard to college and other bills, I will be able, I think, in a week or so to meet them all. . . .

Mama joins in tenderest love. Don't forget our instructions. Continue to pray for us, as we pray for you.

From your affectionate Pa

Other letters written to him that fall provide additional insight into the Hughes home:

Sept. 30, 1876

MY DEAR BOY

. . . The Lord has heard prayer & relieved my mind from anxiety concerning you, but you are continually in my thought. Often I start up to call you to do this or that, only to awake more thoroughly to the fact that we are indeed alone. Well, we trust it is all for the best, & if you are a good, obedient, Godfearing boy, I *know* all things will work together for your good. We were happy in the fact that you passed your Examinations so finely. However we feared that your brain might have been overtaxed. How is it? Are you well? Don't be reticent on this point. Remember advice given & taken in time saves great trouble. I send you enclosed, directions for the use of your medicines. I thought perhaps in the excitement of getting away you might forget. Put them in your box for reference. I also enclose instructions for the regulation of your bed &c. all of which I wish you to heed. One thing more. *Don't forget to hang your flannels & sheets & stockings around the stove when they are returned from the wash.* Some wash women always send home the clothing before it is *dry*. If you were to put on damp flannel or stockings or sleep in damp sheets, the result might be, rheumatism, or, consumption, if not death in a short time.

How I wish I could see your room. Pa says it looks so pretty. . . . Pa sent much love. He misses you so much. He said you must try to send a postal or a little letter in the middle of the week. We can't wait a whole week. With much love & many prayers,

From your loving
MAMA

127 Milton Street,
October 16, 1876

MY DEAR CHARLIE,

We have come to expect a greeting from you before breakfast every Monday morning. We were not disappointed this morning. For which we were thankful to our Father in Heaven. Thankful for the health and strength you report; thankful for the success in your studies; and, above all, that you are able to say: "God has filled my heart with peace and joy." This, indeed, filled our hearts with joy unspeakable. . . .

In respect to your debates, let me say: I do not want you to take any side, pro or con, which you cannot *conscientiously* maintain. *It is a vicious habit.* There are plenty of questions on which there are honest differences of opinion. Let such be selected. . . . But, NEVER *for the sake of argument*, take a wrong side. . . .

Be sure you remember all the advice we give you. Have a little memorandum with a classification of rules. And write down our counsel under the respective heads. eg—Rules for Health—Rules for Conduct, at table, in families, in college, in classrooms, among fellow students, in Society rooms.—Rules for Religion— Scripture Reading, Prayer, Meditation, etc., etc. . . .

Your loving
PA

October 23, 1876

MY DEAR, DEAR CHARLIE,

. . . Let me beg of you, dear Charlie, don't overtax your energies. Your physical constitution is something like my own. You can do good service up to a certain limit. Then you just give out. . . . The barrenness of your mind—when you tried to prepare your composition—is explained on the principle of an overtaxed brain. And you must not accept any Society work when you have a composition to write. And let me caution you again, my dear boy, in respect to accepting so much Society work. I understand that you have 30 members in your Society. If four took part in rotation every week, the same person would not have to take part again under six or seven weeks. But *you* have already taken part two or three times.

Do your regular work in regular time. Do not deviate from your systematic plan. . . . Let nothing but absolute physical inability interfere with your methods of study—I mean your regular daily and hourly routine. Don't ramble over hills on Saturday unless your work for Saturday is done. I regret that you yielded even for once to writing up to 12 o'clock at night. You must not do so again. Believe me, my darling boy, the points I am now making will be found the best in the end. . . .

We were truly thankful, our darling boy, that you could say: "Whatever I do, wherever I go, when the question of right or wrong comes up, it is decided by what will Pa or Ma say if I did it." My dear boy, this has been our prayerful aim all your lifetime—to so instruct you and train you that, if we were called away from you, our teaching would not have gone for naught. Continue thus, dear Charlie, and remember to walk in the fear of God all your days. Ma joins me in love,

PA

Nov. 22, 1876

MY DARLING BOY,

. . . We praise God for these blessings to you every day, but we desire to see manifestations of *quiet* in the midst of your great and numerous duties. . . . I don't wish to lessen your enthusiasm, but I desire to see you pull steadily—with dignity— with quiet composure of soul, so that you may at all times *realize* what you do, why you do it and that it is well and carefully done.

Pa, too, is under the whip all the time,—scarcely gets time to take his meals properly. He looks almost like a walking skeleton—grows thinner and weaker, week by week, and works harder and harder. . . .

Now, I am doing very little better than either of you. I feel like panting for breath all the time—in sympathy with my hurried loved ones. May God in His infinite mercy bless you and keep you is the earnest prayer of your loving mother.

M. C. C. H.

In his first months at Madison, Charlie was responsive to his parents' admonitions, at least in his letters. "You know how it is," he wrote on December 2, "when you have your soul fired with love to God, how you feel. . . . Pray for me that I may be a useful servant in God's vineyard."

Finances were a difficult problem. On October 7 Charlie's father sent him $12, and his mother added this advice:

Pa says, as soon as you get the money, ask Mrs. Thomas for your bill for the month. That will give her an opportunity to decide as to the price per week. You know, we have not asked the question—we have only taken it for *granted* that she will board you for $3 per week. We hope it is all right. Still, *this* method will be a delicate way to relieve us from setting the price. Then, Pa says pay her and take her receipt and send it back to him so that he may know you have done the business, *business-like*.

The precocious freshman from Greenpoint was "rushed" by Delta Upsilon, one of the two national fraternities on the campus, and by a local society, the Adelphian. "My friend Cronkhite," he tells us, "was a member of the Adelphian and some of his society brethren went to extremes in their insistence. They contended that I should be entering on slippery paths if I joined either of the fraternities and went so far as to try to hold a prayer-meeting in my room in the interest of my soul. But I was attracted by the scholastic standing of Call, Terry and Brigham, all of whom were members of Delta Upsilon, and by the obvious good fellowship of others of that chapter, and I joined it with much gratification at the opportunity." [7]

His affiliation with a fraternity gave his parents some concern, and two other youthful requests—for permission to have a roommate and to join a boarding club so that he could "be with the boys"—were at first denied. His father wrote to him on November 6:

[7] CEH's Notes, pp. 52–53.

MY DARLING BOY,

There are two or three things which have caused us both some solicitude of late, and your last letter has increased it rather than diminished it. I refer to your Society matters. There are 3 things which I have always feared in respect to college Societies:

1. The cultivation of a party spirit, which leads to envy and jealousy. . . .
2. . . . the consumption of time which ought to be devoted to private meditation or to thorough and systematic reading—you ought rigidly to pursue a systematic course of reading to which every hour, which can be conscientiously spared for that purpose, may be given. . . .

I notice a parenthetical sentence in your letter which revealed much to me. It is this: "I am quite lonesome some evenings." It indicated to me that there is danger of your losing sight of some of the things to which I have just referred, in respect to the field of exploration beyond the mere narrow routine of college life. You can never feel lonesome if you have enough to do.

3. The third danger arising from college Societies is the difficulty of maintaining a strictly *spiritual* life. I will not dwell on this point. A suggestion must be sufficient to you.

Now, in regard to two requests mentioned in your letter, namely—

1. To board in the DU Club and
2. To take a DU chum.

In regard to the first, it would be a most welcome request financially considered. But there are other considerations. . . . Wait until the close of the present term at all events and then we will *see* you and talk the matter over.

In regard to the second request our judgment is the following . . .

1. It would seriously interfere with your religious privileges. Freedom to throw yourself on your knees frequently and whenever you were inclined to do so, would be out of the question.
2. A chum would increase the number of callers upon your room.
3. A chum would lead to time spent in conversation, which would be better spent in meditation and research.
4. A profitable chum is so rare a thing, that the risk is too great for us to give our permission without being personally acquainted with him. . . .

Write soon and ever believe me, with love from your dear

PA

Three days later the Reverend Mr. Hughes wrote Charlie another long letter beginning:

To say that we were highly gratified and truly thankful to God for the tone of your letter and the excellent spirit with which you took the advice I gave you, coming as it did from the depths of my heart, is expressing our feelings very mildly. O, Charlie, I can sincerely assure you that these evidences of your love for your parents, your pious submission to their counsel, your implicit confidence in their judgment, are to us more gratifying than the most brilliant evidences of unusual genius could be; however much the latter might dazzle and excite and crown you with worldly honor.

Within a few weeks, however, young Hughes had joined a boarding club, along with fifteen or twenty of his new friends. In the following letter he tries to convince his parents of the wisdom of his step:

HAMILTON, December 13, 1876

DEAR MA AND PA,

At present I am perfectly well and hearty and I like it at the DU Club first-rate. Our board is splendid. Mrs. ———— knows how to make good pies. They are not those unbaked crusts as sometimes Mrs. Thomas has, but real good and thoroughly baked. We have pancakes in the morning and they tasted a good deal better than those Mrs. Thomas has. Their bread and butter too is excellent.

Then, in regard to general deportment, I never in my life saw better. There is not even loud laughter but conversation in groups—there being 19 at the table. . . .

In regard to my spiritual welfare. The Lord is abundantly blessing me with tokens of His love and mercy. I am so thankful to Him to think that here I am far away from you and, yet, He has not suffered me to be afflicted in the least, nor a hair of my head to be touched. But I must close. You have my heart's best love more than tongue can tell. So goodbye,

Your affectionate son,
CHARLIE

Eager though he was to get home for the Christmas holidays, Charlie was soon irked by his parents' continuous preaching and overweening concern for his soul. On their part, his parents were obviously shocked by the "worldliness" their "darling boy" had acquired. Shortly after his return to Madison his mother wrote him:

Now, my dear boy, will you remember the counsel of your father and mother. I am so apprehensive that you may be turned from the path of rectitude, by the influence of your worldly associates, that I feel that I was under the shadow of great sorrow. I have committed you to God's care, praying daily that you may be kept from the evil—not only kept from the evil, but be *active* in doing good. . . . In order that you may realize the blessings prayed for, treasure up in your mind the precious promises of God's word, think on them as you used to, write on them also. And, in respect to song, treasure up hymns of praise to God, instead of foolish, pointless college songs—worse than nothing, for it is like feeding on husks, causing one to be full of emptiness.

This week, rather tomorrow, begins the week of prayer, and I trust you will seek opportunity to pray with us sometime between the hours of 7½ and 9 o'clock every evening. Pray for a manifestation of God's power to save in our church and Sunday School and the community, generally.

Well, my *dear, dear* boy, once again I close another letter to you. May you have great success in your studies, the approval of God your Father and Christ your Saviour, and may this year be *characterized* in your life as a year of great progress in Truth and Holiness. May God's word be truly your counsel and your guide is the continued prayer of

Your loving
MOTHER

When he thought of his parents, Charlie felt both penitent and obedient. "In regard to my inner life," he wrote on January 2, 1877, "the Lord is caring for me and watching over me. I am weak & helpless but with his strength may overcome. Pray for me. . . . It is my desire to have my treasure in Heaven where it may be kept free from corruption." But his chief interests were study, fiction reading, and Delta Upsilon. On January 13, he wrote to his mother:

Studies are going on swimmingly and, really, Williams says, if he don't look out, the little tortoise may beat him . . . yet. I found out my standing in Geometry— and it was 4.87, the maximum being 5.00. Williams and I are pretty good friends, and he told me his standing. It was 4.88—only one-one hundredth ahead. We both obtained 5.00 in our examination.

We are still going on with our "Geometrical inventions." Last week we had two demonstrations to work out. . . . The professor asked one day for an original demonstration, ie.—we were to conjure up a figure ourselves and then work out a demonstration. Williams got a very nice one up and was highly complimented. I thought I couldn't let him go ahead there, so I got up a figure even better than his in which I did not even have to draw auxiliary lines, but he had to draw three. The professor said they were better than any in the book. We were the only successful men in that field.

Well, here I am, again, as usual talking about studies. Well, the fact is, I talk and think about very little else than studies. It's my food, my life and my spirit.

On January 24 he wrote again to his mother:

Your letter saddened me somewhat, as it reminded me by the pictures you drew that, indeed, as I richly deserved, your confidence in me had been shaken—if not wholly removed. But, I hope that in the future I may merit better things. I *am* trying to do your will.

But, I must hasten for I have very little time indeed. I had a chance to get a $6 DU pin for $4.50. As this chance will probably never happen again, and as many were after it, I secured it by paying 75 cents down, and saying that I would write and see if I could keep it. If so, I will pay balance when Fortune should give me a chance—if not, he will give me my 75 cents and I, his pin.

Please answer immediately, as there is no time to lose. It is a very pretty pin and awfully cheap. I hope you will consent to my keeping it.

The Reverend Mr. Hughes gave vent to his apprehensions in his letter of February 6:

MY OWN DARLING BOY,

Your long looked-for letter was most heartily greeted yesterday morning. Its tone was more like your own real self than any in some time. The obtaining of that precious prize—a DU pin—opened your *heart*. . . . Is it not so? For me, my dear boy, it gave me great pleasure to have the opportunity of proving to you once more how real, deep, and abiding is our love of you. The marked improvement in your spirit—and I trust in your piety since your visit home—has given us, as your parents, unfeigned gratification. It is, indeed, our constant prayer that the Lord will never allow you again to fall into the snares into which you were inveigled last term. Let Joseph's question be ever uppermost: "How can I do this great evil and sin against God?" There is nothing of permanent value in man except character. . . .

We were glad to see that you make a distinction between what we should have as *aims* and what we should desire as results. Never forget these three essential elements of every true life, and every action of every true life: (1)—*the supreme aim:* THE GLORY OF GOD. (2) *the supreme motive:* THE LOVE OF GOD. (3) *the supreme law:* THE WILL OF GOD. . . .

Again on February 21 Charlie's father wrote:

O, yes, my dear, dear boy, believe it, it is what we *are* that makes our life a success or failure. *Character* is the mighty power, not only of the preacher but of the student, of the boy, of the man. . . . And pray tell me, my dear Charlie, what is the very essence, spirit, vital breath of character, if it be not *true piety*? . . . It is, indeed, what we *are* and not what we *seem* to be, that constitutes real power. O, remember, my dear boy, that there are but two masters—God or Satan. . . . O, see to it ever, child of my heart, that to you God in Christianity shall be your all in all.

Charlie replied on February 24: "I try to follow your injunctions, in regard to everything." But his hunger for scholastic honors seemed to play havoc with his pursuit of piety and moderation. His mixed emotions are clearly evident in his February 11 letter:

I hope, dear Pa, that you will forgive me, for this once, for sitting down on a Sabbath afternoon, but the past week has seen me so busily engaged that it was impossible to write. . . .

I am sure that when you learn what has this week been accomplished, both your heart and Ma's will be in unison with mine, in rendering to God praise. . . . Successes have attended me on every side, and I have done more to raise myself in the esteem of those around me than ever before. . . .

In the afternoon, I spoke before the college and God helped me, and I did better than ever before. But I was very nervous about the evening, for—on account of much drilling—everything in my oration seemed trite to me and unworthy of speaking. I drilled most of the afternoon and after committing all to the Lord, my head and heart grew clearer and more easy—finally I was left without the slightest dread.

When my name was called and as I walked on the platform, every eye was upon me, for never before has anyone in Hamilton so young appeared on the platform of a Society. Every movement I made was watched and, when I had stopped, I found my audience delighted. Success was complete. To God be all the glory! They said I had the best of the evening. . . .

This letter—as usual—is full of *self*, unworthy, abominable, selfish self. How I wish I could—as it were—get out of *self* and know that God's glory is my only aim. Pray for me.

Elocution and literary contests in the 1870's held much of the interest and glamour that today go into college football. Hughes got a good deal of training in Delta Upsilon, which gave part of its weekly meetings to debates, declamations, and essays. His rousing declamation about a cavalry charge in the Civil War won him a place in the Royce contest in his freshman year. In later life he often laughed at the spectacle he must have made—a small boy shouting, "Come on, old Kentucky, I am with you!" But this cry of the cavalry commander seemed to stir the audience, and he took second prize.

When Charlie plunged into Livy and the Orations of Lysias, he realized how inadequate his preparations at home had been. Once this initial handicap had been overcome, however, he carried his courses easily. While he was no "grind" and was sometimes inattentive in class, he seemed always to be prepared. Professor "Jim" confessed in later years that on several occasions he had tried to "catch Hughes napping" but had never succeeded.

By midyear Charlie was able to write to his mother:

Work tells, and all say that indisputably I stand second only to Williams. I can hardly hope to stand any higher. For no one does his work easier than Williams and he has an immense amount of reserve force. Well, for that matter, I have a little too.

A letter written on January 20, 1877, gives us a glimpse of the work he was doing:

In Greek, also, we are having a very interesting time. Next Friday, I have to prepare and deliver an article on Dr. Schliemann and his discoveries. Then, we will have written debates on the question "Has Dr. Schliemann actually discovered the site of Troy?" "Were the Iliad and Odyssey the work of one author?" "Is the Iliad based on historic fact?" "When did Homer live?" So, you see, we are having a very interesting time now. Then, in the "History of Greece" we learn about all the old legends which are very pleasing to study.

This week I have made a splendid bargain. Hearing that, by writing and stating that you were a ministerial student, you could get a copy of "Channing's works" free, and, knowing that it was so, I wrote and got it. It is neatly bound, worth about $3.00, and I did not even have to pay the postage. Besides a full canvassing of Unitarian doctrines, it has fine lectures on "Self Culture,"—"Elevation of Laboring Classes"—"Slavery" and 10 or 12 other subjects.

Pleased though she was by his high standing, his mother sent a note of caution: "Well I always felt your little head was worth a good deal, but don't forget the source of power—all power. It is God who gives wisdom." On April 17 she offered Charlie a pretty stiff bracer for his sense of responsibility:

How truly should gratitude of heart constantly characterize your life. You *are*, highly favored with mental gifts and special privileges for their development—with blessings too numerous to mention in this hurried letter,—for which you will be held accountable in the great future. Make good use of them now remembering the promise, "To him that hath shall be given,"—"He that is faithful in little shall also be faithful in much."

Social life at Madison was meager. Occasionally the Delta Upsilon held a "private-public" (*private* because admittance was by invitation and *public* because others than members were invited) at which members demonstrated their skills in song and speech. These occasions afforded the boys a chance to escort the "sem" girls—students of the Hamilton Female Seminary described by the *Madisonensis* as "handsome, witty and clever as country school marms."

Charlie Hughes became a devotee of whist. Card playing had been tabooed at home, and that made it seem all the more alluring. Occasionally he also played chess with an upperclassman who roomed near him. His venture into baseball, the only athletic sport then in vogue at Madison, is memorable solely because his heroic attitude toward a swift grounder in the sophomore-freshman game cost him a tooth. This misfortune brought a pointed reminder from his father: "Do not forget what I have said about violent exercise and those club competitions in physical skill. *I do not wish you to take part in those things.*"

As spring came to Hamilton, young Hughes reported to his father:

There has been a phrenologist around telling for 50 cents what the boys have in their heads. I would have had mine examined, but I have no money to lose. Well, my birthday passed without my thinking of it. Such is life. My high standing has done one good thing for me, at least. The boys no longer think of me as a little fellow but as one whom they can esteem and regard with respect. My smallness saves me from all rough handling and so I have a happy and unmolested life. . . . My money record for the last week is as follows:

Balance on hand—as of last letter..	$.73
Postage	.03
Crystal for watch	.25
On hand now	.45

On March 3 he had written to his mother:

You ask how my clothing is holding out. I think my shirts will last till June easily. My Sunday clothes are all right. My blue coat and vest is growing shabby. My pants (those you made from Pa's) are threading out. I cannot explain it. The outer thread split. My shoes are miserable. The soles are all right but the leather splits. Two big splits nearly across my foot. . . . My collars and cuffs are all in order but that cravat is about worn out. I wish you would send me one of that kind or some stylish silk neckties for my standup collars.

His father wrote him on May 10:

Well, of this you may be assured,—that there will be two pairs of eyes to speak "Welcome Home" and two pairs of arms to clasp you at home.—O, my dear boy, how little you dream of the height and depth, the length and breadth, of a father's and a mother's love! May the Divine Grace enable you to live worthily of a love that transcends even a parent's love—"The love of God in Jesus, our Lord."

On May 31 his father wrote again:

I was not surprised that you shall be "on for Royce." It was what I expected. Now do your best. But trust implicitly in God for every need and assistance and for success. Do not be too elated, too sanguine or too ambitious. May the Lord help you to do your duty from right motives is my prayer. . . .

It is now quite doubtful whether both your Ma and myself will be permitted to visit Hamilton at Commencement. The truth is, my dear boy, "impecuniosity" has visited us and we do not seem to rally from it. I trust that either the one or the other of us will be there.

Charlie Hughes returned to Madison for his sophomore year in the fall of 1877, and his mother's admonitions soon followed him:

How thankful we are for God's loving care over you & how pleased that you are attentive to your studies & doing well. *Be thorough.* BE THOROUGH. BE THOROUGH in all you undertake. In your reading also, let your motive be improvement. Dwell upon the page long enough to get it into the mind. Inattention in reading injures the mind—weakens the memory. . . .

In respect to your washing neck &c., don't ignore your feet. If you persist in washing them every day, you will cure them of sweating.

Don't play croquet in the evening. I was astonished that you have taken again to the "worn out game." *Well don't play it at night. Take good care of your health in all respects.* HEED THIS WARNING!

Charlie's interest was centered in the Delta Upsilon convention, which brought an engaging group of college men to Madison. Their leader, E. Benjamin Andrews, young president of Denison University, an eminent educator who was later to become the most popular president of Brown University, made a profound impression on Hughes. Here is a man, he thought, who embodies my ideals. The enthusiastic sophomore wrote a detailed account of the convention to his mother on October 27:

DEAR MA:

. . . Well, as you say, our Convention is now a thing of the past. You can't tell how inexpressibly lonely I feel, when all the boys (our delegates) have gone. It seems as if I had known all of them through my whole college life. All our delegates were true men. You may imagine a crowd of about 60—the most of them holding highest positions in our largest and most influential colleges—all of them just completing a long college course and you may form an idea of the strength and talent represented in our Convention . . . some of them I am confident will be heard of throughout our land in coming days . . . all the discussions proved that there were long heads at work behind those shining faces.

On Thursday evening, everything gave way to our grand Promenade Concert. It was the most promising feature of the Convention and it was a grand success. . . . First, our Hall—the largest auditorium in Hamilton was fitted up splendidly. . . . The platform was all festooned and the words—Delta Upsilon—hung over it in letters of evergreen. . . . The most beautiful flowers that could be obtained were placed in urns in the middle of a hall and on the front of the platform. Most of the ladies present were in full dress, and the gentlemen were all dressed as well as possible with white kid gloves. The ladies were escorted to and from the Hall by young gentlemen with carriages. The band was on the platform and discoursed sweet music, while delegates and our own boys became acquainted with [the] ladies . . .

If ever I thought anything of Delta U my thoughts went up 10,000 per cent after our Convention. And, although it will probably cost us a great deal, yet it is in a noble cause. . . .

Now, I come to money matters. This term I am afraid expenses will be large on account of this Convention. That Concert obliged me to buy a pair of white kid gloves. I am sorry I had to get them but I got a six and three-quarter size, so that I can wear them on similar occasions in my college course. My college tuition tax of $13 really ought to be paid now. . . .

I will try to tutor at 20 cents per hour which will help some. I will do anything, but please don't think hard of our heavy tax in D.U.

Charlie's father tried to moderate his excitement and got this reply on November 3:

You speak of the excitement I was laboring under in my last letter. I have now had time to cool off, but I would still reiterate my statements of the DU Convention, and would say in addition, that it did me a great deal of good. We are apt to become narrow and straightened in our ideas, but such occurrences make us liberal and free.

Toward the end of the school year the sophomore class formed a good-fellowship society that indulged in raw oysters, cider, and cigarettes at the old Eagle Hotel. Hughes began to smoke on these convivial occasions. In his Notes he confesses also to taking part in some of the minor pranks at Madison. As a freshman he had joined a group of students campaigning for Hayes and Wheeler, and when (on returning to the campus in the early morning hours after a rally at Morrisville) they had rung the chapel bell in happy disregard of the rules he had felt duly initiated into the ways of college men. But his pranks were as harmless as the snowball fight and mild revolt against overwork that he described to his mother on January 19, 1878:

We met on the hill, and as we were marching downtown, the Academes snowballed us from behind an embankment. The College immediately charged on them, and a vigorous fight ensued, (with snowballs at about two feet apart) which resulted in the entire discomforture [sic] of the Academes. I came out all right, except one bad blow in the ear. A good many of the boys had black eyes the next day and sore heads. Well, so much for college fun.

In studies, we go along as usual. Prof. Andrews kept increasing our lessons until patience ceased to be a virtue, and a committee was appointed to tell him how much we would learn and no more! He acceded to our demands, and though we have hard work enough now, yet it is easy in comparison to what it might have been.

Charlie's parents knew nothing of his smoking, but they kept up a constant effort to keep him in the straight and narrow way. After a brief visit at home in April, he felt very penitent over the heartaches he had caused his parents. On April 13 he wrote to his father:

I am well and happy, but I don't know when I have felt so disconsolate on a return as I have this time. I feel alternately sad and joyous. I am trying to live as a Christian should before the world. But it is so hard. It is uphill work. But it is my aim, by the grace of God, to make my life a truly spiritual one. Pray for me, dear Pa, that I may live to the honor and glory of my Savior and please, please forgive the cruel heartaches I occasioned you on my last visit. I do want to become a truly Christian gentleman.

In April, 1878, the Reverend Mr. Hughes was expelled from the Greenpoint Pastors' Conference, apparently on a charge of unfair proselyting. While the incident caused something of a furor, which was magnified by garbled reports, he was easily vindicated. ". . . blessed be God," he wrote to his son, "I can use the language of Joseph to his Brethren: 'Ye meant this for evil; but God meant it for good.'"

Charlie replied on May 11, almost rivaling the numerous classical references in his father's letter:

DEAR PA,

I am glad . . . to know that you are coming into a safe harbor after a perilous storm. Neptune, with his trident has appeared amid the troubled waters of an Etruscan sea, and ordered Eurus and Notus and Zephyrus to their homes. . . .

However perilous the storm may seem, however violent may be the winds of adversity, the Christian is sure to come off triumphant. In what strange way does Providence lead. Here an attempt to do you the grossest injustice ends in giving encomiums of praise to the pastor of the little church in Greenpoint.

No one knew about it up here until the issue of the last Examiner when I was troubled on every hand by questions of every description. "Is D. C. Hughes your father?" "Quite a gun." "It don't do for them to tackle him." "Tell us all about it."

And so it goes. Well, as you well know, I did all that I could to set you up in the estimation of Hamilton students. You are "quite a gun," and it takes such circumstances as these to show it. I think it will do you and the church good. Nothing like a little stimulating excitement to make the brain quiver and burn with a sense of injustice done and wrong received. How it swells and strains every fibre of one's nature, and what a grand victory it is to establish one's self as inviolable before those who have attempted to stain one's reputation. Self is a mighty power. Bad, when too highly favored. But, when once roused in the cause of right, sets on fire the whole man, and makes him glow with zeal in the cause of truth. . . .

In two weeks from today the ordeal of a thorough prize examination will be passed, the Rubicon crossed—my hard work will be over. O, how I dread it! I will do my best but I cannot beat Williams. I feel it in my bones. If only I can get the second prize. Hoopla! Well, if work will do it it is mine. . . .

Just before the end of his sophomore year, Charlie had one of his few sick spells in college and feared that he was coming down with diphtheria. "Last Tuesday afternoon," he wrote to his mother, "I felt the sore throat coming on me, and before night my throat was nearly shut. I bound it up with a stocking and went to bed. When I got up the next morning, my legs sank from under me, and my eyes blurred, and I was compelled to fall right down on the lounge. It was a long while before I could get down to breakfast. I felt miserably. I couldn't swallow anything and was as weak as a rat." But a doctor supplied him with pills, and he was soon well again.

The extent to which his illness interfered with his competition for the Dun prize is not clear, but he blotted a page of his essay and in recopying it left out ten or twelve lines. Williams got the first prize, as Charlie had anticipated, and he got only honorable mention. "Well," he wrote to his mother, "a disappointing failure. But while sorry, I feel that [it] is a punishment for a pride that must inevitably precede a fall. Well, such is life." There was no cause for disappointment, however, in his scholastic standing. The Madison (now Colgate) records show that his rating was 4.91 in rhetoric (four meaning "superior" and five being the maximum grade), 4.84 in French, 4.71 in Greek, 3.92 in Latin, 4.90 in calculus, and 4.97 in analytical geometry.

Chapter 6

BROWN UNIVERSITY

"EACH man begins with his own world to conquer," Charles E. Hughes once said, "and his education is the measure of his conquest." [1] During his second year at Madison the urge in him to expand the "measure of his conquest" became very strong. He was approaching sixteen. Growing fast in body and intellect, he began to yearn for the more liberal atmosphere and wider opportunities that a larger college could be expected to offer. A survey of the possibilities indicated that the most favorable shift he could hope to make would be to Brown University. Brown, with its Baptist tradition, would appeal to his parents. At the same time it would give him the privileges of city life in Providence besides the freedom of living away from home.

Charlie wrote to Professor Poland at Brown and found that the requirements for admittance were stiffer than he had expected. Brown students finishing their sophomore year had had two years of college French and had begun German and mechanics. It was doubtful whether he could catch up with them by devoting the entire summer to hard study. Professor Poland argued persuasively that, in any event, three years at Brown would give a more solid foundation for his career, and he could still graduate at nineteen. That was early enough. Hughes recognized the good sense of this advice and decided to follow it.

Still there was the question of expense. His entire outlay at Madison (exclusive of clothes) had been $250 for the first year and not more than $275 for the second. At Brown the cost would be higher. Charlie's plan became feasible only when his father got a promise from President Ezekiel G. Robinson of Brown that he could have a scholarship with an income of $60 a year and, as the son of a minister, would not have to pay room rent. On learning the good news from his mother, Charlie wrote:

You cannot imagine how it thrilled me with joy and delight to hear the good tidings of your last letter. It, indeed, was so sudden and so unexpected that I hardly knew how to contain myself. The pent up longing of a whole year to burst forth in such a pleasing fruition was almost too much for me. My joy knew no bounds. How I wish I could see you and have a long talk. How many things I thank you for and how many joyous prospects come up before me.

[1] Address to Brown alumni, Feb. 1, 1929.

43

Entering Brown in September, 1878, Hughes was delighted with the college on the "high and pleasant hill." Manning, University, Slater, and Rhode Island halls and especially Hope College and the new library at Waterman and Prospect streets were soon familiar to him—a familiarity that was to extend throughout his lifetime. The president's house stood opposite the front campus on the site later occupied by the John Hay Library. Slater Hall had just been opened, and its suites were thought to be luxurious. But Dr. Robinson made no effort to conceal his disgust over the "battered doors . . . defaced walls, the gaping flooring" in the halls and "the unmistakable odor of decay pervading" University Hall; and Hope College, built in 1822, was "only a little less uninviting."

Nevertheless, the rooms were in such demand that Charlie Hughes and his roommate, Cornelius W. Pendleton, who had also come from Madison, could not at first obtain accommodations. For a time they lived together in a boardinghouse at 171 Congdon Street, paying $6 a week apiece. Eager to reduce this expense and live on the campus, they moved at the first opportunity to the ground floor of Hope College. Kerosene lamps provided their light, and a Franklin stove with open grate kept them warm in winter. Coal for this stove was stored in one of their two closets. In the other they kept their washstand and clothes. There was no running water or baths, although toilets were provided in University Hall. Servants ("slaves" to the students) kept the rooms in good order. The Hughes-Pendleton pair moved to Hope No. 22 on the second floor in their junior year, and often found it necessary to grope their way up and down unlighted halls.

Brown had about 250 students—a jovial lot with an abundance of college spirit. Hughes got a prompt introduction to Brunonian tradition in the sophomore-freshman class fight called a football game in deference to the fact that a football was somewhere in the center of the melee. A few days later came the forbidden cane rush, which also led to fist-swinging of the free-for-all variety. The specialty of Brown students in forbidden amusements was bonfires. A great blaze was likely to flare up on the College Green in spring or fall whenever there was a varsity triumph or other cause for an eruption of college spirit. Human moths seemed to fly toward the flames, and for a few precious moments there would be boisterous singing and dancing. They would scatter with even greater speed, however, when their sounds of mirth brought Brown's tall, gray-haired, sexagenarian president running to the fire at a deer's pace. Occasionally he would catch one of the students "and act at once as both policeman and committing magistrate." [2]

But not all their fun was of the *verboten* variety. They often gathered on the chapel steps after supper and sang their glees, and accepted rituals were some-

[2] CEH, Notes, p. 63.

times given an amusing twist. Instead of slavishly following the tradition of burying its Chaucer text when the course had been completed, Hughes' class dressed up to represent the characters in *The Canterbury Tales* and paraded through the streets of Providence. Charlie's chief regret about this was that it cost him $4 to help pay for the "grounds, band, advertisements, horses and costumes."

The freedom Charlie found in Providence brought many satisfactions. Up to this time he had never been in a theater. Now he eagerly seized upon every opportunity to see drama, taking the poor along with the good. This experience was high-lighted, however, by such memorable performances as Edwin Booth's in *Hamlet,* Lawrence Barrett's in *Richelieu,* Joseph Jefferson's in *Rip Van Winkle*, and Mary Anderson's in *Ingomar*. His first opera was *Aïda* with Clara Louise Kellogg and Annie Louise Cary. Providence also offered good light opera, such as *The Chimes of Normandy* and in the early part of 1879 the campus resounded with the catching airs of *Pinafore*. To pay for these diversions, Hughes took to tutoring boys who were behind in their work.

Frequently he played poker with his college friends, using matches instead of money. But whist continued to be his favorite. He joined the Brown whist club and played with experts whenever possible. As a mark of his good-fellowship, his friends nicknamed him "Hughsie," "Hughie," or, more frequently, "Huggis." He smoked more than previously. Occasionally, too, he could be seen at a beer garden patronized by the students. When he was studying German, he thought it good sport to drop in at Karl's beer hall and converse with the German proprietor in his native tongue. One day Hughes recited a portion of Schiller's *William Tell* in German for old Karl, who was so delighted that he "set 'em up" for all the boys.

Social opportunities at Brown were few so far as Hughes was concerned. It is more amusing than significant that the satirists of the *Liber Brunensis*, that "amiable catalogue of college follies," as he once called it, listed him as one of the eight foremost members of the Brown University Mashing Association and gave him the special title of "Bewitching Enchanter of Female Hearts." [3]

While Hughes' slight physique and his father's admonitions discouraged any direct participation in athletics at Brown, he became an ardent baseball fan. The Brown team was riding a wave of victories, thanks largely to J. Lee Richmond's mastery of the new curve-ball technique. In the spring of 1880 Brown defeated both Harvard and Yale and won the intercollegiate baseball championship. The fascination that this aspect of college life held for young Hughes stands out from a letter to his father on May 24, 1879:

[3] *Liber Brunensis*, April, 1880, p. 37.

Well, Saturday this afternoon, was taken up with the most exciting game of baseball I have ever witnessed between Yale and Brown, resulting in a victory for the latter by a score of 7–5. The greatest enthusiasm prevails. I can hardly write I am so excited. About a hundred of the Yale boys were down here. In all the games with her rival colleges, Brown has not been beaten once. She has the college championship within her grasp. Even the steadygoing Professors are excited. Professor Lincoln said "it was as good for the college as a new dormitory." You see, the boys always want to go to a college that holds up its head and beats all the others.

Probably, the best game so far this year will be played with Harvard at Cambridge next Saturday. About 150 of our boys are going down. The round trip will not cost more than $1.50, as the Harvard boys will treat all who go to supper and dinner, as they have always done and as we do when they come here. Won't you please let me go with them? Just think, I will be shown all through Harvard University as well as the renowned city of Boston with its historic Green and historic memories. Please grant me this great favor and I will assure you that all I do will be done as becometh a Christian and your son.

Brown University in those days was a classical and literary institution, giving only meager recognition to science and none to the professions. It had a strong faculty. "Such men as J. Lewis Diman, John L. Lincoln, Albert Harkness and Alpheus S. Packard would have been distinguished in any university faculty. Alonzo Williams was an excellent teacher in the modern languages. Nathaniel Davis, in mathematics, had already shown conspicuous ability. The students were brought into direct contact with these and other professors, and there was no reason to complain of lack of competent guidance in the various courses. The president was a powerful directing force." [4]

Hughes started at Brown with light work. Having completed geometry and calculus at Madison, he was excused from mathematics for the first semester. Latin and Greek were easy for him. Consequently, he had an unusual amount of time to give to his French and indulge his passion for literature. On October 21, 1878, he wrote to his father:

Though I am not studying very hard, I am doing an immense amount of reading. I have already read and am reading several of Thackeray's works and miscellaneous Addison's writings in the "Spectator" and Macaulay's essays. . . . I have read a couple of volumes of Addison's work but I don't like him very much. . . . There is in it something which leads me to think more of the great mind of Addison who writes, than of the great thought written. But, when we come to Macaulay's works, all this is gone. Take Macaulay's essay on "Milton." We lose all thought of Macaulay in the thought of the grandeur of the author of "Paradise Lost."

O! How much we lose sight of this all important essential to oratorical success— to make everything bend to the exaltation of the theme. This we see in Demosthenes. The Athenians did not say, "O! what a wonderful speech," but "we must fight Philip." And in this very fact did Demosthenes make the overwhelming power

[4] CEH, Notes, p. 63.

Charlie Hughes with his father and mother, about 1868

Young Hughes at fourteen,
at Madison University

Graduation picture—Brown
University, 1881

The Delta Upsilon Camp at Lake George, 1880
Hughes at the extreme left

of his oratory appear. Well, I must close this sort of thing. But, I have been thinking of this a good while and, at last, it has found expression.

Dickens and Thackeray were his favorites, but dozens of other authors also
held his attention, including Irving, Ben Jonson, Gray, Hugo, Scott, De Quin-
cey, Lamb, Emerson, Carlyle, Sterne, Goldsmith, Hawthorne, Balzac, Kings-
ley, and Schiller. When he learned French, he also read extensively in French
fiction. In his later college years the fiction he read was generally interspersed
by history and philosophy. He had already acquired the habits of rapid reading and absorption of what he read that were to amaze his associates in
official life.

At the end of his first year at Brown, Hughes was a little disappointed
in his Greek course, for while Professor Harkness was a great scholar and a
most gracious and careful teacher, he kept hammering away at construction,
and Hughes felt that they did not fully enter into the spirit of the classics they
were studying. Latin was a delightful contrast. Professor Lincoln embodied
the Latin spirit, and his familiar talks gave the students a sense of the most
charming fellowship. Everyone loved "Johnny Link" with his smooth upper
lip, bearded chin, and winning smile. Excepting only Professor Lincoln's
course, which opened a treasure house of classical literature, Hughes concluded
that he had learned more from his extra curricular reading than from the
classroom. But this did not disturb him; he was now disposed to follow his
own bent, with less concern for marks and credit than he had had at
Madison.

As Hughes settled down to study in his junior year, the ever present problem of paying his expenses seemed to be especially bothersome. He wrote
to his father on October 20, 1879:

I received your welcome letter last Wednesday with the enclosed check for $15.
I paid my three weeks board, got our pail and oilcloth, paid my Society tax ($2)
to meet our expenses at the Convention, paid $.75 for voting and football taxes,
went to a college ballgame (25¢), got a lamp chimney (10¢), got a lead pencil
and a rubber and find myself, at present, with 32¢ in my pocket. How money does
go! I am so sorry to have to keep asking for money when I know how short you
are and how you have to pinch. But, I am trying to spend just as little as possible—
to meet my honest dues and spend none needlessly. I am sorry I went to that ballgame. But it was the closing game of the season between Harvard and Brown and
I very much wanted to go.

Our landlady is very good to us and I can say I never have been so hearty and
had such a first rate appetite right along as now. We have splendid meals. I will
give you an idea of our bill-of-fare. In the morning, first oatmeal, then coffee, baked
potatoes and our choice—generally, between nice beefsteak, tripe, pork steak and
sausage, as well as hot rolls. At dinner—first some nice vegetable soup—then,
vegetables, splendid boiled potatoes and either roast beef, lamb chop, beef pie and

occasionally chicken—as well as nice desserts, consisting of good pies and puddings. At tea, we have tea, toast, cake and sauce. So you see, I live pretty well and feel quite strong and hearty.

I am going to the Gymnasium as soon as I have the money to pay in advance— $3 (for the year). I went once, but was respectfully informed that they must have pay in advance.

My shoes are in very poor condition. . . . My hair also needs cutting and my term's reading room tax ($1) should be promptly paid. Such is the constant demand. But, of course, it lessens as we get along further in the term.

His chronic shortage of funds led him into a shabby ghost-writing venture to pay for a pair of skates. The details come to light in the following letter:

PROVIDENCE,
Feb. 11, 1880

DEAR PA,

I just received your postal, giving me my marks for last term. I believe I am bewitched. By what possible means of legerdemain could my poor work be transmuted into perfection or nearly so? Truly, for ways that are dark & tricks that are vain, the Profs are peculiar. But, however it may be, I am extremely grateful & I know you & Ma will join me in fervent thankfulness to our Heavenly Father, who works everything for our good. . . . In a couple of weeks as soon as my hair grows long enough I will have my pictures taken. I am going to have ½ dozen taken standing up, with my ulster on, open, & hat & cane in hand. Such pictures are very stylish here now. Also ½ dozen in a rational posture. I will send you one as soon as I can get them. . . .

I have bought a pair of skates. You wonder, & think of my promise. Well, I will tell you all about it. Know therefore that when I told you I would never ask you for a pair, on account of my overcoat, I nevertheless intended to have a pair & earn them myself. A fellow hard up, offered me his skates (American Club, like my other pair, in fine condition, polished, sharpened, & new last year & cost $5.00, as you know) for $3.00. I took them. You ask, where did you get the money? A Sophomore came to me one day, told me he had to have an essay in three days, & couldn't spare the time to write it. He only wanted a fair one. I wrote it & received $1.00, which I laid away. He told another one, who is a fine scholar & for him I wrote a fine essay, got him an "ex." & received $2.00, which added to my $1.00 gave me a pair of skates, all for about ten hours work as they had to do the copying.

I shouldn't wonder if I had more such jobs. You see I read over some of the man's essay & imitate his style just as nice as you please. Don't mention this as it is strictly confidential between these fellows & myself. It don't make any difference to me, but the fellows would be in a nice pickle if it got out. We have had skating for a week & I never enjoyed it so much in my life. . . . To-night I am going to a social at Central Baptist Church; to-morrow night I have an engagement out, & Friday, Society, all of which with skating, studying & eating keep me pretty busy. I am progressing nicely in study. 14 ex's out of 15 marks since I have been in Brown. Hurrah! Much love to Ma & you from

C. E. H.

Four months before, Charlie had sharply condemned "one of the boys" who had cribbed an oration from an old magazine. "It doesn't pay in a selfish sense," he had written his mother, "and we all know its real name—*theft*." When his mother chided him for being a party to a similar bit of trickery, however, he vigorously defended his action:

BROWN UNIVERSITY
Feb. 17th, 1880

DEAR MA,

I received your kind letter the other day, & took great pleasure in reading it. For, besides the interest you naturally feel in me, I was much pleased that the way I earned my skates had been a subject of discussion among you. For, I supposed it would be a foregone conclusion. Now, I will give you a few reasons why I think my conduct proper. (1) The aim I had in view. Now you know, skating is a very healthy exercise & also pleasing. It is the very best means of quieting the brain & stimulating physical health. Now to buy a pair of skates without asking my father for money was a very laudable aim. (2) Earning money is also a fine thing for the young. (3) The advantages accruing to myself from much writing. (4) I don't regard myself as placed in any predicament whatever. It is no worse to write an essay for a fellow than to help him out with his lesson. And no blame could attach itself to me in any case. Hack writing, or writing for money is a perfectly legitimate business. I am not supposed to know for what it is to be used. I wrote a certain paper, received so much for it & it is the responsibility of the man himself whether he uses it for himself. (5) Writing like everything else can be bought & sold. If I buy a pencil I have a right to use it as my own, & if a fellow buys an essay of me as merchandise, the only copy in the world, it passes out of my hand & he has a right to do as he wills with it.

Now I wouldn't care if the whole faculty knew of it for with me it was only a business transaction & the other fellows must settle the moral point with themselves. . . . Now about going into society, I think it does a world of good to me, as I am having an easy time with my studies. It polishes one's rough edges & counteracts the influence of being wholly with the boys. Now I don't want you to think I am shirking my work, for I do my duty just as faithfully as I know how.

Although none of the letters written to Charlie by his parents while he was at Brown has survived, it is obvious from his own letter of February 22 that his father also criticized the ghost-writing venture. Charlie then acknowledged his error and asked forgiveness:

As I see it, all your arguments are pointed at the other man. Although you may not see it, I know perfectly well, that my course is not reprehensible before the faculty or before justice. I could cite similar cases in past college history. But, if I have laid myself open to the slightest moral crimination, I am willing to repent and beg your forgiveness. You know the proverbial rashness of youth. You also know my fondness for skating. You know my desire of independence & my aptitude for easy writing. I hope that in view of these facts, you will consider my conduct, if not morally right, as excusable & pardonable. Well, I might as well say out & out that I will pull in my horns & you stand victor of the arena.

Now I have been sick. . . .

Charlie's retreat from his fallacious reasoning was somewhat grudging, but it is evident that his father's strictures found their mark. The net effect of this experience was not to give him a precedent for closing his eyes to moral consequences but to sharpen his conscience. It is significant that at no time in his later career did he use a ghost-writer, and his high sensitivity to moral considerations will be apparent as this story unfolds.

Hughes had plunged into the work of his junior year with the liveliest expectations, and these were not disappointed. Astronomy, chemistry, physics, and German now came within his intellectual ken. On October 27 he wrote to his mother:

> But our work in Chemistry is to me the best of all. It is taught so splendidly. If I ever thought I could be a great chemist, I would make it a specialty. It is more interesting to me than any other study I have yet taken up, notwithstanding my love for Mathematics. Professor Appleton is the best chemist in the state and he never says a single word in class but what means something and which gives some exact information.
>
> . . . A day never passes over my head in which I do not feel profoundly grateful for the advantages I enjoy, and none the less anxious, lest I in my after life— should fail to show the fruit of so much thorough teaching and untiring study.

At the end of the semester he gave his father a rather enthusiastic appraisal of his progress:

> I suppose you will get my marks soon. I expect an ex in German, English Literature and Astronomy and a vg in Physics and Chemistry. I know I won't get an ex in Physics, but I would expect one in Chemistry if the professor wasn't such a hard marker. However, I don't believe a fellow in our class will get five exs, as it is not so easy to recite perfectly in science as in language.
>
> Well, I am glad I am through. I never got so much stuff in my head in a given time in my life. But Chemistry was the worst. I got up at four o'clock Monday morning and worked 'til eight. We had the very hardest possible examination he could have given. I knew it all and wrote just as fast as I could make my pen fly for two hours. But, as I got along very nicely, I felt happy when I got all through —even if I was tired out. . . .
>
> My studies for the coming term are very nice. Logic will, of course, demand much study. Chaucer will be pleasant and easy. Physiology is quite interesting. . . . Political Economy is immense. Our professor, Diman, is about the biggest gun on the Faculty and a clear-headed, shrewd man. You have to pay attention to everything he says and just jot down what you can get of it.

J. Lewis Diman was the pride of Brown. This dignified but unpretending thinker had had numerous attractive offers from Harvard, Princeton, and other universities, but he loved Brown and chose to remain there. When he delivered a special lecture on "Immanent Finality," students flocked in as if it had been a baseball game. His earnest face, creased forehead, and long flowing sideburns were accepted as a sort of symbol of intellectual mastery. He talked with freedom, brilliance, and a fidelity to truth, as he saw it, that lifted the sensitive and receptive Charlie Hughes into a "new and exalted sphere of intellectual activity."[5]

Special notice from Professor Diman was a high distinction. Once Hughes wrote to his father: "On Friday, I was up in History on Guizot's lectures on the Medieval Church. Professor Diman complimented me very highly, saying that it was the best analysis he had during the term." Some weeks later the devoted student again reported, "By the way, Professor Diman bowed to me yesterday and, as he never bows to college boys, it augurs well."

Near the end of the scholastic year Professor Lincoln threw out a challenge: "Hughes, why don't you take examinations for freshman year rank. You ought to do it. You will be sorry in later life if you graduate without class standing." [6] This was a new and appealing idea. By taking a few examinations, Hughes established his class standing and was one of the five members of his class admitted to Phi Beta Kappa at the end of his junior year.

Happy summer days came as a further reward. Marcus C. Allen, scion of the Allen family that had been close to the Hugheses in Sandy Hill, set up a Delta Upsilon camp on an island in Lake George, off Bolton, in 1877, and young Hughes became one of the first to enjoy a vacation there. During the summers of 1879 and 1880 he spent two or three weeks at this rustic camp consisting of tents and a messroom built of rough boards. Hughes and Pendleton (his roommate), Charles C. Mumford, and William Jillson joined a number of fraternity brothers from other colleges, taking along a guide and a cook. They jaunted by buckboards from Glens Falls to the beautiful lake region, and rowed to the island in small boats.

Days at the camp were a merry round of boating, hiking, eating, reading, and tomfoolery. Jillson tells us that Hughes' tent was well stocked with books and that he had a seemingly endless fund of humor and stories. In the evenings the campers sang their college songs so lustily that an audience from the near-by inns often clustered about their tiny island in boats. It was still more fun for the young men to serenade the hotels in their own boats. On these occasions, according to Jillson's account, girls would flock out to the porches. The boys found ways of introducing themselves and sometimes went into the inns to dance—square dances and the Virginia reel.

Hughes returned to Brown in September, 1880, determined to devote to the studies of his senior year all the energy he possessed, but first he became entangled in college politics. He wrote to his father on September 25:

Today was the time for class elections for officers next spring. Each society constituted a clique to run in their men. A combination would be formed & then a

[5] CEH, Notes, p. 67.   [6] CEH, Notes, p. 69.

counter-combination against it. I never saw such a terrible state of affairs. We met this morning & after a two hour's stormy session adjourned in the wildest confusion. For the last three days, class politics have taken the class by storm. The professors are wild & say they have never seen anything like it in the annals of the college. . . .

As I was in it heart & soul, I was naturally terribly excited. I am yet. The class is becoming thoroughly aroused at the mean chicanery of some members, which was brought out today. From morning to night, new schemes are formed, old ones thrown up. Every little while someone comes to my room to know if I will vote for this or that, & then I must go & get the Neutrals to vote in such a way & so & so, it is a complete picture of politics, on a small scale, except it is bitter war to death bet. the secret societies united & the Delta U's & Neutrals. Unfortunately we have just the same number of votes on each side & are fearfully worked up. Pray for me, that I may let my moderation be known. I never was more worked up. I got up this morning in class-meeting & talked about 20 minutes, I haven't the slightest idea what I said only that I sat on cliques generally. But when I got through I was bathed wet through with perspiration & almost wilted out. But the boys all acknowledge that I did more to break up the secret clique than has been done yet. At last accounts, 3 votes have come over to our side.

His studies were now more exacting. There was medieval and modern history under Professor Diman, an elected course in Italian, and psychology and philosophy under Dr. Robinson. At first he thought both history and psychology were "terrible." These two subjects required more work than all his studies combined in junior year. "They give us references every day of 100 pages or so," he complained, "on which we are thoroughly questioned, and the main point of their teaching is to get away from the habit of memorizing a certain number of words, to hard & independent research." But after a few months he was enjoying research—a fact of the utmost importance in his later career. On November 21 he wrote to his father:

You can hardly understand my interest in the term's work. With practical history and philosophy to study and not the ideal and fanciful traditions of Latin and Grecian lore—however beautiful and instructive—I have found a new fondness for research awaken in me. To sit down and develop a closely fact-compacted history is now the same—as a few months ago—to devour the last novel. Sometimes, I look upon this new feature of my character as startling. May it not betoken inconstancy to readily grasp and become enthusiastic in every new branch brought under my consideration?

Dr. Robinson was short on inspiration but had a way of goading his students into self-expression. In his letter of October 6 Hughes gives a vivid picture of how the president badgered him and of his own reaction to it:

We are very busy now looking at the germs of European Civilization among the Goths and Vandals, and deciding that momentous question, as to whether we have a mind or not, or rather whether there is "a conscious cognizing soul or spirit distinct and separable from the material organism, or whether the soul or spirit is a function of the entity called body, i.e. the product of the organs of sense?" This momentous question will probably be decided by the end of the week, and meanwhile I would humbly suggest that all philosophers and sages hold their breath till the decree of fate, personified in E. G. Robinson D.D., LL.D. has gone forth and the question whether there is an entity called soul, distinct and separable from the bodily organism is settled for all generations. Although in this position of undeniable doubt and loss of breath, still I cannot but state that I am perfectly well, and that whatever is learning within me is getting along first rate. . . .

I think I have had the good or bad fortune (as result will prove) of falling into the graces of the aforesaid "fate personified" for whenever with stern eye and solemn phiz he cracks a joke at the other half of the class, he invariably turns suddenly with relentless gaze to my corner only to subdue my hilarious ha ha into a mournfully dying gasp. Then (this is the part of the fortune I deem bad) he always has me up on the hardest parts of the lectures (which I understand is a token of favor), and then suddenly in the midst of my flowing recitation, cuts it off sharply, by asking me what Des Cartes would have thought if I talked such stuff to him. I tremblingly reply, meanwhile flatteringly giving his lectures a better cognomen than stuff, by plunging into Des Cartes philosophy (crammed up the night before) when I am again hauled up with, "What are *you* sir?" That being a much pondered and never satisfactorily answered query, I indulge in a blank stare, which is hewed down . . . by, "Well, if you don't know yourself, what do you expect to know outside of yourself"! I gently advise that a much older and much grayer head than mine attack that problem, when a shout of, "Go on sir," drums my wearied faculties into action & I trot on again in good style when my gait is broken by the following: "What have you been talking about all this time"? This floors me completely, and dissatisfied with all mankind, I repeat my former eloquent appeals to consciousness with broken and failing utterances, when suddenly I find myself sitting down and "fate-personified" telling the class that that is the kind of recitation he likes to hear.

I recover my shattered senses and my spirit once more breathes the pure air, when I am once more sunk in "ungeheures Unheil" by 6–100 pages of references, "which, gentlemen, must be perused by tomorrow morning." No wonder the poet sings "I would not live alway," taking alway in the sense of all manner, method, &c. . . . For my part, if my hair leaves the top of my head, I will never originate a new theory to perplex the students under "fate personified."

On one occasion "fate personified" caught the young man completely off guard but not vacant-minded. As he related it:

I came nearly fizzling yesterday. We are on the question of Moral Taste as contrasted with Conscience. Just as I was called on, the precise point escaped me and, to save myself from a complete flunk, I asked Prex. to answer a hard question I had been thinking of and he entered into a discussion with me about it,— never asked for his point at all and concluded the recitation by saying that nothing pleased him so much as to see original thought on the part of his students. How is that for luck?

A sharp summons to the president's office in October caused Hughes' heart to sink, but he came out walking on air and wrote to his mother:

PROVIDENCE,
Oct. 17th, 1880

DEAR MA,

After recitation in psychology, the President loudly and rather roughly said, "I wish to see Mr. Hughes in my office immediately." Well, I was so scared, I turned white as a sheet, for this is his invariable manner of "hauling up" the boys as it is called. I went quaking to his office with him. He looked me all over carefully and took a piece of paper from his pocket—handed it to me—meanwhile, talking something about "gratifying my father"—"highest marks"—"rhetoric," etc., which in my confusion I did not understand. I hoped most vainly to get from under his stern eye. Slowly, I opened the paper and read an order on the Treasurer for $50 for the Dana Premium. Shortly to say Ma I had received a prize of $50 for having the highest standing in the class in our rhetorical studies, commencing with elocution and rhetoric in sophomore year and ending with our oration and work in English literature. You could have knocked me over with a feather. I thanked the President and made my way to my room and devoutly thanked my Heavenly Father.

I had forgotten all about this prize and if I had thought of it, so many stood high in the rhetorical studies that I could never have supposed myself the highest. The $50 is safe in the best bank in Providence. I want to keep it as a nest egg for my future career. It will be a good thing to have after graduation.

Another honor is put upon me. I am unanimously elected senior delegate to represent the Brown Chapter at the Delta Upsilon Convention at Amherst which means all expenses paid and free leave from college from October 26–29. Think of that! Poor little I am selected to represent Brown in Convention. Well, I will have to buy a new hat and please send me Pa's black coat and vest which I wore last winter as I must have it to go to Amherst with. I will bring it back Thanksgiving or Christmas whenever I go home. *Please, send them as soon as possible.*

Dear Ma, I wish I could see you when you read this letter and kiss you and Pa many times. Think of it, $50 and a delegate to Amherst. Now, please, let me keep that $50 secure until after I graduate so that I can have something to start with. Please excuse this scrawl. You and Pa have my best love, I remain your loving son.

CHARLIE

Write soon

A few days later he was pleading again for his father's coat and vest, for money to buy a new hat and pay his DU tax. "I hope the prize was not too much for you," he wrote. "I have been dazed for almost two or three days."

The Delta Upsilon convention at Amherst in October, 1880, proved to be one of his most memorable college experiences. In the D.U. chapter at Brown he had found stimulating companionship, and many of the friendships formed there were to be lifelong. One of his D.U. friends, William H. P. Faunce, a young man who "represented all that was best in student life," was to be president of Brown University for thirty years. At Amherst, Hughes encountered other keen young fellows who impressed him most favorably. Among them were Starr J. Murphy (later counsel to John D. Rockefeller for investigation of proposed philanthropic enterprises), Frank C. Partridge (later solicitor of the State Department, diplomat, and for a brief period United States Senator from Vermont), and William Travers Jerome, who was to win fame as district attorney for New York County.

It was on this occasion, when he was only eighteen, that Hughes first discovered his power to sway a crowd—a power that was to remain with him throughout his life. Losing himself in his speeches, he demonstrated in marked degree the Welsh *hwyl* that he had so admired in his Uncle John. His excitement over this discovery about himself was poured out in a letter to his father:

PROVIDENCE, Oct. 31, 1880.

DEAR PA,

    . . . Last Monday night was a great night in Providence. The grand state demonstration on behalf of Garfield & Arthur took place & as it was to pass the campus, we were busy all afternoon in illuminating our rooms and the outside grounds. I did not get to bed till quite late & on Tuesday morning, I was very much hurried in preparing for my departure. You must know, that in a certain sense, that was the proudest day of my life. To go out from the finest society in college, which contains the best scholars, speakers &c. to go forth as her representative to meet in convention with representative men from all the principal colleges of the United States, you may well suppose was the highest honor to which I could look in college. . . .

Starting off then as Senior Delegate, at 2-o'clock on Tuesday afternoon, I arrived in Amherst at 9.00 P.M. & was at once met by the Amherst boys, who conducted me to their rooms. . . . I certainly never made the acquaintance of a finer set of fellows. . . . I went to chapel the next morning with the Amherst boys & inspected their buildings &c. . . . The convention assembled at 10 A.M. received the credentials of the delegates, laid out an order of business & adjourned. At 2 P.M. they again assembled & listened to fine reports from all the chapters. I wish you could have been there, to see how high D.U. stands at all the colleges, not from words only but from the immense number of prizes & honors secured. My head was almost turned. You know how ardent a Delta U. I have been, but do not be surprised, when I say that I never had half an idea of the greatness of Delta U. It is wonderful.

When the report of the Brown Chapter was called for, I arose with fear and trembling to tell what the boys were doing at Brown. I gradually warmed with my theme, till it actually seemed as if something gave way in my head & I ran on in the most profuse style, words succeeding words, & climax, climax, without effort and wholly extemporaneous, till I sat down amid sounds of applause & feeling as if I had dropped from a cloud. Please do not imagine me egotistical, for I have been longing to pour out my heart to someone, & I dare do it to no fellow, as I am afraid, he will regard me conceited, but you know how afraid to speak I have been, & you will appreciate my spirit, when I say, that from that morning to this, I have made numerous speeches & in none of them have I had the least trouble in saying just what I wanted to, with well-rounded periods & good climaxes. Well, to return, after that session, I was the centre of an eager crowd of boys, gathering around me & congratulating me on my report. Ever after when I rose to speak, I was greeted with loud applause, and never did my newly-obtained faculty fail me.

In the evening, the question of camping was brought up, & I rose to say only a few words & I spoke to an interested audience for half an hour. Anecdotes, humorous expressions & pithy sentences came unbidden to my lips & when I was through, the Junior delegate said to me—"Hughes, a wonderful change has come over you; you have no idea how finely you have spoken. Why," said he, "the way you kept us laughing & at the same time brought out your point in a steady stream of good English was marvellous." Nor had I an idea of what I was saying. I knew I was speaking very fast & that once in a while I was interrupted with applause & loud laughter & when I sat down I found myself bathed in perspiration & amid a crowd of fellows cheering for the Brown delegate. Now please, dear Pa, don't smile at what you may consider a conceited young fellow, whose head is turned. I have been home two days, am perfectly cool, with my pulse at 70, & I assure you that I never felt more humble than at the present. It seems to me as if a higher power had taken me from myself & given the faculty of unhesitating speech.

Certainly I made many friends & at each session I spoke on some topic or other to an interested audience. I proposed the adoption of resolutions, I had drawn up, with reference to our support of Garfield, the President of the D.U. Fraternity [then the Republican candidate for the Presidency of the United States] & took a prominent part in the business of the convention. I am on a dozen or more committees & never worked harder than when enjoying those two days of respite. . . . Garfield sent us a splendid letter, congratulating the Fraternity, & expressing his sorrow at his inability to meet with us. Then succeeded the banquet & I arrived at Providence at 12 o'clock on Friday & have since been busy in making up lessons &c.

At society meeting, I gave my report & again was blessed with wonderful success. To be able to get away from myself, to live only in my speech, to think only of my point & not of how many buttons there are on my waistcoat, is a gift for which I have longed & sighed in vain till last Wednesday. And, then when thoroughly aroused, not to forget the requirements of rhetoric & accurate oratory, is a matter of constant wonderment to me. The Junior delegate brought back to Brown wonderful accounts of me & the boys have been around me, congratulating & talking to me, ever since my return. Now may my Heavenly Father, the giver of every good gift, bless & sanctify me to his service. This is my constant. Never have I felt more solemn & subdued, than at the very instant of success, when I could hear the echoes of the dying applause.

Your loving son,
Charlie

In spite of his feeling of dedication, religion was claiming less of Hughes' attention. Occasionally he prepared a synopsis for one of his father's expository articles in the *Homiletic Review*, and he often went to church. But the sermons he liked best were those of Dr. A. J. F. Behrends of the Union Congregational

Church and Dr. David H. Greer of the Grace Episcopal Church (later Bishop of New York) instead of those to be heard at the First Baptist Meetinghouse. In a letter to his father he riddled a casuistic lecture by Henry Ward Beecher, and a year later he was challenging and seeking to modify some of his father's views:

Well, you may be sure, I will be glad to greet you next Christmas and we will have many a good chat . . . as of yore. Only I hope my major premise will be more acceptable and my conclusions more worthy of your approbation. I am intent on reforming many of your opinions and I hope, aided by the lectures of our re-doubtable Professors and a little subtly turned English, for once to conquer some of the notions coming out of long established and stereotyped methods of thought. In short, I bring this letter to a close—sending you and Ma my dearest love and throwing down my glove before the most terrible of all debaters.

Yours affectionately,
Charlie

Another letter, written on his nineteenth birthday and signed "Your little Charlie," shows pretty clearly where he stood:

I verily believe you would have wondered at the scion of your stock, if you had seen me argue for three hours yesterday afternoon with one of the boys, impassion-ately & laboriously endeavoring to show the necessity of accepting the whole word of God, of an overruling Providence & a future punishment. I declare it is impos-sible to get outside of one's early training. Whatever I may do or become, there is no danger that I ever will be able to rid myself of the truths implanted in early child-hood.

In November, 1880, Hughes was elected one of the editors of the *Brunonian,* the student newspaper. This he accepted enthusiastically, but when he was elected president of the Brown chapter of Delta Upsilon a few months later he declined to serve because of the extra work it would involve. While his editorials ranged over a wide field, the most notable one concerned a tragedy at Brown. The inimitable Professor Diman, twirling his glasses as he explored the great epochs of history, had become the center of an intellectual ferment on the campus. His lectures seemed more fascinating than ever before. Then, with shocking suddenness, in February, 1881, Professor Diman died. Hughes wrote a vivid account of the incident to his mother on February 6:

On Thursday, as you have probably heard, occurred the death of our much loved Professor Diman. I have never in my life been so stunned. Not only was he my best loved Professor, not only did I reverence him and listen with the greatest respect to all his teaching, but I looked up to him as the greatest embodiment of true scholarship I had ever met. He was taken sick the day after my return from home (Jan. 28). He gave us our first lecture on International Law in the forenoon and returned home to illness and death. . . . On Thursday, noon, I heard he was seriously ill and told the boys so at dinner—but they all laughed at me and said it was all a hoax and so I thought myself. . . . After dinner, Bean [George F. Bean, managing editor of the *Brunonian*] and I got together some of our class and proposed sending a bouquet. So we went down, got a most lovely bouquet and sent it to him at four o'clock. He took it, smelled of it, expressed his gratification very pleasantly and at five-thirty the same afternoon he passed away. . . .

I heard of it first at supper where I arrived late, but would not credit it for a long time, till the blank faces of the boys told me the astounding truth. . . . I felt in a dream. I could not eat. Had I heard of anything incredible I could not have been more stunned. I thought more of him than any man living, outside of my own relatives. . . . You, who know how often and how fondly and reverently I spoke of him, can imagine my utter bewilderment . . . I went to my room and remained in a stupor for some time. About eight o'clock, Bean came to me and said, as the Brunonian was already in press for Saturday, we must get out a great supplement with a memorial.

We immediately went to Prex and Professor Lincoln for facts of his career and at nine and a half o'clock sat down to write. Bean wrote the little editorial at the head and I wrote the account of his life up to the last week and Bean wrote the account of his illness and death, and then I finished with the eulogy (the last column and a half beginning with "The Sudden Removal"). We distributed the parts before we sat down and wonderful to tell it was finished at ten and a half and carried down and was printed by next morning. I wrote faster than Bean and, as you will see, wrote the larger part of it. We were both under a spell and it would be utterly impossible for us to do the like again except as then under the greatest nervous excitement. The next morning, in chapel, Pres. Robinson arose and in a broken voice read and prayed, and then postponed college exercises till after the funeral. Among the Seniors there was not a dry eye and we all left chapel sobbing as if suddenly deprived of parents and friends. . . .

A pall seemed to fall on everything. The boys (Seniors) talked to each other in whispers and burst into tears when vivid recollections would occur. It did seem as if the stars had fallen. . . . In this time of gloom and sadness, it seems as though the joy had faded from the world and, as I try to shake off this mournful feeling, every now and then there rises before me that manly form, whose like I shall never again behold. Oh! if I could but give you an adequate description of him and our relations to him. All I can say is that, in his death, the University has suffered the greatest possible loss and the class of '81 has lost its kindest instructor, its most cheerful advisor, its most cherished friend.

Sickness at Brown caused much concern that winter. Hughes complained in an editorial that students in chilly classrooms were "whirled from serene meditation on . . . modern philosophy to a sudden consciousness of freezing feet and hands." [7] Before Professor Diman's death one of Hughes' intimate friends, Frederick L. Gamage, had gone to bed with typhoid fever. For a time Hughes took care of him, as there was no college infirmary. The consequent loss of sleep, added to his hard work, drained him of his vitality, and he went home sick for the first time in five years at college. After a week of his mother's

[7] *Brunonian*, Feb. 5, 1881.

nursing, however, he was back at Brown for the final sprint toward graduation.

As his senior year approached an end, he wrote to his parents, "I am thoroughly tired of college life, and when once, I grasp my diploma it will be with no mawkish or sentimental sorrow at leaving the Lyceum of my youth." In part this feeling may have resulted from the continued struggle to pay his bills. It seemed a last straw when he had to ask his father for $18 for the alumni dinner. "Think of paying $18," he wrote, "to see a lot of gray-haired alumni gorge themselves. Then I am having the hat made over $3.00 & the pictures (extra dozen standing ones) $3.00 more & I suppose the Finance Committee ought not to be obliged to delay their wonderful proceedings to accommodate the downtrodden and poverty-stricken Senior. At least they will not."

One other worry was what he would turn to when he left college. Dr. Robinson had told the father of one of his students that there were two or three men in the class who would "amount to something"—Hughes, Chase, and Bean. He had also given Hughes a suggestive bit of advice: "Now above everything else don't let yourself sink out of sight after you graduate." But Hughes had only vague ideas as to how his talents might be employed. On November 7, 1880, he had written to his father:

I am quite intimate, now, with a DU graduate of '80 who is studying medicine in the city. I have become quite interested—picking up information here and there and have attended one dissection and one operation. Who knows? I may become a doctor. Hoping the Lord will direct me in the way He has chosen for me, I am looking in all directions to ascertain my fitness for some pursuit.

A week later he was very much at sea:

I was somewhat amused at your observation on my courage and my approaching manhood. I assure you, that I really am afraid that I am too much the dear little boy of yours and not enough the dignified and reverent Senior whom Prex thinks is so responsible for the well-being of our Seminaries of learning. However, I never could be and never hope to be anything else to *you* than a dear little boy, although in Providence it is Sir, Mister, etc. That is one reason why I also feel as if I have tumbled off an elevation to which I had no right and been respectfully reminded of my real position when I come home. Well, my dear Ma, a long intercourse with the world has taught me much that will be of benefit to me (please supply after "long" in the above, "for my age" and be sure you don't laugh).

Well, if I only knew what I should do when I left college, I would feel more cheerful and manly than I do now. I never was more respected in college than at present, never was more honored, yet, I always feel as if—when I left college—I would drop unminded into oblivion as far as the professors and the boys are concerned.

Dave Call has now been made President of Des Moines University, Iowa. Think of it and the rapid rise of that most fortunate young man. It is truly wonderful. Now, don't think I am ambitious, but I would like to be something in this world.

Within a fortnight he was talking of medicine again, although in a rather facetious vein:

I am thinking more and more of medicine as a profession. During vacation, I have talked several times with my friends—and, in fact, am almost enthusiastic over dry bones and sticking plasters. There is something enchanting about the study and, were it not for the long course necessary, I am almost afraid, dear Ma, I should usurp your functions and take your place as the family doctor. What a team we would make! I would have you to entertain and nurse the nervous—Pa can give them lectures on morals and myself to supply the pills. . . .

The one certainty was that he did not wish to go into the ministry. Replying to his mother's urgings, he made this clear on December 7:

I have carefully weighed what you said in your letter & have reached this conclusion. I want to do just that which will enable me to do most for the world around me according to the divine will. As yet, I feel no *call* to the ministry, & I know that such a sphere of life is not exactly suitable to my abilities. In the other professions, I see no special choice, except I have felt of late a drawing toward medicine, although all the boys declare that my business should be that of law. Now I know that I [could do] well in law, but the profession is repugnant to me.

This letter is the first indication that he had given any thought to the legal profession as his life's work. His fellow students continued to point to his special talents in this field, and the law gradually became less repugnant to him. By January 9, 1881, he was at least neutral toward it:

I had a good sober talk with the boys last night on our future, and everyone said that, in every respect, I was cut out for a lawyer—that I would be foolish to think of anything else. Well, time will tell. At present, I am grateful to do my regular work, trusting in Providence for future favors.

A month later he was "thrown into a whirl of excitement" by the prospect of becoming a university professor. In response to a letter from Hughes' father, David Call, Charlie's esteemed friend from Madison who was now president of Des Moines University, wrote that, while he could offer no opening in 1881, he would be happy to give young Hughes the chair of modern languages and belles-lettres the following year. Overjoyed by this promise, the young man began to dream of spending the intervening year on a scholarship at Johns Hopkins University.

By March 6, however, he was definitely warming up toward the law. He wrote to his mother:

The more I think of the future, the more I incline toward the legal profession, as the one for which I am most fitted & the one most favorable to a high ambition. However, I am now settled down into a quiet, inoffending drudge, whose pleasant anticipations of the future are mere dry leaves blown about by the present duties, which operate on my mind like a chill October gale.

There are other indications of his growing interest in the legal field. Digging into the antiquated rules of the university, he wrote two editorials for the *Brunonian* ridiculing the prohibitions against playing cards, using profane language, going to the theater, or entering a tavern where liquor was sold. It was already evident that his investigative instinct, his logical mind, his quick grasp of intricate problems, and his powers of lucid expression were made to order for the law. But the question of his future was still wide open as he finished his work at Brown. Having been chosen class prophet, he was pondering over the future careers of his fellow students one day when John Murray Marshall, the songfest leader, came in and asked, "And what are you prophesying about yourself?"

"I don't know," Hughes admitted, ". . . I rather think I'll take up teaching."

"Of course, you'll be a lawyer," his friend retorted. "I've picked out law for myself, and if you are not a lawyer too I'm no prophet." [8]

Young Marshall's confident prognostication gave Hughes another strong push toward the legal profession. For the present, however, all dreams of the future had to be subordinated to the pressing realities of commencement week. As usual, Hughes had made an enviable record. In his sophomore year he had earned nine ratings of "excellent" and one of "very good"—in Latin; in his junior year all his marks were at the maximum, excepting a "very good" in physics. Only his French dropped one notch below the maximum in the first term of his senior year, and in the last term he had the coveted "ex." in everything.[9] After the final examination he was assigned the "Classical Oration" at commencement, which meant that he stood third in the class. He and Charles C. Mumford (later associate justice of the Superior Court of Rhode Island) were singled out for the Carpenter awards; in the judgment of the faculty they united "in the highest degree the three most important elements of success in life, ability, character, and attainment." Although he was the youngest member of a class of forty-three, Hughes' intellect and capacity for work had made a deep impression upon professors and students alike.

The commencement festivities began with class day on Friday in mid-June. Custom dictated that the seniors wear full-dress suits and silk hats throughout the day and every day following until the commencement exercises came to a close the next Wednesday night. In this garb they went to the formal

[8] CEH, Notes, p. 76.   [9] Brown College Register, 1880–1881.

class-day ceremonies, to a tree-planting in the afternoon, a promenade concert in the evening (balls had not yet come in), and then to their class supper. This convivial affair began about midnight after the seniors, escorted by their band, had marched down college hill to the Narragansett Hotel. It was on this occasion that Hughes delivered his "Class Prophecy." At the end of their festivities, about four or five o'clock in the morning, the hilarious seniors marched back to the campus and attempted, in accordance with the tradition, to play a baseball game.[10] With his "swallowtails" and pumps and his pompadour haircut, young Hughes must have been an amusing spectacle on the baseball field at sunup that morning.

On Wednesday the academic procession formed on the campus and the "Officers of the Corporation, the faculty, the seniors and alumni marched to the old First Baptist Meeting House, 'built for the worship of God and to hold commencements in.' " Walter J. Towne, who was to become a teacher in the schools of Providence, delivered the valedictory. Hughes' classical oration was on "The First Appearance of Sophocles." George F. Bean (a future lawyer and mayor of Woburn, Mass.) was salutatorian; William C. Ladd (later professor of French at Haverford College) gave the philosophical oration; Frederick R. Hazard (future president of the Solvay Process Company of Syracuse, New York) was class president. Among other prominent members of the class were William Sheafe Chase, who was to become a canon of the Episcopal Church and a noted crusading reformer; John Murray Marshall, who was to practice law in Los Angeles; and Morgan Brooks, future professor of electrical engineering at the University of Illinois.

Looking back at his college experience across half a century, Hughes once remarked that he was impressed by two facts—"first, that there was so much that we did not learn, and, second, that we learned so many things that were not so." [11] But this whimsical hindsight does not obscure the extraordinary intellectual growth that his letters from Brown reveal. In those three years he had felt the inspiration of Diman and the imperious challenge of Robinson, and he had discovered the power of his own mind. While he had turned definitely away from the ministry, the moral essence of his home background had been transfused into his thinking and his new activities. The young man had found himself. Throughout his days Hughes never ceased to be grateful to Brown for the good fellowship it afforded, the standards it upheld, the scientific method or "way of knowing" that it taught, and the windows it opened upon "a world so full of riches of culture that no one with eye and ear need ever be poor." [12]

[10] CEH, Notes, p. 74.
[11] CEH's address to Brown alumni, June 15, 1931.   [12] *Ibid.*

Chapter 7

LAW TAKES COMMAND

WITH college days behind him, Hughes' uppermost thought was that he must begin to make a living. The idea that he might become a lawyer now fascinated him. He nursed it fondly every time he went over the question of his future career. But he did not feel that his parents should be burdened with the expense of a law-school course. Law was something to reach for in the future. Just now he had to make some money by means already available to him.

In the days when he thought of teaching as his métier, Hughes had a vague notion that he might make enough money to enable him to study for a year or two in Germany in preparation for a college position. That dream was now fading before the onslaught of a new ambition, but teaching still seemed to afford him the best opportunity of earning some money in the year ahead; so he registered with a teachers' agency, hoping for a place as an instructor in Latin or Greek in a secondary school.

Several schools showed an interest in his application. When they learned that he was only nineteen, however, negotiations were quickly terminated. One of his best prospects seemed to be the Pennsylvania Military Academy (now College) at Chester. Colonel Hyatt, the principal, had been pleased with Hughes' letters, but when they met for an interview in New York he exclaimed, "Why, you could never maintain discipline with my cadets!" [1] The only satisfaction Hughes was to get out of this experience was postponed until 1928, when, on receiving the degree of doctor of laws from the Pennsylvania Military College, he told the alumni how much easier it was to get that degree than to enter the faculty.

Young Hughes was keenly disappointed over these rejections. Yet he could scarcely complain; for, while he had attained his maximum height of five feet eleven inches, he was still slight and looked younger than he was. The beard that was to become famous in many lands had not even begun to grow. He had a fine, intelligent face, but it was the face of youth and inexperience.

Turning to other fields, Hughes secured his first job in the midsummer of 1881—a truly novel undertaking. Property in certain parts of Brooklyn had been heavily assessed for local improvements in advance of immediate needs, and the unpaid taxes and assessments exceeded the then assessed valuation of

[1] CEH, Notes, p. 77.

the property. The legislature offered the owners relief, and it became necessary to calculate the amounts of the arrears in each case. The owners offered this job to the young master of mathematics from Brown University. Hughes worked ten hours a day for six weeks at a wage of $6 a week.

Just as he was finishing this job, he was pleasantly surprised by an offer from the Delaware Academy at Delhi, New York. The salary was only $200 for the school year, with board and room. But he would be free each afternoon, and if he desired to study law he could do so in a good office. Hughes accepted with alacrity and went to Delhi at once.

Dr. James O. Griffin, principal of the academy, went to the station on a September afternoon to meet his new teacher. When the lanky young man from Greenpoint alighted from the train and introduced himself, he could see a shadow of disappointment cross the principal's face. Dr. Griffin held his tongue until he had reinforced the eager young man by taking him home to supper. Then his misgivings could no longer be restrained. "I had not supposed," he began, "that you looked so young—quite as young as many of my students." [2]

One account of this interview has the principal exclaiming, "Why, you've no more beard than an egg." Such a statement would have been accurate, but Hughes carried away no recollection of such bluntness on the part of Dr. Griffin. Certainly the inference that this chiding caused Hughes to grow a beard in later years is without foundation. The significant point is that Dr. Griffin voiced his fears that Hughes would be unable to handle the job, and Hughes, seeing his last chance to teach that year slipping away, summoned all his powers of persuasion. What he pleaded for was a test of his teaching ability. At least he had self-confidence and enthusiasm, and, in the circumstances, a tryout could scarcely be denied him. Dr. Griffin assented.

One reason for Dr. Griffin's initial reluctance became apparent when Hughes was shown to his room. It was near the center of a long hall on the second floor of the dormitory, with the girls' rooms on one side and the boys' on the other. He was expected to maintain order in the hall. The academy had all grades from the primary to full preparation for college. Some of the young farmers who would come in later for a winter of schooling—steady, industrious, and ambitious fellows—were older and huskier than the new teacher. But from the beginning Hughes' students responded to his enthusiasm and vitality, and, except on rare occasions, noise in the hall ceased to be a problem. Even without a whisker to shave, he had enough magnetism about him to command a rare combination of loyalty, attention, and respect.

"Do I stay longer?" Hughes asked the principal as soon as he dared to raise the issue.

[2] *Ibid.,* p. 78.

"You may stay the rest of your life if you wish," Dr. Griffin replied.[3]

Delhi was a charming village among the hills. The academy had a delightful setting in spacious grounds with beautiful trees. Its main building, with cupola and broad veranda, and the separate hall which served as a commodious dormitory had the atmosphere of an old and honored institution. Professor Griffin, a man of exceptional talent who had studied abroad and was later to become professor of German at Leland Stanford University, came to be listed among Hughes' best friends. Teaching in this congenial atmosphere proved to be one of the happiest experiences of a long lifetime.[4]

Hughes fell in with a number of forward-looking young men at Delhi. As an informal club, they would meet at the American Hotel on Saturday evenings for whist and other games and "raids" upon the hotel larder at the invitation of the proprietor's genial son, who was one of the intimates. Hughes' reputation as a wit also won him an invitation from the townspeople of Scottish descent to eat the haggis in honor of Robert Burns and respond to a toast. At Dr. Griffin's urging the young instructor also "broke through the fetters" of his work-study system and "sought both health and pleasure in a genuine fishing excursion." Describing this experience to his father, he wrote on April 30, 1882:

We reached Delhi about six P.M.—bringing home as nice a mess of trout as could well be caught—they numbered 42 in all, and a large number were these large, beautiful ones, which make the heart of the angler palpitate. Although I did not do as well as Mr. Griffin, I secured some rare beauties, and with the exception of a slight lameness, feel much the better for the trip, which we hope soon to repeat. I wish you could make such a trip. It would do you more good than a pound of medicine—put new blood in your veins and harden your muscles. . . .

I am making the most of my time and trying to do my work in a conscientious manner. I have countless desires and yearnings, which I repress in paying strict attention to the demands of the present. That is the best cure for all mental ailments—*work*.

The following week Hughes wrote to his mother:

I was thinking over my relations with Delhi people the other day. I never found more cordial and whole-souled friends. I never received so many kind attentions, and I don't think that I have a single enemy. May these blessings continue. My health is good. I weighed 130 the other day. I hope to return to you without any ill health caused by my year of hard work.

At the academy Hughes taught Latin, Greek, algebra, and plane geometry and drilled the boys in their declamations. One of his outstanding students was

---

[3] Clipping in Mr. Hughes' personal papers, quoting Cornelia Raymond, Delhi teacher.
[4] CEH, Notes, p. 78.

James E. Russell, who became dean of Teachers College, Columbia University. "Many of our students are so eager & enthusiastic," Hughes wrote to his mother, "that I find myself passionately fond of instructing them." "They were 'my boys,'" he said in later years, ". . . and . . . I have never had a warmer glow of satisfaction than I felt when the boys of the academy came through their tests and went forth to justify their training." As a sideline, he tutored two young women of Delhi in advanced French. At first he declined to attempt French conversation, but when the girls insisted (one of them was soon to be married and go to Belgium) he guided them in a series of talks based on a French translation of *The Vicar of Wakefield.* Apparently this was the basis of his quip when he was Secretary of State that he did not speak French but had once taught it.

Hughes began his study of law in the office of William M. Gleason, former Delaware County judge and a lawyer of high repute in up-State New York. Especially stimulating was his association with the judge's son and partner, John B. Gleason, a graduate of Yale and of Columbia Law School, who had one of the keenest minds Hughes had encountered. First he read Maine's *Ancient Law* and followed with Kent's *Commentaries* and the first volume of Washburn on *Real Property,* making elaborate notes. Most of his afternoons and many evenings were spent in the Gleasons' law offices. Occasionally John Gleason would prod him with questions. During this period he also got his first glimpse of the judiciary in action by attending sessions of the New York Supreme Court held regularly in Delhi, the county seat.

The sense of duty that his parents had implanted in him was driving him to great efforts. Two days before his twentieth birthday he wrote to his mother:

When I cast myself into a reflective mood, and think how I have been cared for, how every wish has been met, how every want provided for, I am constrained to cry out at the terrible responsibility that rests upon me, and as I look at the future, that distant shadow gradually creeping on and becoming lost in the light of the present, I feel a weight resting on me, and a consciousness of utter lack & need, such as almost to overwhelm,—but the power, which has led & cared for & protected me for the past 20 years . . . is able to hold me to the end . . .

Before commencement time rolled around, Hughes had made a decision. The law had hold of him. He was determined to have a career at the bar, and he was not satisfied with his progress from reading in a law office. Only a few months ago he had pleaded for a chance to teach at $200 a year. While he had found that experience most congenial, and Dr. Griffin now offered him $800, with board and room, for the ensuing year, he turned it down. Nor would he consider the offer from David Call, his friend at Madison, to join the faculty of Des Moines University. Some of his Delhi friends suggested that, if he were admitted to the bar and practiced in an up-State community, he would have political opportunities. But this prospect had no more interest for him than further teaching. He was intent on thorough preparation in law and had sufficient confidence in himself to move directly toward that goal. "If you could possibly see me through two years at Columbia," he wrote to his father, "I am sure it would pay in the end." [5] Apparently the Reverend and Mrs. Hughes were by this time reconciled to their son's rejection of the ministry; but they still believed he would have a great future and agreed to put him through law school.

Hughes returned to New York in June, 1882, found a job for the summer, and soon embarked upon an eye-opening experience. His employer was handsome and agreeable Edgar Gray, then in his forties, promoter of the Gill Rapid Transit Company. When Hughes answered Gray's advertisement for a secretary, the latter spoke of his cab service enterprise in the most alluring terms and offered the young man $200 a month, which he thought a princely sum. So attractive was the opportunity, the promoter said, that Hughes might give up the idea of studying law and become a permanent officer in the company.

Hughes was asked, incidentally, of course, to make a small investment in the company "so that he would feel identified with it." He did not like that idea, but he was eager to have the job and thought he could recoup from his salary the small amount required. After making inquiry of W. Fearing Gill, the originator of the company, and of its bankers, a reputable Wall Street firm, Hughes' father borrowed money from a parishioner and made a small payment to Gray for stock to be delivered later.

One of the new secretary's first assignments was to index Gray's press-copy letter books. Uneasiness began to creep into his mind when he saw letters apparently in Gray's handwriting signed by other names. One day Gray blandly informed him that, not wishing to be known personally in a certain matter, he was signing his (Hughes') name to a telegram. Further use of his name was apparent when he found a note addressed to him by a woman, expressing regret that he had not kept an appointment of which he knew nothing. The young secretary was alarmed. The affairs of the company seemed to be in good order, and he did not wish to lose his job, but he felt that this duplicity could not be tolerated. His anxiety sent him to the Astor Library to see what information about Mr. Gray and his enterprises could be gleaned from the newspaper files.

Hughes soon discovered that Gray was a notorious character. Armed with extensive data from the newspapers, he went straight to Mr. Gill, who again assured him that Gray had been introduced to him by General Daniel E.

[5] *Ibid.,* p. 81.

Sickles and was "all right." Hughes disclosed his ammunition, and Mr. Gill was greatly shocked. He said they must confront Gray in his office the following morning and promised that the money "invested" by Hughes' father would be returned. Mr. Gill, too, was eager to get back the power of attorney he had given Gray.

There was a dramatic scene when Hughes and his father called on Gray the next morning and Mr. Gill promptly joined them. Hughes told Gray that he had learned his real name—William E. Gray. He recounted the charges that Gray, while employed by a Wall Street banking firm, had raised the amounts of checks and fled the country with about $300,000; that Gray had been arrested in London, where he had been for several years a dashing member of the Prince of Wales' set; that he had escaped and had again been arrested after a long period in Paris; that he had been extradited to New York, tried and convicted, and that on appeal he had won the right to a new trial. Hughes also said that he knew of the failure of Gray's electric-light venture during the period (apparently several years) while he had been awaiting a new trial. With his employer thus completely unmasked, the aspiring young lawyer-to-be demanded the return of his father's money.

The suave Mr. Gray could not blot out his record, but he insisted on his right to take stock subscriptions. Mr. Gill denied it, and Gray then flashed his power of attorney. Hughes asked to see it and then handed it over to Mr. Gill. "As a result," he once wrote, "my father got his money back and I left Gray's employment with my salary for two weeks' services and with a new insight into the ways of men.[6]

Even before entering law school, Hughes thus conducted his first successful investigation into financial corruption. Apparently Gray was never brought to retrial. Hughes saw him some fourteen years later as Gray—in evening dress, escorting a beautiful woman—entered the dining room of the Hotel Victoria in London. Despite the repeated exposure of his operations, he was reported to be engaged in an investment business.

Left without a job, the young investigator decided to resume his preparations for Columbia. A friend of his father gave him a letter of introduction to General Stewart L. Woodford, United States Attorney for the Southern District of New York. The general assigned the young man to a desk in a room adjoining his own in the Federal Building and thus made it possible for him to use the library of the Law Institute on the floor above. Hughes was delighted and made the most of his privilege. When Elihu Root became United States Attorney in March, 1883, Hughes, coming last in the line as the office staff paid its respects, explained his status and said that his desk was, of course, at Mr. Root's disposal. Root had already acquired an enviable stature in the

[6] *Ibid.*, p. 84.

law, and Hughes looked upon him with the admiration of a young hero worshiper. "The impression," he said forty-two years later, "was too deep ever to be effaced."

The Columbia Law School had a two-year course, with each of its classes divided into morning and afternoon sections. Entering in the fall of 1882, Hughes chose the afternoon section and continued to spend his mornings in the Law Institute Library. His class began with Chase's *Blackstone*. Then came a course in Contracts, guided by Parsons' treatise, and in the second term they concentrated on Washburn's *Real Property*. Hughes had the good fortune to take both the latter courses from Professor Theodore W. Dwight, a teacher of remarkable powers, who had fascinated him as a youth peering through the windows of the Columbia Law School. Dwight's head was "crowned with the distinction of age while his countenance gleamed with the fire of youth." [7]

The "Dwight Method" was frequently contrasted with the Harvard system. This eminent Columbia professor used no case books. His method was to assign portions of the textbook and hold recitations accompanied by his running comments, with an occasional dictated note. By this means he gave his students a ready grasp of fundamental legal principles. Of course he did not ignore the leading cases, and he supplied a profusion of citations. But in the absence of daily drill in the analysis of cases, many students left his classes with "a delusion of acquisition, which was the undoing of those inclined to avoid toil." Hughes knew little of the different methods of teaching law at the time, but he ran down the cases that Professor Dwight cited and carefully digested them in his notebook. This library work brought to his attention numerous other cases which he also digested. By systematically adhering to this practice, he doubtless taught himself more law than he learned from even the brilliant Professor Dwight. "The great lawyer," he once said, speaking of his illustrious predecessors, "has always been a great teacher and his best pupil is himself." [8]

Hughes was soon filling his nights as well as his days with law. He joined a small private "quiz" conducted two nights a week by capable young lawyers—Walter Leggat and Lewis Burchard. Other nights were given to the moot court and "quizzes" sponsored by his legal fraternity, Phi Delta Phi. Some of the latter were conducted by his rival from Public School No. 35, R. Floyd Clarke, who had been graduated by Columbia Law School the previous June. Hughes was also one of the seven members of "The Law Club," which held a moot court fortnightly at the home of John S. Melcher, its organizer. In this exclusive group were Frank C. Partridge, his old friend of Amherst, and Sherman Evarts, son of William M. Evarts. Hughes was making new friends and going ahead at full steam.

[7] CEH's address to Dwight Alumni Association, April 12, 1917.
[8] Address to Alumni of Harvard Law School, June 21, 1920.

Not content with living and breathing the law in a scholastic atmosphere, Hughes thought he ought to have his foot in a law-office door. With this in mind, he went to see Eugene H. Lewis, the junior member of the well known firm of Chamberlain, Carter & Hornblower. He had a letter of introduction from a young lawyer in his father's congregation at Greenpoint, but Mr. Lewis was not interested. He did not even seem to remember the lawyer who had taken the liberty of introducing the young man. Crestfallen and preoccupied by this rebuff, Hughes was making an inconspicuous retreat when, turning at the doorway, he bumped headlong into Walter S. Carter. That was a most fortunate collision which was to change the whole course of his future career. Chance, fate, or Providence had given him a jarring introduction to the best friend of young lawyers in New York—a man who was to be his future partner and father-in-law.

While Hughes was apologizing, Mr. Carter gave him a sharp glance and asked him what his business was. Hughes said that he had been seeking a place in the Carter firm. To his surprise, this brought an invitation to step into the lawyer's private office. There the young man was put through a stiff examination concerning his antecedents and aspirations. Mr. Carter, the antithesis of his junior partner, was a man of hobbies. He "collected" young men with the same enthusiasm with which he collected etchings. Having by accident encountered an interesting specimen, he proceeded to advise the young man as to his future education. German universities, he said, offered some remarkable opportunities. As he was planning ambitiously for his son George, then a student at Yale, he drew German university catalogues from his desk and described their courses in jurisprudence.

"If I were your son, sir," Hughes replied, "I might hope for such advantages. But I am not your son—I must earn a living right away. What I would like to know is whether I may enter your office." [9]

This brought from Mr. Carter a sharp attack upon the idea that anyone should attempt to work in a law office while going to law school. Before he dismissed the young man, however, Mr. Carter told him that if he wished to come into his office during the summer "to see the wheels go 'round"—on "the usual terms"—he could do so. Hughes eagerly accepted the invitation, and as soon as the law-school term ended he became a nonsalaried clerk.

At fifty, Walter S. Carter, with his iron-gray hair and closely trimmed beard, was a successful lawyer of most pleasing personality. Since coming to New York from Chicago, he had had partnerships with such able men as Leslie W. Russell, later attorney general of New York, and Sherburne B. Eaton, who became counsel for Thomas A. Edison. When Daniel H. Chamberlain, former governor of South Carolina, joined the firm, it became Chamberlain, Carter &

[9] Brooklyn *Daily Eagle*, Feb. 9, 1930; author's interview with CEH, Nov. 19, 1947.

Eaton. Then William B. Hornblower, a graduate of Princeton and of Columbia Law School who was rapidly rising to eminence in the profession, took the
place of Eaton.

Mr. Carter had also gathered around him a notable group of young men.
He was perhaps the first of the New York lawyers to make a practice of keeping in close touch with the law schools so as to single out their most promising
students and take some of them into his office after their graduation. As a
result, students trooped from Harvard, Columbia, and other schools to interview him, and, aside from those who entered his own office, he was able to
place many of these young men in law offices throughout the country. In this
he was aided by a wide acquaintance with lawyers and the remarkable ability
of remembering the names—even the middle names—of everyone he had
met. The achievements of his "kids," as Mr. Carter called them, were a source
of great satisfaction to him.

When Hughes entered Mr. Carter's office in the summer of 1883, the managing clerk was Lloyd W. Bowers, valedictorian of the class of 1879 at Yale.
Bowers was to become, in the opinion of the Justices of the United States
Supreme Court, one of the best solicitors general ever to appear before them,
and he probably would have been appointed to the supreme bench had it not
been for his untimely death in 1910.[10] Next to Bowers sat James Byrne, a
graduate of Harvard Law School in 1882, who was to become one of the
leaders of the New York bar and chancellor of the University of the State of
New York. On the other side of the clerks' room sat Starr J. Murphy, Hughes'
friend from the Delta Upsilon convention at Amherst.

Association with this group of brilliant young men became a great stimulus
to Hughes. His chief assignment was to assist Bowers. This was a pleasure, for
Bowers possessed personal qualities conducive to the highest professional
success. Both Bowers and Hughes worked largely on cases in charge of Mr.
Hornblower. This was less of a pleasure, for the third member of the firm
was irritable and difficult to work for. Nevertheless, he had a keen intellect, a
clear voice, and an incisive manner which commanded respect. A decade later
Mr. Hornblower was to be nominated as Associate Justice of the United States
Supreme Court, but Senator David B. Hill was to block his confirmation out
of resentment over the part Hornblower had played in investigating a contested election.

One of the most memorable events of the summer was a blunder. Mr. Hornblower was engaged in a savage fight with E. Payson Wilder, a terror of the
New York bar, over the assets of an insolvent firm. Throughout their battle
of motions, appeals, and so forth, Wilder never failed to begin his argument
by saying, "My friend, Mr. Blowhorner, I beg pardon, Mr. Hornblower"—

[10] CEH, Notes, pp. 89–89a.

a jest that left the victim livid with rage. An important brief in the case was given to Bowers one Friday afternoon to be printed, proofed, and put in readiness by Monday morning. Being addicted to italics, capitals, and bold-face type, Mr. Hornblower had reached the climax of his argument in this outstanding line: "And the firm paid *seven thousand dollars* in CASH." On Monday morning the printed brief was on his desk, but he soon appeared at the door of the clerks' room so full of wrath he could hardly speak. As he pointed to the climax of his brief, the two young men who had labored over it read with amazement and horror: "And the firm paid *seven thousand dollars* in COAL."

"Bowers and I did not know which one of us was responsible for this egregious error," Hughes wrote many years later, "whether it was due to a misreading of Mr. Hornblower's script or to a failure to catch the mistake in the print, and we both took Hornblower's unsparing denunciation with abject humility and contrition. Thenceforth, I was the most careful of proof-readers, quite sure that the mistake most likely to be overlooked would be on the title page or in some conspicuous place where it would stand out like a monument." [11]

Adhering to his agreement, Hughes left the office as soon as the law school opened. At their parting, Mr. Carter sent a tingle up the young man's spine. "Hughes," he said, "when you get through the law school, you can come back and I will put you on a salary." The lawyer-to-be walked home on air, thinking his future was now secure.

At Columbia, Hughes plunged into Equity under Professor Benjamin F. Lee and into Torts, Evidence, and the New York Code of Civil Procedure under Professor George Chase. He also took the course in Common Law Pleading, not because he had any intention of practicing outside New York but because he wished to be familiar with the subject. Chase was utterly unin-spiring; he had none of Dwight's magnetism; but he was precise and accurate, and the students came to have a high regard for him. Hughes and a number of his classmates made a practice of attending the junior as well as the senior lectures in order to review the previous year's work.

During the summer this young disciple of the law had spent his evenings in a commercial school studying stenography. He left with a diploma saying that he could write 150 words a minute. This new skill enabled him to make copious notes of everything Professors Dwight and Chase had to say, and those notes proved invaluable when he later began teaching law. After leaving law school, however, he never used shorthand.

In the spring of 1884 Hughes' father resigned his pastorate in Greenpoint and moved to Jersey City Heights, where he had become pastor of the Summit

[11] *Ibid.*, p. 92.

Avenue Baptist Church. Not wishing to lose his residence in New York, young Hughes went to live with a classmate, Emerson Hadley. They shared a small room—fourth floor back—in West Thirty-fourth Street, then a desirable street of brownstone fronts. Here they crammed for the final examinations. Hughes did not enter the voluntary competition for the law-school prize given for the best essay and the highest marks in a special examination, but he was given the prize fellowship for his class. Columbia thus rewarded the outstanding graduate of each senior class with a salary of $500 a year for three years, in return for tutoring in the law school. Hughes accepted gladly with the understanding that his duties would involve only the holding of a "quiz" two nights a week, and would thus not interfere with his plan to become a law clerk in Mr. Carter's office.

Then came the New York County bar examination. Hughes passed with a high mark, took the oath, and was admitted to the bar in June, 1884. Sixty years were to elapse before the star performer at that bar examination was to learn of his real standing. One day in the late fall of 1944, Michael H. Cardozo IV called at the home of Chief Justice Hughes, then retired, carrying the original record of the bar examinations which his grandfather, Michael H. Cardozo, had helped to conduct in 1884. Hughes' mark in this record is 99½.

Chapter 8

FIRST YEARS AT THE BAR

CHARLES E. HUGHES had invested his lifeblood as well as his father's money and all of his own time in a legal education. After his admittance to the bar, even he had to acknowledge that his relentless toiling day and night had impaired his health. Fully clothed, he weighed only 124 pounds. A severe cold had left him with an obstinate cough. It was evident that he would have to take a long rest if he were to enter upon his duties as a law clerk with his customary zest.

Good fortune came his way. De Witt J. Seligman, who had been a classmate of Hughes in law school, asked him to tutor Larry Bernheimer, Seligman's brother-in-law, in preparation for the bar examination in the fall. Since the young man's family was to spend the summer at Long Branch, Hughes could thus have several months at the seashore. The tutoring would require only two hours a day. Hughes was very pleased with the arrangement and systematically applied himself to the task of improving his health.

During his sojourn at Long Branch, Hughes escorted two girls from the boardinghouse where he was staying to a "hop" at the West End Hotel. While they were sitting on the veranda, up came Albert Cardozo, a friend of one of the girls, with his young brother, Ben, a shy lad of fourteen, in knickerbockers.[1] They spent a large part of the evening together, not dreaming that in a distant future the gay law-school graduate and the shy lad would sit together as judges of the highest court in the land.

Later on, Hughes moved to Asbury Park but returned by train every day to do his tutoring. His summer of leisure was terminated by a note from Mr. Carter in these words: "What do you say to coming 1st Sept. instead of 1st of Oct.? We need you now." [2] Hughes was ready. A summer of sunshine, sea air, and exercise had added eight pounds to his weight, fully restored his health, and left him in the best of spirits.

Several changes had taken place in the firm of Chamberlain, Carter & Hornblower since Hughes had watched "the wheels go 'round" during the previous summer. When Eugene H. Lewis left the firm, Lloyd W. Bowers had succeeded him as junior partner. Bowers, too, had left to form a partnership

---

[1] CEH, Notes, p. 95; G. S. Hellman's *Benjamin N. Cardozo*, p. 221.
[2] Hughes Papers, Library of Congress, Item 24.

with Judge Thomas Wilson of Winona, Minnesota, and James Byrne had stepped up to the position of junior partner. About the same time Robert Grier Monroe, a grandson of Mr. Justice Robert C. Grier of the Supreme Court, entered the office as a clerk.

Hughes was full of regret over the departure of his brilliant friend Bowers and the circumstances contributing to it. Bowers had suffered an unmerciful tongue-lashing from Justice Abraham R. Lawrence, a choleric gentleman with wavy white hair and florid complexion, who seemed to have a special contempt for young lawyers. In closing his argument on a motion, Bowers had ventured to suggest that it was highly important that the question be speedily decided. Procrastination being a well known failing of Justice Lawrence, his vanity was wounded. Pounding with his gavel, he shouted that "it did not lie in the mouth of a young lawyer whom he had never seen before to tell him when to decide his cases"; he wanted "the young lawyer" to know that he would not "tolerate such an innuendo by any member of the bar"; that "a more experienced lawyer" would have known better than to make such an "unjust imputation." [3] Bowers went back to his office fuming and vowed that he would never set foot in a New York court again. Apparently he never did. The incident deeply impressed Hughes with the importance of good manners on the bench.

In those days the best law firms were engaged in general practice, with many cases in the courts, and the most highly prized professional opportunities in New York City still lay in advocacy. The business of Chamberlain, Carter & Hornblower was largely commercial. Most of it was brought in by Mr. Carter, but he did little law work himself. His attention was given chiefly to managing the office, correspondence, and interviewing clients, whom he would usually turn over to Hornblower or Byrne.

Hughes' job was to assist members of the firm in whatever was assigned to him. He helped on briefs, acted as junior in cases in court, and did general office work. For this he received $30 a month, with an increase of $5 every two months. His chief reward was experience. He especially prized the privilege of being about the court house, "for any morning one might see Joseph H. Choate, Benjamin F. Tracy, Frederic R. Coudert, Edward C. James, or some other distinguished advocate, ascending the stairs to one of the court rooms and one might find a few minutes to hear part of some important trial and observe a great lawyer in action." [4]

Hughes' first case proved to be a dramatic affair. Mr. Carter brought in a German street broker named Wellenkamp, who had suffered painful injuries and some disfigurement in rescuing his two young children from a fire in his home. While Wellenkamp had been recovering in a hospital, his wife had

[3] CEH, Notes, p. 97.   [4] Ibid., p. 98.

deserted him and thereafter refused to allow him to see his children. Mr. Carter correctly concluded that there was no prospect of a fee in the case, but he liked to give young lawyers a chance to prove themselves; so he dumped the Wellenkamp mess into young Hughes' lap and told him to see what he could do with it.

His first step was to bring a habeas corpus proceeding to assert Wellenkamp's rights as a father. There followed a long and bitter controversy which attracted a good deal of attention in the press. Mrs. Wellenkamp was defended by her brother into whose home she had gone when she deserted her husband. "This precious pair," as Hughes called them, "she a virago and he a pugnacious lawyer and glib witness, piled up accusations regardless of truth or decency against the unfortunate Wellenkamp." [5] The hearings before a referee continued for many months, and almost every detail of the Wellenkamps' married life was laid bare. Hughes almost lived with Wellenkamp for a year. By rigorous cross-examination of the brother and sister he succeeded in breaking down the stories they had fabricated. The referee, Samuel A. Blatchford, decided in Wellenkamp's favor, awarding him custody of the children. The court confirmed the referee's report. The children were well cared for by their father, and years later Hughes had the pleasure of hearing from the daughter, who was then living under much happier circumstances.

Under his scholarship at Columbia, Hughes was quiz master for about two hundred students two nights a week, and two other nights were given to a private quiz which he undertook at the request of about a dozen seniors. At the end of these grilling two-hour periods, he had a long journey every night— by the elevated railroad to Cortlandt Street, by ferry to Jersey City, and by horsecar for twenty-five minutes to Jersey City Heights, where he was living with his parents. This extra work thus proved to be a heavy burden, but it gave him a wide acquaintance with, and a most favorable reputation among, the coming young men of the bar. One of his former classmates, Scott Hopkins, was so firmly convinced that Hughes was destined for the Supreme Court that he always greeted him as "Mr. Justice." But Hughes thought this ridiculous.[6]

Meanwhile his reputation in the Carter firm was rising with the swiftness of the morning sun. Mr. Carter declared that of all the young men with whom he had been associated "not one of them, in pure intellect and legal scholarship, compared with Hughes." [7] That amiable connoisseur of men was delighted by his young clerk's industry, his searching mind, his thorough knowledge of the law, his systematic habits, personal honesty, and high pro-

[5] *Ibid.*, p. 99.   [6] Author's interview with CEH, Dec. 4, 1945.
[7] Burton J. Hendrick, in *McClure's Magazine*, March, 1908.

fessional ideals. But Hughes was by no means swept off his feet by this happy appreciation of his qualities.

"Mr. Hughes," said his employer in one of their early conferences, "I am told that you are the brightest man ever graduated from Brown University."

"Mr. Carter," Hughes replied, "hearsay evidence is not trustworthy." [8]

In terms of financial reward Hughes was also doing remarkably well. The firm paid him $500 for his year's work. His fellowship brought him $500, his private quiz a similar amount, and fees from cases coming to him from outside the firm amounted to nearly $1,000, of which he was allowed to keep 50 per cent. His total income for his first year at the bar amounted to nearly $2,000.

Worn out but happy over his initial success, Hughes concluded in the midsummer of 1885 that he should take a good vacation. The firm agreed. With Colin S. Carter, son of his employer, as a traveling companion, he sailed on the *State of Nevada* for Glasgow, taking advantage of the old State Line's return-trip fare of $75 for first-class passage. The two young men parted at Glasgow, and Hughes went to Oban and Inverness, then to Edinburgh and through the Trossachs. Journeying then to Wales, he visited his Aunt Jane Jones and Uncle John Richard Hughes, crossed the St. George Channel to Dublin and went north to Belfast.

On the return voyage Hughes made an acquaintance that brought him into a highly sensational affair. His stateroom companion was Gerard Murray, son of the "keeper of the petty bag" of the British Court of Chancery, who was traveling with his brother, an Episcopal clergyman living in Virginia. Young Murray soon confided to Hughes that he had failed in an attempted elopement with the daughter of a tavern keeper and was being shipped to America to finish his medical education at the University of Virginia. He swore that he would marry the girl in spite of his family. This he did a few months later after returning to England on funds supplied by his prospective mother-in-law. Bringing the girl to New York, he left her in a boardinghouse while he went to Charlottesville for his books and clothes. She disappeared, and detectives found her in a brothel whence she had been taken by a merchant with whom she had struck up an acquaintance on the voyage while Murray had been seasick. When Murray was arrested for allegedly threatening to kill his bride, Hughes defended him in police court and later got the charges dismissed. The girl was sent back to England, and shortly afterward Murray died of a sudden illness.

During part of the second year of his fellowship at Columbia (1885–1886) Hughes taught, at the insistence of Professor Chase, the regular course in

[8] Recorded in letter, Frederick L. Gamage to Hughes, July 27, 1945.

common-law pleading, also continuing his private quiz. At the office, Hughes stepped into the position of junior member of the firm. Governor Chamberlain withdrew to practice alone, and the firm became Carter, Hornblower & Byrne, with Hughes as fourth man. He was kept on salary, as was customary with the junior, but his bimonthly increases brought his salary for the second year to nearly $900. His own business also expanded, and occasionally he was asked to write briefs for other lawyers. Eugene H. Lewis, who had turned Hughes away so abruptly when he first knocked at the door of the Carter firm, now asked him to write briefs in two or three important cases and to join the staff of Eaton & Lewis. A large firm, Turner, Lee & McClure, offered Hughes a place at more than twice the salary he was receiving, and several young lawyers sought a partnership with him. But Hughes appreciated the special opportunity he already had for important work and continued advancement in a firm of excellent standing, and this meant more to him than larger compensation.

Hughes and Colin Carter went abroad again in 1886. After jaunting about Holland, the young men roved through Paris and London. In London, Hughes read in a newspaper that Parliament was assembling. "Listen to this, Colin," he said, ". . . I'm going to try to get in." Young Carter laughed and insisted that any such attempt would be futile on the opening day, without a card from the American Legation; he refused to go. As the more venturesome traveler encountered a "bobby" near the entrance, he had an inspiration. "Where are Mr. Parnell's headquarters?" he asked. He followed the "bobby's" directions and presented his card showing that he was an "Attorney and Counsellor at Law, 346 Broadway, New York City." "I was soon introduced," Hughes recalled, "to an agreeable young man who said he was on his way to the House and would take me over. He was none other than John Redmond, then at the outset of his parliamentary career and destined to become the leader of his party. Full of inquiries about the States and our public opinion on the Irish question, he proved a most amiable escort. He took me to the lobby of the House, pointed out some of the most distinguished members who were about, and left me with one or two of his friends,—an exciting and unforgettable adventure." [9]

The young travelers returned on the *W. A. Scholten,* an ancient vessel that went down a short time later. Their adventure abroad together had been so pleasant that they now decided to live together in New York. Hughes had concluded that he could no longer endure the inconvenience of living in Jersey City Heights. He and young Carter took rooms at the Murray Hill Hotel, then new, with a first-class clientele, rivaling the Windsor. The arrangement did not last long; for when the Reverend Mr. Hughes accepted a call to the Trinity

[9] CEH, Notes, p. 105.

Antoinette Carter and Charles E. Hughes
at the time of their wedding, 1888

Mrs. Hughes with Charlie and Helen, Cornell University, 1892

The uncompromising investigator

Baptist Church on East Fifty-fifth Street, New York, his lawyer son returned to the parental roof at 110 East Eighty-first Street.

In the third year of his Columbia fellowship, Hughes was relieved of the course in pleading and acquired a partner in his private teaching. Mr. Carter had asked him who was the most promising man in his quizzes. Hughes had replied, "A great big fellow by the name of Cravath." Paul D. Cravath, the six-foot-four prize fellow of the class of 1886, thereupon became a clerk in the office. Cravath agreed to share Hughes' private quiz so that each would give only one night a week to it. Hughes' happy relations with his students was warmly attested when, at the end of his fellowship, they presented him with a handsome gold watch that he was to carry for more than sixty years.

His most disagreeable experience in this period was an emergency appearance before Justice Van Brunt, known as "Sitting Bull." Mr. Byrne was seeking an attachment on the ground of fraudulent disposition of property. Moving with all possible speed, this ordinarily meticulous practitioner based his case on a sheaf of affidavits, without waiting to assemble his facts in more orderly form. When a motion to vacate the attachment came up before Justice Van Brunt, Byrne had a severe cold and sent word that Hughes should appear for him. Hughes had not previously worked on the case, and before he had a chance to master all the facts he found himself in court listening to a vehement attack upon the papers Byrne had offered. Abram Kling, counsel for the defendants and a companion of Justice Van Brunt on summer trips, used the strategy of selecting insignificant affidavits and holding them up to ridicule. His close friend on the bench was favorably impressed.

"Who appears on the other side?" the judge shouted. "It's an imposition on the court to present such papers. I'll vacate the attachment!" [10]

Hughes arose, inwardly trembling with excitement but giving the impression of cool discipline and determination. The judge's tongue-lashing was then directed straight at the young lawyer. He remembered the searing experience of his friend Bowers, and his fighting disposition was aroused. He insisted on being heard. In the circumstances he could have disavowed all personal responsibility for the state of the papers, but his loyalty to his firm prevented him from doing so. In spite of repeated interruptions by the judge, he succeeded in pointing out certain affidavits containing admissions by the defendants which, under a decision of the General Term, justified the issue of the attachment. Doggedly he held his ground, and Van Brunt (who was an able judge in spite of his overbearing attitude) eventually sustained the attachment rather than risk reversal on appeal. Throughout the ordeal Hughes "suffered keenly" and was once more deeply impressed by the importance of judicial manners.[11]

[10] *Ibid.*, p. 107. [11] *Ibid.*

Hughes' work load was too heavy to permit another vacation abroad in 1887, but his two weeks at Block Island brought unexpected pleasures. As he sat in the smoking room of the Ocean View Hotel on the evening of his arrival, an imposing man of stocky build appeared at the door, glanced about, and asked, "Young man, do you know how to play whist?" Hughes admitted that he did.

"Come into my apartment," the imposing gentleman commanded, "we need a fourth hand."

Chance thus threw the energetic young lawyer into the company of Mr. Justice Samuel F. Miller of the United States Supreme Court, and he had the "inestimable privilege" of playing whist with this eminent jurist every evening of his stay at Block Island.

"To be his partner," Hughes wrote, "was a tough experience. He played without signals and expected one to divine his hand without the aids which modern whist had provided. When things went wrong, he used his objurgatory vocabulary without restraint. We cut for partners every rubber and it was a joy occasionally to get the best of him. Despite his brusquerie, he had a very kindly disposition and took a genuine interest in young lawyers." [12]

Justice Miller plied Hughes with questions about the practice of law in New York. "It is hard to make a good lawyer in New York," he once observed. "You try to get an injunction or an attachment or something right at the start, and if you don't get it you drop the case. What we want at the bar is thoroughness." On the last evening of their play together the Justice made up for the severe discipline to which he had subjected the young lawyer by saying, "Well, Hughes, if you will practice law as well as you play whist, I think you will get along." [13]

During his stay at Block Island, Hughes also encountered Justice George C. Barrett of the New York Supreme Court, whom he regarded as the best of the New York judges. Justice Barrett asked the young lawyer to join him in an afternoon walk and talked at length on the legal points at issue and the basis for his rulings in the trial of Jacob Sharp for bribery in obtaining the Broadway street-car franchise. When Hughes returned to work, he had been intellectually stimulated as well as physically refreshed.

There is other evidence that young Hughes was very pleasant company. Within his circle of friends his wit and his skill in self-expression made him a favorite toastmaster at dinners. In June, 1885, Charlie Hughes, Mark Allen, "Ned" Bassett, Fred Crossett, and "Ot" and "Robe" Eidlitz went to Easton to install a Delta Upsilon chapter at Lafayette College. Hughes was the youngest member of the group, but he entertained his fraternity brothers in the sleeper until late into the night with an "inexhaustible fund of stories." [14] At

[12] *Ibid.*, p. 108.   [13] *Ibid.*, p. 109.   [14] New York *Herald*, Jan. 5, 1908.

Easton he took the initiative in carrying out the business of the trip. In the fall of 1886 he was toastmaster at the Delta Upsilon convention at Madison University. As his reputation grew, he was frequently invited to add sparkle to a festive occasion.

Hughes had no time for politics. His first vote had been cast for Seth Low in the Brooklyn mayoralty election of 1883. In the following year he lost his opportunity of voting for Blaine or Cleveland by moving from New York to his parents' home in Jersey City. After settling once more in New York, he joined the Republican Club and the Association of the Bar. With other young lawyers, he campaigned unsuccessfully in 1887 for De Lancey Nicoll, prosecutor of Jacob Sharp and rising hope of the independent bar, who was running for district attorney. But these were minor events in a life given almost wholly to law. "Many nights Hughes and I sat reading law together," Cravath once said, "but at two o'clock in the morning I was usually on the sofa, dozing, despite black coffee and wet towels, but Hughes was still reading." [15] One of Hughes' resolutions was to get in a good deal of reading outside the law, but that sort of self-education was confined largely to weekends and to his devouring of the daily papers on horsecars and elevated trains.

William Hornblower's practice in connection with the Grant & Ward receivership and the New York Life Insurance Company had become so extensive and so lucrative that he decided to pull out of the Carter firm in the fall of 1887. James Byrne agreed to go with him. Their decision was a matter of deep regret to Hughes. Hornblower's clarity, precision, and exacting demands upon his associates and Byrne's extreme care and caution had afforded an excellent discipline. Intimate contacts with these men had given their junior partner "a constant awareness of the best traditions of the bar."

Walter Carter looked around for an outstanding lawyer to fill the gap in his firm. When he discussed several possibilities with Hornblower, the latter suggested, "Why not take young Hughes?" Mr. Carter repeated this to Hughes, and he was "greatly surprised and overjoyed at the opportunity." [16] "But," he said, "we should hold Cravath." Mr. Carter agreed.

That evening the jubilant new second partner took Paul Cravath to dinner at the famous Martinelli restaurant, where they reviewed the whole situation over a bottle of Chianti.

"Cravath," he said, "this is an extraordinary chance. We would be a young firm with a good business at the start and every opportunity for making an independent reputation instead of virtually being clerks." A young firm, indeed! Hughes was twenty-five and Cravath twenty-six. Mr. Carter was the business-getter and gave little attention to legal work as such. To clinch the argument with his associate, who had had a tempting offer from Hornblower

[15] *Outlook*, Oct. 20, 1906.   [16] CEH, Notes, p. 110.

and Byrne, Hughes declared, "We will make the firm Carter, Hughes and Cravath."

"Make it Carter, Hughes *and Cravath*," the big fellow thundered, bringing his fist down on the table, "and I'll join."

Carter, Hughes & Cravath it became. They agreed to a division of the fees from the general business of the firm, giving Carter, who owned the library and office furniture, 60 per cent, Hughes 24 per cent, and Cravath 16 per cent. In addition, Hughes and Cravath continued to have 50 per cent of the fees from business that each brought in. Their junior partner was John W. Houston, a graduate of Harvard Law School who had shown exceptional talent as a clerk. Among the new crop of clerks were such promising men as Thaddeus D. Kenneson, Howard A. Taylor, and Harry W. Mack.

Hughes could scarcely believe that fortune had smiled upon him so favorably. At the age of twenty-five he had become the number one lawyer of a highly respected firm with an extensive practice. By dint of industry, intelligence, and frequent reorganizations he had moved from the bottom to the top rung in the firm, so far as handling the legal work was concerned, in only three years. That remarkable success was shortly to lead to the happiest venture of his life.

Chapter 9

OVERFLOWING CUP

LOVE had little chance to blossom in Charlie Hughes' heart in his first quarter-century. At Madison he had shown some interest in the "Sem" girls, but at Brown and Columbia Law School his experience was almost devoid of social contacts. In his first years at the bar his work and his quiz classes four nights a week left little time for dates. When girls whom he had known elsewhere came to visit New York he used to "beau them around." [1] But the law had first call upon him. Feminine charm was a negligible factor in the range of interests that he permitted himself to pursue.

He had been with the firm a year before he knew that Mr. Carter had a daughter. One day Mr. Carter took from his drawer a watch—a birthday gift to his daughter—and showed it to Hughes. A few months later the young clerk met the daughter herself. The firm had hired two new graduates of Columbia Law School—Ethelbert Dudley Warfield (later president of Lafayette College) and Charles B. Storrs. In December, 1885, Storrs accepted an offer to teach law at the University of Tokyo, and the firm gave him a dinner at old Delmonico's. Standing with Mr. Carter as he received the guests was his tall and attractive twenty-one-year-old daughter Antoinette. She was dressed in black and seemed to Hughes a vision of loveliness. He had "but a word with her," and the opportunity of taking her in to dinner was not to be his. Instead, he escorted Mrs. Thomas Wilson. But at the table, he once related, "I happened to catch Miss Carter's eye when we both saw the same joke which others seemed to miss, and a certain understanding was then and there established, although it was some time before this ripened into the love that never failed." [2]

Hughes made no immediate effort to follow up this favorable introduction. Months of hard grinding in the law enveloped him—months in which Antoinette Carter was only a vivid and pleasing memory. Then he was invited to the Carter home for Sunday dinner, and on various occasions he played whist in the same alluring environment. On one of these visits he stayed overnight with Antoinette's brother Colin. About 2:00 A.M. Antoinette awakened the young men and asked them to go for a doctor; her stepmother had become dangerously ill. She spent the night taking care of her stepmother, but

---

[1] Author's interview with CEH, Dec. 5, 1945.   [2] CEH, Notes, p. 103.

the next morning Hughes found her as radiant and good-humored as if nothing had happened. Such poise and even temperament were typical of her. His admiration was lifted several notches higher. Still Hughes made no concerted effort to court the young lady.

Antoinette Carter had attained her sunny disposition in spite of a harried childhood. Born in Milwaukee on September 14, 1864, she was christened at the funeral service for her mother, Antoinette Smith Carter. Her father, a direct descendant from Elder William Brewster of the *Mayflower*, had gone to Milwaukee as a young man and returned there to practice law after fighting in the Civil War. As the youngest of four children orphaned by her mother's death, Antoinette was placed under the care of a nurse, Mrs. Sarah Williams. In her old age Mrs. Williams remembered Antoinette as "an unusually beautiful little child with dark hair and eyes and sweet little vivacious ways" [3] and a captivating lisp that gave special charm to her recitation of "A Little Thip Thailed on the Thea."

Mr. Carter married again, but his second wife died within a year. A sister of the second Mrs. Carter (Mrs. W. J. Bridges of Baltimore) then induced him to "lend" Antoinette to her for a few months. The child's sojourn with the Bridges lengthened to six years—until she reached the age of ten. At Washington, Pennsylvania, Antoinette went to a private school kept by Miss Nannie Stewart in West Maiden Street. Later she moved with the Bridges to Princeton, having become so much a part of the family that she was often called "Nettie" Bridges.

Meanwhile Mr. Carter had moved to Chicago and then to New York and had acquired a third wife who became the mother of Walter F. ("Dutch") Carter, the great Yale pitcher of his day, and Leslie Carter. When Antoinette rejoined her father's family, therefore, she came under the influence of her fifth mother. Yet she remained a serene and sweet-tempered girl. At Wells College in Aurora, New York, and at Wellesley College, she was a good student and acquired the habit of extensive reading. Like her father, she found much interest in art and music as well as literature. But she was also athletic, and her face was a beaming reflection of good health. Hughes regarded her as a perfect specimen of womanhood.

For two and a half years after their meeting at Delmonico's, Antoinette Carter and Charlie Hughes were merely friends. During the second year of their acquaintance, he took her to the theater twice and saw her on a few other occasions. But he would not permit himself to fall in love with her. She was the daughter of his employer. Contrary to the oft-repeated statement that Hughes "married the boss's daughter," he deliberately avoided courting her so long as he was a clerk in her father's firm. The idea of marriage to further

[3] Undated letter in the Milwaukee *Daily News*.

his ambition was highly repugnant to him; [4] it stood as a barrier between them. And that barrier was not removed until after he had become a full-fledged partner in the firm of Carter, Hughes & Cravath.

Meanwhile Antoinette had gone to Rochester, where she and her friend Marie B. Pond opened a gymnasium for women and children on November 3, 1887. When she returned to New York the following summer, Hughes (now a full-fledged partner with excellent prospects) saw her more frequently. In the course of their excursions to Manhattan Beach, Bridgehampton, and elsewhere, their mutual attraction ripened into a close friendship—so close that Hughes began to unburden his heart to her concerning a personal matter that was troubling him. Antoinette proved to be not only a delightful companion but also an eager confidante and clear-headed adviser. It must have been apparent to everyone but him that she loved him.

After she returned to Rochester in September, Hughes became a persistent correspondent. One of Antoinette's letters in reply seemed to strip a blindfold from his eyes, and love for her suddenly filled his whole being. No longer could he suppress his feelings. Proposing by letter, he got a prompt and favorable reply and almost flew to Rochester with an engagement ring. From that moment to the end of their days his devotion to her was intense and unwavering.

Antoinette's happiness was bubbling over when she wrote the good news to her father. He replied on October 11, 1888:

MY DEAR DAUGHTER:
  The subject called for a good letter and *you wrote it*.
  Yes, that is all right. There are *very* few abler, and certainly there are no better, fellows than Hughes. If I'd been going to choose for you, I should have selected him over all I know.

For the remainder of the autumn, Hughes was a faithful week-end visitor in Rochester. Stopping at the Powers Hotel, he would take a sitting room so that they could be indoors together, but as tongues began to wag, they soon shifted their meeting place to the home of Miss Pond's sister. Each visit deepened Hughes' conviction that his fiancée was the one woman in the world with whom he could be happy.

We get some indication of Antoinette's emotions (as well as an index to her disposition) from the following letter which she wrote on October 16 to her future mother-in-law:

MY DEAR MRS. HUGHES:—
  My heart was full of gratitude when I read your letter welcoming me as a *daughter* to your "heart and home."

  [4] Author's interview with CEH, Dec. 5, 1945.

Office of
Carter, Hughes & Cravath,
Attorneys & Counsellors at Law.

346 Broadway.
New York, Oct° 11ᵗʰ, 1888.

Walter S. Carter.
Charles E. Hughes.
Paul D. Cravath.
John W. Houston.

My dear daughter:

The subject called for a good letter & you wrote it.

Yes. That's all right. There are very few abler, & certainly there are no better, fellows than Hughes. If I'd been going to choose for you, I should have selected him, over all I know.

In loving,

Father.

For Charlie's sake, because you are *his Mother,* though we have but met, I love you and think of you as *my Mother* already. When I come to you, I shall love you, I know, for your own sake as well as his and find you indeed a Mother. All that I feel for you, I feel for your husband also. Will you tell him for me, and I hope it will not be long before we shall see each other face to face.

If I could not rely upon your charity it would be with grave fears of sadly disappointing you that I look forward to that day, for do you not know that Charlie paints me in colors altogether too bright, that he looks at me with a lover's eyes, blind to faults and seeing virtues which I do not possess? If however *love* for *him* and his can "cover a multitude of sins" and over balance many failings, all will be well.

You will spare Charlie to me next Sunday? Even gladly, if you knew how I long to see him and how anxiously I am awaiting that day.

Many bright visions of the future float through my mind. I see a *very* happy, a very united family, myself one of its members and as such to be to each all that I should be is my fondest hope, the most earnest prayer of

Your daughter to be

ANTOINETTE CARTER

They were married on the following December 5. It was a simple ceremony at the Carter home, 176 Brooklyn Avenue, Brooklyn. Officiating were Hughes' father and the Reverend Mr. E. H. Dickinson, husband of Antoinette's sister Emma, and only members of the families were present.

"Hughes," said Mr. Carter as the newlyweds were leaving the house, "you'll find that Nettie is a good person to live with." [5]

The groom concluded that this was the most masterly understatement of which his father-in-law was capable.

Plans for their honeymoon were a deep secret. When Mr. Carter asked where they intended to go, Hughes replied, "You might guess Canada." But he did not deceive his shrewd father-in-law. Mr. Carter telegraphed to Judge Thomas Wilson (then in Congress) to expect the newlyweds at the Arlington Hotel in Washington. The judge was on hand to greet them. On the train they had encountered Mayor Hugh J. Grant of New York, and it was to him that Hughes had the privilege of first introducing his "wife."

Washington favored them with delightfully mild and sunny weather. They drove about in one-horse victorias and went by steamer to Mount Vernon. Visiting the Supreme Court, they watched its solemn proceedings with reverence. Hughes was proud to point out to his bride his erstwhile partner in whist, Mr. Justice Miller. The memory of this first glimpse of the Supreme Court in action would often flash upon his mind when he himself came to look out upon wide-eyed visitors from that mighty seat of judgment. But in December, 1888, his imagination would not stretch so far as to place himself on the supreme bench. To friends who assumed that at least he must

[5] CEH, Notes, p. 121.

have cherished such an ambition, his reply was always: "Not for an instant! . . . I dreamed of nothing more than a reasonable measure of professional success." [6]

The blissful days in Washington, and a few more in Baltimore, passed all too quickly. Back in New York, Hughes took his bride to live with his parents in the three-story brownstone house at 129 East Sixty-second Street. Being relatively prosperous, he had become responsible for the rent ($1,200 a year) when the family first moved to this house the previous May. With his mother still inclined to call him to account for any shortcoming, real or imagined, the arrangement was probably not a happy one; but within a few months his parents moved to Scranton, where his father had accepted a call from the Jackson Street Baptist Church.

The newlyweds spent most of their first summer together at Lake Mahopac, with Hughes commuting to and from New York every weekday. His exacting legal work was interrupted for a vacation of two weeks in the Adirondacks. On November 30, 1889, a son was born to them and promptly named for his father. His coming convinced them that they should establish a permanent home, and, thinking Brooklyn might be the most desirable location, they rented a house on the Park slope, No. 117 St. John's Place.

Hughes had found new bearings. His love for his wife knew no bounds, and that love was now extended to include his son. The marriage on which he had embarked was to be one of the happiest imaginable. It made all his other causes for satisfaction seem "trivial by comparison." To draw further upon his own words, written after more than half a century of married life: "Our cup of happiness was full at the beginning and has been full and overflowing ever since. In all my privileges and responsibilities, in good times and bad, in success and defeat, in joy and sorrow, we have had a perfect union of minds and hearts. Whatever I have accomplished has been made possible by that strong, unselfish, ever radiant spirit, constantly by my side." [7]

In the summer following the birth of his son, Hughes also acquired a new badge of identification—his beard. His decision to join the ranks of his be-whiskered elders—his father, father-in-law, grandfather, and several uncles—had nothing to do with his prolonged beardlessness as a youth. The family took a little cottage at Siasconset, Nantucket, for the summer, and Hughes let his beard grow during his holiday of three weeks as a matter of convenience. He had never learned to shave himself. When he returned to the office, he simply rebelled at the idea of resuming his daily visits to the Hotel Astor barbershop, where he had kept a shaving cup for several years. He had previously worn a mustache by choice, but the auburn stubble on his chin was allowed to take its own course solely as a matter of saving time. Had safety

[6] *Ibid.*, p. 122.   [7] *Ibid.*

razors been in use at the time, the famous beard would never have been grown.[8]

After living in Brooklyn for a year, Charles and Antoinette Hughes concluded that the upper west side of Manhattan was a more desirable place for a permanent residence. Early in 1891 they bought the house at No. 318 (apparently later numbered 320) West Eighty-eighth Street, near Riverside Drive. That is, they bought the equity subject to the building loan. This four-story red brick house, with its bay windows and spacious rooms, was a very attractive residence, and they decorated and furnished it to their complete satisfaction. Their cup of happiness was truly overflowing. Only one circumstance arose to cloud their bliss, and that can better be seen from the vantage point of Hughes' law office.

[8] Author's interview with CEH, Dec. 26, 1945.

Chapter 10

BREAKNECK STAIRS

IT WAS a proud moment for Charles E. Hughes when, on the first day of 1888, he took possession of Mr. Hornblower's room and assumed the leading role in the legal work of Carter, Hughes & Cravath. At an age when most young lawyers are pleased to be clerks, he was the head of a little legal domain.

Compared with present standards, the firm was small and its equipment meager. Indeed, when Hughes had first joined the firm, it had but one telephone placed in the outer hall of the office and but one stenographer who copied all the important court papers (when not printed) in "copperplate" longhand. By 1888, however, typewriting had become the rule. Carter, Hughes & Cravath began with two stenographers and two law clerks, and their staff was soon reinforced by two graduates of Columbia Law School—Philo P. Safford and Frederic R. Kellogg.

While office arrangements were simple and staffs small in even the best law firms, the 1880's were, in several respects, the golden age of the bar. The legal profession was riding a high wave of prestige. Roused by the scandals of the Tweed régime, William M. Evarts and Samuel J. Tilden had led public-spirited lawyers in founding the Association of the Bar in 1871. Its meetings still brought forensic clashes among great men of the law. Hughes was especially intrigued by the verbal battle over the advisability of codifying the common law in which James C. Carter led the opposition and David Dudley Field defended the proposed code of which he was the author.

The art of advocacy had reached a high state of development. Evarts was approaching the close of his distinguished career. Joseph H. Choate, James C. Carter, William Allen Butler, Frederic R. Coudert, Wheeler H. Peckham, and other leaders were in their prime. These giants of the profession seemed to hold an enduring grasp upon the best professional opportunities and to leave little room for young aspirants outside the favored groups. But this gave Hughes little concern. He was "intent on the day's work with the single ambition to do it well." As the years passed, he was impressed by the gradual disappearance of the old masters and the emergence of new leaders in a constant fructification of the bar. "If the young lawyer sees to it that his work is of the best and if by intelligence and industry he stands well in his own generation," Hughes reflected, "he can afford to await his share of the privileges and responsibilities which to that generation are bound to come." [1] This is precisely the course that he followed.

The practice that Hughes began to direct was largely in the field of commercial law. Among the firm's clientele were importers, jobbers, commission merchants, and leading houses in the drygoods business with many claims against insolvent debtors. Since there was no bankruptcy law and the state insolvency law was seldom invoked, failing debtors usually made general assignments for the benefit of creditors. Often, however, they concealed property or made separate transfers to relatives and friends on pretended claims. Shrewd and unscrupulous lawyers aided these fraudulent schemes. It required both mental agility and resourcefulness to unmask such operations and induce the courts to set aside transfers and assignments tainted with fraud.

In one difficult case involving a general assignment without preferences, Hughes succeeded in getting attachments sustained by the Special Term, but they were upset by the General Term. While the proceedings were under way, an employee of a brokerage house told Hughes that the debtor in question had purchased shares of stock shortly before his assignment. The stock had not been delivered to the assignee or even mentioned to him. When the debtor was examined in supplementary proceedings, he again concealed this information. Hughes brought a creditors' bill and successfully resisted a motion for a bill of particulars. A long time elapsed before the case was tried, but Hughes kept his secret, and the devious debtor walked straight into the trap. After he had given his testimony without a word about the concealed transaction, Hughes produced his evidence to the debtor's dismay. That dramatic exposure clinched the case for the creditors, and the assignment was held invalid as part of a fraudulent scheme.[2] Hughes' success in so difficult a case did not go unnoticed at the bar.

Early in 1888 Hughes tried a case involving the ownership of a deposit with the Consolidated Stock and Petroleum Exchange before Justice Alton B. Parker. He won both the case and a friend. Parker was a man of pleasing personality and courtly demeanor as well as an excellent judge. He did not get Hughes' vote when he ran for the Presidency against Theodore Roosevelt in 1904, but their friendship was broken only by Parker's death.

That tantrum of nature known as the Blizzard of 1888 dealt roughly with Hughes. Not accustomed to being intimidated by either man or weather, he went to the office as usual on Monday, March 12, in disregard of a heavy fall of snow, which had left the streets impassable to vehicles and stalled the elevated on Third Avenue. Wading over to Second Avenue, he took the elevated to Chatham Square and again waded to his office on Broadway. No one else

---

[1] CEH, Notes, p. 115.
[2] *Passevant* v. *Cantor, Cases and Points,* Vol. I. (This set of eight volumes consists of Mr. Hughes' printed records and briefs assembled in 1891.)

had arrived. Indeed, most New Yorkers had recognized that they were snowed in and had stayed home. Seeing that no business could be done on such a day, Hughes decided to get home as soon as possible.

By this time the trains as well as the cabs and buses had stopped running. Hughes and a number of other defiant souls plowed up Broadway single file, stopping to rest at the hotels. The chance of getting home was nil, but he thought he could make it to the Murray Hill Hotel. "A furious blinding gale that made exposure to it an exquisite torture"[3] disputed his decision. The upper layers of a snowfall that would reach a depth of 20.9 inches were being distorted into fantastic drifts. All the perils of polar exploration seemed suddenly to have invaded the great metropolis.

"Fifth Avenue between 23d and 40th Streets," according to Mr. Hughes' account of the storm, "was a wild scene. There were no vehicles and almost no pedestrians. The wind was blowing a gale and the drifts not only covered the street but the lower parts of the dwellings. There was no place to stop on that leg of the journey and it was all I could do to finish it. I arrived at the Murray Hill almost exhausted and remained there for a couple of days while the City sought with difficulty to renew its life."[4]

Hughes had scarcely any acquaintances in business circles other than those he had made through the office and consequently brought in little business of his own as distinct from that of the firm. Cravath was in a very different position. His uncle, Caleb H. Jackson, who was the right-hand man of George Westinghouse, began to direct Westinghouse cases to Carter, Hughes & Cravath. Within a year the firm was almost swamped by this new type of business.

The most important litigation resulting from this contact was the overhead wires case. The New York electric-light companies were furnishing current by means of poorly insulated wires strung on poles above the streets. One lineman had been roasted alive from contact with a defective wire in front of the courthouse; deaths from this cause became so common that the city was aroused. Relying upon an act of the New York Legislature requiring the companies to put their wires underground, Mayor Grant ordered the overhead wires to be torn down. The companies, including the United States Illuminating Company represented by the Hughes firm, brought suit for an injunction against the city.

Hughes drew the papers and prepared the brief, and on the motion for injunction he opened the case, stating the facts and the questions involved. The firm retained Joseph H. Choate as counsel, and one of the other light companies brought James C. Carter into the case. This array of legal talent induced the Special Term to give the companies an injunction, but the General Term, not unexpectedly, found "a shameful condition of affairs" and sustained the right

---

[3] New York *Tribune,* March 13, 1888.   [4] CEH, Notes, p. 121.

of the city to remove wires that were not adequately repaired and constituted a public nuisance.[5]

A good deal of criticism has been directed against Hughes for his participation in this case. The companies' negligence had properly aroused intense public feeling. But there is not the slightest indication of any unethical conduct on his part. He argued against destruction of an essential utility in the process of abating a nuisance. The companies had erected their poles and strung their wires with proper authority, and bad though the situation was, they could not shift to underground cables immediately because only a small part of the city had been supplied with the necessary subways.

With the overhead wires outlawed, the fight for underground conduits became intense. The Westinghouse interests arranged to make use of subways to be provided by a new company under authority granted by the Board of Electrical Control. But the board's action was challenged in two suits, one brought by a group of taxpayers and the other by Elihu Root in behalf of an electric-light company.[6] Wheeler H. Peckham, one of the most eminent lawyers of his day in spite of his rejection when nominated for the Supreme Court, appeared in support of the board, and Hughes helped to prepare his briefs. Once more they were successful in the Special Term, but the General Term held that the contract between the board and the new subway company was invalid.

The part Hughes played in these complicated legal tussles was relatively minor, but they gave him experience in a new field and brought him into close personal contact with the top men of the bar. He made the most of this by observing the great lawyers' methods. James C. Carter, he shrewdly noted, bore heavily on the legal rights of property and was not as persuasive as Choate, who skillfully presented the practical problem of supplying current to consumers and the earnest efforts of the companies to repair the defects in their lines.

Choate was a delightful personality as well as a brilliant advocate. When Hughes would arrive at the Choate home in the early morning, eager and tense after a long night of labor, he would find the great lawyer in his library reading some literary work and serenely looking forward to the heavy tasks of the day without a suggestion of strain. His invincible calm in difficult situations, his easy mastery of his cases, his unvarying geniality and air of complete confidence won the younger man's unbounded admiration.

The great lawyer's advice thus fell upon fertile ground. It was a mistake, he told Hughes, for a busy professional man to accustom his system to more physical exercise than it was feasible for him to take. Find some method of

[5] *U.S. Illuminating Co.* v. *Grant,* 55 Hun 222.
[6] *Manhattan Electric Light Co.* v. *Grant,* 56 Hun 642; *Armstrong* v. *Grant,* 56 Hun 226.

moderate daily exercise, he advised, that would not take much time and would yet keep one fit despite hard day and night work. Walking could best serve the purpose. Hughes followed this counsel for the remainder of his life. Choate also talked about the great importance of being able quickly to relax and find some agreeable diversion. "Hughes," he said, "if you don't get your fun as you go along, you will never have it." [7]

In studying the technique of eminent practitioners, Hughes had no thought of emulating Choate's scintillation, Coudert's charming pleasantries, or James C. Carter's profundities. He realized that "there are gifts which belong to one's native endowments and are not to be had by laborious effort." While the young lawyer can "aim at equanimity, clarity and force," he said, "he must succeed, if at all, by being himself." [8] But Hughes proved to his own satisfaction that the young lawyer can improve his technique by observing the most able of his elders.

When the firm established a branch office for Cravath at 120 Broadway, because of his rapid development of a distinct line of legal business, Hughes tried to keep abreast of the firm's commercial cases while at the same time helping Cravath to carry the Westinghouse load. This finally proved to be an impossible task, and they agreed to dissolve the firm. Cravath took Houston with him. Carter and Hughes advanced Frederic R. Kellogg into third place in their firm, and the fourth place went to Edward F. Dwight, nephew of Professor Dwight and a prize fellow at the Columbia Law School.

The new firm had plenty of work. Hughes and Hornblower won a ten-year-old case when the Court of Appeals ruled that the promoters of a corporation must account to subscribers to its shares for secret profits.[9] During the following year Hughes took several cases to the Court of Appeals, writing the briefs and presenting the arguments. In one of these he succeeded in convincing the court that a section of the Code of Civil Procedure was unconstitutional as depriving his client of real property without due process of law.[10]

Despite his gratifying professional success and his happy marriage, Hughes was worried and nervously depressed. In seven years of practice he had driven himself at a terrific pace. His steady grind of day and night work had reduced his weight to 127 pounds in his shirt sleeves. Every application he had made for life insurance had been rejected. The examining doctors could find no ailment or physical defect; they classified him as a poor risk solely because of his emaciated condition. "I found it easier to get married," he once remarked to a group of incredulous insurance men, "than to get insured. She thought I was a good risk. The life insurance companies thought I was a lightweight." [11] His

[7] CEH, Notes, p. 125a.　　　[8] Ibid.
[9] Brewster v. Hatch, 122 N.Y. 349.　　[10] Gilman v. Tucker, 128 N.Y. 190.
[11] Address to Life Underwriters Association, May 22, 1906.

anxiety over the lack of protection for his family and the seemingly endless drain upon his strength was intensified by the fact that he was soon to be the father of a second child.

Hughes had been stimulated to extraordinary efforts by an ambition that was deeply imbedded within his nature. It was not political ambition, nor was it a passion for wealth. He labored as indefatigably on cases involving small fees, or no fee at all, as he did on cases that might bring large returns and professional distinction. It was the work itself that drove him on, and when he had a vacation he applied himself to the task of recouping his strength so that he could return to the legal treadmill with renewed vigor.

"I inherited a continuing ambition to excel in good work," he said, "and to do my job as well as it could be done. I couldn't bear the thought of leaving undone anything which could be done or of not doing my particular work as well as it could be done within my limitations." [12]

What troubled him was that his driving passion for self-fulfillment seemed to lead only to more of the routine drudgery that was impairing his health and thus threatening to blight his fondest hopes. His faculty for cool self-analysis and his profound respect for facts, however disagreeable they might be, led to drastic action. He decided to give up his great opportunity in New York and go back to teaching.

The door of escape was opened by Hughes' old friend James O. Griffin under whom he had taught at the Delaware Academy. Griffin was now assistant professor of German at Cornell University. Visiting the Hugheses in New York, he asked if his friend would consider a professorship of law. "I would jump at the chance," [13] Hughes replied. Professor Griffin repeated this conversation to President Adams, and he asked Hughes to come to Ithaca. At the conclusion of their interview, he offered a full professorship in the Law School, and Hughes accepted it.

Mr. Carter was dumfounded. The idea of giving up a promising career at the bar for a professorship, he told his son-in-law, was absurd. Hughes had done remarkably well at the bar. He had a great opportunity, Mr. Carter insisted, to build up a practice that would bring him "opulence." [14] But "opulence" was not an irresistible attraction for the younger man. It was the intellectual stimulus of the law, the interests of his clients, and especially the opportunity for advocacy that had appealed to him. Now he was tired, and the offer of an academic retreat, affording what he thought would be abundant time for study and reading, seemed so attractive that he could not reject it. Mrs. Hughes, with characteristic loyalty and unselfish interest in her husband's well-being, strongly supported him despite her father's opposition. In September, 1891, they gave

[12] Author's interview with CEH, Dec. 4, 1945.   [13] CEH, Notes, p. 129.   [14] Ibid.

up their new home in New York, after living in it only a few months, and moved to Ithaca.

Dejected, Mr. Carter gave Hughes' place in the firm to George M. Pinney, Jr. His sharp disappointment over the loss of his young partner may nevertheless have been tinged by prophetic insight, for at the luncheon given Hughes at the Lawyers' Club before his departure the firm presented him with two volumes—*Lives of the Lord Chancellors* and *Lives of the Chief Justices*.

Chapter 11

HAPPY INTERLUDE

HUGHES went to Ithaca with a sense of emancipation from the grinding toil, the hustle, and tension of the great metropolis. For one in this mood, Cornell was a charming refuge with its broad lawns, stately elms, and quiet walks, with its superb setting on the hill—"far above Cayuga's waters." The Hugheses took a house on State Street about halfway up the hill, and the new professor walked to and from the campus. The air, the exercise, and the associations were exhilarating, and he soon found himself gaining in vigor and thoroughly enjoying life.

Being only twenty-nine, Hughes believed himself to be Cornell's youngest full professor, but he and Mrs. Hughes were received with the utmost cordiality. This was not surprising, for the outstanding members of the university faculty were still young. Jacob Gould Schurman, who was to become president of Cornell a year later, was only thirty-seven. Benjamin Ide Wheeler, future president of the University of California, was about the same age. Liberty Hyde Bailey, at thirty-three, had begun his climb toward recognition as one of the country's most distinguished agricultural experts. James Laurence Laughlin, future head of the political economy department of the University of Chicago, was forty-one. Harry Burns Hutchins, soon to be dean of the Cornell Law School and later president of the University of Michigan, was forty-four. Among these men on the threshold of outstanding careers Hughes formed lasting friendships.

The social life into which Professor and Mrs. Hughes were initiated was most agreeable. Andrew D. White, cofounder of Cornell, still had his residence on the campus, and in the town Henry W. Sage and his sons had large mansions in which they gave generous entertainment. "On the campus," Hughes recorded, "the professors had frequent dinner parties which were simple, but conducted with *savoir-faire*, and afforded the most delightful contacts. Some of us became close companions, playing whist from time to time in each other's homes, trudging about the campus in daily walks, or bowling in the excellent alley of the Town and Gown Club." [1]

Hughes' thoughts were much upon his family as the year 1892 dawned, with

[1] CEH, Notes, p. 131.

the result of enhancing his appreciation of his own parents. On January 3 he wrote to them from Ithaca:

DEAR PA AND MA,

Antoinette continues extremely well. Baby, ditto. They told me in New York that I had not looked so well in many years. Certainly, I am highly favored— and would much prefer my pleasant, quiet and healthful life in the retirement of this small city than the active, abnormal existence (however materially successful) of those who are devoting all their energies to the pursuit of gains in the great centers.

Baby grows more and more lovely. His mind is expanding rapidly. He has a wonderful memory and a love of humor which daily gives us new cause for wonder. What a happy home ours is! And it is not rarely that I think of my great debt to you, for the quiet, wholesome training in childhood—the learning to live contentedly without luxury or extravagance—the fondness for books—for the really good things of life—above all for the constant incitements to probity and integrity, which your examples will ever furnish. I begin now to realize and appreciate the love you have lavished upon me as I begin to know the daily strengthening hold our little one has upon my heart, which he, in turn, will take as a matter too much of course, until, if he has his father's and his grandfather's rare happiness, he will find a corresponding love welling up within him, for a child born out of the pure love which only a true and noble woman may inspire. So that these days, I revisit the scenes of boyhood the more frequently—and I think the more tenderly of the kind hands that led me and the care that kept my feet from slipping, as "with heedless pace I ran." With me the New Year is full of thoughts of fatherhood—thoughts which embrace not only my own duty but my own privilege. Antoinette joins me in much love to you both,

CHARLIE [2]

His domestic bliss rose to new heights on January 11 when his daughter Helen was born. Antoinette Carter Hughes was indeed proving to be an ideal wife and mother. She managed the household without the slightest friction. She was never ill, except in her periods of confinement, and, while she had plenty of spunk and determination, she never lost her serenity. She knew precisely how to handle the children—how to keep them well and happy and how to train them in the essentials of civilized living. Little Helen was not a strong child, but she responded well to her mother's expert care. So adept was Mrs. Hughes in the delicate art of rearing a family that her husband could devote himself to his work without a moment's anxiety about the children.

Her presence was also sweet balm to Hughes' nervous tension. He had come to think of her as "a perfect companion whose spirit was a constant benediction." [3] His reliance upon her was evident whenever they were separated.

[2] CEH's private papers.
[3] Author's interview with CEH, Oct. 24, 1946.

"There is no doubt of my need of you," he wrote her in this period. "You are my 'strong tower.' Without you, I feel helpless (sort of a one-legged feeling, if you know what that is)—Such a sense of incompleteness." [4]

At the first opportunity the Hugheses moved to the campus. With a few thousand dollars of savings, they bought at a bargain the commodious frame and shingle house that Professor William Gardner Hale had built at No. 7 on shady East Avenue before he left Cornell for the University of Chicago. Cornell encouraged its professors to acquire homes on the campus by renting plots at nominal sums and making substantial building loans. This house had an especially fine library and an attractive outlook over the campus. Moving there in the summer of 1892, the Hugheses seemed to be settling down to a long period of campus life.

Cornell was completing an extensive building program that would add Barnes, Morse, and Boardman halls and the library to its plant. During Hughes' first year the Law School occupied the top floor of Morrill Hall. In the fall of 1892, however, attractive Boardman Hall, built of gray Ohio sandstone, provided ample quarters for the two hundred law students.

The faculty was small but painstaking and full of zeal. Judge Francis M. Finch of the New York Court of Appeals, was the titular dean. As acting dean, Professor Hutchins handled the administrative work with tact and dispatch. Professor Charles A. Collin, the oldest member of the law faculty, was an expert in corporation law and legal adviser to Governor Hill. William A. Finch was an able associate professor.

Hughes had many subjects: elementary law, contracts, agency, partnership, mercantile law, suretyship, sales, and evidence. To cover all this ground, he taught no less than fifteen hours a week, in addition to holding moot courts, and, in his second year, giving considerable time to graduate students taking advanced work. While he used textbooks, he insisted on the study of cases, with analysis and discussion of the leading cases in the classroom. Already well versed in the law of New York, Hughes determined to make up for any deficiencies in his own legal training by giving himself a course in the Harvard casebooks. Langdell's, Ames', and Thayer's casebooks became his guides in this one-man venture. "Whether or not the students were benefitted by my teaching," he commented, "I got the advantage of a self-conducted but thorough post-graduate course which in my later practice proved to be invaluable." [5]

In the minds of his students there was no doubt about the value of his teaching. "He created in all of us," wrote Harry L. Taylor, justice of the

[4] CEH to his wife, Sept. 15, 1892.
[5] CEH, Notes, p. 134.

New York Supreme Court, "respect for his extensive and (so far as we could judge) accurate learning, his uncanny memory and his ability to 'put over his messages.' " [6] President Schurman's appraisal was:

Hughes would lecture for three hours, always without a note, citing perhaps a hundred cases, and quoting the opinion verbatim. It is a matter of record, too, that his pupils did not "cut" his lectures. Nor should one miss the human note amid all this labor. Apart from his regular hours, Professor Hughes gave up his own time, his own recreation periods, to help the less brilliant . . . among his pupils. Students who marveled at his scholarship were still able to profit by his friendship.[7]

The New York Law School made a bid for Hughes' services in December, 1891, offering a salary of $5,000 and a share in receipts that would bring it close to $6,000. Gratified by this recognition, Hughes nevertheless declined for reasons stated in a letter to his father and mother:

I shall stick to Cornell, however—as I prefer the quiet of this University town to the attempt to teach law in the midst of the busy metropolis with all of the *dis*advantages of a metropolitan residence and none of the *ad*vantages in the way of money-getting. I assure you that I appreciate the offer—coming, as it does, from my former instructor [Professor Chase]. I found the "office" thriving—and all friends revelling in a prosperity and living in a luxury which seemed dazzling to my already-grown-provincial eyes.

In his second year at Cornell, Hughes was asked to take over the course in international law while Professor Herbert Tuttle was away on sabbatical leave. His protests on the ground that he was not familiar with the subject were overridden. While he embarked upon this new assignment with misgivings, because it meant devoting all the time he could spare from his other courses to a study of international law, it proved to be a "most satisfying diversion." "Little did I dream," he tells us, "that many years later I should find that year of special and exacting study a highly important, if not an indispensable, preparation for my service in connection with our foreign relations." [8]

The Hugheses had been settled in their new home on the campus for only a few months when they came face to face with a difficult decision. Messrs. Carter and Pinney had come to a parting of the ways, and Carter and Kellogg insisted that Hughes should resume his old position. Their offer was tempting, but the genial atmosphere of Cornell still had a strong appeal. To be sure, the Law School had proved to be a "hive of industry," and Hughes had found little of the leisure that he craved for general reading and contemplation. Nevertheless, his purpose in coming to Ithaca had been attained. He had re-

[6] *Cornell Law Quarterly*, December, 1940.
[7] *Outlook*, Oct. 20, 1906, p. 405.   [8] CEH, Notes, p. 134.

gained his poise and a sound physical condition, and had been accepted for life insurance. The strongest argument for returning to practice was the fact that he was drawing upon his savings to make both ends meet. In his last year of practice Hughes had earned $13,500. At Cornell he had dropped to a salary of $3,000. With his increased family responsibilities and two mortgage loans to repay (he had been unable to sell his house in New York and had carried it for some time without a tenant), he concluded that he would have to increase his income or retrench to the point of serious inconvenience.

Eager to have Hughes back, his father-in-law bore down heavily on the financial sacrifice that a professorship entailed. On December 21, 1892, he wrote to Hughes:

I felt, when you first spoke to me of going to Cornell, that you were making a very great mistake, and time has only served to strengthen that conviction. More-over, I have never yet talked with a friend of yours, who did not agree with me,—with the exception of Houston and I have always thought that he was so much of a friend of yours that he felt he must offer some sort of a defense of your course. . . .

I want to say this, not only for your eye, but Antoinette's also. Nothing has ever made me more furious than to hear it urged that you left because you were afraid of your health. Who under the sun ever asked or ever wanted you to work your-self into the grave? You know—and no one knows better—that I am never happier than when I have an office full of bright young fellows whom I have a patent on being able to find. I don't know but you thought, at the time, that if you didn't do these things, they wouldn't be done well. But, Kellogg and Dwight and Rounds have shown since—by uniformly good work in this office—that they are able to take up and carry forward successfully any work which you may not have time or strength to do. You can come back and play just as ornamental a part as anybody at the Bar. You can come down late and go home early and get something more than $3,000 a year! In a word, there is open to you today here, an opportunity the like of which has never been offered to any man of your age in this country.

The business will be the most varied that ever came to a law office. It is going to come from all nations and tribes and kingdoms under the sun, and there is going to be a great deal of it. . . .

I don't know whether you have found it out or not, but I want to say to you that the man who has a wife and two children has got to everlastingly twist and turn—economize in all directions—to get along and make both ends meet. Of course, he can do better on $4,000, but even that is pretty scanty. Here you can have income enough from the very start to live as you please—with the probability that it will grow every year. . . .

Tell that girl, A. Carter Hughes, that I should think life in a one-horse town like Ithaca would remind her that "a little thip was on the thea" and that both "thip" and "thea" were very small. The very idea of bringing up two such light-ning calculators as you have got in Ithaca! You ought to be "batted in the beak" —both of you—for even thinking of such a thing.

Walter Carter followed up this tour de force with further argument on December 27:

So, you see, the way is clear for you to come so far as things here are concerned. Now, let me say, that I want you to come first and foremost on my own account. I shall be 60 years old in a few days, and I ought not to be compelled to undergo the agony of change of firm anymore. There is going to be business enough—the opportunity is a magnificent one—and, in asking you to do this, I am sure I am demanding no sacrifice.

Of course, I realize that you will not have the pleasure of life in a university town, but you will have in its place plenty of money for all reasonable wants, and the leading Court position in one of the best equipped and successful law firms in the country. . . .

And, now, I want to record a prediction which I would like to have you remember. It is this—that the firm of Carter, Hughes and Kellogg, in 1893, with you away nine months of the year, will do a cash business of at least $60,000:—that, in 1894, with you present *all* the time, its cash receipts will be at least $80,000 . . . and that before the 1900 point shall have been passed, we will have a business where the net amount to be divided is $100,000 per year.

Now, if you don't preserve this letter as a whole, just clip this part out, put it away in an envelope, seal it up and write across the face of the envelope— "Mr. Carter as a Prophet."

The letter found its mark. Receiving it at Palmer House, Chicago, Hughes read it and reread it. His father-in-law's logic seemed irresistible. The lawyer-professor went out and bought a hat—one of the slouch variety that made him "look like a cross between a minister and a cowboy." Then he read the letter again and sat down in a whimsical mood to write to his wife:

He [Mr. Carter] asked no sacrifice—if it were a sacrifice he would not ask it, but would suffer in silence (heroic). He only asks that I should not sacrifice *myself* and thus he hopes to prevent what our theatrical friends would call a "grand double bill" consisting of two high class immolations on the altar of consummate folly.

I do not see (at present) my way clear to destroy your Father's hopes and to frustrate his cherished plans when I'm by no means sure that the course he wishes me to take is not the best for us both . . . the strongest argument he could have used was to appeal to me to show *him* some consideration as well as to protect myself.

I do not mean that I think this argument so well founded that I would be led by it to do what I otherwise could not approve—but the case on its merits is so nicely balanced that this is enough to turn the scale. And I think before you have this letter, I will have telegraphed him that I will come—if interests are adjusted harmoniously—as I've no doubt they will be. . . . But, after sleeping over it, I may change my mind.

The next morning his resolution was strengthened. It was the natural and proper thing, he told himself, to help retain the large business his father-in-law had built up. His desire to stay at Cornell was a fancy—a whim. It was doubtful whether, after a few years of routine, he would continue to enjoy teaching more than practice. In any event, he had the dearest wife in the world, the most promising son, the sweetest daughter. It was his duty to make their future secure. He wired Mr. Carter that he would come and dictated letters to Dr. Schurman, Judge Finch, and Professor Hutchins. When the letters were finished, however, he withheld them from the mail, visited some lawyer friends, and went to see *The Professor's Love Story*, a "most charming comedy."

Late that night he wrote a full account of his doings and thinking to his wife with this conclusion:

And now last and best of all. I got this evening your dear letter. Oh my darling, I would give up all for you—and when I am asked to stretch forth my hand and take the good things of life for your sake—how can I refuse? Yes, I will take them and if there is anything in this big moneymaking world I can win, I will win it for wife and babies. I have no business to be out of the great rush. There is my place —and, if I fail and troubles come, you will know, dearest, that I did what I thought best for the little family. I could not do otherwise and think of you. Now goodnight, sweet one, it will be all right. We have each other and that makes everything right.

Back in Ithaca, however, Hughes ran into a powerful barrage of arguments from his associates as to why he should not go. When he went to New York to consult Messrs. Carter and Kellogg, Professor Hutchins telegraphed that the trustees had agreed to raise his salary to $4,000. Hughes felt that his family could live comfortably on that. Touched by this evidence of his high standing at the Law School, he again wavered. He was not yet finally committed to the law firm. Going to see President Schurman, who was also in New York, Hughes was strongly inclined to accept the anticipated offer. But Dr. Schurman said nothing about the action of the trustees and merely urged Hughes to remain because of his interest in teaching. This lack of candor provoked the professor into a firm decision to return to practice, and when Schurman got around to offering the salary increase it was too late.[9]

Dr. Schurman expressed his regrets on January 3, 1893:

I greatly regret, but I must accept as final, your decision to leave Cornell. To the University it is a loss whose magnitude I do not care to contemplate. In view of the splendid opening before you, your decision is not surprising,—and though your colleagues would all fain have prevented it, now that the die is cast, they will, I am sure, all join me [in] wishing you all success and happiness.

In expressing my own sincere regret at your withdrawal from Cornell, I desire to add that nothing could have been more courteous, honorable, and straightforward than your conduct of this business.

[9] *Ibid.,* pp. 136–137.

Mr. Carter celebrated his victory with this note to his daughter:

December, 30, 1892

Well, Madame Hughes OF NEW YORK, how are you?

There never was anything so "perfectly lovely" as the way we have fixed things for the prodigal's return. . . .

We shall welcome you all gladly. Love to the young folk,

WSC

Hughes left Cornell in June, 1893, thus ending one of his happiest experiences. "As I look back over a life of varied activities," he said nearly a half-century later, "I think that I enjoyed teaching most of all." [10] In September the family moved back to New York, settling at 229 (later renumbered 329) West End Avenue. The burden of their frequent moves fell upon Mrs. Hughes, but she bore it with patience and good humor. No lack of cooperation on her part would ever interfere with her husband's career.

Back in the role of advocate, Hughes in some small measure satisfied his urge to teach by returning to Ithaca for a week in each year to lecture on "Assignments for the Benefit of Creditors." He also lectured for several years at the New York Law School. Despite his enjoyment of these contacts with the oncoming generation of lawyers, the increasing pressure of his practice finally drove him out of the teaching field.

[10] Letter from CEH in *Cornell Law Quarterly,* December, 1940.

Chapter 12

ATTAINING STATURE

BEFORE Hughes had a chance to plunge into practice again in New York, he went to the Far West to safeguard Rowland Hazard's investment in bonds of the Oregon Pacific Railroad. While he had regained his poise at Ithaca, he was still far from being sure of himself. One of his letters to Mrs. Hughes, written from Portland on June 20, 1893, contains this revealing paragraph:

MY DARLING WIFIE,
Today I have written for about six straight hours. Then my long letters to Mr. Martin. I suppose I'm foolish to write them. Better to be Napoleonic and give a word and a hint—saving myself trouble and increasing his respect. As it is, I turn my mind inside out, tell him just what I'm doing—everything as to my proceedings. So that if I'm not coming up to his standard, he has full chance to know it. I'm not posing a bit, wifie, treating him as a real friend & giving him my complete confidence. I lack *nerve*—wifie—*confidence, cheek*—I could [do] so much better if I had it. And the older I get the less I have. I'm so anxious that he shall be satisfied, I go far to make it likely that he will not. So I write—when I'm tired out—hurriedly to catch the mail, etc. But I really think I am doing well. Between you and me I don't see how any one could do more or better. Only others might appear to be doing more than any one could, or at least leave something to a friendly imagination.

Lonely but full of faith in her husband, Mrs. Hughes replied:

SWEET DARLING —
Do not wish yourself other than you are. Your perfect candor and frankness with Mr. Martin, I am sure he will appreciate, and as for the work you are doing, that will tell, as your thorough and self-sacrificing work has ever told. . . .
Dear darling, I want to tell you of my love each time I write you. I long to but how can I? Words are inadequate. . . . I can but assure you, not of the continued existence of that love but of its growth. Oh, dearest, it is so sweet to love and be loved.

Goodbye,
WIFIE

The Oregon Pacific case was a difficult one involving a grandiose venture promoted by a notorious character—T. Egenton Hogg. The railroad was projected to run from the Oregon coast to Boise, Idaho, but one disillusioned bondholder described it as connecting "a snowbank on the Cascades to a mud-hole on the Pacific." [1] Hogg had induced Rowland Hazard and other Eastern investors to put $15,000,000 into Oregon Pacific bonds. His success in collecting money had not been matched by the laying of rails. When the depression of 1893 hit his mismanaged enterprise, Hogg had nevertheless become the receiver and induced the bondholders to take receiver's certificates to the amount of several hundred thousand dollars.

In one of their conferences Hogg told Hughes that in his younger days in Illinois, on an occasion when he had hired a rig to take him to Springfield, an innkeeper induced him to take along a lawyer who could find no conveyance. It was Abraham Lincoln. On arriving at Springfield, Lincoln thanked Hogg and said, "If I can ever do anything for you, let me know." Hogg remembered this, and when he was thrown into jail for hauling down a Union flag in the early days of the Civil War, he succeeded in having his card taken to the White House. Lincoln sent for him, asked "what scrape he was in" and what he wanted.

"I want to go South," said the Confederate sympathizer.

"What for?" asked Lincoln.

"I want to save my country," Hogg replied.

Lincoln turned to his desk and wrote on a card addressed to the commander of the defenses of Washington: "Pass the bearer T. Egenton Hogg through the lines. He is going to save his country. A. Lincoln." [2]

Hughes later learned that Hogg's effort "to save his country" consisted of a scheme to seize a merchant vessel in the Port of Panama and convert her into a Confederate cruiser. He was caught, convicted, and sentenced to be hanged,[3] but succeeded in having his sentence commuted and then in obtaining his release. With similar adroitness, he had later exploited Eastern investors and Western dreamers of empire.

Hughes made a careful firsthand examination of the whole enterprise, spending several weeks at Corvallis, Oregon, where the railroad crossed the Willamette Valley. Returning to New York, he reported that the Oregon Pacific could not pay expenses unless it was extended at a cost of several million dollars. Without further improvement, it was not worth anything like the amount of the receiver's certificates. On the basis of this report the burnt-fingered bondholders organized a committee to seek a solution. Hughes worked with the committee, and his self-confidence grew as he began to submit plans of his own "instead of being merely a reservoir of facts and a critic of the plans of others." [4]

In December, 1893, the bondholders sent Hughes and Fabius M. Clarke to

[1] CEH, Notes, p. 138.   [2] *Ibid.*, p. 140.
[3] Footnote in *Ex Parte Quirin* (saboteurs' case), 317 U.S. 32.
[4] CEH to wife, Aug. 31, 1893.

Oregon to bid in the property at the foreclosure sale. They succeeded in doing so at a price of $200,000—the minimum fixed by the court and the maximum fixed by the bondholders. But confirmation of the sale was violently opposed.

In his letters to his wife Hughes gives a vivid account of his discouragement over the case and his loneliness. It was the first time they had experienced a lengthy separation. On December 23 he wrote from Portland:

MY OWN DARLING,

. . . Of course, our position is one easily understood by reasonable men—but these men are not reasonable. We have put up all the money our principals are willing to invest in an almost hopeless enterprise & if it is not enough to pay these claims [for wages, materials and so forth], we are sorry—but we cannot give more for the luxury of owning a railroad in the condition this one is in. . . . Then certain attorneys here—who think we have supplanted them have worked hard to prejudice us. Pressure of every sort has been brought to prevent the Judge from confirming the sale—& we think it will succeed—nor in view of the conditions will we be very sorry if it is not confirmed.

The next day, Christmas eve, he wrote again:

MY OWN SWEET WIFIE,

. . . the Angel Gabriel couldn't do much with this situation and would be extremely fortunate to escape with his wings in good order and a good note in his trumpet. . . .

God bless you my darling—I cannot keep back the tears as I think of your loving heart—your true devotion. And how I love you—and the dear babies—well, well, this is not a merry Xmas for poor ———. I rebel when I think of how I have toiled for these past few years and the little I have to show for it.

In court Hughes argued earnestly that the only hope of saving the Oregon Pacific and protecting the community lay in confirmation of the sale. Never again, he said, would the court see an offer of as much as $200,000 for the railroad as it stood. But Hogg's fantastic visions still dominated the thinking of the local people. At a junction hotel where Hughes was waiting for his train, the proprietor told him that the barroom below was filled with cursing railroad men who were threatening to avenge their wrath upon his person in good old Western fashion. "Come this way," the proprietor said, "I have a rig waiting at the back to take you to the neighboring town."

"Where is this barroom?" Hughes demanded, suddenly finding more nerve than his task required, in spite of his meager 135 pounds. Walking into the midst of the hostile crowd, he said: "Good evening, gentlemen. Will you join me? What will you have?" Hughes stayed in the barroom until a few minutes before train time, discussing his clients' offer man to man.[5]

[5] John Palmer Gavit in New York *Evening Post,* June 10, 1916.

Because of the unfriendly atmosphere, the bondholders obtained the consent of the court to withdraw their offer, take their losses, and give up the enterprise. The road is reported to have been sold later for half the sum Hughes offered. Incidentally, his pessimism as to his own reward proved to be well founded. Two years later at a Swiss resort he met one of his Oregon Pacific clients, the wealthy J. J. Belden of Syracuse, and reflected bitterly that Belden had not paid his bill. "The old boy, . . ." Hughes remarked contemptuously, "hasn't sensibility enough to maintain the ideals of a wild boar." [6]

His trips in connection with the Oregon Pacific case gave Hughes his first opportunity to see the West, and he made the most of it. What impressed him deeply were the great pine forests along the projected line of the railroad, the trip to San Francisco by way of Siskiyou Pass, and the acute depression he found in that city as well as in Portland, Tacoma, and Seattle. Despair pervaded everything. Lawyers who had gone to new settlements in Washington and Oregon with the brightest prospects found themselves in wretched plight.

In New York, too, the bar felt the effects of the depression. There was no diminution of work in the office of Carter, Hughes & Kellogg, but fees had shrunk and were not easily collected. The firm was established at a new location—96 Broadway in the old Schermerhorn Building (later replaced by the American Surety Building). Arthur C. Rounds, graduate of Amherst and the Harvard Law School, had become a strong pillar of the firm. Randall J. Le Boeuf (later to practice in Albany and to be appointed to the New York Supreme Court by Governor Hughes) had become managing clerk on his graduation from Cornell Law School, and Hughes now brought into the office one of his graduate students, George W. Schurman, brother of President Schurman. Rounds' keen mind and thorough training and Schurman's special aptitude for legal work won Hughes' admiration, and they were to remain associated with him for many years.

Kellogg left the firm about 1896, and it became Carter, Hughes & Dwight, with Edward F. Dwight as third man. Within five years, however, Dwight was stricken with a fatal illness. George W. Schurman, who had left the office to become assistant district attorney under William Travers Jerome, then returned, and the firm became Carter, Hughes, Rounds & Schurman. In June, 1904, death again invaded the firm, this time claiming Walter S. Carter. After his father-in-law's funeral, Hughes sorrowfully reorganized the firm once more as Hughes, Rounds & Schurman.

Activities of the organized bar claimed Hughes' interest and support whenever his work permitted. At a meeting of the Montreal bar he addressed the banquet as a representative of the American Bar Association and met many leading Canadian judges and lawyers. For the last two years of the old century,

[6] CEH to wife, Aug. 20, 1895.

he was a member of the committee on admissions of the Association of the Bar of the City of New York, and from 1906 to 1908 he was a member of its executive committee.

That "legal monstrosity," the Code of Civil Procedure, engaged his special attention in 1898. Numerous changes and additions had robbed the code of its simplicity and made it an instrument of confusion. As a member of a New York State Bar Association committee, Hughes helped to bring to light the code's shortcomings and pleaded for its revision.

Hughes, the reformer, came to the fore again with a denunciation of the imprisonment of men for debt. The New York law was "unsound in principle" and stupid in practice. "While it is ordinarily ineffective as a remedy for *bona fide* enforcement of just demands," he declared, "the existing law is easily made a means of extortion and oppression in the case of the ignorant and friendless poor. It is a ready instrument of blackmail." He called for complete abolition of imprisonment for debt, save in cases of contempt of court.[7]

Nor was his interest in civic and human affairs narrowed to legal outlets. His face became familiar at the Social Reform Club, where he met John Spargo, the prolific Socialist writer. That club was, as Spargo said, "both a symbol of racial and religious equality and a conscious protest against every kind of intolerance and bigotry." Some forty-six years later Spargo would look back over the years and congratulate his friend for never having compromised on these aspects of "genuine liberalism." [8]

Hughes' political activities were casual and local. He always attended the primaries in his district and voted the Republican ticket in state and national elections. The Democratic Party was associated in his mind with the rebellion, the fight against Lincoln, and, more currently, with the heterodox economic schemes of William Jennings Bryan. That was enough to keep Hughes steadfastly Republican. On election days he served as legal watchdog for the Republican Committee on the lower East Side. Local fusion campaigns and independent candidates for judicial office had his support. Frequently he was named vice chairman of a political meeting, but no one asked him to make a political speech, and he made none.

Abe Gruber, Republican leader, argued that the wholehearted manner in which Hughes threw himself into every case gave him a natural aptitude for public office. In the late 1890's the New York County chairman suggested that Hughes come around to the Republican Club more often. "We might want to run you for the Supreme Court some day," he said.[9]

"I'm too busy," Hughes replied, "and I don't want a judgeship or any other office."

[7] Speech before New York State Bar Association, January, 1905.
[8] John Spargo to CEH, April 8, 1947.
[9] Author's interview with CEH, Dec. 3, 1947.

A few years later he replied in the negative when a White House intimate asked if he would be interested in a federal district judgeship. Considering his family obligations and the salary then paid federal judges, he thought he could not afford to go on the bench.

The church claimed more of Hughes' time than did politics. He joined the Fifth Avenue Baptist Church about 1889, when his college friend William H. P. Faunce became pastor, and resumed active relations with that congregation on his return from Ithaca. Actually the church was not on Fifth Avenue. A wave of depression had induced the parish to sell its Fifth Avenue lots and build its edifice on the adjoining property facing Forty-sixth Street. But the authorities held doggedly to the name. At a meeting of the Baptist Association, Dr. Robert S. MacArthur, pastor of the Calvary Baptist Church, took occasion to twit the Fifth Avenue Baptists for perpetuation of this misnomer. The dry rejoinder of Dr. Thomas Armitage was, "The Fifth Avenue Baptist Church is a great deal nearer to Fifth Avenue than the Calvary Church is to Calvary." [10]

Dr. Faunce asked his college chum to teach the young men's class in the Sunday school. Hughes consented with the understanding that, instead of following the scheduled lessons, he would be at liberty to concentrate on the teachings of Jesus. "While I maintained my Baptist connection," he tells us, "I had long since ceased to attach any importance to what many regard as the distinctive tenets of the denomination. Rather, I cherished the noble tradition of the Baptists as protagonists in the struggle for religious liberty. I wished to throw what influence I had to the support of Christian institutions, and so far as the dogmas of the creeds were concerned I saw nothing to be gained by leaving the Church in which I had been brought up and joining another denomination." [11]

At Cornell he had conducted a Sunday afternoon course in the Old Testament prophets, with special reference to their place in the evolution of religious thought. At the Fifth Avenue church his lessons on the ethical and literary aspects of the New Testament brought together a large group of interested young men, and Hughes continued to teach the class for several years. When the pressure of his legal work finally compelled him to give it up, the class continued under one of his pupils, John D. Rockefeller, Jr., and became widely known as the Rockefeller Class.

Hughes was elected a trustee of the Fifth Avenue church and held that position until shortly before he entered public life. For two or three years he was president of the Baptist Social Union in New York and presided at its dinners. At one of these he invited Booker T. Washington to be the principal guest and was surprised at the protests from some of the good Baptist brethren.

[10] CEH, Notes, p. 156.   [11] Ibid., pp. 158–159.

They were especially resentful over the fact that Mr. and Mrs. Hughes escorted the eminent Negro educator and Mrs. Washington to seats at the guest table. Hughes thought this display of prejudice on the part of those who were supposed to be the least susceptible to it was ridiculous and tried to ignore it.[12]

Membership on the board of the Fifth Avenue Baptist Church brought Hughes into frequent contact with its president, the elder John D. Rockefeller. In his church work the tycoon of Standard Oil was unassuming and affable. Occasionally he asked Hughes to join his golf parties at Pocantico Hills. But Hughes had no business dealings with him or the companies in which he was interested. At Rockefeller's request, Hughes did take up the case of a young church member in need of legal advice, and he reported on the case several times to the multimillionaire, also at his request. But his service was rendered gratis, and he received only Rockefeller's thanks.

Many good stories passed between members of the board. Rockefeller was fond of telling about the Swedish immigrant in his employ who wandered into a Salvation Army meeting on the Bowery. One of the army lassies sat down beside him and said, "Wouldn't you like to work for Jesus?" The Swede stiffened and shook his head. She would not be put off. "Why wouldn't you like to work for Jesus?" Again the Swede shook his head: "I have a very good yob with Rockefeller."

While he was Governor of New York, Hughes was chosen president of the Northern Baptist Convention, and continued to respond to the church's demands upon him whenever it was feasible. The essence of what he distilled from Christian teachings may be found in the following excerpt from his remarks to the Vaughan Class of the Calvary Baptist Church in Washington:

We need to cultivate the spiritual life, not by centering our attention upon dogma, or by sacrificing intellectual honesty, but by reflection upon the spiritual verities of the Sermon on the Mount.

A truly Christian character is revealed in a balanced life. . . . What does the Christian character or balanced life mean? It is this:

Faith without credulity; conviction without bigotry; charity without condescension; courage without pugnacity; self-respect without vanity; humility without obsequiousness; love of humanity without sentimentality; and meekness with power.

That is our ideal.[13]

Hughes' disinterest in ritual and his lack of orthodoxy was a continued source of grievance to his mother, and she never ceased to let him know it. On August 31, 1893, he wrote to his wife:

I got a sermonic letter from mother this morning. (Poor mother, she didn't expect to see me so soon, when she wrote it.) I know just how she feels. Sermons

[12] *Ibid.*, p. 158.   [13] Address, Feb. 20, 1925.

prompted by a sense of duty may be ignored, but this was an appeal of love—the result of Ocean Grove experiences. Well, dearie, it's hard to be misunderstood by those we love. But it would be cruel to meet such a loving appeal in any other way than lovingly.

On November 30 he replied to his mother with a touching defense of his own convictions and a sad realization that she would never understand his feelings:

DEAR MOTHER:—

You must not think that my silence indicates indifference to your reproaches. I have felt them keenly. I have been anxious to write you fully in regard to the questions which trouble you, but I have not had the opportunity. Then, too, I may say frankly that I have had little hope that you would understand me. You know, of course, to what I refer.

I know how far short I fall of that ideal you have always set before me and which I have set before myself. If you knew my heart you would not think me complacent and certainly you would not find me indifferent to those interests which we would both call highest.

But, when we come to formal religious observances, your thinking and the circumstances of your life make it difficult for you to judge me either justly or leniently. Many things you would have me do, I cannot do with sincerity and I know that you would not wish me to act otherwise. But you grieve that I cannot enter—as you do—into certain religious exercises and this you attribute to a "religious declension." It cuts me to the heart that you should grieve and the more painfully that it should be on my account. But, while in important matters we are in entire accord, you give special prominence to certain forms which in many cases are indeed "means of grace," but which cannot be or, at least are not, in mine.

Now, I hold what religious convictions I have, as sacredly as you do yours. I am perplexed by many questions, but I believe my heart is open to the truth. I want to be honest with myself. I do not want to use the form of prayer when I am not praying, and whatever may be the mysterious connection between ourselves and the unseen world, and whatever the secret of that communion with the Father of Spirits for which we all yearn, it is too wonderful and mysterious and sacred to be cheapened by formalism and vain repetitions. When I really want to *pray* I want to be *alone*—and it is at those times when the reality of the unseen comes upon one irresistibly and the sense of one's own littleness and helplessness draws one, half-doubtfully—half-trustfully but altogether reverently to the Father of all.

Would that I were always, or often, on the "mountain top"! But one thing's certain, I will not imitate this most sacred communion by unworthy pretense of devotion. I believe in the "life of prayer," in the ever-abiding spirit of prayer—in the sense that we may live always conscious in a meaure of a connection, however ill-defined, with the unseen. But they are few—who take their places in the world's conflicts—who are not compelled to draw themselves away to the secret place to fit themselves for prayer. You and Father are peculiarly circumstanced. Your daily work is intimately connected with your religious emotions. As for me, I try to be true and do right, but the attempt to adopt your methods would end sadly enough.

And whatever else my children may find to condemn, I do not wish to be found guilty of trifling with that which is Holiest or of setting a daily example of insincerity. For most people, prayers before meals and the so-called family prayers are a wretched business. There is a *life*, of the possibilities of which I am keenly sensible, so far above these petty observances,—a *faith*, of which I sometimes feel the power, so transcending the narrow limits of our church creeds that I have little patience with the tests commonly proposed to determine one's religious condition. And it sometimes seems to me that these tests should be wholly done away with. But this is not so. They have their uses. But they are not for many, of whom I am one.

So believe me, dear Mother, though you may not understand, though you may grieve, we have the same desire to serve God though the methods of our service may differ.

I cannot write you more fully. I had hoped to see you before this. Can you not make it convenient to visit us soon? Any time! We would all be so glad to see you and Father, too, if he could come with you. . . .

I manage to keep well despite the work. I hope you and Father are in good form. Antoinette sends her love and, whatever else you may think, you know you have the devoted love of your boy,

CHARLIE

In his practice Hughes was unassuming, independent, and increasingly effective. Almost everything he did was carefully planned and reduced to order and system. His planning was especially fruitful because of his faculty for seeing the possibilities for trouble in every situation. Instead of merely fussing over such difficulties, he went to extraordinary pains to overcome them. "Hughes never wins a case," his father-in-law used to say, "until it's won."

Nor was planning enough. He taught himself to work rapidly with a minimum of error. As he improved his technique, he could dictate a brief with such precision that the first draft would be ready for the printer and would stand with only minor changes in proof. His method was to assemble all the data he would need and make a brief outline high-lighting his chief points. Then he would begin dictating. Augustus L. Richards, who went to the firm's office hoping, as he said, to "hitch his wagon to a star," found Hughes "pacing the floor like a lion in captivity, roaring dictation to a stenographer." [14] His method accounted in large measure for his fabulous capacity to get work done.

At no time did he accept a general retainer that might have required him to render all kinds of legal service. In this respect he was not a corporation lawyer. To be sure, he took many corporation cases, but always on his own terms. Clients came to him because they knew they would get a candid and independent opinion of what the law required.

Judges began to take special note of his work and to send him hotly contested or highly entangled legal controversies. Judge Alton B. Parker told

[14] Richards to CEH, March 25, 1940.

friends that of all the lawyers appearing before the Court of Appeals none was abler than Hughes, who was still in his thirties.[15] "I guess we better take that to Hughes" became a common reaction to a complicated legal problem.[16] He could carry a thousand details in his mind. He was always ready for any emergency. The man who wished to remain a professor had become one of the most resourceful lawyers in New York.

Hughes acted as junior to James C. Carter in *Stokes* v. *Stokes,* writing the brief in the Court of Appeals and drafting the papers in subsequent proceedings. In Albany the two lawyers discussed the case in a hotel lobby the night before Mr. Carter was to make his argument. Hughes excused himself and said that he would like to make a memorandum on certain points they had talked over. Suspecting that Hughes would work most of the night, Carter related that on one occasion, after he had worked until 4 A.M. boiling down an argument, he lost his train of thought before the court and found it impossible to continue. "Hughes," he advised, "never work the night before an argument." To the younger man this seemed a "counsel of perfection." For many years he put in his hardest licks at night in preparation for trials and arguments.

Hughes won an interesting case against the New York *Sun*. Chester S. Lord, managing editor of the *Sun*, had chartered a yacht to obtain news in Cuban waters during the Spanish-American War. When the yacht was lost by stranding, the owner brought suit in admiralty against the *Sun*. The owner's attorney, George Zabriskie, took sick and Hughes was retained to try the case. The publishers insisted that their managing editor had no authority to bind the *Sun*. Hughes brought in an abundance of evidence to show the broad authority of the managing editor to get the news. Addison Brown, the eminent admiralty judge, decided against the *Sun*, awarding judgment for the agreed value of the yacht ($75,000) less the amount of the charter hire ($10,000),[17] and this decision was upheld by the United States Supreme Court.

A happier contact was soon established with the New York *World*. Several leading lawyers had given Joseph Pulitzer cautious and conflicting opinions as to whether his newsprint contract was enforceable. At the suggestion of Justice Edward Patterson of the New York Supreme Court, Bradford Merrill, managing editor of the *World*, walked into Hughes' office and asked for his opinion. He got a candid and forthright reply.

Pulitzer then asked Hughes to visit him at Lakewood for a consultation. Almost blind, the famous publisher passed his hands over Hughes' face to get an idea of his features. For an hour or so he then put the lawyer through a rigorous examination on all the points involved in the paper contract. As he left, he called a stenographer and asked Hughes to dictate what he had said.

---

[15] Cuthbert W. Pound to CEH, April 27, 1910.
[16] Burton J. Hendrick in *McClure's Magazine,* March, 1908, p. 521.
[17] *Moore* v. *Sun Printing & Publishing Ass'n,* 95 Fed. Rep. 485 (1899).

Staying for lunch, Hughes was fascinated to see a journalistic genius in action. Surrounded by his editors and secretaries, Pulitzer seemed to be in touch with everything of importance. "One would have supposed that Mr. Pulitzer was sitting as the judge of all the earth," Hughes said, "and I was vastly entertained by the way in which this man, so physically dependent, dominated all by his intellectual power." [18]

During an afternoon drive Pulitzer consulted Hughes about his will. Their conference left each with the most favorable impression of the other. They were not to meet again, but representatives of the publisher frequently came to Hughes for legal advice, and he drafted contracts for the *World*. When Hughes entered public life, Pulitzer became one of his most enthusiastic supporters. In 1910 the publisher named Hughes in a codicil to his will as a trustee of the Press Publishing Company, with the understanding that, at Pulitzer's death, Hughes would become the directing influence behind the *World*. When he ascended the bench a few months later, however, Hughes informed Pulitzer that he would not be able to continue as trustee. A cablegram from the publisher on May 1 begged Hughes to let the arrangement stand, insisting that it would "not interfere with your high integrity and sensitive independence." Pulitzer died in October, 1911, leaving a will that still named Hughes as trustee and provided that he should receive a fee of $100,000 for his services— twice the amount fixed for the other two trustees.[19] But Hughes could not imagine himself directing the policies of a newspaper from the inner sanctum of the Supreme Court. He renounced both the appointment and the fee.

The most important retainer in this period, in its relation to Hughes' future career, was that in the beet-sugar case. A group of enterprising young men of Detroit had employed a German firm to build a beet-sugar factory at Caro in the Michigan Thumb. The work was miserably botched. When the antiquated machinery installed by the contractor went to pieces under use, the owners sued Speyer & Company of New York on their bond of $300,000 guaranteeing performance of the contract. Hughes was brought into the case because his firm was correspondent in New York for Charles Beecher Warren, who represented the factory owners in Michigan. Other lawyers were shaking their heads over the case because of the extensive technical knowledge required to prove the inadequacy of the machinery. But Hughes went to Caro, made a thorough study of beet-sugar manufacturing, and came back with enough technical details and expert testimony to overwhelm the opposition.

After many months of testimony-taking, the referee died. As Henry W. Taft, the opposing attorney, would not stipulate before the new referee the evidence already taken, Hughes began the weary task of presenting it a second time. Baffled at last by the thoroughness of the case he had built up, the opposi-

[18] CEH, Notes, p. 150.   [19] *Ibid.*, p. 151.

tion caved in, agreeing to a settlement which gave Hughes' clients a very substantial sum. Hughes did not know it at the time, but he was acquiring a reputation in legal circles that was certain to carry him to a wider field of activity.

Retained by David Belasco, Hughes successfully resisted an attempt to stop the production of *The Music Master* starring David Warfield. In 1903–1904 he gave an opinion as to the validity of the charter of the New York, Westchester and Boston Railway Company, which was seeking, and finally attained, a franchise to lay tracks in New York City. Critics attempted to discredit him in this case as a tool of J. Pierpont Morgan and the New York, New Haven and Hartford Railroad in attaining the franchise to promote a monopolistic scheme. But Hughes represented neither Morgan nor the New Haven. He appeared only for the local company, which was later acquired by the New Haven; his work was confined solely to the legal issues and had nothing to do with any negotiations for absorption of the New York, Westchester and Boston project by the New Haven. The senior attorneys in the case were John G. Johnson, leader of the Pennsylvania bar, and William Hornblower.

In the year that Theodore Roosevelt was elected President, Hughes had his first brush with the life-insurance scandal. James W. Alexander, president of the Equitable Life Assurance Society, who had locked horns with James Hazen Hyde in one of the most famous struggles in the history of American finance, hired a number of lawyers to back up his efforts to mutualize the company. Among them were Bainbridge Colby, William D. Guthrie, William N. Cohen, Adrian H. Joline, Hornblower, and Hughes. They consulted and prepared opinions while New York seethed with excitement over the threatened crumbling of a great financial empire. Within four months, however, Hughes dropped this engrossing task for a much larger undertaking.

Increasingly he had become a lawyer's lawyer, with wide recognition of his talent within the legal profession. Yet he was not conspicuously successful financially. Associates estimate his income during this period at $20,000 to $25,000 a year. Often he reduced by half the fees suggested by his partners. Hughes had acquired none of the beautiful houses, private art galleries, or spacious country estates that were common to successful New York lawyers of the day. While some of his friends were making fortunes out of corporate mergers and reorganizations, he was plodding along with difficult cases and modest rewards. Up to this time (1905) he had had no opportunity to argue a case in the United States Supreme Court, although three of his cases were then on their way to the highest bench. His independent course and herculean efforts often seemed to be leading nowhere.

To the public he was quite unknown. Seldom did his name appear in the newspapers. One evening, as he and Mrs. Hughes sat in their library looking at the papers, the absence of his name from stories about an important case on which he was working seemed especially strange because his associates were mentioned.

"My dear," Hughes said, "you must know that I have a positive genius for privacy." [20]

Little did they realize that he was soon to be caught in a wave of publicity that would broadcast his name throughout the land, or that the public eye would be focused upon his activities for the next thirty-seven years.

[20] CEH, Notes, p. 160.

Chapter 13

STRENGTH FROM THE ALPS

Two powerful forces were at war within Charles E. Hughes. His irresistible will to succeed repeatedly drove him close to the breaking point of his nervous and physical strength. At the same time his yearning for a fullness of life stirred up rebellion against this seemingly endless drudgery. The clash of these inner stimuli left him alternately happy and miserable.

Nature had given him an unusual mind. His home training and his own philosophy of life made intensive use of that mind one of the imperatives of his being. In spite of his moments of self-deflation, he recognized within himself the makings of a great lawyer. For realization of that dream no effort was too strenuous. But it was a well rounded self-fulfillment that he sought, and this often seemed to be thwarted by the heavy drain upon his energy and reserve.

No greater mistake could be made about Hughes than to assume that he was merely a thinking machine. On the contrary, he was a bundle of nerves. Having inherited a mercurial temperament from his Welsh-Irish-Scotch forebears, he shifted easily from elation to depression and back again. At the office he was called "the ship," and his associates would say that "the ship" was "plowing along steadily" or sometimes that it was "in stormy seas" and "pitching heavily."

Such a volatile personality could not thrive on the dry dust of the law alone. Greater than the law was life, and the life for which he was struggling was made up of love, freedom, aesthetic interests, humor, and bracing mountain air no less than of professional achievement. His eager pursuit of the good things of life and the resulting conflicts within must be given a good deal of attention if we are to understand the complex forces that shaped his career.

Along with most other New Yorkers, he and Mrs. Hughes found pleasure in bicycling in the gay nineties. On holidays, whenever possible, they took long cycling excursions into the country as far as Babylon, Long Island. The theater, too, was a constant lure. The Hugheses found keen delight in the productions of the stock companies, notably the Daly company with Ada Rehan, John Drew, and George Lewis, and the Frohman company with Herbert Kelcey and Georgia Cayvan, in addition to the more famous stars of the period. "Musical comedy still had standards of decency, and such inimitable comedians as

Francis Wilson, De Wolf Hopper, and Jefferson De Angelis, afforded the best light entertainment." [1] Occasionally they went to the opera, but more frequently Mrs. Hughes attended the afternoon performances, sometimes, after the turn of the century, taking her son.

Sunday was Hughes' day with the children, who were devoted to him. It was rarely that he allowed his work to interfere with a Sunday-afternoon excursion with young Charlie and Helen. They rowed or took swan boats on the Central Park lake, visited the zoo, the Museum of Natural History, and the Metropolitan Museum of Art, went coasting or took sleigh rides in the winter and victoria rides in the warmer weather, took the ferries to Fort Lee or Staten Island or the "Iron Steamboats" to Coney Island, and generally availed themselves of whatever made for a companionable afternoon. One memorable day, when the fleet came up the river after the Spanish-American War, they visited the battleship *Indiana*. On another there was the first ride in one of the "horseless carriages." Sometimes the whole family spent Sunday afternoon visiting the children's grandparents. Often, too, Hughes took long walks with his son, discoursing zestfully on many subjects and punctuating his talk with such enthusiastic gesticulations that the lad, who was at the self-conscious age, thought his father ought to be ashamed to make such a spectacle of himself in public. [2]

At home Hughes found time to read to the children, usually dialect stories such as "Uncle Remus" or "Mr. Dooley," and to write whimsical rhymes for their birthdays. He was especially adept at reproducing Mr. Dooley with a fine Irish brogue. Being a born mimic, he was in danger, even in later years, of unconsciously slipping into the accent of anyone he happened to be conversing with. Being also an incorrigible tease, his humor sometimes cropped out at the least suspected moments. He had a habit of reading aloud interesting bits from the newspapers while the family was at breakfast or in the study after dinner. Then, with his face still in the paper and without changing his expression, he would tell a fictitious story involving a member of the family in some humorous situation. His pretense to be reading this imaginary tale would continue until the credulity of his listeners would give way to laughter.

Sometimes he would "blow off steam" at the piano. The only piece he ever played certainly did not come from his music-lesson days. It was a rollicking number of unknown origin, in octaves for both hands, and devoid of harmony. He played it presto and fortissimo, with great verve, and ended by running up and down most of the keyboard with his thumb and adding a couple of resounding thumps. His "piece" was reserved for moments of extreme exhilaration, and when he played it without urging from the children, the family knew that something good had happened at the office. To amuse the children, there

---

[1] CEH, Notes, p. 160.   [2] Author's interview with CEH Jr., Aug. 13, 1948.

were also "stunts" carried over from his boyhood, such as the "Evangeline Walk" and a series of rapid manual convolutions ending with crossed hands pinching his nose and ear, which he performed with a comical expression of self-consciousness.[3]

The Hughes household was a place of relaxation and happiness as well as an intellectual workshop. The rugs, books, and pictures contributed to its quiet, harmonious atmosphere. There was evidence of refinement and comfortable living, without ostentation. The study was the favorite room. In this second-floor retreat looking out over West End Avenue, the walls banked with book-cases and a large picture of Gladstone giving a legal touch, Charles and Antoinette Hughes spent many an evening together; she in an easy chair with a book, he at a great central desk covered with manuscripts, letters, and telegrams.[4]

Any placid attorney at law might well have found in these happy circumstances an ample offset to the tensions generated at his office. Hughes did not. With the approach of summer, he would be physically worn out and subject to "fits of depression."[5] By 1894 his "unrequited drudgery" had pulled him down so near to the breaking point that both he and Mrs. Hughes concluded he would have to have the relaxation of an ocean voyage and a few weeks of complete freedom. It was a difficult decision to make, for Mrs. Hughes, with a baby only two years old, could not go, and her husband was as loath to be parted from her as she from him. As he boarded a Dutch steamer for Boulogne, regret thus mingled with his determination to regain his strength and peace of mind.

Mrs. Hughes and the children spent the lonely weeks in a cottage in the Connecticut hills. On the boat her husband wrote to her:

DARLING WIFIE,

I have slept every afternoon from one to three hours and managed about eight more at night. . . . I have about as much thought as a jelly fish. Reading is out of the question—talking is laborious—and this is my first attempt at writing. . . .

I am afraid I am reputed to be rather misanthropic—at least I have not tried to be "sociable." Aside from two or three pleasant men—who know how to enjoy their hard-won leisure, I have talked with few. . . .

But to sit by the hour and watch the sea is my chief enjoyment—though my stare is a vacant one. I have tried desperately to get up a little mental friction by worrying—but it's out of the question. There is an abiding peace of mind which resists all shocks. I feel like one benumbed or bewitched—and the senses, or rather the faculties—you see how my psychology has suffered—won't work.

Darling, it is hard for me to realize that I am "here" and you are "there." I have not allowed myself to get moody or "maudlin" but "from morn to afternoon, from afternoon to night, from seven o'clock till two, from two till broad daylight," you have been in my thought—the thought of my heart. "Far and away to me is

[3] *Id.*   [4] New York *Evening Post,* Oct. 20, 1906.   [5] CEH, Notes, p. 160a.

near." And I shall have you with me every hour of my trip. Too bad you can't know at the time how much fun we are having—you and I. . . .

I am daily renewing my youth. By the time I get back, I shall skip like the "little veals" a German doctor on board talks of.

Now, darling one, you said you loved me well enough to let me leave you. I love you too much to leave you again. And when I take a similar outing, we will have a "vacation built for two" and wifie will be the other.

Darling, this voyage would have been of three times the benefit if you had been with me. As you once said, every pleasure is halved when it might have been doubled. But all in good time. This trip will accomplish the purpose for which it was taken, I don't doubt, and I shall be happier for it. . . .

Bye bye, darling. Kisses for the babies and a wealth of love for them and for the dearest one on earth.

CHARLIE [6]

After a day in Paris he left for Lausanne. His first glimpse of the Alps from the pass over the Jura almost took his breath away. An intense lover of mountains, he found here the greatest exhilaration that nature had ever afforded him. The transformation that came over him is evident from the letter he wrote on August 8:

MY DARLING WIFE,

. . . The day has been perfect—the scenery all beautiful but the last few hours gave me a delight I shall never forget. We went through the Jura Country—the mountains richly wooded—the valleys richly cultivated. And then about seven the Alps rose before us en masse—peak above peak—dark, rugged, snow-capped. And at 8:30 after twelve hours travelling, I reached Lausanne—near the shore of Lake Geneva—with the grand mountains on the other side. A "petit diner" enjoyed all the more for the reason that a "station lunch" was all that I had had, a pipe—and then my letter to my darling. I want to say *mon ange—mon trésor—ma femme, la femme, la plus belle et la plus chère dans le monde*. But I will forbear, and you can dream in English all that I cannot say in French.

Oh! my love—if you could share this with me. You would have been in ecstasy today. . . .

This letter, darling, if it represents my feeling has love all over it—"not jes' bedobbled but jes' civired" as Uncle Remus would say.

But I must add it in words, my love; you are my idol—and the wealth of this beautiful world is nothing in comparison with my darling's true heart. Kiss the little doddies and tell Charlie his papa is riding on the funniest "choo-choos"—little Brownie "choo-choos." Tell both Charlie and Helen how much their Papa loves them.

Bye bye, darling,
CHARLIE

He took the boat to Geneva. Then came Chamonix, where he again wrote on August 10:

[6] All the letters quoted in this chapter are in CEH's private papers.

MY DARLING WIFE,

. . . Your letters have thrilled me many times—but I have never had such a thrill as your little letter of this morning gave me. Darling one, I do love you so devotedly.

Well, at last, I am in the Alps and my vacation seems to be just beginning—that is, I feel that sense of freedom, that exhilaration which is borne to one on the cool mountain breezes. Here I am at Chamonix with the great peaks of the Mont Blanc range towering above me—Mont Blanc itself—monarch of the European mountains—rising to a height of 15,780 feet. Even this valley is 3445 feet above sea level. The great glaciers are close at hand, stretching their icy arms toward the valley—but all about them are fine trees and grassy slopes. It is such a contrast—grim death and verdant life side by side—for you know the vegetation extends even to the ice line.

Before dinner I took a three-mile walk and observed the "lay" of the valley. I am feeling very well, and have improved twenty-five per cent since I reached here. . . .

I am delighted to get away from the cities and out into the open—into God's country. . . . I shall not be content until you can make this trip with me. I could almost hear your outcries of delight as we drove into the valley. In fact, most of the time I am thinking—"What would wifie say? What would wifie do?"

On the "diligence" from Cluses, where the train journey then ended, Hughes fell in with a young Londoner who proved to be a good companion. Together they walked up to Montanvert, crossed the Mer de Glace, and found shelter in a little inn at La Flégère on the other side of the valley. A thick fog obscured the mountains, but at five o'clock the next morning the excited traveler from New York had a thrilling view of the Mont Blanc range in the gleaming sunshine. Nature had lifted her curtain on one of her most inspiring sights at the most dramatic moment.

Hughes and his new-found friend returned to the valley and set out for Martigny, walking over the Col de Balme. Taking the train, they traveled through a gorge and emerged into a "valley of rare beauty" where "under the Matterhorn—lies quaint little Zermatt." [7] They walked to the Riffel Alp, and, the following day, to Gornergrat and back to Zermatt. Here they parted, and Hughes went on to Leuk, where he took to his boots again to cross the Gemmi Pass to Kandersteg. Then came Spiez, Interlaken, and Meiringen. In passing over the Grimsel Pass to the Rhone Glacier he was caught in a snowstorm.

At the inn Hughes sent his only suit to the drying room and went to bed to await its return. The gong for table d'hôte awakened him out of a sound sleep at seven. His clothes had not been returned, and the electric bell would not ring. He was ravenous and could scarcely face the thought of missing dinner. Opening his door a crack, he summoned a chambermaid and tried to explain his predicament. She brought him "nearly everything in the hotel" except his

[7] CEH to his wife, Aug. 15, 1894.

clothes. Finally he made her understand that he was *"sans habits"* by shaking his foot at her through the doorway, and his clothes were returned in time for him to "connect with dinner in good shape."

Crossing Furka Pass by "diligence," he took a boat to Lucerne and returned to Boulogne by way of Basel. "Thirteen glorious days!" [8] Hughes came home a new man. No outing had ever given him so much reinvigoration of body, mind, and spirit. In consequence, walking in the mountains became his hobby. While he was never to become a real mountaineer, he "did all that a sedentary man, with a young family dependent upon him, should attempt." [9]

In the following winter, Amelia Edwards' *Untrodden Peaks and Unfrequented Valleys* filled the ambitious climber with a desire to visit the Dolomites. Again it was impossible for Mrs. Hughes to go, but she raised no objection to his plan. After he had sailed she wrote to him on August 9, 1895, from Chesham, New Hampshire:

My darling,

. . . you are nearly two days and a half out now and I am constantly wondering how you are faring on the "Teutonic." . . . I know that you can't but enjoy it my darling—and wifie is glad for you. I can't say that I don't miss you, dearest. On the "Priscilla" Wednesday evening after the babies were tucked away in their little berths . . . I went out on deck alone and saw the moon rise. I was very sure that on another ship deck you were looking at the same . . . sight—and though very near to you in spirit I longed to be *really* near you and was so oppressed by the thought that each moment took you further from me that I couldn't stay out under that starry sky very long, though it was so beautiful and in a way so fascinating. I went in to my little ones and busied myself with practical affairs. . . .

ANTOINETTE

When Hughes wrote a few days later, he was again looking forward to the trip they would someday take together:

My dearest,

. . . Sweet wifie, you have spoiled me for friendship. The sweet quiet restful companionship of love unfits me for the conventions of social intercourse. [There follows a complaint about the passengers encroaching upon his rest.]

I have a room picked out for "wifie" when we can go together—with the little ones "hard by." What wouldn't I give to take you and them into my arms at this moment. My darling, I must try to get into a normal condition so that we may make more of our home life. A separation like this makes us feel its worth. I feel guilty in running away from you—but I know it will be best for us all.

Hughes had been near to nervous exhaustion when he left, and he had some difficulty in regaining his composure. After a walk of seventy miles in three days (over the passes to Caprile, Canazei, St. Ulrich, and Bolcano) he felt

---

[8] CEH, Notes, p. 161.   [9] *Ibid.*

reinvigorated, but the edge of exhilaration was dulled by loneliness. From Pontresina he wrote on August 30:

My precious one—were it not for my constant—rather "continual" journeyings what would I do? As soon as I halt there comes over me such a sense of loneliness and homesickness. One by one my illusions are passing—and now the illusion of travel is fast going. I realize that after all my soul anchor is wifie. Oh my precious one—how dreary, dreary would be life anywhere and everywhere were it not for your love—not that your *love* alone is everything, but it is *your* love—the love of the dearest, truest, noblest woman on earth. And how blessed we are in having such sweet little ones to care for and treasure. It is at a time like this, when I am away from the cares of business, that I fully understand how small a part of life they are.

Their separation was brief in 1896. Mrs. Hughes spent July at Chesham with the children, while Hughes' mother and father came to stay with him in New York. On July 4 he wrote a self-revealing letter from his library:

DARLING WIFIE,
This is Independence Day—but I find myself more dependent than ever—on wifie. . . .
Mother is watching the books and making valiant struggles toward economy. Poor mother—she is so tyrannized by trifles. It's in the blood. I have a big dose of it. But everything is going smoothly and both father and mother are doing all possible to make me comfortable—and I am comfortable. Happy? Well, that requires wifie. Love and kisses to the doddies.
Lovingly,
C.

At the end of the month his father and mother went to Chesham to stay with the children while Hughes introduced his wife to the beauties of Switzerland. In happy anticipation he wrote on July 19:

DARLING "WIFIE,"
. . . at the prospect of our outing I'm as happy as a tinker. Only ten days— and what's more only six days till I see "wifie." Then opens a "vista!" Well, dear one, you have had the burden and heat of the day—and very little freedom from care since we have been married. And if I can make this little excursion pleasant for you—I will. How often I thought yesterday of our walks on Manhattan [Beach] about eight years ago. We haven't much to regret have we? Our sorrows are yet to come. And with the love that soothes and sustains we can bear whatever there is in store. Our separation, darling, is a good appetizer for the coming feast— isn't it? I have a very busy week ahead, but I can't very well break down in five days. . . .
By by, Sweetheart
C.

They reached Switzerland by way of Liverpool, London, and Paris. Starting at Lausanne, they covered much of the charming mountain and lake country that had so fascinated Hughes on his first trip. Arriving at Zermatt in a fog, the Alpine enthusiast from New York could scarcely wait to show his wife the Matterhorn. "Can't you just see it through the mist!" he exclaimed, as he outlined the position of the famous peak from their hotel window. When the sun lighted up the mountains the next morning, the Matterhorn was indeed visible from one of their windows but in the opposite direction from where Hughes had described it.

From the Riffel Alp above Zermatt they walked to Gornergrat, and on the way to the Rhone Glacier they ascended the Eggishorn, Mrs. Hughes riding a mule halfway up. The day was bright, and they could "see plainly most of the great peaks of the Alps." [10] At Interlaken they visited Mürren and Grindelwald and then went on to the blue waters of Lake Lucerne.

Having planned another jaunt to Switzerland alone in 1897, Hughes began to protest the separation from his wife before he embarked. Mrs. Hughes was at Littleton, New Hampshire. On July 11, he wrote to her from Asbury Park:

MY DEAREST,

. . . I thought I might get rid of my loneliness, or some of it, as well as the heat, but the sight of these papas and mammas and the host of little ones makes me feel worse than ever. And so while gazing at the blue ocean what I have really seen is the peaceful cottage under the elms and the widespread view of wooded hills stretching far away to the southwest and wifie dear in her chic little summer dress (with the pink ribbons) and little Charlie and Helen playing gleefully on the lawn. And every now and then I must wipe my glasses to get a better view. Oh! my darling, how I rebel against this cruel separation. Why should it be so, I ask again and again, only to review all the "logic of the situation" and once more come to the conclusion that it is for the best. I have been over my continental time tables which I got yesterday and planning my trip in detail—not a difficult task—for I know pretty well what I want to do. Only I don't want to do it at all. The present is but an earnest of the wretchedness to come. Even when I think of Pontresina and try to picture that lovely valley—the most vivid recollection is that of my lonely tramps on each one of which I vowed I would never do it again. Really if I hadn't that return passage and my tickets paid for, I should give it up. What I should do, I don't know. But anywhere *with* wifie—nowhere *without*, I would like to make my motto. Sweet one, our lives are so intertwined, neither is complete without the other. And to make one happy, both must be made happy. We can have no separate pleasures. . . .

I haven't met a soul I know—and if I don't uncork soon, I shall "bust."

Bye-bye, wifie dear. To think that you—so even, so normal—so reasonable—so sane—should have such a neurotic, abnormal, cranky, crotchety, absurd husband. I think you are my steering gear and when I lose you, I flounder about like an old hulk in a swell.

[10] Mrs. CEH to Mrs. D. C. Hughes, Aug. 24, 1896.

Dearest, I owe so much to you. As the years go by, I feel that I am accomplishing very little—but I know that I am far more of a man than I ever should have been, had we not met and loved.

Now a thousand kisses and a heart full of love.

C.

After saying goodbye and just before sailing, he wrote her:

How is my brave little wifie this morning? How fondly we shall cherish the memory of yesterday, darling. I must confess that I was badly broken up last evening. The little girl's sorrow touched me deeply and brought such a vivid realization of all I had to be thankful for and the beautiful love of our home life that I couldn't control myself. That last incident I shall never forget and the darling one's remembrance—"The Shield of Faith" never meant so much to me before—I shall always have with me. Now that our separation has actually begun and the ordeal of parting is over, I feel stronger. As you say, "I have shut my teeth." I'm going through with the program and get all the benefit I can out of my vacation, which costs us so much in many ways, and come back as vigorous as possible to do my best for the dear ones I love so devotedly and of whose love I feel so unworthy.

You are the most unselfish—the bravest, truest wife a man ever had. You let me go without a murmur—indeed, urge me to go because you believe it best. Darling, I know what it means to you—I know what must be the monotony of the life at Elin Cottage and how eagerly you will follow my travels and how much you long to be with me. I know it all—and it makes me feel like a worm in the dust. . . .

The next day Mrs. Hughes wrote:

I am trying to fix my mind to the weeks of separation to come. As you say there is a great deal in what you set your mind to—and I believe it. The hope of our sweet reunion buoys me up. . . .

But, my sweet one, I must stop. I know you won't have time to read a long letter, and you know how truly and undividedly *I love you.*

On the boat he took to imagining that he was walking the deck with her:

I have seen your nose wrinkle with delight as you entered with me into the pleasures of this delightful journey.

My own—I feel newly wed—I want to say it all over again. And yet if you were here, I should probably be silent. For we have been too long together to need *words*. To be with each other—to see love in every glance of the eye—to have the joy of constant companionship—that is what we want. And we shall have another happy year—my loved one—and if I can, by being happier and more thoughtful of you, repay you for the unselfishness which permits a vacation like this—darling one—you shall be repaid.

Pontresina now fascinated him more than any other retreat. From that delightful spot he wrote on August 8:

The past two years seem almost like a dream, and the old spell is over me. For one thing, the air is so exhilarating that Chamonix with its lower level is not to be compared with it for healthfulness, and one has that *joie de vie* which gives so much zest to every undertaking. Then there is so much more that the ordinary mortal can do than at Zermatt, while the town itself is clean and picturesque. . . .

I am not as worried as I was two years ago—I distinctly remember my endless calculations. Now I am at peace. . . .

Do the little ones think of Papa sometimes—or is he simply one who works and plays all by himself?

Climbing Piz Languard (10,715 feet), he found the view "too wonderful to describe," conversed in a high state of good humor with a German couple, and came away so excited that he left his Baedeker on top. In the course of a letter to Mrs. Hughes he wrote on August 11:

If I could only feel as well as this in New York! My heart is where wifie is, my business is in New York—but my "Gesundheit" is in the Alps. I went up the Piz Languard two years ago. I would like to go up every year. Precious one—I have just been up a mountain and I am very happy. But this after dinner—when I wander about in solitude, I am so lonely. But luckily I am tired and can sleep. And so I drown in slumber the thought of our separation.

At first Hughes spoke to hardly anyone at the inn. "Almost everybody is in some party and somehow opportunities for making acquaintances have been rare," he reported. "I have a pleasant neighbor on my right, a recent Cambridge graduate, but after a half hour of 'No, really!' 'Well, rather,' and 'Very jolly, isn't it,' I give it up." [11] As the days passed, however, he became better acquainted. Every night he dressed for dinner—"for the honor of my country," he said. "No Englishman could be more fastidious. Every man at our table is in full dress—'thriving' is a mild description."

Before leaving on a jaunt to the Italian Lakes, he wrote on August 16:

This is certainly the air I need. I have never anywhere felt so well—continuously. No "downs"—all "ups" in this climate. . . .

One thing [is] sure. This is my last trip to Switzerland without wifie— For I have done Pontresina so thoroughly, I know I shall not want to come again *alone*—and I love Pontresina so much, I shall not be contented to go anywhere else. So some day, when we can come together, we shall—and until then we shall stick together and to our own country. For Switzerland, for me eclipses all else—and Pontresina is the best of Switzerland. . . . Well I have had four great years. And possibly hard work may drive me over here again—but the charm of novelty will be gone and the other charms can only be enjoyed with "my charmer." . . .

Well, dearest, two weeks from today I sail for home. Sometimes I feel uncertain as I think of that dreadful office with its constant demand—but I am inclined to be stout-hearted—and ready to do my best. The most disheartening thing is the growing

[11] CEH to his wife, Aug. 14, 1897.

conviction that my best is not much. But I have what counts most—a happy home and what counts next—good health—and to tell the truth what I have not weighed in true balance is not worth much—that is money and fame.

The birth of their third child kept the Hugheses away from Switzerland in 1898. They took a cottage at Twilight Park in the Catskills so that Hughes could spend week ends with his family and be close by at the time of Mrs. Hughes' confinement. Daughter Catherine arrived earlier than was expected, however, and caught her father off guard. He had gone to Canada for a few days and learned at Quebec of her advent on August 11. Hurrying to Twilight Park, the happy father had scarcely made the acquaintance of his daughter when he was summoned to New York to handle litigation over a city bond issue. Returning again to his family, he was soon snatched away by Frederick R. Hazard for a business trip to Belgium.

The Hugheses returned to Twilight Park the following summer, but the call to Switzerland would not be denied. When Hughes had to go to London in June to take depositions in a will case, he finished his work and went straight to Geneva. Soon he was off to Fayet and St. Gervais to make a tour of the southern side of Mont Blanc. Here is his own account of it:

> I walked over the Col du Four and the Col du Bonhomme, passed through L'Allée Blanche—directly below the great massive of Mont Blanc, and by the Lac de Combal to Courmayeur, which lies across the Mont Blanc range from Chamonix. I then proceeded to Aosta and Valtournache. From there I walked over the Theodule Pass to Zermatt. On the way I stopped at the Alpine hut on the side of the Theodule Glacier and from there made the ascent of the Breithorn, for me a memorable climb.[12]

Back at Zermatt, he described the climb in a letter to Mrs. Hughes on July 17:

> . . . at half past three in the morning, I am waked and make ready for the Breithorn. The stars are shining peacefully in the dark blue sky and we are sure of a clear sunrise. We take our coffee black (we have no milk) and set out. I am securely fastened to my guide by a stout rope—and away we go over the snow, now hard and firm. The morning is beautiful—every mountain unclouded. Soon the Matterhorn is tipped with rosy light and one by one the mountain peaks are lit like torches. We cross the Theodule Glacier, then on over a fairly steep ascent of snow until we reach the Breithorn plateau and so to the base of the summit, if I may so express it. . . . We climb the steep sides, digging our shoe nails vigorously into the snow and zig-zag up. There is no suggestion of danger, and there was none beyond the risk of losing one's head and consequently his footing, and sliding "quite indefinitely." Once we came to a little level space and stopped to rest. "No," says the guide, "you are over a crevasse." So I must rest on the steep slope leaning

12 CEH, Notes, p. 163.

on my stick. The morning air is cool and we go rapidly and reach the top in 2½ hours—all over snow and ice. The summit is a ridge of ice . . . with precipitous descents on both sides. I spread out my mackintosh and sit down to enjoy "the finest view in Europe." So many call it and I have never seen anything approaching it. Well, I won't say that, but anything as superb. . . . I have had the best the Alps can give, and that is saying a good deal.

In another letter written at Vevey he described himself as "frisking like a youngster, sleeping like a deacon." After a "wheel voyage" of thirty-six miles, he reported, "I was all right, though, of course, after so many revolutions, the seat of government was much disturbed." There were some discouraging moments. "The weather changed," he wrote, "and I left [Bel-Alp] yesterday in the midst of thick clouds, picking my way along the path I could hardly see and followed by my pack mule who no doubt thought me more of an ass than he himself for coming out on such a beastly day." [13] By the time he finished his excursions on the Aletsch Glacier, however, and visited Sass Fee, he concluded that this was his best trip.

Meanwhile the family had taken up a new diversion. Hughes returned to find his wife, his son, and his father playing golf on a little course near their cottage in the Catskills. He joined in the fun and soon became a golf enthusiast. Almost every free Saturday or holiday thereafter he could be found chipping the turf at the Scarsdale or the Englewood golf club. Hughes "played with his nerves" and never became a good golfer, but his zeal was boundless, as illustrated by the fact that on one Washington's birthday he played with red balls in the snow. Years later, when he golfed with his debutante daughter Elizabeth, he used to call her "Deb, the daughter of Dub."

In 1901 Hughes also began to bolster his strength with regular exercises. At first he followed, morning and night, a system prescribed by Swoboda. After a few years he trimmed this down to a workout of about ten minutes each morning. His slender frame began to fill out. Within two years his previous maximum of 140 pounds had been increased to 153 pounds. By 1907 another twelve pounds had been added. When he attained "a proper weight" of 173 pounds (stripped before breakfast), he was to hold it with little variation for more than twenty years by the simple expedient of adding a slice of toast for breakfast when he began to lose and reducing the pile of toast when he began to gain. His regimen of exercise was to be faithfully adhered to until he reached the age of seventy-seven.

The enthusiastic Alpine climber had to be content in 1900 with a summer place at Mount Menagha near Ellenville, New York, and a two weeks' holiday with Mrs. Hughes on the Maine coast. But the following year they sailed together again, visiting Bremen, Hamburg, Berlin, Dresden, Prague, Vienna,

[13] CEH to his wife, July 26, 1899.

Salzburg, Munich, and Innsbruck as a preliminary to Thusis and The Enga-
dine. Then came the Italian Lakes and the thrill of their first trip to Venice.

Left behind with Grandpa and Grandma Hughes at Mount Menagha, young
Charlie and Helen, then aged eleven and nine, experienced difficulties which
they had not sensed during their parents' first European trip five years earlier,
and to which Catherine, being only three, was even then immune. The grandparents were not convinced that their son and daughter-in-law had put sufficient
zeal into training the children along religious lines, and they devoted themselves assiduously to supplying the lack. When Charlie was caught with a
Sweet Caporal breath, which he had not had time to disguise, he was knelt
down by the bed, between the grandparents, who prayed alternately for nearly
an hour for his salvation from evil companions. The crowning indignity for
both children was when their grandparents assembled them on the porch of
the cottage to sing old revivalist hymns, grandpa singing a resonant and
breathy bass and grandma a piercing, flutelike treble. Thoroughly miserable
because of the snickers of their playmates from the near-by cottages and
hotel, the children would steal away hand in hand to some secluded spot and
hold an indignation meeting.

At the age of twelve Charles Junior was initiated into the pleasures of European travel. His father took him on a jaunt to London, Paris, Switzerland, Germany, and Belgium. The trip was especially notable, however, for an event
which temporarily robbed the elder Hughes of the peace of mind he customarily found in Europe. At Strasbourg they visited the cathedral, and being
fresh from the Alps, decided to climb the spire. Charlie and the guide went
rapidly ahead. Hughes followed at a slower pace with increasing concern over
the narrowness of the spiral stair and the great Gothic apertures in the spire,
which gave a full view of the street 464 feet below the pinnacle.

The steps became almost too narrow for a secure footing. Hughes wanted to
turn back, but his son was nowhere in sight. He had to go on. As he came
to the final pinched stairway, he spied the guide standing on the outside of the
spire above, with only one foot on a narrow perch quite devoid of protection.
In his best German, Hughes shouted, "Where is my son?" The guide pointed
upward and said something like "Hinauf." Keeping far ahead, Charlie had
passed the precarious spot where the guide was now standing, and, without
the slightest concern, climbed a straight metal ladder outside the spire to the
highest point that could be reached.

"Get him down!" commanded the frantic father.

There followed a period of mental torture while the agile youth came down
the ladder, squeezed himself into the spire, and joined his elders in descending
the open stair, which seemed to Hughes as unprotected as a great corkscrew

reared into the sky. He reached the ground in a nervous chill. It is scarcely necessary to add that the incident became a family saga.

In the summer of 1903, the Hugheses returned to the delights of Maine, camping on the western side of Moosehead Lake about ten miles north of Kineo. One of their excursions took father and son to Lobster Lake and to the summit of Spencer Mountain. Another took them by canoes and carries by way of Chesuncook, Chamberlain, Eagle, Churchill, and Umsaskis lakes and the Allagash River to Fort Kent. On the return trip they climbed Mount Katahdin, reaching the summit in a driving rain. Moose and other big game often crossed their trail, but Hughes never carried a gun. Nor would it likely have been different if his tramping had been done in the hunting season. He went to the wilds for relaxation and a sense of inward enrichment, without the slightest desire to kill anything.

Every trip into the mountains was an uplifting experience. Hughes thrived on the high altitude, the bracing air, the sense of achievement in climbing, the awareness of natural beauty, and the delight of satisfying an appetite whetted by exercise. As he found renewal of vigor year after year, even at a heavy cost of loneliness, he came to believe that Switzerland had saved his life and made it possible for him to carry a work load that otherwise would have pulled him down in middle age. Not only that; the mountains calmed his feverish ambition, gave him perspective, and in this sense prepared him for the larger responsibilities ahead.

Chapter 14

THE GAS INQUIRY

AMERICAN industrialism was undergoing what is probably its sharpest transformation in the early years of the twentieth century. Big corporations were in their heyday of mergers. Sprawling financial empires were in the making. Men of vision and daring were creating vast new industries and amassing fortunes, and unscrupulous promoters were taking their toll through the watering of stock, the capitalization of franchises, the exaction of exorbitant rates, and, not infrequently, the corruption of lawmaking bodies.

Against this background the great investigations that made Charles E. Hughes a national figure were undertaken. New York was most concerned in 1904 and early 1905 about the exorbitant rates charged for gas and electricity. The city was fighting the trust over the cost of municipal lighting. "For Half Light," screamed a New York *World* headline, "New York Pays Double Price." [1] Mayor George B. McClellan was advocating construction of a municipal lighting plant. The City Club and the Merchants' Association were clamoring for an investigation. Rousing editorials protested that the people were being "shamelessly robbed." Even "thief-ridden Philadelphia" was getting light at rates much lower than those prevailing in New York.[2] The Board of Aldermen concluded that something would have to be done, but when Charles F. Murphy, leader of Tammany Hall, poured cold water on the idea of an investigation the Tammany aldermen once more turned their backs upon the scandal. At last, in the spring of 1905, the legislature at Albany was goaded into ordering an investigation, to the dismay of the gas lobby, which was said to be offering high prices for opposing votes.

Governor Francis W. Higgins hastened to name the investigating committee, representing both the Senate and the Assembly, with Senator Frederick C. Stevens as chairman. The committee went to New York in March and began its search for an eminent lawyer to direct the inquiry. At the suggestion of former Judge William N. Cohen, Governor Higgins had recommended Charles E. Hughes for this assignment.[3] Cohen and Hughes had crossed swords years before in several hotly contested creditors' suits involving the analysis of complicated accounts, and the judge was keenly aware of Hughes' resourcefulness. But the Stevens committee was not immediately impressed. It was looking for

[1] Dec. 7, 1904.   [2] New York *World,* Dec. 8, 1904.   [3] CEH, Notes, p. 169.

132

a lawyer with a name that would instantly command public confidence. The assignment was offered to Henry Taft, brother of the Secretary of War, and to several other eminent lawyers. Obviously inspired by his defeat at the hands of his auburn-whiskered friend in the beet-sugar case, Taft advised: "Take Hughes; if any one can take you through the maze of technical testimony about the practical business as well as the stock manipulations, it is Hughes." [4] Suggestions to the same effect came from other lawyers and from Bradford Merrill and Frank McCabe of the *World,* without any knowledge on Hughes' part that his name was being mentioned to the committee.

Senator Stevens then went to Hughes' office and encountered another rejection. "I knew nothing of the gas business," Hughes later explained. "I had little or no confidence in the integrity of legislative investigations, and I feared that, with the great financial interests involved, the investigation would be thwarted in some way and I should be in a position of apparent responsibility and debited with a conspicuous failure in a matter in which there was intense public interest." [5] His skepticism was shared by the public. So many investigations had fizzled that the new venture was looked upon as just another excursion in political plunder.

Stevens would not take No for an answer. "The more I think about it," he said on his second visit to Hughes' office, "the more I am convinced that you're the man to take charge of the investigation." [6] The committee was determined, he further insisted, to make a thorough inquiry without political hindrance. As counsel, Hughes would have a free hand to bring out the facts and would have assurance in advance that he would not be "called off." Stevens also sent Senator Page around to reassure the lawyer of the committee's intentions.

Hughes then began to think more seriously of the offer. His first step was to investigate the committee chairman. Senator Stevens had been president of an electric-lighting company in Washington, D.C., but he was a man of independent mind and complete integrity. Although he was a millionaire and "desperately solvent," as Job Hedges put it, his devotion to the public interest seemed to be well established. Satisfied on this score, Hughes then scrutinized his own qualifications. He had had no experience whatever in legislative investigations. He distrusted his capacity and "hated the idea of work where the public eye would be upon every step, with the newspapers keen on the scent for any political intriguing and the Hearst press ever ready to make sensational charges." [7] All these objections he laid before Senator Stevens with complete candor.

"Mr. Stevens," Hughes then said, "I belong to the same church as Mr. Rockefeller."

[4] *Outlook,* Oct. 20, 1906, p. 406.   [5] CEH, Notes, p. 170.
[6] Beerits' Memorandum, II, p. 4.   [7] CEH, Notes, p. 171.

"What bearing does that have on the matter?" the senator asked.

"Well," the cautious lawyer replied, "some might mention it later." [8]

Stevens assured him that the committee was convinced of his integrity, and Hughes finally concluded that it would be "cowardly" to reject the committee's urgent appeal to him on grounds of his own inadequacy. "There is a public service of importance to be rendered," he told himself, "and if I go at it with the single purpose of doing a thorough professional job, that attitude will be recognized and in some way I shall get through." [9]

In announcing the committee's choice of counsel, Stevens said: "It was purely a Diogenes search, and we found an honest man. Furthermore, I think it will be conceded that we obtained one of the most eminent as well as one of the most able attorneys in the city." [10] Hughes promptly nailed down the pledge he had received by telling the reporters who swarmed around him: "I told Senator Stevens that I would not become counsel to the committee unless I could be absolutely free from political dictation of any and every sort. When we get this investigation started we will follow the trail that leads us to the information we desire, no matter where that trail takes us. . . ." [11]

But skepticism was rampant. The press introduced Hughes "with a groan." He was a friend of Rockefeller (who was supposed to control the gas monopoly) and a former partner of Cravath, now attorney for big utilities. William Randolph Hearst's *New York American* carried a three-column headline on the front page: "Friend of Rockefeller, Long a Fellow Trustee of his Church, Leader in his Son's Sunday School Class, Counsel for Gas Investigators." Beside this smear in words was a cartoon depicting Rockefeller and Hughes, Bible in hand, passing the plate. Hughes' straightforward attitude was described by cynical newsmen as being "hard, cold, and flinty." His recreation was said to be "climbing icy crags." When he gave his days and nights to preparing for the inquiry, he was suspected of being closeted with the gas tycoons. Before the hearings got under way, he had been associated in the public mind with "coldness, solitude, aloofness, silence, frigidity, ice." [12]

The first few days of the inquiry did nothing to alter the gloomy forecast that it would be a "whitewash expedition." Hughes offered only dull figures for the record. The press yawned. Even the company officials under investigation acquired a feeling of reassurance. "If Hughes gets out of a witness anything he does not wish to reveal," one journalist wrote, "it will be a surprise to those who watched his initial operations." [13] Senator Owen Cassidy described the committee members as "running around like a lot of children with toy bal-

[8] Stevens, quoted in *New York American*, March 26, 1905.
[9] CEH, Notes, p. 171   [10] *New York Journal*, March 24, 1905.
[11] New York *Daily Tribune*, March 25, 1905.
[12] William Brown Meloney in *Everybody's Magazine*, October, 1916, p. 389.
[13] James Montague in the *New York Journal*, March 31, 1905.

loons, gas balloons, you know." [14] Here was, in strident and voluminous detail, precisely the sort of public reaction that Hughes had feared.

The investigation went forward, nevertheless, without heeding the skeptics. Hughes had had only a week to prepare for the hearings. He was still feeling his way. Then a deluge of malodorous facts began to pour out of the aldermanic chamber of City Hall where the inquiry was being held. Through the press and by word of mouth it flowed out through the city in astonishing volume. The public attitude was changed almost overnight. At last it appeared that an investigating committee was actually investigating.

NEXT!

From the *New York American*, 1905.

Hearst's yellow journals, which had ridiculed Hughes and called him a "trust lawyer," now begged their readers to follow the reports of the investigation. Even some of the chief counsel's friends were surprised at his ability to elicit vital information from reluctant witnesses, without bluster, rudeness, or even impatience. With the suddenness of an eruption, a striking new figure burst in upon the public consciousness.

Newsmen took great delight in publicizing their "discovery." Here is a sample of many descriptions: "Mr. Hughes is a large man, not burly, but with the appearance of one who is built on big, broad lines. He looks strong. His shoulders are square, his limbs solid, his teeth big and white and his whiskers thick and somewhat aggressive. His voice is loud, but not rasping, his manner that of one sure of himself and his position." [15] Photographers and cartoonists exploited his whiskers with brashness characteristic of the great

[14] *New York Times*, March 26, 1905.   [15] New York *Evening Mail*, April 1, 1905.

untamed metropolis, and the *World* assured its readers that "in real life they are broader, braver, bigger, bushier" than they appeared in pictures, and that "when in action they flare and wave about triumphantly like the battle-flag of a pirate chief." [16]

In three toilsome weeks Hughes examined the chief executives of all the gas and electric companies operating in the five boroughs of New York, in addition to various city officials and Boss Murphy and his brother. He showed that the Consolidated Gas Company (popularly known as the gas trust) was charging the city $80,000 for the same amount of electric current it supplied to large private consumers for only $25,000. One unit of the monopoly was supplying electric current to the city at a cost of 4.86 cents per kilowatt hour and reaping a profit of 2.44 cents per kilowatt hour. [17]

Small private consumers were similarly "gouged." Hughes proved that the New York Gas and Electric Light, Heat and Power Company, which was entirely owned by the gas trust, produced and distributed electric current at a cost of 3.664 cents per kilowatt hour and sold it at an average rate of 8.042 cents, the net earnings being substantially larger than the costs. [18] Many consumers were paying 15 cents a kilowatt hour for this current.

The chief target of the inquiry was the gas trust itself. This gigantic combine had absorbed six gas companies back in 1884. Only one company manufacturing and selling gas in New York, the Mutual, had been able to remain outside the trust, and that was only because its charter provided for the imprisonment of its officers if they should consent to its merger with any other company. In 1902 even Mutual had surrendered by entering into an agreement to supply all its gas to the trust.

Hughes compelled officers of the monopoly to admit that when the consolidation was effected the plants and other property belonging to the six companies, which had cost them $20,942,632, were capitalized at $37,971,419 without any additional contribution. Good will, franchises, and rights had been capitalized at $7,781,000. Hughes vigorously challenged the right of the company to base its earnings on any such inflated valuation. "The fact that the company, by rendering competition impossible, has been able to earn large dividends," he wrote into the report he prepared for the committee, "does not justify it in adding to the value of its plant an additional amount for good-will or earning capacity, and thereby justify a continuance of excessive charges. If this were permitted, . . . extortion for a series of years would be sufficient excuse for further extortion. . . . The company is entitled to a fair return upon its capital actually invested, but it is not entitled to capitalize its grip upon the public." [19]

[16] March 25, 1905.   [17] *Committee Hearings*, I, 802.
[18] *Committee Report*, p. 94.   [19] *Ibid*, pp. 17–18.

In attempting to justify its exorbitant rates, the trust claimed a book value of $47,183,455 for its assets employed in the making and distribution of gas. But when it reported to the State Board of Tax Commissioners, the trust cut this down to $35,079,576. The actual value of the company's plant, the investigation showed, was little more than $27,000,000. When various trust officials were unable to explain these appalling discrepancies, Hughes called Robert A. Carter, secretary of the company. The suave witness drew elaborate distinctions in terms of high finance, but before his grilling was completed he had entangled himself in the ridiculous contention that the value of the company's plant was greater than its worth and that its worth was greater than its value. There was no escape from the fact that the trust was juggling its figures to the extent of more than $12,000,000 in order to keep taxes down and rates up.

The company's inflated valuation had been built up by adding the cost of every new unit and every improvement of its plant, with only meager allowances for depreciation. "For eighty or a hundred years we have been building up this plant to an investment of $48,000,000," cried Charles F. Matthewson, counsel for the trust. "It is utterly preposterous to say that you can take what it might cost to reproduce a plant today."

"I once had an umbrella . . . for fifteen years," Hughes replied dryly. "I had it recovered every year . . . and I suppose that covering of the umbrella dating back would amount to $50 or $60 at the end of that time. Would you say therefore that the value of that umbrella might be $50 or $60?" [20]

Even with its inflated capitalization, the trust's profits were so enormous as to be embarrassing. In 1904 its dividends were 10 per cent, not on the real value or even the inflated book value of the plant, but on the $80,000,000 par value of the stock. Hughes also brought out that the stockholders were receiving an additional 6 per cent on $19,857,600 of debentures convertible into stock of the company at par. When new stock was issued, favored stockholders reaped additional millions through the privilege of buying it at from forty to fifty points below the market price.

Nor was Hughes content to expose financial trickery and ruthless profiteering. One of his witnesses testified that adulteration of the gas created a deadly poison, even when it was burning. New York had suffered 130 accidental deaths from gas in a single year. The investigation also brought forth charges that the company increased the pressure in its mains in order to make a poor quality of gas supply the required illumination, thus forcing unwitting consumers to pay for wind as well as gas. There was no inspection of gas pressures, except occasional inadequate tests in Manhattan.

[20] *Committee Hearings,* I, 383.

Taken as a whole, the picture was one of brazen corporate pillage and governmental ineptitude. At last an unassailable case for reform had been made. New York's exploited masses were delighted. The press applauded heartily. "Admirably conducted," exclaimed the *World.* "The people wanted to know the facts; and the facts have been brought out beyond cavil." [21] "A model inquiry," said the *Globe,* "under able and adroit direction." [22] The Stevens committee, which had remained true to its pledge giving Hughes a free hand, was no less pleased. "Mr. Hughes has shown ability of a high order," Senator Stevens commented. "The committee is more than satisfied with the way he has handled the case." [23]

Hughes had no time to contemplate the plaudits that came his way. The inquiry had ended abruptly, leaving some leads unexplored, because of the committee's rush to get corrective bills before the legislature while it was still in session. Taking his voluminous data to the Fifth Avenue Hotel, Hughes plunged into the writing of the report and did not leave the hotel until it was finished a week later at two o'clock in the morning. Six and a half hours later he was on the Empire State Express en route to Albany, where he delivered the report to the committee.

The report was factual and restrained. Hughes concluded that the gas company could earn a reasonable return upon its capital actually invested in the gas-making business by charging 75 cents per thousand cubic feet for its product instead of a dollar; that electric current could be furnished for light, heat, and power purposes at a maximum of 10 cents per kilowatt hour in place of the 15 cents then being charged; and that charges to the city for street lighting should be substantially reduced. On the basis of these conclusions he submitted specific recommendations.

The proposal for 75-cent gas and 10-cent electricity won the warmest response from the public. Far more important, however, was Hughes' last recommendation calling for a public service commission to supervise all the activities of the gas and lighting companies in New York State in order to compel their operation in the public interest. "The gross abuse of legal privilege in overcapitalization and in the manipulation of securities, for the purpose of unifying control and eliminating all possible competition," he wrote, "shows clearly that there can be no effective remedy by general legislation or through ordinary legal proceedings, and that for the protection of the public there should be created a commission with inquisitorial authority, competent to make summary investigations of complaints, to supervise issues of securities and investment in the stocks or bonds of other companies, to regulate rates

---

[21] Editorial, April 24, 1905.   [22] April 24, 1905.
[23] *New York Press,* April 22, 1905.

and to secure adequate inspection, or otherwise to enforce the provisions of the law." [24]

Hughes turned his back upon the vain hope that competition could be restored. Only through effective governmental regulation could the public hope to obtain fair treatment from the giant utilities that had made their services indispensable. In that forward-looking stand he was joined by all but two of the investigating committeemen.

At Albany, Hughes spent several days briefing legislators in gas economics. Six weeks before, he had known nothing of the gas business or of legislation controlling it. Now he was generally regarded as the leading expert in this field. His close-up view of the New York Legislature in action was not impressive. Before settling down to a morning conference, Chairman Malby of the Finance Committee, Speaker Merritt, Senator Raines, and others fortified themselves with whisky. After observing their hard drinking and irregular living for a few days, Hughes told one of his companions: "I'll give those fellows five more years. They can't live any longer than that." Within a few years the only survivor of the group was in a sanatorium.

All the bills which Hughes helped to draft to carry out the recommendations of his report were promptly passed, except the eighty-cent gas bill, which was rejected by the Senate and did not become law until 1906. Timorous legislators had lifted Hughes' maximum price by five cents. Nevertheless, the trusts challenged the constitutionality of the act, and Hughes led the fight to have it upheld in the courts, serving entirely without compensation. The legislature also created a State Commission of Gas and Electricity with the powers Hughes had requested for it. Saving in New York City's light bills alone were later estimated at $780,000 a year.[25]

The lift in spirits that came to Hughes through this experience was temporarily reversed, however, as he was taking his son to Old Point Comfort for a breathing spell over Memorial Day. He chanced to pick up a paper carrying an editorial to the effect that, since he had been restrained in his treatment of Boss Murphy on the witness stand, Tammany Hall might use its influence to have him nominated for justice of the New York Supreme Court.[26] Hughes had tried so hard to avoid any appearance of currying favor with any person or group that he was unprepared for such a cynical jibe. Wounded and perturbed, he yearned for the bracing air and the majestic detachment of Switzerland. As soon as he could tie up the loose ends of his neglected practice, he followed Mrs. Hughes and the children to Europe.

[24] *Committee Report*, p. 94.   [25] New York *Evening Post*, Oct. 20, 1906.
[26] Beerits' Memorandum, II, 8.

Chapter 15

THE INSURANCE INVESTIGATION

WHILE Hughes reveled in his freedom, New York was seething with excitement from a new source. The almost sacred temple of life insurance was being shaken by dissension within and sensational rumors without. As early as February 12, 1905, the *World* had dragged into public view the dramatic struggle between James Hazen Hyde and James W. Alexander. This put many hounds of the press on the trail, and they brought in, as Mark Sullivan has recorded, "morsels of rumor about scandal in the very highest financial circles of New York, of charges and counter-charges, of rival committees wrangling, of the pot calling the kettle black, of violent quarrels, of bitter invectives hurled across mahogany tables in closed directors' rooms. . . ."[1]

There had been no sudden revolution in the life-insurance business. Rather, the public had acquired a new awareness of long-standing exploitation, and the chief eye opener seemed to be young Hyde's unbecoming display of his inherited wealth and power. He affected French clothes and spiced his conversation with Gallic witticisms. His fabulous parties at his "château" on Long Island, the elegance of his town house and of the private hansom that carried him to his office caused widespread wagging of tongues as well as the clatter of typewriters. "Dumas' riotous, turbulent imagination," cried the *World*, "never conceived of such a situation."

Five years after his graduation from college, Hyde was drawing a salary of $100,000 as vice president of the Equitable Life Assurance Society. Under the terms of his father's will, moreover, he was about to inherit absolute ownership of 502 shares of Equitable stock, which carried with it control of a company with assets of more than $400,000,000. So fastidious and so favored a youth, strolling jauntily through the Wall Street jungle, was "little Red Riding Hood to the wolves."[2] Financiers and directors of life-insurance companies as well as policyholders were alarmed. James W. Alexander, president, and thirty-five other officers and agents of Equitable brought serious charges against Hyde and asked the board of directors to mutualize the company. It was in connection with this effort that Hughes had been retained by Alexander before he took up the gas investigation. Hyde countered with charges against Alex-

[1] *Our Times* (New York, Scribner's, 1933), III, 49–50. Copyright, 1933, by Charles Scribner's Sons.
[2] *Ibid.*, p. 35.

ander. Henry Clay Frick, hard-boiled steel magnate of Pittsburgh, was named chairman of a committee to sift the charges, and his report called for dismissal of both Hyde and Alexander, drastic reorganization of the company, and restitution of certain ill gotten profits. When the report was rejected by the board, Frick, E. H. Harriman, and Cornelius N. Bliss resigned. The following week Hyde sold his 502 shares to Thomas Fortune Ryan for $2,500,000.

This turn of events convinced thousands of people that their policies were mere pawns in the hands of unscrupulous czars of finance fighting among themselves. Under the law, dividends on Hyde's stock could not exceed $3,514 a year. Yet before he parted with it under pressure for $2,500,000, Frick had offered him $5,000,000 for it and George W. Young had offered $7,000,000.[3] Obviously it was not an investment they were seeking but the privileges of high finance manipulation that control of the Equitable would afford.

The demand for an investigation grew so loud that it could no longer be ignored. The *World* carried a series of more than one hundred editorials under the heading "Equitable Corruption," numbering them one, two, three, and so forth, for greater effect. Still the major facts behind the life-insurance scandals remained unknown. Only a full-fledged legislative investigation could bring them to light. At last Governor Higgins yielded, although insisting that "nothing is to be gained by it," and the legislature approved his request for an investigation just before its adjournment.

Senator William M. Armstrong was named chairman of the investigation committee, the other members being Senators William J. Tully and D. J. Riordan and Assemblymen James T. Rogers, Robert Lynn Cox, W. W. Wemple, Ezra P. Prentice, and John McKeown. Armstrong, Tully, and Rogers went to New York to employ the ablest lawyer they could find having no connection with insurance litigation. They called on Ervin Wardman, editor of the *New York Press*. Wardman telephoned Don C. Seitz of the *World* to ask for his suggestion.

"What's the matter with Charley Hughes?" asked Seitz, remembering the gas inquiry.

"He's in Europe," the committeemen replied through Wardman.

"Well, there are cables aren't there?" was the journalist's response.

"They will cable," came the reply.[4]

"The committee could do no better," the *World* declared editorially, than to select as its counsel "the patient and persistent prober of the gas trust abuses. . . . Mr. Hughes would get the facts." [5]

---

[3] *Hughes Report*, p. 94.

[4] Don C. Seitz, *Joseph Pulitzer, Life and Letters*, (New York, Simon and Schuster, 1924), pp. 278–279. Copyright, 1924, by Simon and Schuster, Inc.

[5] New York *World*, Aug. 4, 1905.

Apparently the committee had similar advice from various sources, including Governor Higgins. At first Hughes' connection with the Alexander case had caused some hesitation, but inquiry showed that he was one of the few outstanding lawyers in New York who were free from entangling alliances with corporate wealth. "No one," as Ida Tarbell said, "held a mortgage on his ability." His independence and unquestioned integrity, in addition to his ability as a fact-finder, had singled him out as the logical director of the great investigation.

Hughes himself was oblivious to all this. Catching up with his family for a happy reunion at Nuremberg, he concentrated all his energies upon the thrilling business of showing his two daughters, his son, and Mrs. Hughes through the Dolomites. They took delightful excursions out from Cortina. Father and son wheeled to Belluno, on a trip to Venice. After leaving the Dolomites, the Hugheses journeyed to the Carinthian Alps and set up new headquarters at idyllic Heiligenblut. In this remote and picturesque retreat the stern-faced investigator was a youth again, drinking in the beauty around him. New York with its toil and corruption seemed a million miles away. The climax of his enjoyment came in a long day's trip to the Gross-Glockner Glacier. Tired and happy, he was eating a hearty dinner with his family when a messenger put a cablegram from Senator Armstrong into his hand.

Hughes was almost stunned.[6] There was little sleep for him that night. At 4:00 A.M. he aroused his family and began a thirty-mile drive down the valley to the nearest railway station. All the glory of morning in the Alps burst upon them as they jaunted from Heiligenblut to the Pusterthal, but now it was Antoinette Hughes who repeatedly exclaimed over the panoramic views unfolding before them.

"Look, sweetheart!" she finally chided him for his silence, "we may never see such a scene again."

"My dear," he expostulated, "you don't know what this investigation would mean. It would be the most tremendous job in the United States." [7]

Hughes' first thought was that he was not free to act because of the work he had done for James Alexander. At the railway station, he so cabled Senator Armstrong before taking the train for Munich so that cable communication could be more readily maintained. Armstrong brushed this objection aside. Hughes then insisted in his second cable that the committee chairman see Hornblower, Cravath, Alexander, and others to make certain that the Alexander case left him under no disqualification. Again he was reassured. Still he was tempted to decline. The responsibility that would go with this assignment would be staggering. When the showdown came, however, his sense of duty and his ambition to advance in his profession pushed him forward. His next

[6] CEH, Notes, p. 172.   [7] *Ibid.*

From the New York *World*, September 14, 1905.

THE GRIDIRON

cablegram laid down the condition that he be given a free hand to conduct the investigation. When the committee gave such a promise, he at once cabled his acceptance, arranged for passage home, and arrived about the middle of August, "bubbling over with enthusiasm for the work ahead of him." Doubt and hesitation had given way to determination supported by boundless energy.

There was no time for adequate preparation. The press was hammering away at the Equitable scandal, and the committee felt that it had to open its hearings at the earliest possible moment. The Hyde-Alexander imbroglio was only one phase of a much broader degeneration of standards that threatened the whole life-insurance business. The investigation would have to deal comprehensively with all the New York companies and with many kinds of slick practice. Facts and responsible recommendations would now have to take the place of rumors and sensational reporting. A hurried survey of what the newspapers had disclosed gave few leads of importance. After subpoenaing records and books of the insurance companies and obtaining transcripts of many accounts, Hughes outlined a tentative plan of procedure and plunged into the taking of testimony.

Several hundred persons were in the aldermanic chamber of City Hall an hour before Chairman Armstrong, "watchdog of the Senate," brought down his gavel at the first public hearing on September 6. The committee occupied an improvised platform in front. Reporters, photographers, and sketch artists swarmed into the hall as if the proceeding had been a notorious murder trial.

Forty-four company officials, some under subpoena and some voluntarily present to get the lay of the land, occupied conspicuous seats, flanked by a cordon of lawyers. Among these distinguished fellow practitioners, now lined up in bitter opposition to what Hughes was undertaking, were former Governor Frank S. Black (Equitable), Paul D. Cravath, personal counsel to Ryan; James M. Beck (Mutual), and Richard V. Lindabury (Metropolitan). With so many adroit legal minds seeking to thwart him and so many nimble writers itching for sensation, Hughes would have to watch every move. Keenly he realized that he was walking the edge of a precipice, with his future career at the bar the price of a serious misstep.

James McKeen, associate counsel, made the opening statement for the committee. Then Hughes quietly began the examination of witnesses. From that point on, the investigation was unmistakably a Hughesian performance. His reddish-brown beard, piercing steel-blue eyes, and large teeth (which the *New York Times* spoke of as rivaling "the famous Roosevelt collection in size, prominence and regularity") made him a striking figure at any gathering. More impressive than physical features, however, were the wit and mental agility that kept him in the center of the controversy.

James McKeen had been named counsel to the committee on ostensible terms of equality with Hughes. Actually, however, McKeen's appointment was a sop to the interests opposed to the investigation. Some soft-pedaling committeemen had sought to have him appointed chief counsel and consented to naming Hughes only on condition that McKeen should be associated with him. In spite of this, Senator Armstrong informed Hughes that he was expected to take full charge of the examination of the witnesses. The latter chose as his general assistant Matthew C. Fleming, who had been with him in the gas investigation, and Miles M. Dawson, an independent actuary. Fleming worked with Hughes at his home in the evenings preparing for the public hearings. There was no time to consult McKeen on every step; so Hughes was soon playing virtually a lone hand.[8]

When Emory McClintock of the Mutual Life Insurance Company took the stand, McKeen asked if he might conduct the examination. Hughes readily assented, but after the questioning had proceeded for some time Chairman Armstrong intervened.

"You must take charge of this," he whispered to Hughes. "McKeen is not getting anywhere. McClintock hasn't even opened his brief case." [9]

Hughes replied that he did not wish to offend his fellow counsel; if the chairman wished McKeen to step aside, he himself should make the request. The Senator then asked McKeen to give way, and within a few minutes Hughes had McClintock diving into his brief case. McKeen did not again attempt to examine any witness. Indeed, he appeared quite willing to let Hughes take the full responsibility, as the investigation began to rock the insurance business to its foundations.

Hughes moved slowly at first, as he had done in the gas inquiry. A publicity seeker would have plunged into the seething Equitable scandal. Hughes began with almost colorless details about Mutual and New York Life. The hungry press had to be content with the disclosure of a few exorbitant salaries and the farce that some companies were making of "mutualization." Mutual had boasted that its governing authority rested with more than 400,000 policyholders. Under Hughes' prodding, however, vice president Robert A. Granniss confessed that in practice voting was confined to about 200 policyholders, nearly all of them officers or employees of the company. And in case the policyholders should manifest any tendency toward independence, the officers were ready to squelch it with 20,000 long-standing proxies.

The disclosures began to take on a sensational cast as soon as Hughes was able to follow up the leads he gleaned from detailed examination of company books and records. Often he was as surprised by the outcome as anyone else. Great scandals grew out of the most trivial clues. He would plan each day's work, "but almost invariably something would soon be developed in the

[8] *Ibid.*, p. 174.   [9] Author's interview with CEH, Dec. 3, 1947.

course of the examination of witnesses which would give a lead that had to be followed up at once,—and in so doing new and important facts would be elicited." [10] Headlined in the press, these disclosures became very disquieting to the companies, the politicians, and even to some committee members.

At first the insurance executives were reluctant to unburden their souls. "Those relations are confidential, sir," one of them replied to Hughes' searching questions, "and I must decline to answer."

"There is nothing confidential about the insurance business now," he replied, and went right ahead with his probing. He asked several New York Life representatives what had happened to the money received for some Erie stock that had been carried as a nonledger asset. No one seemed to know. The mystery whetted his interest. Finally a bookkeeper produced a card on which sale of the stock was recorded, with no indication as to what had happened to the money. In one corner were three tiny letters, "H.B.O.," so inconspicuous that they might easily have escaped notice. "What do these letters mean?" Hughes asked. They signified the Hanover Bank Office, he was told.

So New York Life had an office at the Hanover Bank! Hughes demanded the books from that office. Officials promised to produce them at once. Hours passed, and the books did not arrive. Visibly annoyed, Hughes went to the bench and whispered to Chairman Armstrong, "I think I shall have to have those books by four o'clock or issue a public statement drawing attention to the fact that the company has failed to submit for examination the books we have requested." [11] Armstrong urged patience, and Hughes agreed to wait until the next morning.

Political temblors of alarming proportions shook New York that night. Every influential person in the state seemed to be telephoning members of the insurance investigating committee. Former Governor Odell, the Republican boss, summoned Senator Armstrong and said it would be inadvisable for the committee to demand the missing books. Armstrong replied that the committee had accepted its assignment with the understanding that it would go to the bottom of the insurance irregularities. Odell frowned and mumbled that he was afraid the missing evidence "might actually lead to the door of the White House." [12]

The next morning the committee asked Hughes what he wanted from the missing books. With complete candor, he replied that he did not know but that it was essential to examine the books to make his investigation complete. At last the books were brought in. Hughes scanned them eagerly, finding many items that he wished to explore. Near the end of one book was a mysterious item of $48,702.50 which the witness then under examination could not

[10] CEH, Notes, p. 174.   [11] Ida Tarbell in *American Magazine*, March, 1908.
[12] James Creelman in *Pearson's Magazine*, September, 1907, p. 246.

explain. "Who can explain it?" the patient counsel asked. "George W. Perkins," was the reply. Perkins was called to the stand.

This suave partner of J. P. Morgan & Company and vice president of New York Life began by telling the story of his life and expatiating upon his principles and motives. Hughes let him ramble on, then gradually brought him around to the business at hand. When the committee adjourned for lunch, with the mystery still unexplained, Perkins sought the investigator's private ear.

"Mr. Hughes," he said, "you're handling dynamite. That $48,000 was a contribution to President Roosevelt's campaign fund. You want to think very carefully before you put that into the evidence. You can't tell what may come of it."

"After lunch," Hughes replied, "I'm going to ask you what was done with that $48,000; and I expect a candid answer." [13]

When Hughes put the momentous question, he had already offered the telltale check as evidence.

"What was the payment for?" he persisted.

"That was money paid to Mr. Cornelius N. Bliss," Perkins admitted, with a characteristic flourish, "on account of the Republican National Committee Campaign account of last year. . . . I am very glad you brought that out." [14]

"Yes," Hughes replied with a broad grin parting his whiskers, "I intended it should be brought out."

Reporters raced to the telephones. Telegraph wires throughout the land clicked out news stories of "widows' and orphans' money" swelling the coffers of big politics. Meanwhile Hughes coolly drew from the hapless Morgan partner the fact that similar sums had been contributed to the Republican Party by the New York Life in 1896 and 1900. A later parade of witnesses showed that Mutual had contributed $40,000 to the Grand Old Party in 1904; Equitable had given $50,000; and smaller companies, lesser sums.

"If no other or further information about the life insurance business were elicited by the Armstrong Committee," said the *New York Times*, "the ordering of the inquiry would be fully justified. . . ." [15] The *World* expressed doubt, "if any legislative investigation in the history of the state was ever conducted more ably or more acutely or more rationally." A wave of resentment against giant corporations marshaling stockholders' and policyholders' funds for political purposes swept over the nation and hastened the outlawing of that vicious practice.

"Hughes calls himself a Republican," the bosses wailed, "but he's ripping the party wide open." Under the bosses' badgering, several members of the committee became restive and asked for an executive session to seek a show-

---

[13] Beerits' Memorandum, II, 19.
[14] *Armstrong Committee Hearings*, I, 751–752.   [15] Sept. 16, 1905.

down with Hughes. Instead of openly opposing him, however, a spokesman complained that the committeemen never knew in advance what course the investigation would take. They were caught utterly unprepared for Hughes' shocking revelations. Could not their counsel keep them informed as to what line he was going to take?

Hughes protested that this would be impossible. Usually he did not know what he would find until he came to the end of the trail. How could he give them information he did not have? Some members were nevertheless persistent. After all, they intimated, it was the committee's investigation.

"I understand that perfectly," Hughes replied. "I am only your counsel. Of course, you are free to give me explicit instructions, and if you do so I shall follow them, or I shall resign and tell the public why." [16]

Senator Tully walked over to the lawyer's side. "I am with Mr. Hughes," he said. Others followed suit. Public sentiment was such that the committee could not have provoked Hughes' resignation on the issue of continuing the investigation free from boss domination without committing political suicide. Every member knew it. Hughes had become, as one commentator said, "the personification of outraged America." From this point on there was no further effort to interfere with his direction of the inquiry.

Outside the committee, however, tremendous forces buffeted the determined investigator. A clamor arose for further light on the "buying of public office" with corporate funds. Hughes had courageously exposed the tie-in of his own party with the "big three" in life insurance. Now, the argument ran, he must summon Cornelius Bliss and Postmaster General George B. Cortelyou, chairman of the Republican National Committee, and probe further into the relations between big business and the political machines. The pressure behind this demand was especially intense because it came chiefly from those individuals and newspapers (including the *World*) that had given the investigator the most enthusiastic support. But Hughes refused to budge. He was investigating life insurance, not political corruption. He fought with dogged persistence to get a complete picture of the hidden campaign expenditures of insurance companies spread upon the record; these were part of the mismanagement that he had been retained to expose and correct. At the same time he refused to jeopardize the insurance inquiry by going off on a tangent. If he deviated from his central aim, the inquiry would be smothered by politics and nothing of value would be accomplished. His friends were no more successful in diverting him from his purpose than were his opponents.

Meanwhile the Republican bosses advanced his name as the logical candidate for mayor of New York City. Hughes correctly saw that it was a plot to break up the insurance investigation and tried to withdraw his name from con-

[16] CEH, Notes, p. 175; author's interview with CEH, Dec. 3, 1947.

sideration. Odell persisted, however, in refusing to believe that a hitherto obscure lawyer would turn down a chance to be mayor of New York when the final showdown came.

The evening of Friday, October 6, 1905, was one of the few occasions during the insurance investigation when Hughes found it possible to snatch two or three hours for relaxation. He took his wife to the theater. Meanwhile a drama of a very different sort was taking place at Carnegie Hall, where cheering and waving of flags greeted Senator Nathaniel Elsberg's declaration that Hughes was "the man to meet a great emergency." Returning from the theater, the investigator found his house brilliantly lighted and the street full of cabs and excited people. He had been nominated for the mayorship in spite of his prior refusal to run. A large delegation of party leaders was awaiting his return, determined to high-pressure him into acceptance of the honor.

Hughes took the "notification committee" up to his library. There were Herbert Parsons, the county chairman; Julius Mayer, attorney general of the state; Senator Page and Ezra Prentice of the insurance investigation committee, and several others. Flattery was the foremost arrow in their quiver. Hughes was the only man, they said, who could beat Mayor McClellan. If he should refuse to run, McClellan would be reelected mayor, then governor, then President of the United States. Hughes must step in, he was told, to save his party and his country from this dire chain of contingencies. His nomination had been pressed against his wishes because of these peculiar circumstances, and now he could not let his party down.

The dilemma confronting the party leaders, Hughes replied, was entirely of their own making. He had told them in unmistakable terms before they had acted that he could not accept the nomination. Their heedlessness had not in any way changed his situation. Nor would he attempt to look into the future. It was enough that he had an immense job to do in the present.

"If I were free to take the nomination for mayor," the harassed investigator continued, "I cannot say what I would do, for I have never desired to enter public life. My wish is to practice my profession and to support my family with my earnings from that work. If I were free, however, to take a nomination, it might seem to be my duty to do so against my wishes and the interests of my family. But I am not free." [17]

Every suggestion that he could continue the investigation and run for mayor at the same time he brushed aside. To permit entanglement of the investigation in politics would be to defeat its purpose and subject himself to justifiable attack. Such G.O.P. wheelhorses as Platt, Depew, and Odell were yet to be called. How impossible it would be to question them if he were their candidate for mayor! The argument went on until two o'clock in the morning, the pressure

[17] An eyewitness, Ervin Wardman in *Review of Reviews,* November, 1906, p. 552.

gathering such intensity that Mrs. Hughes, listening in an adjoining room, did not see how her husband could hold out. No one present would accept his point of view. Finally the politicians implored him to delay announcement of his decision until Monday. When he agreed to this, they went home.

The telephones at Hughes' home and office buzzed almost incessantly through Saturday and Sunday, and his desk was banked with telegrams. Every cog in the Republican machine seemed to be grinding out an appeal to him to bow to the good of the party. Nor was the pressure confined to Republican sources. So intense was Hearst's bitterness against McClellan that he sent a message to Hughes through Ervin Wardman, editor of the *New York Press*. If Hughes would run, the message informed him, Hearst would support him, or, alternatively, Hearst himself would run in order to split the opposition and ensure the election of Hughes.[18]

The investigator remained unshaken. On Monday he issued a crisp statement explaining why it was impossible for him to accept the nomination:

In this dilemma I have simply to do my duty as I see it.

In my judgment, I have no right to accept the nomination. A paramount public duty forbids it. . . .

You know how desirous I have been that the investigation should not be colored by any suggestion of political motive. Whatever confidence it has inspired has been due to absolute independence of political consideration. It is not sufficient to say that an acceptance of this nomination, coming to me unsought and despite an unequivocal statement of my position, would not deflect my course by a hair's breadth, that I should remain, and that you intend that I should remain, entirely untrammelled. The non-political character of the investigation and its freedom from bias, either of fear or favor, not only must exist, they must be recognized. I cannot permit them, by any action of mine, to become matters of debate. . . .

Were I with the best of intention to accept the nomination, it is my conviction that the work of the investigation would be largely discredited; its motives would be impugned and its integrity assailed. To many it would appear that its course would be shaped and its lines of inquiry would be chosen, developed, or abandoned as political ambition might prompt or political exigency demand.

Such a situation would be intolerable. There is but one course open. The legislative inquiry must proceed with convincing disinterestedness. Its great opportunities must not be imperilled by alienating the support to which it is entitled or by giving the slightest occasion for questioning the sincerity and single-mindedness with which it is conducted.[19]

Ten days after Hearst had failed to induce Hughes to accept the mayoralty nomination, his *New York American* (October 16, 1905) was denouncing the Republican bosses for trying "to take away the brilliant and uncompromising investigator who is following the trail of financial perfidy and crime" in the in-

[18] Author's interview with CEH, Dec. 3, 1947.
[19] New York *Evening Post*, Oct. 9, 1905.

surance investigation. "It is to the everlasting honor of Charles Evans Hughes," Hearst's organ continued, "that he saw through this intrigue and refused to be the dupe of Ryan and Odell." Hearst ran against McClellan and William M. Ivans, the Republican nominee, and came close to equaling McClellan's vote.

Hughes assumed that he had burned his political bridges. His chance of receiving another Republican nomination seemed about equal to that of the bosses putting their fingers twice into the same fire. But this consequence of his independence did not disturb him, and it immeasurably enhanced his standing with the public. ". . . his refusal to be a Mayoralty nominee is as praise-worthy as his nomination by the party managers in convention was reprehensible," commented the *New York Herald*. "This action," chimed in *World's Work*, "is a good measure of the quality of the man." "His declination was so fine," declared the *Evening Post*, "that everyone wishes his duty had allowed him to make it an acceptance." In contrast to the "mire of moral rottenness" that the insurance investigation was exposing, Hughes' conduct stood out as a beacon of new hope for democratic government.

The investigation went forward without interruption. Hughes keenly felt its responsibility. The future of a great business and billions of dollars belonging to policyholders were at stake in addition to the reputations of numerous business and political leaders. Because the committee did not allow counsel to appear for witnesses or to cross-examine them, Hughes took special precautions to avoid any unfairness. He encouraged witnesses to explain or defend any conduct that had been brought into question. When the phalanx of lawyers in the front seats suggested questions, he himself would pass them along to the witnesses.

Not content to get the whole truth into the record, Hughes often called in the newsmen to make certain that they understood complicated or elusive testimony. The public as well as the committee, he felt, was entitled to the facts. Almost to a man, the reporters were friendly to him, although some were doing their utmost to sensationalize the investigation. By his frequent seminar sessions Hughes took the rough edges off many stories and convinced the reporters that he was "trying to cut out a cancerous growth and restore the victim to health—not to slay dragons for the sake of public applause." [20]

Sometimes the burden seemed too heavy to be borne. Night work, often continuing as late as 2:00 A.M., repeatedly cut into his rest. When he did get to bed, his nerves would be too taut to be relaxed in sleep. Indeed, his capacity for quick relaxation was permanently impaired. He began to take an alcoholic drink each night before going to bed to help release his mind from its charge.

"I can't see an end to this," he exclaimed to his wife on several occasions when his feeling of depression seemed especially acute. "It is too much.

[20] Author's interview with CEH, Oct. 17, 1946.

I simply can't go on." [21] But after a night's rest he would start again with unrelenting vigor.

Great reputations began to crumble. Men who dealt in millions and were mentally conditioned only to the giving of commands suddenly found themselves accounting to a lean and persistent lawyer for transactions they had supposed to be safely hidden by the trickery of bookkeeping. It became a common experience for them to come into the hearing room with lordly self-assurance and leave in a gray fog of disgrace.

Portly Richard A. McCurdy, president of Mutual Life, came breezing into the limelight with an air of aloofness to petty inquisitions. Elegantly dressed and wearing a large seal ring, McCurdy seated himself with enviable composure, removed his gold-rimmed pince-nez, and asked that the shades be drawn to shut out the glare of the sunlight. Having seen a dozen insurance investigations that had come to nothing, he intended to take this one in stride.

When Hughes pressed him on the exorbitant salaries and commissions paid by his organization, McCurdy expatiated grandly upon the virtues of life insurance. It is no ordinary business, he boasted. The men who organized Mutual did so "from a pure spirit of philanthropy" on the theory "that it was a great beneficent missionary institution."

"Well," Hughes replied, "you have made a very full explanation. . . . The question comes back to the salaries of the missionaries." [22]

"Well, all right," the witness snorted.

Hughes showed that "Missionary" McCurdy and his vice president held enough proxies from policyholders to control the election of the trustees who had increased his salary over a period of years from $30,000 to $150,000 annually. Another of the "missionaries," Robert H. McCurdy, the president's son, had received $530,788 from the company in sixteen years, in addition to commissions on the company's foreign business (at first calculated at 5 per cent and later reduced at his own request) amounting to $1,268,390, part of which was paid to an associate. The president's son-in-law, Louis A. Thebaud, had drawn $147,687 in commissions in 1904. The *World* estimated the "take" of the McCurdy clan, including syndicate and trust-company profits, at $15,000,000 [23] during their reign over this "autocracy, maintained almost without challenge."

In an effort to determine how much the $150,000 president knew about the business of the company, Hughes asked him a simple question about calculation of premiums.

"You are trying to prove me a fool," McCurdy retorted. "I refer you to the actuary."

"Without commenting upon that, Mr. McCurdy," dryly replied the investi-

---

[21] CEH, Notes, p. 177.   [22] *Hearings*, II, 1842.   [23] Oct. 15, 1905.

gator, "I want to ask *you*. . . ."[24] He repeated his question about premiums. McCurdy stubbornly refused to venture upon any such demonstration of his knowledge of the business. But in the course of his examination he said enough to show that his ignorance of his own company was astounding.

From the *Denver Post*, October 19, 1905.

SOME OF THEM ARE COMING OUT OF
THE LITTLE END OF THE HORN!

What Mutual called "legal expenses" amounted in 1904 to the exorbitant figure of $364,254. Many payments from this "legal expense" fund were made at the behest of Andrew C. Fields, head of the "supply department." Fields maintained a house at Albany—promptly dubbed the "House of Mirth" by the press—at which lawmakers were entertained in gratitude for their work in controlling legislation. Senators William J. Graney and Charles P. McClelland, of the Senate's Insurance Committee, had lived at the "House of Mirth" as the guests of Fields. Before his election McClelland had had $3,000 a year from Mutual as an "adviser on legislation." For other favored legislators there were poker games in which lawmakers always won.

Fields left for parts unknown soon after the committee began its hearings.

[24] *Hearings*, II, 1870–1872.

But Hughes showed that all the expenses of the "House of Mirth," including the wages of the cook, the rent, and all the supplies used, were charged to "legal expenses." Fields also acted for Equitable. The investigation brought to light numerous memoranda from Equitable's Thomas D. Jordan (who also had disappeared) instructing Fields to oppose, or in some cases to promote, legislation in which the big insurance companies were interested. The evidence also showed that an examiner in the State Insurance Department had been appointed on requests from Fields and a Senator living at the "House of Mirth."

Hughes laid bare an organized scheme on the part of the big insurance companies to control legislation throughout the United States. To avoid duplication of effort, they had divided the country into four districts. Lobbyists for Mutual undertook to "kill" all "unfavorable" legislation in one of these districts; New York Life lobbyists took over the second, and Equitable lobbyists the third, the fourth being regarded as open territory.

"They have been organized into an offensive and defensive alliance," Hughes concluded, "to procure or to prevent the passage of laws affecting not only insurance, but a great variety of important interests to which, through subsidiary companies or through connections of their officers, they have become related." [25]

In addition to large gifts to the Republican war chests in 1896, 1900, and 1904, Mutual had helped to elect Republican congressmen and New York legislators. McCurdy claimed not to have heard of any Mutual contributions to state or local campaigns; but Senator Platt later admitted that he had had $10,000 from Mutual "from time to time," and his recollection was that it had come in response to his requests to McCurdy. The president of Mutual admitted that the company had paid $1,000 to William Barnes, Sr., father of the Albany boss, for fighting a change in the insurance law.[26]

Insurance money also flowed freely for the purpose of corrupting the press and influencing public opinion. The companies paid some newspapers for advertisements disguised as news and greased the palms of venal reporters. Even during the investigation, Hughes showed, Mutual sent out "colored statements of its proceedings," which were published in numerous papers throughout the country "at a cost of one dollar a line." [27]

While the income of executives and concealed expenditures for illegitimate purposes had skyrocketed, Mutual's dividends had taken a nosedive. Between 1885 and 1904 the company's total income had increased from $20,214,954 to $81,002,984, but dividends to policyholders had fallen from $3,183,023 to $2,674,207. Total payments to policyholders had also fallen drastically in

[25] *Hughes Report*, p. 394.   [26] New York *World*, Oct. 18, 1905.
[27] *Hughes Report*, p. 22.

relation to total income. McCurdy's explanation was that "large rewards" are justified in return for "large achievements."

Not all the foregoing details about Mutual were elicited from President McCurdy himself. But his "terrible hours" of writhing, twisting, and blustering on the witness stand brought the story of scandalous mismanagement of a great enterprise to a fitting climax. As McCurdy's confessions entangled him deeper and deeper in a web of ignominy, his counsel, James M. Beck, arose and charged Hughes with giving cues "to the most sensational newspaper attacks." "I don't impute to Mr. Hughes any intention to be unfair," he said, "but I do say that the net result is quite as unfair to the witness as if it were Mr. Hughes' intention that it should be unfair."

"The record is far more eloquent than anything I can possibly say," Hughes replied, "of the extreme courtesy and fairness with which this investigation has been conducted. . . . The witness who gets himself into a false position has only himself to blame. Candor and straight-forwardness will ever be treated as they deserve to be treated, and evasion will always be held up to the contempt which it also deserves." [28]

Round after round of applause came from the big audience in the chamber. Chairman Armstrong pounded with his gavel and threatened for the seventh time to clear the room. As soon as he had a chance to speak, McCurdy cut the ground from beneath his counsel by saying: "May I avail myself of the opportunity to express myself in entire concurrence with the remarks of Mr. Hughes . . . the self-restraint that he has imposed upon himself . . . I have noticed with admiration, not to say gratitude." [29]

Probably McCurdy realized at the time that he was ruined. Within a month he voluntarily slashed his salary from $150,000 to $75,000. Several weeks before the investigation was finished, he resigned from the company, as did his highly paid son and son-in-law and vice presidents Granniss and Gillette. Broken in health, McCurdy went abroad and died. The McCurdy family restored $815,000 to Mutual.[30]

John A. McCall, president of New York Life, was 225 pounds of self-assurance when he took the witness stand. A former superintendent of insurance in New York and a man who commanded wide respect in business circles, he drew a salary of $100,000 and completely dominated the company through proxy votes.

"As president of the New York Life Insurance Company," Hughes asked, "have you had occasion, from time to time, to direct the drawing of checks on executive order?"

---

[28] *Hearings*, III, 2021f.   [29] *Ibid.*, p. 2024.
[30] Marquis James, *The Metropolitan Life*, (New York, Viking, 1945), p. 161. Copyright, 1945, by Viking Press, Inc.

"Yes, I have," McCall replied.

"Without approval or reference to any committee of the company?"

"Absolutely."

"Has that been a frequent occurrence?"

"Daily."

"For large amounts?"

"For large amounts."

"Amounts in excess of $25,000?"

"Yes."

"In what way is the propriety of the payment determined by other officers of the company?"

"I am the sole judge of that." [31]

Of the $48,000 gift to Theodore Roosevelt's campaign McCall said: "I took the responsibility. The blame is mine." He defended his action as a legitimate effort to maintain a proper monetary standard, although sound money was not an issue in 1904. In addition to by-passing the trustees in this matter, he had made every effort to conceal the nature of the item in the company's books. In the "Hanover Bank Office account," which had concealed the political contributions, Hughes also found a disbursement of $235,000 which tripped McCall into a pathetic series of evasions and contradictions. McCall had authorized the spending of this money, but he would give no clear indication as to what it had been used for. Public confidence suffered a reverberating shock.

Hughes knew precisely how to deal with quibbling. "If a witness evades him," said the *New York Times*, "he is willing to go around the irresponsive answer with infinite patience and elicit a whole body of collateral facts." [32] Sometimes he was criticized for not being brutal enough, but his method brought results. When McCall came back to the stand, Hughes had already assembled proof that the $235,000 could not have been used for any legitimate aspect of the insurance business. No avenue of escape from candor was left. Shaken and worried, McCall began to unfold the full story of his relations with "Judge" Andrew Hamilton.

Hamilton was the key lobbyist of the whole corrupt alliance between the political bosses and the insurance magnates. Supplied with enormous resources, he made a big business of influencing legislators and press agents in many states. McCall admitted that Hamilton was expected to deal with the men who could "produce the results" and "to do whatever was necessary to prevent the attacks the companies feared." In defense of the system he insisted that the insurance executives in every state were "badgered and harassed to death . . . by the introduction of bad bills." "I believe that three-quarters of the

[31] *Hearings*, I, 788.　　[32] Oct. 1, 1905.

insurance bills introduced in the United States," he said, "are blackmail bills." [33]

New York Life had paid Hamilton $1,312,197 in eleven years. In addition, he had been getting substantial sums from other life-insurance companies. Big insurance was "feeding a monster whose appetite could not be sated."

Hamilton himself had fled to Paris, claimed to be ill, and refused to return until after the investigation was finished. When the committee demanded an accounting for the funds that had been turned over to him, McCall sent his son, John C. McCall, the company's treasurer, to Paris. Young McCall brought back a statement from Hamilton purporting to account for $720,550 which he had retained as compensation or expended during the years 1899 to 1905. But Hamilton had not kept any books or accounts; he had obtained no vouchers from the people to whom he had paid money; he offered no checkbooks, since most of his disbursements had been made in cash—for obvious reasons. In these circumstances his statement was obviously worthless.

Most embarrassing of all was the mysterious $235,000 which McCall had secretly advanced to Hamilton in 1903 and 1904 without authorization from any source. The lobbyist already had ample funds to carry on the work of his "department of legislation and taxation." No purpose whatever could be found for advancing him an additional $235,000. McCall said it had been anticipated that this money might be used in connection with the purchase of a mortgage, but Hughes showed that that purchase had not been made. The fact that Hamilton had charge of purchasing land for the company's "Home Office Annex" was used as a pretext for charging the $235,000 to the real-estate account. But Hughes dug into the records and disclosed the cost of every piece of property bought for the annex and the source of the money used to pay for it. Hamilton could not have spent the $235,000 for that purpose. Moreover, he had cashed the mysterious checks in Albany. At last McCall admitted that the $235,000 belonged to the company and gave a pledge to repay it by December 31, 1905, if Hamilton had not previously done so.[34]

In order to comply with the prerequisites for doing business in Prussia, New York Life had pretended to sell 15,300 shares of stock and thereafter reported to the Insurance Department that "the Company does not invest in stocks of any kind." Actually, Hughes proved, it had not sold its stock. The shares were in the keeping of the New York Security & Trust Company, but they were held as collateral for "dummy" loans in the names of a New York Life bond clerk and a messenger in an aggregate amount of $3,357,000.

Before the inquiry ended, McCall's health was shattered, as well as his reputation. Making arrangements to repay the New York Life the mysterious $235,000 he had turned over to Hamilton, McCall resigned his presidency

[33] *Hearings*, II, 1415.   [34] *Hughes Report*, pp. 51–53.

and in a few weeks was dead. His tragedy left him without resentment against the man who brought about his undoing. "Mr. Hughes has been eminently fair," the broken executive told Haley Fiske, later president of the Metropolitan Life.[35] Hughes had only disclosed the truth. It was McCall's misfortune that this lighting of dark corners tended to obscure the constructive work he had done for life insurance in his long career.

George W. Perkins was in a less vulnerable position, but Hughes bore down heavily upon his dual role as a vice president of New York Life and a representative of J. P. Morgan & Company. In a $4,000,000 bond deal Perkins had represented both Morgan, the seller, and New York Life, the buyer.

"When you bargained for the bonds," Hughes asked, "did you bargain for them with any person other than yourself?"

"I can't recollect," Perkins stammered, "but I think I did it myself, probably."

"You were dealing with yourself," Hughes persisted.[36]

Perkins also provided details of a trick to deceive the public and the Insurance Department. New York Life had participated in the Navigation Syndicate and received an allotment of $4,000,000 from the Morgan company. Upon this $3,200,000 was called in 1902, and this amount appeared in the company's annual statement. But the Navigation Syndicate proved to be one of Morgan's most disastrous ventures. When the remaining $800,000 was called in 1903, the insurance company was loath to admit any additional involvement. So it effected one of those familiar year-end "sales" of the stock to Morgan. Three days later, however, it repurchased the stock at the same price—far above its market value. Obviously there had been no bona fide sale. Having arranged this deceptive loan for both companies, Perkins insisted that he had acted "to protect our situation."

"But the only situation you had to protect . . ." Hughes retorted, "was the situation exigent by reason of your making your report to the superintendent of insurance." [37]

New York Life ultimately lost $80,000 on this venture. Perkins was forced to admit the anomalous nature of his dual role and resigned from the insurance company.

James Hazen Hyde's appearance on the witness stand was almost an anticlimax. Hyde had already sold his Equitable stock. The company that he had planned to dominate had undergone an extensive housecleaning. Claiming to act out of philanthropic motives, Thomas F. Ryan, purchaser of the Hyde stock, had placed the shares in a voting trust composed of former President Grover Cleveland, Justice Morgan J. O'Brien, and George Westinghouse. The

[35] Address by Haley Fiske to Association of Life Insurance Presidents, Dec. 4, 1925.
[36] *Hearings*, II, 1219.   [37] *Hearings*, I, pp. 758f.

From the *Brooklyn Eagle*, December 8, 1905.

THE PIED PIPER OF LIFE INSURANCE

new chairman of the board of directors, Paul Morton, had effected economies estimated at more than $600,000 a year before the investigation was completed.

After trying to explain to the committee his lavish use of policyholders' funds to give a party for the French ambassador, Hyde's conscience prompted him to repay the $12,000 in question. Hughes also focused attention upon numerous slick practices in which the men of Equitable had indulged. Equitable controlled the Mercantile Trust Company and had very large interests in two other trust companies. "The relations to the Trust Companies have been used," the investigator showed, "to aid in carrying of irregular accounts and to further the interests of individual officers." [38] Equitable maintained cash balances, largely in these trust companies, in the enormous sum of more than $36,000,-000 in 1903 and 1904. The obvious purpose, Hughes said, was to enhance the prosperity of the trust companies in which various Equitable bigwigs were interested. To conceal the extent of these unprofitable cash balances, year-end loans were made to Kuhn, Loeb & Company (later in the name of clerks of that company), the cash balances being correspondingly decreased for a few days while the Equitable made its sworn report to the Insurance Department. With the annual report thus safely falsified, the "dummy" loans were promptly canceled.

The inquiry brought out that Jacob Schiff of Kuhn, Loeb & Company had sold to Equitable, of which he was a director, securities valued at $49,704,408 in five and a half years—in the teeth of a state law requiring the dismissal and permanent disqualification of any life-insurance director who profited by "selling or aiding in the sale of any stocks or securities to or by such corporation. . . ." But the basic complaint ran deeper than manipulative abuses and laxity in enforcement of the law. In his report Hughes deplored the whole tie-up between insurance and speculative finance.

The insurance companies were not chartered, he asserted, to make money by speculation, barter, or the development of industry. "They were chartered to furnish life insurance, and the true measure of their power and their duty in the handling of their funds is to invest them with due conservatism, to the end that they may be able to discharge their obligations." [39] The mingling of life insurance with banking and industrial finance was tending toward vast combinations of capital. That dangerous trend should be broken up, he concluded, by forbidding insurance companies to invest in stocks.

Edward H. Harriman brought the committee a tale of sordid intrigue that had failed. With his 16,000 miles of railroad and forty steamships, the hard-boiled financier said that he had little time to think about life insurance. Yet he had moved in to shape the destiny of the great Equitable Society when dissension arose among its officers. Under Hughes' probing, he admitted that he

[38] *Hughes Report*, p. 122. [39] *Ibid.*, p. 384.

had prevented bills from being introduced in the legislature to aid James Alexander's efforts to mutualize the Equitable. Incidentally, Alexander was in a sanatorium and did not appear at the investigation.

"I had the matter watched at Albany," Harriman said, "to see what attempts were being made to use legislation improperly." [40] The men on whom he relied for this service, he claimed, were Governor Higgins and Speaker Nixon.

Harriman had boasted to Hyde that he controlled the New York Legislature.[41] Now he openly proclaimed his political prowess.

"Were you in politics?" Hughes asked.

"No, sir."

"Did you have any political influence?"

"I think I have," Harriman responded.

"Well, it has been openly charged that through your relations with Mr. Odell you have political influence: what would you say to that?"

"Well," the railroad magnate boasted, "I should think Mr. Odell [the former governor and at the time of the inquiry Republican leader in New York] had political influence because of his relations to me." [42]

Harriman's confidence in his political power had led him to believe that he could recoup his lost opportunity even after Ryan had tricked him by buying Hyde's Equitable stock. Apparently he had helped Ryan get his nominee, Morton, elected chairman of the Equitable board and Ryan had then agreed to consult Harriman before taking any further move in the matter. Harriman waited in vain for a call from Ryan. When a message finally came, through Ryan's attorney, it was to the effect that the controlling Equitable stock had been purchased. Harriman was furious. He offered to buy half the stock from Ryan, on condition that he be permitted to name two additional trustees, and, according to Ryan, threatened his rival with adverse legislative action if he should refuse to comply. "Ryan," the *World* aptly commented, "assumed he had become the Equitable. Harriman assumed he was the government of New York." [43] Harriman left the witness stand very little ruffled, but he had contributed greatly to public knowledge of the corrupt working arrangement between the lions of finance and the jackals of politics.

Thomas Fortune Ryan, cool and reserved, came to the witness stand assuming that he could withhold from the Armstrong Committee whatever he did not care to see in print. When Hughes asked him about Harriman's alleged threats, Ryan flatly refused to answer. Here seemed to be an opportunity to entangle the inquiry in a legal contest. Ryan's attorney, Paul Cravath, who had been one of Hughes' first partners, called the investigator by telephone and said that if Hughes would get out an order to show cause, he would be glad to

[40] *Hearings,* VI, 5155.   [41] Philip C. Jessup, *Elihu Root,* p. 440.
[42] *Hearings,* VI, pp. 5152–5154.
[43] Editorial, "Equitable Corruption," No. 150, Dec. 13, 1905.

cooperate in having Mr. Ryan's right to decline to answer the questions tested in court.

"Oh, no!" Hughes instantly replied, "I'm going to have him indicted." [44]

Cravath was indignant, but Ryan came back a few days later and answered everything Hughes asked him.

That incident alone is enough to dispose of Hearst's trumped-up charge, in the 1906 campaign, that Ryan had selected Hughes as counsel to the committee. And it does not stand alone. A few weeks later, when Hughes probed into the affairs of the Washington Life, he showed that, under Ryan's management, it had become a heavy buyer in what were known as "Ryan securities," and most of its stock and bond purchases had been made through a brokerage firm of which Ryan's sons were members. Hughes' treatment of Ryan was the same fair, fearless, and impartial treatment that was accorded every other witness.

Senator Thomas C. Platt was probably the most candid of the New York bosses who paraded before the committee. Before leaving his office to testify, he put into his pocket letters from several members of the committee asking contributions in their campaigns of former years.[45] But no committeeman attempted to prevent Hughes from calling the "easy boss" or to interfere with his examination.

Platt confessed that each of the big insurance companies customarily gave him $10,000 which he turned over to the Republican State Committee for the election of pliable legislators. After some preliminary fencing, the ugly truth came out in this colloquy:

HUGHES. Now, isn't that the way it really comes about, Senator, that the use of these contributions in the election of candidates to office puts the candidate more or less under a moral obligation not to attack the interest supporting him?

PLATT. That is naturally what would be involved.

HUGHES. But isn't that really what is involved?

PLATT. I should think so.

HUGHES. That is what you meant when you said that they would expect you, through your relations to the State Committee, to defend them?

PLATT. Yes, sir.[46]

Platt had previously admitted that, in return for these contributions, he held himself in readiness to fight bills in the legislature hostile to the insurance interests. It was a triangular arrangement. The "interests" controlled the bosses by paying them "boodle"; the bosses controlled the legislature by use of this money in campaigns; and the legislature protected the "interests" in their exploitation of the public. "The frank admission that moneys have been obtained

---

[44] Author's interview with CEH, April 16, 1946.
[45] *Outlook*, Vol. 84, pp. 404–407.   [46] *New York Times*, Nov. 23, 1905.

for use in state campaigns upon the expectation that candidates thus aided in their election would support the interests of the companies," Hughes wrote, "has exposed both those who solicited the contributions and those who made them to severe and just condemnation."

Senator Chauncey M. Depew shamefacedly told of drawing a $20,000 annual retainer from Equitable, of which he was a director. The arrangement had been made by the elder Hyde, whom Depew advised as to investments and various "troublesome questions," and was continued by his successors for many years. "The testimony as to the services [rendered] is very general," Hughes commented with characteristic understatement, "and it does not appear that outside of those which the society was fairly entitled to receive from him as a director, the services were such as to warrant the payments made." [47] The reformed management cut off this retainer, and Depew resigned as a director. An attempt was made to force his resignation from the Senate, but he held on until the end of his term.

Benjamin B. Odell, Jr., came before the investigators haggard and angry. The man who had refused to accept nomination for the mayorship of New York at Odell's hands now put the former Governor through a searching examination as to an alleged shakedown of the Mercantile Trust Company. Odell had invested $184,171 in bonds of the United States Shipbuilding Company, for which Mercantile was trustee. Having sold the bonds at a loss of $125,482, he brought suit against Mercantile to make it good. Before the suit was filed, however, bills were introduced in both houses of the legislature for repeal of the law incorporating the Mercantile Company.

In these circumstances the Mercantile Company settled Odell's claim through negotiations for $75,000. Odell vehemently denied that any threat was made and insisted that the bills had not been introduced at his request. Yet the fact remained that he knew about and approved the bills to repeal the company's charter before they were introduced, and his guardian in the financial world, Mr. Harriman, had suggested to Mr. Hyde, vice president of the trust company, that the claim be settled "in view of the powerful interests in Albany which were antagonistic to the Mercantile Trust Company."

The nature of Hughes' findings was not changed much when he turned to the State Insurance Department. Superintendent Francis Hendricks' stock reply to questions put to him on the witness stand seemed to be, "I don't know." For six years he had been complacently examining insurance companies' reports without exposing any of the irregularities that Hughes uncovered within a few months. Ample authority was at his command, but he had not used it. Companies were deceiving the department by "glaringly false returns," and the department did not even recognize the fact. No attempt had

[47] *Hughes Report*, p. 106.

been made to ascertain the nature of the companies' expenditures. Not one of the sinkholes into which vast sums were being poured for lobbying and vote-buying had been uncovered. In short, the reports of the superintendent of insurance were nothing more than misleading propaganda. "Most of the evils which have been disclosed by the investigation," Hughes concluded, "would have been impossible had there been a vigorous performance of the duties already laid upon the department." [48] Hendricks recognized that his position was untenable and retired.

In spite of the drama of crumbling reputations and falling official heads, Hughes was not primarily concerned with personalities. Wasteful, hazardous, and dishonest practices were his chief target. When District Attorney Jerome started a movement to have Hughes prosecute all the culprits exposed as law violators by the insurance investigation, the latter promptly scotched it.[49] His job was to diagnose the sickness of the business and to prescribe a remedy, and he refused to be diverted to the building up of criminal cases. Several insurance-company officials were later indicted, but the cases against them came to nothing. It was the housecleanings that the investigation inspired and the legislation that it brought about which gave it a significant place in American history.

Every detail of the policies that the companies sold to their patrons came under scrutiny. Were the terms fair to policyholders? What was the record of performance on the contracts? Was the cost of getting new business excessive? Frequently it was an idea that cracked up under Hughes' cyclotronic bombardment. That is what happened to the idea of deferred-dividend policies which had been popular with various companies. The scheme of these policies called "tontine" was to hold back for ten, fifteen, or twenty years all accumulations that would otherwise have been available for dividends. In the case of death before the expiration of the fixed period, only the face value of the policy would be paid. If a policy lapsed, everything would be lost. At the end of the period, the survivors would share the accumulated profits.

The advantages of such policies went largely to the companies. "They permitted the accumulation of profits for long periods without accounting," [50] and the tendency was for those profits to be frittered away through exorbitant salaries, commissions, and other expenses for obtaining new business. Hughes concluded, with the concurrence of the full committee, that no more deferred-dividend policies should be written in New York.

Through fifty-seven public hearings over a period of four months the exposé continued. The press carried the story to every town and city. University presidents and preachers joined editors and humble citizens in condemning the

[48] *Ibid.*, p. 356.   [49] Author's interview with CEH, April 16, 1946.
[50] *Hughes Report*, pp. 421–422.

men in places of trust who had proved to be "reckless speculators" and "pil-ferers with the savings of the poor." The life-insurance business throughout the country was shaken to its foundations, but the result was to dislodge the exploiters and their practices and leave the business infinitely sounder than before.

The investigation had not been a complete success. The committee decided to close its hearings before Hamilton, Fields, Jordan, and other key figures could be found within its jurisdiction. "At the close of the investigation," Hughes said, in a statement praising the committee for its fairness, courage, and intelligence, "I am impressed more with what we have failed to do than what we have done. So many phases of life insurance developed that it is a matter of regret to me that we have not been able to go on and do thorough work in all the directions that have been suggested." [51] But that modest ap-praisal found slight echo in the public response.

The investigation, said the *World*, "has restored faith in legislative com-mittees as a means of bringing the truth to light. It has given us Charles E. Hughes as another magnificent example of the man who is willing to serve the public, who has a service of the highest order to give to the public, and who can be neither intimidated nor betrayed." [52] "Nobody in New York," agreed Hearst's *American*, "will question the excellence of the work done by the counsel for the people, Mr. Charles E. Hughes. . . ." [53] Hughes, the chorus continued, is "the chief figure on the right side of the most important inquiry of its kind in recent American history." "This man ought to be kept in public life if possible, why not make him governor?" [54]

Probably the most significant comment was that of the *Outlook*: "It has been a dash of cold water upon the face after a time of moral drowsiness. It has set the public conscience stirring." [55] Hughes, too, believed that the public awakening was the most striking aspect of the inquiry. A "vindication of the sound moral sense of the American people," he called it. He had brought into public life in New York a new standard of morality, a new concept of the public interest and of the power of the people to make their will prevail.

In Montreal, where he had gone with Mrs. Hughes for a few days of rest, the acclaimed investigator was amused to encounter, at the top of Mount Royal, an exiled lobbyist by the name of Buckley whom he had been trying to subpoena. One glance at the whiskered nemesis put Buckley in flight, while Hughes laughed heartily.

Back in New York, Hughes plunged into the writing of the report. Several insurance men had importuned the committee to forgo a formal report, and

[51] New York *World*, Dec. 31, 1905.   [52] Jan. 1, 1906.   [53] Dec. 30, 1905.
[54] Public reaction reported by Ida Tarbell in *American Magazine*, March, 1908.
[55] Nov. 4, 1905.

Counsel McKeen emerged to support the argument. But Hughes insisted that a comprehensive report be made. Chairman Armstrong and a majority of the committee agreed and gave Hughes a broad mandate to finish his work. In six weeks of day and night toil he brought together in fewer than five hundred pages the salient facts about every New York life-insurance company, summarized the abuses he had found, and concluded with sweeping recommendations for legislative action. Every word of the report was his, although it carries only the names of the committee members.

From the *New York Herald*, January 2, 1906.

PREPARED FOR THE WORST

After conferring with the committee, Hughes also drew up bills to carry out his recommendations. Then he went to Albany to explain the bills to legislators and the press. By April, 1906, the legislature had completed enactment of these bills, giving New York what Haley Fiske later declared to be "the best insurance legislation the world has ever known." [56]

One of these measures prohibited insurance companies (and other corporations) from making contributions to political campaigns. Another forced

[56] Fiske's address to the Association of Life Insurance Presidents, Dec. 4, 1925.

the registration of lobbyists, with public disclosure of the nature of their services, expenses, and compensation. Congress soon followed the first of these leads with its Corrupt Practices Act of 1907, but forty years passed before it similarly required the registration of lobbyists at Washington.

The acts dealing more directly with insurance provided machinery for mutualizing stock companies; outlawed existing proxies and required new elections with wider policyholder participation; prohibited the writing of the unsound deferred-dividend policies and required dividends to be paid annually; prescribed standard policies "simple in form and clear and concise in language"; required the companies to give to policyholders who discontinued the payment of premiums policies representing an appropriate ratio to the premiums already paid; limited the amount of new insurance that any company could write in one year so as to minimize the wasteful scramble for new business; required action by the full board of directors to approve all salaries over $5,000 a year; limited commissions and other expenses; required vouchers for all expenditures of a hundred dollars or more and annual reports in much greater detail, including data on lobbying expenditures; tightened up the law against making false reports; made triennial examinations of all companies mandatory; required the companies to dispose of speculative securities within five years and forbade them to hold stocks in banks, trust companies, or other corporations; forbade participation in syndicates; prohibited officers and agents from holding pecuniary interests in transactions with their companies; and opened the courts to suits by policyholders against the companies.

These laws were widely copied in other states and became the foundation on which modern insurance in America rests. Temporarily the investigation and the new laws hurt some of the New York companies. A survey in 1909 by William H. Hotchkiss, New York superintendent of insurance, indicated that insurance in force with New York companies decreased $126,213,453 in 1906, the first year following the investigation. But in the same period the business of companies organized outside of New York increased by more than twice that sum, and the purged New York companies soon regained their losses.

More significant is the estimate by Hotchkiss that in 1908 the savings in general management expenses of thirty-four New York insurance companies amounted to $4,817,500. Savings in the cost of writing new policies he placed at $4,864,500, making a total saving of $9,682,000 to policyholders in a single year as a result of the insurance investigation.[57]

Some resentment against Hughes lingered among insurance men. One critic went so far as to denounce the investigation as a "Socialistic assault on the pillars of civilization." But the more intelligent insurance men realized that he had given their business an invaluable charter of reform. When he addressed

[57] Hotchkiss' report, CEH's private papers.

the Life Underwriters Association of New York shortly after the new insurance laws had been enacted, he was greeted by applause, cheering, and waving of napkins for "what seemed an interminable length of time." [58] Thirty-four years later Frederick H. Ecker, chairman of the board of the Metropolitan Life, concluded that Hughes was "in considerable part" responsible for the prosperity of the life-insurance business.[59] Especially during the great upheaval of the thirties, insurance men and informed policyholders alike felt in their bones a deep thankfulness to Charles E. Hughes. He had transformed the insurance business from "a public swindle to a public trust."

[58] *Life Insurance Notes*, June, 1906.   [59] *St. Louis Post-Dispatch*, March 26, 1939.

Chapter 16

THE CAMPAIGN AGAINST HEARST

PRESIDENT THEODORE ROOSEVELT had followed the insurance investigation with keen interest and approval. Apparently he took no offense at Hughes' exposure of the lavish corporate gifts that had gone into his campaign fund in 1904. In any event, he concluded that he could make good use of an investigator of Hughes' ability and asked him to take charge of an inquiry into combinations in restraint of trade and other illegal practices in the coal industry. Hughes acquiesced.

Roosevelt tested the temperament of his new investigator by asking for advice on an appointment. He wished to know whether the insurance investigation had reflected upon the individual in question so as to make his appointment inadvisable. Hughes answered the President's letter with great care, setting forth the facts in the case and concluding that the proposed nominee had not really been discredited. Roosevelt was "DElighted" and said that Hughes' fair and impartial answer reflected a commendable freedom from vindictiveness.[1]

These two striking personalities met for the first time on Easter Monday, 1906. A conference on the coal investigation had taken Hughes to Washington. He found Attorney General William H. Moody eager to get the investigation completed before the transfer of Secretary of War William H. Taft to the Supreme Court, then scheduled for the coming fall. Actually it was Moody and not Taft who went to the Supreme Court, and the coal investigation, too, was to be left to other hands. Indeed, the President was already thinking of Hughes in a quite different role. When the investigator went to the White House with the Attorney General—his second visit there that day—Roosevelt and his secretary, William Loeb, were standing by a window in a holiday mood. Hughes joined them in watching the Easter egg-rolling festival on the lawn. As his guest was leaving, the President said, "In the next Republican convention you will have two votes for governor—mine and Loeb's." [2]

Pleased by this compliment, Hughes nevertheless dismissed it as "only a pleasantry." [3] The idea of exploiting his prestige as an investigator to win public office struck no responsive chord in him. His primary interest still lay in the

[1] Beerits' Memorandum, III, 8.   [2] *Ibid.*, p. 9.   [3] CEH, Notes, p. 178.

169

law, and, aside from some preliminary work on the coal inquiry, his whole energy was devoted to picking up the threads of his neglected practice. But talk of his nomination for governor spread like ripples on the disturbed surface of a pond.

Hughes got a firsthand report on these political reverberations when he chanced to drop in at the University Club while working with Samuel Untermyer on a big shipbuilding case. There he met Frank H. Simonds, Albany correspondent for the New York *Daily Tribune*, whom he had come to know well through the insurance investigation. Simonds predicted with remarkable foresight that his whiskered friend would be the Republican nominee for governor and that William Randolph Hearst would run against him.

Hughes protested that during the insurance investigation he had been gall and wormwood to many Republican leaders. By exposing the failings of the Insurance Department he had subjected the Republican régime at Albany to an avalanche of criticism. When he refused to run for mayor after his nomination in 1905, the party leaders had been highly irritated. They would never consent to his nomination for governor, Hughes said.

"But the governor elected this year may occupy the White House in two years," Simonds persisted.

"That, too, has no attraction for me," Hughes replied. "My one desire is to be left alone in my profession." [4]

In June, 1906, Brown University conferred an honorary degree of Doctor of Laws upon her distinguished alumnus and trustee. President Faunce's salutation is still remembered: ". . . investigator without malice and without fear, skillful to use the probe but not the rake, through whose labor the public conscience has been quickened and purified." Charles Junior proudly witnessed the ceremony as a freshman completing his first year at Brown.

More concerned with recuperation from the strain of past toil than with any political future, Hughes took his son to Europe in July. His disinterest in politics stands out from the following paragraph of a letter written to his father and mother from Edinburgh on July 26:

I was informed yesterday by the Cable Company that a code name had been registered for Communications with Timothy L. Woodruff—and I suppose there will be cables ere long. (Keep this to yourselves of course.) As soon as I have an opportunity I shall put a quietus on the whole business. It's the only thing that worries me. It gives me a cold sweat to think of going through a Campaign with the alternative of defeat or two years at Albany. I don't [know] which would be worse. I can be of more service and far happier in my chosen profession. So "fling away" any political ambition you may have for your son—and take counsel of your philosophy—for of all vanities there is no vanity like that of politics.

[4] *Everybody's Magazine,* October, 1906.

In his letters to his wife it was their separation and not politics that concerned him most. His letter of August 3 reechoes a familiar refrain:

You Dear Old Sweetheart,
To think of one at my age receiving such a love letter as I received this morning! Dearest, we must arrange in the future not to be separated in our holidays—life is too short and our love is too strong. Your letter was like a long draught from the old home well. And the sweet poem, darling, I shall always cherish. You must *not* worry about me, sweetheart—I am doing pretty well. . . .

C.

While Hughes and his son were "doing London," he wrote:

Charlie left his watch under the pillow at Oban and I was duly superior, paternal and severe. But alas! I left my drawers at Edinburgh (Ramie's at that) and I have walked humbly (and somewhat coolly) ever since. If I do not recover my reason, I may have to come home in kilts—à la "Hielan Willie." Charlie wrote for his watch and it came today—wonderful to tell! I didn't have the nerve to write for my panties and of course they haven't come. Charlie is a good boy and doesn't say much.[5]

Walking quietly together one evening, each began to wish they were in Switzerland. As soon as they realized they were of the same mind, they changed their plans and revisited the old haunts they loved so well. While there, Hughes received word that Odell had suggested his nomination for governor, but he refused even to nibble at the bait. Continuing his relaxation into September, he returned to New York only two and a half weeks before the Republican state convention at Saratoga.

Governor Higgins, who was too ill to consider another term, had thrown his support to Lieutenant Governor M. Linn Bruce. But astute politicians saw no hope of victory in Bruce or in any candidate from their own circle. The people of New York were in open revolt against bossism and the exploitation that had characterized Republican rule for many years. Even Theodore Roosevelt, who had been elected governor by a narrow margin in 1898 on the strength of San Juan Hill, had sought his reforms by working with the bosses. Once when he had a judge to appoint he had said over and over again to Odell that he wanted to name a certain individual. "Well," Odell had replied, "why don't you?" "Can I? Can I?" T. R. had queried.[6]

After Roosevelt, Odell had given the state four years of direct boss control. Then came the Higgins administration, carried into office by the strength of the Roosevelt presidential campaign in 1904. Quiet and honest, Higgins had ousted some of the exploiters but he could not control the organization. By 1906 even the bosses had to admit that only a miracle could save them from

[5] CEH to his wife, Aug. 10, 1906.
[6] Odell to Hughes to author, interview April 16, 1946.

resounding defeat. In their desperation it became increasingly difficult to suppress the name of the now famous insurance investigator.

Hughes himself remained silent, apparently forgetting the quietus that he had talked about in July. To his friends he said: "I do not desire office; I am not a candidate; any man who knows me knows that. But, in the present emergency, to declare myself out of the field would be to put myself forever beyond the possibility of rendering a public service, if the peculiar conditions now prevailing should later lead that way." [7]

Herbert Parsons, the Republican committeeman for New York County, took the lead in pressing for a candidate who could arouse the enthusiasm of the people. That meant Hughes. Parsons aired his views at the White House and obtained a hearty endorsement from the President. Going to Saratoga for the convention of September 25, he began to sound out the delegates. He found Odell, who controlled about one-third of the delegates, trying to swing the nomination to former Governor Black. Other bosses were promoting their favorites. In a long conference before the final session of the convention, Parsons and Senator Page talked earnestly in favor of Hughes as "the strongest man." But the bosses were not convinced. What assurance did they have that Hughes would be loyal to the party?

"I never spoke to this man," blurted William Barnes, Jr., boss of Albany, whose letter chiding an insurance company because of its delay in forwarding the "usual honorarium" to his father had been read at the insurance investigation.

"I never saw him," protested George W. Aldridge, chief political dictator of up-State New York.

"Gentlemen, I have met him—once," [8] lamented Francis Hendricks, boss of Syracuse and former superintendent of insurance, with understandable acerbity.

Parsons and Page sent word to Oyster Bay that they needed help. Roosevelt replied through Postmaster General Cortelyou and Congressman William W. Cocks: "I think that Mr. Hughes is the strongest candidate before the convention. We need just his qualities in the coming campaign." [9] With this emphatic endorsement on record, the convention could not reject Hughes without also repudiating Roosevelt. The bosses bowed to "mournful necessity." The next morning Job E. Hedges presented Hughes' name, and he was unanimously nominated by a convention in which he had no instructed delegates, no partisan politicians and only hostility on the part of the bosses. His only asset was the confidence of the people.

Hughes responded with a telegram that rubbed salt into the bosses' wounds:

[7] *Outlook,* Oct. 20, 1906.   [8] *Ibid.*
[9] B. J. Hendrick in *McClure's Magazine,* March, 1908.

I thank you for your confidence. . . . I shall accept the nomination without pledge other than to do my duty according to my conscience. If elected, it will be my ambition to give the State a sane, efficient and honorable administration, free from taint of bossism or of servitude to any private interest.[10]

President Roosevelt wired Hughes, "I rejoice for the sake of the cause of good citizenship in your nomination." T. R. was enjoying "the astonishment of many of the Republican leaders of my native State and city at finding how very respectable their party has suddenly become." In some measure Roosevelt shared the bosses' concern about the rise of a popular and independent figure in his home state. At the moment, however, it was a welcome alternative to "disaster at the polls." "Hughes' nomination," the President wrote, "is an excellent thing for the morale of the Republican party . . . he is identified in the public mind as a reformer, but a sane and sincere reformer, who really has fought against the very evils which Hearst denounces, while yet free from any taint of demagogy." [11]

The President's attitude failed to dispel the gloom at Saratoga. Some of the organization men hoped that their candidate, in divorcing himself from bossism, was indulging in campaign buncombe. But those who knew Hughes best saw in his declaration of independence a gage of battle within the party. Dark forebodings were held in check only by the ominous news that had come from Buffalo, where the Democratic Party had nominated William Randolph Hearst for governor.

Hearst was at the apex of his political career. In 1904 he had spent $600,000 trying to get the Democratic presidential nomination and had won a substantial following in the West. His drive for a political stronghold in the East had carried him within a few thousand votes of capturing the mayoralty of New York in a three-cornered race in 1905. Now he was making a determined drive to obtain the New York governorship so as to strengthen his bid for the Presidency in 1908.

When Hearst lost the mayoralty, he had accused the Tammany boss, Charles F. Murphy, of stealing the election. Murphy had been cartooned in the Hearst press in prison stripes and called an "evil specimen of a criminal boss." [12] A year later, however, Hearst accepted Murphy's support in grabbing the Democratic gubernatorial nomination. His ambition had to be gratified at any price. Edmund Wetmore caught the essentials of the situation in a verse in which he had Hearst saying,

> So I lashed him and I thrashed him in my hot reforming zeal,
> Then I clasped him to my bosom in a most artistic deal.

[10] New York *Daily Tribune*, Sept. 27, 1906.

[11] *Selections from the Correspondence of Theodore Roosevelt and Henry Cabot Lodge*, (New York, Scribner's, 1925), II, 239. Copyright, 1925, by Charles Scribner's Sons.

[12] Oliver Carlson and Ernest Sutherland Bates, *Hearst: Lord of San Simeon*, p. 150.

Murphy was willing to team up with his former enemy because he had broken with Mayor McClellan and was frightened by Hearst's vote-getting power. Together they took control of the Democratic convention by throwing out anti-Hearst delegates from twenty-one districts and seating rival groups that were prepared to do their bidding. The powerful Tammany machine was thus harnessed with the country's greatest journalistic rabble-rouser. Hearst also had in his favor a wave of popular sympathy resulting from the widespread belief that he had been swindled of the 1905 election.

It was against this background that Hughes weighed his "call to duty." "If there appeared to be a contest between two forces equally worthy," he told an interviewer, ". . . there would be nothing in the office for which I have been nominated that could appeal to me." [13] His innate modesty did not prevent him from seeing that he was the only man in the state who had a chance of defeating Hearst. Roosevelt also saw it; the Republican bosses saw it; and so did a great majority of the informed voters.

Hughes mapped out the strategy of his campaign the night after his nomination. His acceptance speech at the Republican Club in New York City on October 3—the first political address he ever made—set the tone of his appeal. It began with a bow to "the achievements of our great leader, Theodore Roosevelt," and then swung sharply to state issues. In contrast to the "noisy pretensions of the hour," he pointed to the substantial achievements of the gas and insurance investigations and the legislation they had produced. But the real issue was not the Republican record or any difference of principle between the old-line parties. It was not a partisan issue at all. "It is," he said, "the vital issue of decent government. The question is whether the unholy alliance that succeeded at Buffalo shall capture the State of New York." The choice between orderly reform and the play upon ignorance to further selfish ambition, he felt, should array on one side all lovers of truth and sobriety, whether they be Republicans, Democrats, or Independents.[14]

Some feared that Hughes would not be an effective campaigner. The insurance investigation had given rise to rumors that he was a "mental machine, a human icicle" devoid of emotions and lacking any warmth of personality. A cartoonist had pictured the ship which brought him back from Europe on a hot day in 1906 as draped with icicles and smothered with frost because of his presence on it. Many who had witnessed the intensity of his efforts in the two legislative inquiries were ready to accept this view. In those tense and dramatic situations he had had no time or inclination to be a good fellow. Nor did he play to the galleries with the expectation of emerging a popular hero. In this sense Hughes *was* unusual; there was a good deal of justification for writing

[13] Ervin Wardman in *Review of Reviews,* November, 1906, p. 550.
[14] CEH, *Addresses 1906–1916* (New York, Putnam, 1916), p. 60. Copyright, 1916, by G. P. Putnam's Sons.

him down as a *rara avis*. But the assumption that he was a cold fish or a sort of legal calculating machine without human feelings was a mile wide of the mark.

When he began to campaign, people were relieved to note that he told amusing stories, that he laughed spontaneously with his whole body, that he was a good handshaker, and that he met men and women in all walks of life with friendliness and keen interest in their problems. The public began to learn what Hughes' close friends had always known—that beneath his reserve he was "a buoyant and joyful person, fond of books of all sorts, music, golf, mountain climbing, friends, family, college and church." [15] John Palmer Gavit of the *Evening Post* described him as "the most straightforward, intellectually honest, transparently sincere person I ever have known; at the same time one of the most companionable, most *human* men it has been my fortune to meet." [16]

Hughes often turned the reports of his icy disposition to good account. Once when some one urged him to "warm up" and suggested that every candidate had the duty of kissing babies, he replied, with a twinkle in his eye, "No, I will not make any appeal to the passions of the populace." [17] On another occasion when he encountered a ridiculous yarn illustrating his supposed frigidity, he exclaimed, "I hope that, if an autopsy is ever performed upon me, you will find something besides sawdust and useful information." [18]

As the campaign warmed up, Hughes bore down heavily on Hearst's demagogy while sparing his private life. "The man who would corrupt public opinion," he declared, "is the most dangerous enemy of the state. . . . As against reckless denunciation, I set fair criticism. As against indiscriminate attacks upon business organizations, I set a serious and determined attempt to ascertain the evil and to remedy it." Here is an issue, he continued, which transcends all the questions on which we may differ. "When, in a flame of passion, you once get a feeling existing which ignores reason and dispassionate discussion, how are you going to make progress? Flame feeds flame . . . let us settle once for all that this is a government of sound public opinion and not a government of insanity and appeal to the passions of the ignorant and the thoughtless." [19]

His faith in public opinion ran deep. "We have in this country," he declared, "but one security. You may think that the Constitution is your security—it is nothing but a bit of paper. You may think the statutes are your security—they are nothing but words in a book. You may think that elaborate mechanism of

[15] Ida M. Tarbell in *American Magazine*, March, 1908, pp. 451–464.
[16] New York *Evening Post*, June 10, 1916.
[17] Frank H. Simonds in *Putnam's Monthly*, October, 1907.
[18] B. J. Hendrick in *McClure's Magazine*, March, 1908.
[19] *New York Times*, Oct. 6, 1906.

government is your security—it is nothing at all, unless you have sound and uncorrupted public opinion to give life to your Constitution, to give vitality to your statutes, to make efficient your governmental machinery." [20]

When Hearst assailed him as a corporation lawyer, Hughes showed that Hearst himself was the head of fourteen corporations, some of them organized to evade taxes and responsibility for libel. Hearst's response took the form of ridicule and defamation. His newspapers pretended to believe that Ryan had chosen Hughes as counsel in the insurance investigation. One of his papers said that the attorney general of New York had retained Hughes to assist in arguing a case growing out of the gas investigation and that Hughes had taken the fee and gone to Europe. Actually, Hughes had argued the case and had neither asked nor received one cent of compensation for it.

Hearst reached the zenith of his campaign when he called his bewhiskered opponent an "animated feather duster." Hughes made no effort to reply in kind. Ridicule was the weapon of petty or malicious minds. Keeping his speeches and his thinking free from animosity, he drove home the importance of the choice voters had to make without the slightest effort to insurrect the public mind or to match the extravagant promises of his opponent.

Traveling widely over the state, Hughes sometimes attended five or six rallies in an evening and made as many as twenty speeches in a single day. Mrs. Hughes did not attempt to take the strenuous up-State trips, and experienced newspapermen grew weary of trying to follow him, but Hughes kept up his pace until the end. "Whatever the result," he would say, "I want to know that the fight has been fought for all it is worth."

At home Antoinette Hughes watched the campaign with great interest. On October 25, 1906, she wrote:

DEAREST,

I have just been reading of the demonstrative welcome accorded you in Cortland—and I can't help rejoicing through and through that the good work goes on. I know how you feel about it all in your inmost heart, and I wish you might be spared the immense personal sacrifice. But, as the wife of a Columbia professor said to me this morning, "When I think of Hearst, it must be, it *must* be!"

We are following your strenuous career through the papers and in thought and spirit, darling. I am with you *always*. I am not without my anxieties, of course, for you were weary when you left us. I hope you are standing the heavy strain in your usual, wonderful and surprising manner and that your voice is holding out well.

Devotedly,

ANTOINETTE

The non-Hearstian press was strongly for Hughes. Every man who is not "ready to see the Empire State sold to a reckless adventurer," said the *Daily*

[20] Speech at Kingston, Oct. 23, 1906.

Tribune, was lined up behind the investigator.[21] The *Sun*, the *New York Times*, and the *Evening Post* were working for him, but it was the *World* that continued to give him the most spirited and effective support. "I am simply crazy about Hughes, so vitally important do I regard his work," wrote Joseph Pulitzer to Frank I. Cobb, chief editorial writer of the *World*. "Support Hughes with all the fire and force you possess." [22]

President Roosevelt repeatedly put in his oar. Returning to Washington from Oyster Bay after the Saratoga convention, he asked Hughes to join him at Jersey City and ride to Trenton. They went over the strategy of the campaign and agreed upon the desirability of concentrating all effort on state issues. Roosevelt was fearful of trickery and fraud on the part of the Hearst-Murphy combine. On October 2 he wrote to Hughes:

> The situation is certainly very serious in New York, and we must get out the reserves of decent citizenship in order to upset the apostles of unrest and their huge and misguided following. Hearst will of course use money like water and with shameless corruption wherever he gets a chance. . . . I earnestly hope you will thru Woodruff see to it that our up State leaders are thoroly on the alert and watchful about any . . . move by Hearst's people to cut down our vote in the Republican counties, either by downright corruption or by an unrebuked and un-contradicted appeal to envy and hate. I regard your triumph as of more conse-quence than anything else at stake in this election.[23]

"I cannot tell you," Hughes replied, "how much I appreciate your cordial support. This fight must be won." [24] To this he added on October 7: "Your letter was a most inspiring one. Needless to say that in the campaign for decency and sanity you and the achievements of your administration are our tower of strength."

Roosevelt offered his advice on the importance of appealing to the Catholic vote. Hughes replied that he had addressed the YMCA at Carnegie Hall by invitation accepted before his nomination, but that he would not speak before any other Protestant group. Parsons was making the candidate acquainted with the labor leaders. Roosevelt drew attention to his own speech at Harrisburg to emphasize the difference between sensibly curbing the great corporations and the "hideous orgy of misdoing" that would follow a victory by "a mixt crowd of wild zealots and crafty corruptionists." [25] T. R.'s enthusiasm for Hughes reached its zenith in these words:

> My dear Sir, I feel that you are fighting the battle of civilization. If you were an ordinary time-serving politician, if you had the slightest taint of subserviency to the great moneyed interests, I would not give a rap for your success. But you are

[21] Sept. 27, 1906.   [22] Don C. Seitz, *Joseph Pulitzer, Life and Letters*, p. 309.
[23] Hughes Papers, Library of Congress.   [24] CEH to T. R., Oct. 4, 1906.
[25] T. R. to CEH, Oct. 5, 1906.

an honest, fearless, square man, a good citizen and a good American first, and a good Republican also—a Republican who believes in Abraham Lincoln's principles. You believe in reforming the relations between the Government and the great corporations as drastically as is necessary to meet the needs of the situation; but you believe in having it done in a spirit of sanity and justice. If I were not President I should be stumping New York from one end to the other for you. As it is I can not do much of anything save to hope that my own record and the way I stand towards these questions will help and not harm you.

The first differences between Roosevelt and Hughes arose over the "Judiciary Nominators' " ticket. It had been named by a committee of lawyers of which Hughes, Henry Taft, and Judge Cohen had been members. They chose outstanding men who would make good judges. The ticket was weak from the viewpoint of the party leaders because no Republican lawyer of real stature in New York thought he had a chance of being elected. The organization was dissatisfied and appealed to the President. Roosevelt complained to Hughes. The candidate replied that the situation had been straightened out in Brooklyn, but he stood firm against loading the judicial ticket with politicians and especially against any deal with Hearst and Murphy. To select men who had been more active in politics than at the bar, he wrote the President, would "turn a current of criticism against us at a critical time. It would seriously reflect upon the sincerity of the position we have taken." [26] Secretary of State Root took a similar view. But the President was not wholly satisfied. "As you know," he lectured Hughes two weeks later, "I did not think they [the judiciary nominators] displayed great wisdom in their ticket in any event, and nothing but the fact that the Republican organization was in mighty good hands enabled us to avoid a break. We are going to have with us anyway the people whom the great lawyers could influence. We don't want to drive away the others." [27]

In itself this disagreement was of little significance. But it was symptomatic. Hughes would not bid for votes by any sacrifice of principle that he considered vital to good government, while Roosevelt was willing to play the game of politics in the politicians' way. Such a difference between two men of strong will and tough fiber could scarcely portend a smooth relationship. Their cordiality would, however, outlast the campaign.

The New York managers were "continually having fits" over the strategy of the campaign. National issues were rigorously excluded. Only one Cabinet member—Root, a New Yorker—was to speak. Then the strategists became panicky over what Hearst might say of Root's former connections with Ryan and the big corporations. Contrary to Hughes' wishes, they decided that Root's speech might be a liability. Before the campaign ended, however, the man-

[26] CEH to T. R., Oct. 7, 1906.   [27] T. R. to CEH, Oct. 21, 1906.

agers' fears were running in the opposite direction. Hearst's followers were interpreting the seeming aloofness of the White House as indifference. So the strategists frantically urged the President to come to New York. Instead, he persuaded Root to carry out his original plan to speak at Utica and issued the following statement: "Anyone who believes or tries to convey the impression that I am not heart and soul for Mr. Hughes is either wilfully or inadvertently laboring under a delusion. I am first, last and all the time for Mr. Hughes, because I know he stands for concisely [sic] the same principles that I stand for. I authorize you to make that statement to your friends, and to my friends on the East Side with all the emphasis that is in you." [28]

Root prepared his speech before leaving Washington and took it to the White House. Roosevelt penciled in stiffer language in one portion to express his view of Hearst. In Utica, Root and Hughes rode together from the station to the hall. Newsboys threw into their carriage Hearst's reply to Root, as the latter's speech had been given out in advance to the press. Across the front page was a cartoon of "Root, the Rat" nibbling at the defenses of the common people. Republican supporters were buying up these copies of the *Evening Journal*, tearing them into shreds, and littering the streets.

Tammany Hall had sent a gang to Utica to break up the meeting. But every act of rowdyism was suppressed by the spirited audience. One of the hecklers yelled at Root, "It's a lie!" The crowd roared, "Throw him out!" Root quelled the uproar with his raised hand and said, "No, let him stay and learn."

Root rebuttressed Hughes' accusation that the publisher-politician was using his great wealth to sow the seeds of dissension, strife, and hatred throughout the land. "Once only," he said, "has this method of incendiary abuse wrought out its natural consequence—in the murder of President McKinley. For years, by vile epithet and viler cartoons, readers of the *Journal* were taught to believe that McKinley was a monster in human form, whose taking-off would be a service to mankind."

From Hearst's *New York Journal*, Secretary Root quoted the fatal quatrain:

> The bullet that pierced Goebel's breast
> Cannot be found in all the West:
> Good reason; it is speeding here
> To stretch McKinley on his bier.

"In President Roosevelt's first message to Congress, in speaking of the assassin of McKinley," Root continued, "he spoke of him as inflamed by the reckless utterances of those who, on the stump and in the public press, appeal to the dark and evil spirits of malice and greed, envy and sullen hatred. . . . I say, by the President's authority, that in penning these words, with the horror

[28] *New York Times*, Oct. 28, 1906.

of President McKinley's murder fresh before him, he had Mr. Hearst specifically in mind.

"And I say, by his authority, that what he thought of Mr. Hearst then he thinks of Mr. Hearst now." [29]

Election day came with forecasts ranging erratically from a 200,000 majority for Hughes to a similar majority for Hearst. Party lines had been extensively broken. The first returns suggested that the voters had administered a severe drubbing to the entire Republican ticket. But the gloom in Hughes' headquarters was short-lived. Soon it was evident that he was pulling ahead of the other Republican candidates and ahead of Hearst. The final count stood: Hughes, 749,002; Hearst, 691,105, giving Hughes a comfortable plurality of 57,897 votes. Hearst had spent $500,000 out of his own resources and brought upon himself probably the bitterest disappointment of his career. Hughes' campaign had cost him only $619, largely spent for travel and secretarial service,[30] and he had won a striking manifestation of public confidence even while the party which sponsored him was being repudiated. All the other Republican candidates for state executive offices were defeated.

"I am much gratified," the new Governor-elect said as soon as the returns seemed to leave no doubt of the outcome, "but, regardless of the size of the plurality, my feeling is not one of elation, but of deep responsibility." [31]

The staggering obligation he had taken upon himself was all too apparent. He would go to Albany to preside over an administration composed of his political opponents and cope with a legislature still in the grip of the bosses who had fought his nomination. For the moment, however, there was great rejoicing over his victory. The President was elated. "I doubt whether in this crisis," he wrote to Hughes, "we could have elected any other man but you. . . . I feel that you and I, my dear Mr. Hughes, approach our work in the same spirit: and I wish you Godspeed in performing the heavy task which the people of the State of New York have laid on your shoulders." [32]

The 1906 campaign left Hearst so discredited that he would never again become "a national peril." Some writers expressed the belief that this elimination of Hearst as a contender for the Presidency was perhaps Hughes' greatest public service. Today that negative view is amply contradicted by history, but in November, 1906, when Hughes' ability in public office was yet to be tested, his awakening of the people to the distinction between fair reforms and hate-producing slander could well be regarded as his crowning achievement.

[29] Reprinted by permission of Dodd, Mead & Company from *Elihu Root* by Philip C. Jessup, p. 120. Copyright, 1938, by Dodd Mead & Company, Inc.

[30] Sworn statement to New York Secretary of State, Nov. 16, 1906.

[31] New York *Daily Tribune*, Nov. 6, 1906.

[32] T. R. to CEH, Nov. 7, 1906, Theodore Roosevelt Papers.

Chapter 17

FIGHTING GOVERNOR

THE GREAT battle of 1906 was followed by brisk maneuvering for position among the victorious forces. Woodruff, Barnes, and Parsons took the initiative. The chairman of the Republican State Committee invited Hughes to relax at Camp "Kill Kare" in the Adirondacks, along with Dr. Schurman, Senator Page, and other friends. Hughes accepted the invitation and found himself surrounded by the Old Guard instead of the friends he had expected. This did not interfere with his enjoyment of the sleigh riding and other sports that the camp offered, but it excited the newspapers. When he returned to New York, they were expressing fear that he had been "taken into camp" in more ways than one. Woodruff clearly won this first skirmish.

William Barnes, Jr., Republican boss of Albany, followed up his none too subtle suggestions at Camp Kill Kare with a letter bluntly denouncing several reforms that the Governor-elect had favored and arguing for restoration of "the power of the organization." [1] The implication was that the bosses understood the purpose of Hughes' campaign oratory, but with the votes safely counted, they expected him to be a regular Republican. Hughes countered in a friendly vein, although he rejected Barnes' major premise. Harmony was not enough, he said. The party would also have to give "aggressive and convincing" leadership in the public interest.[2] While he was trying to avoid an immediate showdown, he held stoutly to his own principles.

Parsons, who was a man of character and in general a "good-government" Republican, kept his maneuver strictly under cover. As committeeman for New York County and one of Roosevelt's close friends, he suggested that the Governor-elect go to Washington to write his message. Hughes interpreted this as a White House hint that the President would like to keep his hand on the Governor's shoulder.

"No," he replied, "I'll gladly talk with the President about the points to be dealt with in my message; but the people of this state elected me to be Governor of New York and not an agent by which they might be governed from Washington. To write the message in Washington wouldn't be a good thing for the

[1] William Barnes, Jr., to CEH, Nov. 26, 1906.
[2] CEH to Barnes, Dec. 3, 1906.

181

party, or for the President, or for me. But I hope that the President and I will have the most cordial relations." [3]

This skirmish was a Hughes victory, but the public knew nothing about it.

The President's direct maneuver was to give a stag dinner for Hughes at the White House in December. It was a sort of initiation for a neophyte into big-league politics. Secretary Taft, Senator Henry Cabot Lodge, Speaker Joseph G. Cannon, James S. Sherman (later to become Vice President) and most of the other Republican leaders were there to take the measure of the rookie Governor. Roosevelt was the acme of cordiality. After dinner he accompanied Hughes to his room, sat on the edge of the bed, and chatted about New York politics in the most entertaining Rooseveltian manner for an hour and a half.

Hughes entered fully into the spirit of the occasion. With complete candor, he discussed the high points of what he intended to do as governor; Roosevelt gave his endorsement, and the two seemed to have reached a cordial understanding.[4] T. R. was especially pleased with Hughes' idea of recommending a recount of the Hearst mayoralty vote of 1905. The President and Governor-to-be parted in an aura of friendship and apparent mutual admiration.

If this meeting can be regarded as a skirmish, it ended in a draw. Hughes took the oath of office on January 1, 1907, with the question as to who would actually exercise the powers of governor in the Empire State still wide open.

The Hughes family moved to the Executive Mansion on Eagle Street shortly after Christmas. On inauguration day the Governor-elect was escorted from the mansion to the Capitol by a parade. Promptly at twelve o'clock a colorful ceremony was held in the assembly chamber. Hughes and his staff marched to their appointed places following the official entrance of the outgoing Governor and his staff all decked out in uniform. Ailing Governor Higgins spoke briefly; then Hughes took the oath from Secretary of State John S. Whalen and delivered his inaugural address while Mrs. Hughes and the children looked on beaming with pride. At the public reception which followed in the executive chamber, the bewhiskered chief of state and his graceful spouse had an opportunity to greet almost every outstanding figure in the state.

The façade of gaiety at the official ceremonies could not dispel the awareness of impending upheaval that pervaded Albany and radiated through the state. New York seemed to be on the verge of a revolutionary shakeup of the established political and economic order; yet the nature and extent of the changes to be effected remained a mystery.

Hughes' inaugural address heightened the tension without offering any specific clues as to what his course would be. "We have reason to congratulate ourselves," he said, "that coincident with our prosperity, there is an emphatic assertion of popular rights and a keen resentment of public wrongs. . . .

[3] Beerits' Memorandum, III, 17.   [4] Author's interview with CEH, Jan. 7, 1946.

Slowly but surely the people have narrowed the opportunities for selfish aggression, and the demand of this hour . . . is not allegiance to phrases, but sympathy with every aspiration for the betterment of conditions. . . ."

The speech was Lincolnesque in its sense of dedication:

I assume the office of Governor without other ambition than to serve the people
of the State. I have not coveted its powers nor do I permit myself to shrink from
its responsibilities. . . .
I believe in the sincerity and good sense of the people. I believe that they are
intent in having government which recognizes no favored interests and which is
not conducted in any part for selfish ends. They will not be, and they should not
be, content with less.[5]

The next day came a detailed Hughesian program outlined in his message
to the legislature. He requested a recount of votes in the Hearst-McClellan
contest in 1905 and amendment of the law to provide a summary recanvass in
any future contest. "Our entire system of government," he said, "depends upon
honest elections and a fair count." [6] The victor was demanding justice for his
bitterest enemy not only because it was the right thing to do but also because
a recount would probably deprive Hearst of an issue that had won him much
sympathy.

Disregarding the advice of Boss Barnes, the Governor asked for reforms in
the method of voting and limitation of the amount that a candidate could spend
"to procure his election." Defying all the bosses, he asked for an experimental
direct-primaries law to be applied on a voluntary basis. More important still,
he urged abolition of the Board of Railroad Commissioners (a haven for boss-
controlled timeservers), the Commission of Gas and Electricity, and the Rapid
Transit Board of New York City. In their place he suggested two broad-gauged
public service commissions, one to operate in New York City and the other
in the remainder of the state, with ample power to control utility corporations
in the public interest.

Here was the direct and powerful blow to special privilege that the bosses
and the utilities had feared. In the teeth of their opposition, the new Governor
had translated his campaign promises into specific legislative proposals. That
seemed intolerable conduct for a tyro who had no standing in political circles.

While the bosses fumed, the press and public loudly applauded. "Mr. Hughes
presents the first comprehensive plan advanced by any governor within a generation," declared the exultant *World*, "for dealing adequately with the complicated questions of election reforms and the regulation of public utilities." "It
is pregnant with enormous possibilities," said the *New York Press*. ". . . filled
with words of wisdom," echoed the *Binghamton Herald*.[7] "Specific, candid and

5 *Public Papers of Charles E. Hughes 1907*, pp. 7–9.   6 *Ibid.*, p. 24.
7 Fuller Collection, New York Public Library, Vol. 49.

progressive . . ." added the *Outlook*. "Seldom has a . . . message been so freighted with promise to American democracy." [8]

"It is none of my business," wrote President Roosevelt, with unmistakable irony, "but I cannot deny myself the pleasure of writing to congratulate you as well as our party and our State upon your admirable message and upon the admirable way in which you have begun your term." [9]

The response of the Republican organization was to assign the key posts in the legislature to anti-Hughes men. The time-honored custom at Albany had been for the machine to boss the governor and the governor to boss the legislature. In accord with this tradition leaders of the Assembly and Senate called on Hughes and asked for his views as to the selection of committee chairmen. He replied simply that that was the task of the Senate and the Assembly. While he was eager to cooperate in every way in suggesting legislation and putting it into proper form, he had no intention of trying to control the committees or of resorting to any kind of dictation. As a practical matter, he could not have organized the legislature to his own liking without inviting its leaders to make patronage demands upon him; and Hughes was determined that the employees of his administration should be chosen for their competence in the jobs at hand—not for their service to any party machine.

The party leaders guffawed over this strict regard for constitutional functions and entrenched the Old Guard in the committee chairmanships. The liberal Senators, including Page, Saxe, Agnew, and Tully, were given insignificant assignments. The only concession to the Hughes men was the chairmanship of the Committee on Miscellaneous Corporations assigned to Senator Harvey D. Hinman. The vital Railroads Committee went to Senator Benjamin N. Wilcox, who for years had produced a stream of procorporation laws, and the Judiciary chairmanship to Senator George Davis, who had fought Hughes' 80-cent gas bill after the 1905 investigation. "So offensive to decency" was the committee list, one observer said, "that there was a state-wide howl of rage when it was published." [10]

Governor Hughes was shocked. His education in the ways of politicians had been greatly enhanced by the gas and insurance investigations and his gubernatorial campaign. By the time he took the oath of office he knew all the political leaders of the state and was no "babe in the woods," as some of the party leaders supposed. But he had misjudged the temper of the Republican leaders. He had supposed that, after his election, they would accord him some degree of loyalty in spite of disagreements over policy. Instead, they had unmistakably thrown down the gage of battle.

Hughes took up the gage, but without any show of hostility toward the or-

<hr />

[8] Jan. 12, 1907.   [9] T. R. to CEH, Jan. 6, 1907, Hughes Papers.
[10] Christian MacDonald in *Harper's Weekly*, Feb. 2, 1907.

ganization leaders themselves. In reply to questions from the press, he completely dissociated himself from the committee assignments. About an hour later came the first inkling of what his course would be. "The only strength that I or my Administration may have," he said in a speech to the Albany Chamber of Commerce, "is the confidence of the people of this State, and, in any difficulty that may arise, to the people of this State I propose to appeal." [11]

The bosses laughed at this sally. Nor was the Governor's talk of going to the people the only executive antic that set legislative tongues to wagging. Hughes was actually trying to conduct the public business in public. The press was talking about "daylight government." The politicos who gathered in the bar of the Ten Eyck Hotel close to the Capitol alternately snickered and cursed as they reviewed the indignities to which their fraternity was being subjected.

The New York executive chamber is a large, high-ceiling room in the southeast corner of the Capitol beautifully paneled in Santo Domingo mahogany. On two sides are five huge arched windows; on the walls are the portraits of past governors, a sprinkling of presidents, and other historic figures. Here the governors had presided at occasional hearings and conducted ceremonies of state, but until 1907 none of them had ventured to use this room as an office. Rather, they had secluded themselves in the inner sanctum reached by way of a swinging panel in the wall of the great chamber. Tradition said that a secret stair gave the political bigwigs access to this private suite without danger of being observed in their comings and goings.

Hughes surveyed the situation and decided to see visitors in the big room. It was a symbol of his break with the back-door methods of the past. Of course, his private office remained open to department heads and others who came in by appointment with important state business to transact. But during his "morning hour," which was given over to the hearing of complaints, suggestions, and comments from citizens, he operated almost exclusively in the big room. The rule was first come, first served, whether the visitor was a humble farmer or a powerful boss. It amounted to a revolution in the conduct of state affairs.

The Governor sat at an elaborate desk in the far corner of the room beneath the "fighting and squinting" portrait of Theodore Roosevelt. On the right was his secretary, Robert H. Fuller, a former newspaper man. On his left was his military secretary, Colonel George Curtis Treadwell, who had a fondness for swank uniforms and decorations. Waiting visitors occupied the chairs and sofas around the room and moved over to the big desk as their turns came. Hughes listened attentively, kept the discussions on the points at issue, and usually promised to give prompt attention to the problems laid before him.

As one delegation moved away, a clever little man darted back to the big

[11] New York *Evening Post*, Jan. 10, 1907.

desk. "Now, Governor," he said, "I know a lot about this thing that you ought to hear. I'd like to talk to you about it."

"There is no time better than the present," Hughes replied. "I want to get all the facts."

He instructed his messenger to call back the other members of the group who were leaving the room. The puzzled citizens returned, but the little man who had stayed behind, hoping to whisper privately into the Governor's ear, had little to say.

The politicians were furious over having to wait in line and then talk with the Governor under the watchful eyes of other citizens. The size of the executive chamber made it possible to carry on a conversation at the Governor's desk without being overhead by visitors awaiting their turn, but the atmosphere conducive to undercover bargaining was gone. And to put the party hierarchy on a par with ordinary citizens added insult to injury. Hughes was not only taking over powers that the bosses had traditionally exercised; he even made a show of his independence. Woodruff publicly complained that "things are in a bad way at Albany."

The press was delighted with the arrangement. It meant that the state government would be operating out in the open where editors and reporters could see the wheels go around. "Sly party Nicodemuses no longer go to the executive chamber by night . . . or the back door," rejoiced the *Evening Post*. "We have a governor again." [12]

The showdown with the party leaders was not long in coming. Woodruff and Parsons were in agreement that two political plums—the offices of superintendent of public works and superintendent of elections for the New York Metropolitan district—should fall promptly into their hands. At their behest Governor Higgins had given Lewis M. Swasey a recess appointment as superintendent of elections, but his tenure would soon expire unless Hughes renominated him. Before acting, Higgins had asked the Governor-elect for his advice, and Hughes, knowing nothing about Swasey and being preoccupied with his message and other affairs, had declined to commit himself. After his inauguration he inquired into the nominee's fitness and found no evidence of the ability and character which he thought a superintendent of elections should have. Swasey was a Republican district leader in Brooklyn, "a mere tool of the machine." To entrust the supervision of elections to him would make a mockery of Hughes' promise to give the state a clean and efficient administration "free from taint of bossism."

Woodruff rounded up the legislators from Brooklyn and sent them to the Governor to plead the cause of Swasey. "While I thank you very much for what

[12] Feb. 6, 1907.

you have said," the Governor responded, "I shall have to use my own judgment, even though it may be erroneous." [13]

Woodruff then insisted on making the reappointment of Swasey a test of power. He and Parsons called on the Governor and bluntly told him that Swasey would have to be retained. Hughes replied with equal candor that he did not intend to renominate the unqualified Swasey, but he would be glad to appoint anyone else whom they might recommend, "provided he was a fit man for the place." [14] His offer was spurned. The party leaders were thinking only of maintaining their power.

The issue was much broader, Hughes told them, than the question of this particular appointment. The people had elected him governor because they trusted him to stand on his own feet and use his best judgment in directing the affairs of the state. If he should appoint Swasey, the people would know that he was sacrificing their interest to party organization. Woodruff and Parsons ought to sympathize with his efforts to bring the Republican Party back to popular esteem, he told them, and not take a stand that would hinder essential changes.

At one o'clock in the morning Woodruff and Parsons were still insisting that Swasey be appointed. Hughes ended the argument at that point with a flat No. As the conference broke up, Parsons turned to the Governor and said, "I think we'll find a way." [15] Hughes did not know what the New York County leader meant, but it was soon to be evident.

The press detected the scent of battle and knew that Hughes would have to win this fight if he were to make good his promise of an unbossed administration. When the Speaker of the Assembly, James W. Wadsworth, Jr., went to Washington, therefore, amid reports that he would bid for the President's support of Swasey, the outcome of his mission was followed with intense interest. Roosevelt apparently concluded that in this instance "opportunism could be one of the major virtues." Washington dispatches of patent White House origin reported that the President had no intention of giving Governor Hughes any advice on appointments or other state affairs unless the Governor should ask for it, and Wadsworth told reporters that he had not received any "orders or instructions." [16]

When he called on the Governor, however, Wadsworth did have a message—a message which, he said, he was sorry to have to deliver. "The President said," the Speaker reported, "that while of course he thought the Governor should do what he thought right, he felt that he should appoint Swasey, and that if he (Roosevelt) were governor, he would appoint him." [17]

[13] New York *Evening Post*, Jan. 10, 1907.   [14] CEH, Notes, p. 182.
[15] Beerits' Memorandum, IV, 5.   [16] New York *Evening Post*, Jan. 14, 1907.
[17] Beerits' Memorandum, IV, 5.

"I'm sorry to get this message," Hughes replied. "I would be very glad if it were possible to accept the President's advice. However, I wish you would tell the President that I have thought over this matter very carefully and that I'm sending in the nomination of William Leary this evening." He had already ordered the nomination to be written out and saw no reason to reconsider it.

Leary's name had been suggested by Job E. Hedges, one of Hughes' most enthusiastic supporters in the 1906 campaign. The nominee was a Republican of good standing, a friend of Roosevelt, and Parsons' former campaign manager. He also had the endorsement of many independents. Hughes felt that Leary was so well qualified both as a public servant and as a party man that the Senate could not turn him down.

The implied rebuff to Roosevelt was a matter of "deep regret" to the Governor.[18] He was eager to maintain friendly relations with the President and to have his advice. But when the issue was whether he should be governor in his own right, Hughes felt that he had to adhere to his own principle. Woodruff and Parsons had acted foolishly in trying to dictate to him and then in bringing the President into the affair. It was they who had insisted on a showdown, and only they could be blamed for the outcome.

Scarcely less jolting to the organization was the appointment of former Senator Stevens of Attica to be superintendent of public works. Stevens was a man of integrity and executive talent whose business and political experience especially fitted him for this major administrative task. Hughes had learned to trust him when Stevens was chairman of the gas investigating committee. But Stevens was anathema to the Wadsworth clan of western New York. He had helped to unseat James W. Wadsworth, Sr., from Congress, and the Wadsworths had gerrymandered him off the political map. The junior Wadsworth, Speaker of the New York Assembly, now visualized Stevens using the vast Public Works Department, which was constructing the new Erie Canal at a cost of more than $100,000,000 as a source of patronage for anti-Wadsworth men.

Hughes had discussed this appointment with several advisers without reference to politics. He was determined to rescue the department from the aura of scandal surrounding it and did not know that Stevens was involved in a political feud.[19] To quiet the furor he issued a statement explaining why Stevens had been chosen and disavowing any antagonism toward Speaker Wadsworth. It was nevertheless a bitter pill for a high-minded legislator whose aid the Governor needed.

There was no foundation, however, for the Speaker's fears that the Public Works Department might become an anti-Wadsworth machine. "I want you to conduct this office with an eye solely to efficiency and the public interest," Hughes instructed his number one administrator. "The one thing you must

[18] CEH, Notes, p. 183.   [19] Ibid.

not do is to try by the use of patronage to build any 'Hughes machine.' " [20]
This was typical of his attitude. He preferred to appoint Republicans and gladly
accepted the candidates of professional politicians whenever they measured up
to the standard he set. But the primary consideration was to get trained and
competent men.

Friendship with the Governor was likely to be a liability to job seekers.
After the new public service commissions had been authorized, Job Hedges
dropped into the Governor's office, reminded him of the part he (Hedges) had
played in the campaign, and said frankly that he would like a place on one of
the commissions. Hughes expressed his high regard for Hedges. "But you see,
Job," he added, "I can't very well appoint you because you're a personal
friend." "By God," Hedges replied, "you need no longer consider that an
obstacle."

In spite of its shock, the Senate promptly confirmed the Leary and Stevens
appointments. The anti-Hughes men had not surrendered. They were merely
waiting for firmer ground on which to make their stand.

Meanwhile the public found new hope and amusement in the turn of events
at Albany. Frank H. Simonds declared that Woodruff had been eliminated as
a political figure and that the reactionaries would now have to fight or run. "To
listen to the stupefied comments of the old-line politicians," he wrote, "to
watch the inextinguishable mirth of the independents and unaffected onlookers,
and to mark the confusion of the people who said two weeks ago, 'Oh, Hughes
will be a Republican,' is to understand fully what has happened, and why the
appointments for two comparatively small jobs are regarded as indicative of a
revolution. It is worth recalling, also, that the Hughes Administration is not
yet two weeks old." [21]

John Kendrick Bangs expressed the prevailing sentiment in verse:

> O woe is me! O woe is us
>   That it should come to pass!
> That gum-shoe King Politicus
>   Should go at last to grass.
> It is the dee-dash-dernedest thing
>   That ever we did see!
> A Governor a-governing
>   At ancient Albanee.[22]

Hughes himself managed to squeeze more than a little ironic humor out of
the situation when he spoke at the dinner welcoming James Bryce, the new
British ambassador to the United States. Dipping into Bryce's *The American
Commonwealth*, which other speakers had been lauding extravagantly, Hughes

[20] John Palmer Gavit in New York *Evening Post*, June 10, 1916.
[21] New York *Evening Post*, Jan. 15, 1907.   [22] *Current Literature*, June, 1907, p. 622.

came up with a passage saying that the men who managed state governments "turn out to be insignificant" persons who fail to hold the public interest.[23]

"I find no flattering word for the governor in *The American Commonwealth*," Hughes bantered—to the great amusement of an audience keenly aware of what was happening at Albany.

"Oh, yes, Governor," Lord Bryce spoke out, "there is another passage there."

"Perhaps our good friend refers to this," the Governor replied, quoting again: " 'The State Executive, it is said, has little to do and comparatively small sums to handle. . . . A State Governor, however, is not yet a nonentity.' Now, while there is life there is hope," Hughes commented, "that we may be able to supply material for a new edition."

Whatever his discomfiture may have been at the time, Lord Bryce wrote to the Governor two months later, congratulating him on his "great success" and penciling on the bottom of the note: "I shall indeed have to rewrite that chapter in my 'American Commonwealth' in order to show what may be accomplished by the firmness, tact and courage of a State Governor." [24]

[23] Speech of March 23, 1907, Hughes Papers, Library of Congress.
[24] Bryce to CEH, June 18, 1907.

Chapter 18

THE BOSSES RUN RIOT

BEFORE he had been in office a week, Governor Hughes embarked upon a systematic housecleaning. His pledge to the people made it necessary to break the hold of the political machines and the big corporations upon the state's service and regulatory departments. In the face of the opposition now lined up against him this was a herculean task; yet he could not fail without risking loss of all the public confidence that he had attained.

His first effort was successful. Banking Superintendent Kilburn stepped out and was replaced by Charles Hallam Keep, a trained executive of high standing recommended by President Roosevelt. The Insurance Department presented a more delicate problem, but the Governor hoped that by tact and candid reasoning he could quietly effect a change there also. In this he was to suffer a sharp disappointment of historic consequences.

Otto Kelsey was strongly entrenched as superintendent of insurance. A former legislator and comptroller, an ally of Odell and a friend of the Speaker, he commanded powerful support and had a reputation for simple honesty that seemed to make him invulnerable to attack in the 1907 political climate in and about Albany. In deference to these facts Hughes looked for a less strategic position into which Kelsey could be eased without loss of face.

When Kelsey refused to budge, the Governor laid his case before a group of the superintendent's organization friends. Eight months had elapsed since the insurance reforms had been enacted, and Kelsey, ostensibly named to make the new laws effective, had done nothing. Senator Armstrong and Hughes had met with Kelsey shortly after he took office and explored the relationship between the department's laxity and the insurance scandals.[1] Kelsey had seemed sympathetic to reform at the time, but he went right on operating his department as if the insurance investigation had never been held.

"If I can appoint Kelsey to any other position for which I think he is qualified," Hughes promised the organization men, "I'll do it. He is honest, and I don't want his removal to reflect on him. But he is not the man to head this department. I want you to get him to resign." [2]

Kelsey stood pat. Being an amiable and spineless fellow, he might well have yielded to avoid a fight if the organization had left him free to make a choice.

[1] CEH, Notes, p. 184. [2] Beerits' Memorandum, IV, p. 9.

But the political satraps could not afford to let the Insurance Department—one of the foremost political levers in dealing with big business—slip out of their control. Nor could they let an "honest man" be ousted for any such reasons as the Governor advanced. The case against Kelsey was that "he owed a duty to the people of the state" and had failed to perform it. Albany understood the eclipse of political figures for opposition to a boss or a governor or for conduct bringing the individual into open disgrace. But here was a new and frightening test. Kelsey was to be sacrificed because he had been loyal to the machine instead of the people. Judged by this criterion, who would be safe? The Governor's revolutionary idea could obviously be turned against every bosslet holding a political job.

The leaders felt especially sure of themselves because, under the statute, Kelsey could not be removed without the consent of the Senate. How could Hughes go before the Senate and demand the removal of a public servant admitted to be honest when no well defined charges had been brought against him? Certainly this time they had an issue on which they could show up the Governor for the babe in the woods they believed him to be.

As Kelsey consulted a wide circle of friends, the story leaked out to the press. Further scrutiny of his record then indicated that the assets of a savings and loan association of which he had been receiver had dwindled disastrously. Five million dollars' worth of stock-transfer stamps, almost as good as money, were reported to have disappeared while he was comptroller. Ostensibly they were burned because of defects, but no record had been kept. These disclosures further stiffened Kelsey's fighting spirit.

Defeated in his persuasive efforts, Hughes openly demanded Kelsey's resignation. Kelsey flatly refused to make any such "admission of wrongful conduct in office," but invited the Governor to tell him what he wished to have done in the Insurance Department. To Hughes' mind this was a confession of Kelsey's unfitness. The Governor's demand was not for a lackey but for a superintendent who could clean out the department's dead wood and corruption and administer it as an alert and virile instrument of public policy.

The fight was temporarily interrupted by the death and funeral of former Governor Higgins. Then Hughes took the offensive with a brilliant maneuver the like of which Albany had never seen. In response to Kelsey's request for further consideration of his fitness, the Governor unearthed an old statute authorizing him to "take proofs" before recommending a removal and summoned Kelsey to the executive chamber on February 18 for an informal examination.

Kelsey came to the hearing wrapped in his honesty, which the Governor had not challenged, but utterly unprotected against the sort of probing to which he was subjected. The superintendent admitted that the negligence of the examiners he had inherited from his predecessor amounted to a "public scandal," but he had not dismissed any of them. The chief examiner of the old regime had resigned of his own accord. Other examiners who could see no evil and hear no evil were still at their desks because Kelsey did not wish to hurt their feelings and felt a need for "experienced men." Oblivious to the revolt against the old order which he represented, Kelsey had plodded along with his eyes fastened on routine trivialities.

Ida M. Tarbell called the examination of Kelsey the most cruel stripping of a man in public ever seen.[3] In answer to the Governor's searching questions, Kelsey had prepared his own indictment before the Senate. Some critics who knew nothing of the Governor's efforts to save Kelsey's face felt that this public exposure of his incompetence was unnecessarily harsh. But it was Kelsey himself who had brought the case into the open. Hughes could only choose between making an example of Kelsey and making a shambles of his own program. The Governor "has handled the case of the people vs. Kelsey with such skill and fairness," rejoiced the *New York Press*, "that we almost hesitate to praise him for fear of intoxicating ourselves with the adjectives that flow in streams to the lips." [4]

By this time it was evident, however, that Kelsey was only a pawn in a major struggle for political power. The men who had said at Saratoga that "even Hearst wouldn't hurt *us* as much as Hughes" were now shaking their heads and telling each other how right they had been. The Governor could not be controlled. He would not play the political game. The only course open to the bosses was to attack him and all that he stood for. Kelsey had merely supplied a name, as Frank H. Simonds said, "for Hughes' political rubicon." "Henceforth," he added, "the issue is not Kelsey, but progress or reaction at Albany." [5]

For weeks the Senate did nothing in response to the Governor's appeal for Kelsey's removal. The Republican leader, John Raines, whose long drooping mustache seemed to symbolize the old order, formed a coalition with Democratic legislators captained by the sharp-faced and sinister Patrick H. McCarren and Thomas F. Grady in order to block the Governor's reforms. They braced themselves for what they believed to be the inevitable swinging of the Governor's patronage and veto clubs. But Hughes made no effort either to coerce or to punish them for their opposition. Instead, he announced that his powers would be used solely in the interests of good legislation and efficient administration. The Senate would have to act on its own responsibility without fear of retaliation against Kelsey's supporters or promise of reward for those who stood by the Governor. This strict adherence to the principles of

[3] *American Magazine*, March, 1908, p. 460.   [4] Feb. 20, 1907.
[5] New York *Evening Post*, Feb. 18, 1907.

representative government amused the rough-hewn legislators and spurred them to bolder measures of revolt. Hughes' prestige in Albany visibly sagged.

Throughout this period the Governor was fighting doggedly—in his own way. He held two press conferences every working day that he was in the capital, talking freely with the news-gatherers about what he had done and what he planned to do. In confidence he unfolded background information and news not yet ready for release to the public, thus discouraging uninformed speculation and preparing the way for intelligent handling of each story when it broke. Hardheaded newsmen paid him the great compliment of saying, "Hughes is on the level." [6] Such keen observers of public affairs as Louis Howe, who represented a Saratoga paper, John Palmer Gavit of the Associated Press, and Frank H. Simonds of the New York *Evening Post* became enthusiastic exponents of the Hughes policies. The newsmen's confidence in the new Governor filtered through to editorial offices that were already friendly, and Hughes had an exceptionally favorable press.

The extraordinary flow of good will between the Governor and the press was demonstrated when newspaper men pretended to "impeach" him at a dinner of the "Amen Corner" in the Fifth Avenue Hotel. Hughes was acquitted of the accusation that he was a Republican. But the most "heinous crime" charged against him was a different matter. "He does wear upon his face," the "impeachment" read, "certain long and dark curtains, portieres, lambrequins or draperies of an impenetrable texture, which make it impossible to tell whether he is stringing a statesman or not." Hughes laughed heartily at this ribbing. When he arose to speak, several diners shouted, "The next President of the United States," and the audience roared its approval. [7]

As a novel and striking figure in the political firmament, Hughes was much in demand as a speaker. He accepted as many invitations as possible for the sake of acquainting the public with his program. In his campaign he had promised that he would be close to the people. Now he realized that he would have to rely upon their support if he was to accomplish anything at Albany. His heavy duties as Governor left him little time to prepare speeches, but he talked out of the fullness of his daily experience, hiring stenographers in relays to take down his extemporaneous remarks so that accurate copies would be available to the press a few minutes after he had finished speaking.

Often he spoke at three dinners in a single evening by hurrying from one to another. If the audiences expected to hear oratorical gush or sparkling pleasantries, they were disappointed. Hughes packed his speeches with facts about the public business and reasoning on the basis of those facts, laying each issue candidly and persuasively before the people for their own decision.

[6] Samuel G. Blythe in the *Saturday Evening Post,* March 16, 1907.
[7] *New York Press,* Feb. 10, 1907.

The Governor threw his challenge directly into the teeth of the politicians when he spoke to the Republican organization of Albany on February 27. He knew that Barnes had asked him to dine with the machine in the hope of softening him to its pressures. The big red-faced, loud-talking Albany boss was clearly the most formidable leader of the Old Guard. Keen and eloquent in a bullish sort of way, a graduate of Harvard University and a grandson of Thurlow Weed (one of the founders of the Republican Party), his dominant purpose was to restore the party machine in New York to "fighting trim." To Barnes' mind this meant tight control of the three P's—patronage, privilege, and police. In his letter written shortly after the election, he had warned Hughes: "There are breakers ahead unless the faddist [meaning reformer] as well as the political crook is exposed in his folly." Apparently Hughes decided that one of the best places for a breaker to strike was the organization dinner.

Party harmony was desirable and party loyalty was a fine quality, he told the machine. But they did not require support of anything wrong either in policy or administration. Organization too was essential, of course. But "no matter how skilfully constructed or astutely led," Hughes solemnly warned, "the people will smash any organization that is devoted to selfish interests." They had rebuked the Republican Party for overreaching itself. Hughes supplied the facts and figures. "It is clearly evident," he insisted, "that on state issues the Republican Party will be doomed to defeat unless it gives new assurances to the people of its capacity to govern in their interest. No man is a friend of the Republican Party," he continued, "who asks me or anyone in authority to appoint a man or to retain a man who is not equal to his job. . . . Let there be a demonstration that we are a party of the people and that the interests of all citizens are safe in our keeping." [8]

The politicians who had come to believe that Hughes was already beaten and in retreat were stupefied. "It was like a skeleton in armor," one of them exclaimed. Barnes' anger flared openly. As soon as the Governor had left— apparently to make another speech—the bullish boss unloosed a passionate tirade in defense of the old order and in denunciation of the Hughes reforms.

As the months passed, Hughes' appeal to the people became increasingly direct. "When any proposal is made that is right . . . which the people recognize as demanded for mischiefs that exist," he urged, "then let public opinion assert itself and make it impossible to defeat such a proposition upon any ground of expediency or because of the opposition of any interest." [9] But while the Governor talked, the situation at Albany went from bad to worse. Near the end of March, John Raines, leader of the Senate, let it be known that he had "decided to fight Mr. Hughes tooth and nail for the rest of the ses-

[8] Text of address in Hughes Papers, Library of Congress.
[9] Brooklyn *Daily Eagle*, Feb. 12, 1907.

sion." [10] The legislature had done nothing. Two irreconcilable forces were locked in what seemed to be hopeless combat that thwarted the plans of both.

A wave of dissatisfaction swept in upon Albany, and some of it hit the Governor. Several newspapers commented sharply on the apparent failure of his tactics. The people will look elsewhere for a Governor, next time, said the *Hornell Times*, unless Mr. Hughes can produce results.[11] Some of the legislators themselves, accustomed to being told what to do, were obviously embarrassed by the freedom and responsibility that Hughes forced upon them. Many resented his inclination to play a lone hand and his genius for holding the spotlight of publicity on his own program.

Then came an incident that seemed to align the White House with the bosses. President Roosevelt was eager to see the Hughes Administration succeed. At the same time he was irritated by Hughes' uncompromising attitude toward the organization. The party leaders ran down to Washington with numerous complaints, and the Governor did nothing to counteract their wailing. When the Kelsey incident produced an open split, Roosevelt saw in it dangerous potentialities. He called Woodruff to Washington and urged him to swing the organization behind the Hughes program in order to keep New York in the Republican column in 1908.

About the same time the President ousted Collector of Customs Archie Sanders of Rochester, one of the minor figures in the anti-Hughes fight. Undoubtedly he thought he was doing Hughes a favor. Superintendent of Public Works Stevens had visited the White House and asked for Sanders' political scalp, apparently not mentioning that he spoke without Hughes' knowledge or consent. Roosevelt may well have assumed that Stevens was reflecting the Governor's wishes. As Sanders was a partisan of the Wadsworth clan, however, both Stevens and Roosevelt had personal motives for moving against him, apart from any interest in the Hughes program.

Congressman James W. Wadsworth, the Speaker's father, had denounced Roosevelt's meat-inspection bill, and, losing his fight, had called the President "a humbug and a faker." [12] Wadsworth's "federal appointees" were thereafter removed "one by one." [13] When the ax fell upon Archie Sanders, Wadsworth accused the President of persecuting his (Wadsworth's) friends because of his opposition to the meat-inspection bill. Reporters carried the accusation to the White House, where a statement was given out saying Sanders was being removed to "uphold the hands of Governor Hughes." "It is the President's intention," said the *Tribune*, "to strengthen Governor Hughes' stand at every opportunity." [14]

[10] *New York Press*, March 29, 1907.
[11] Fuller Collection, New York Public Library, Vol. 101.
[12] CEH to Mark Sullivan, Oct. 22, 1929.   [13] Brooklyn *Daily Eagle*, Dec. 13, 1907.
[14] April 20, 1907.

Hughes read this news with dismay. The President's interest in what he was trying to do was indeed gratifying, but Roosevelt was using patronage as a club in Hughes' behalf—a method the Governor had repeatedly pledged himself not to use. If he had had any inkling as to what Stevens was up to, Hughes would have scotched the proposal before it had been made. Newsmen flocked into the executive chamber to learn whether he had changed his policy. In response to their questions, he admitted that he had not requested the President to remove Sanders. Even at the risk of offending the President, Hughes would not be a hypocrite. He told the correspondents the simple truth, without authorizing quotation of what he had said.

"It was stated from excellent authority today," the *New York Times* reported the next morning, "that Governor Hughes was not consulted . . . and knew nothing about it [Sanders' resignation] until it was announced to the public." [15] Hughes' matter-of-fact explanation was to be grossly distorted by another newspaper to feed the fires of personal resentment. But that story can best be told in another connection. For the moment it is sufficient to note that the Governor's failure to fall in with Roosevelt's "big stick" tactics brought a sudden cooling off at the White House.

At first the order for Sanders' removal had been a jolt to the bosses. Opposition to the Hughes program was temporarily relaxed. But when the Governor dissociated himself from the Sanders incident and the resentment of the White House became evident, the anti-Hughes forces cut loose. Albany witnessed the amazing spectacle of Republican leaders in the Senate violently denouncing the Republican Governor. "Even the Governor's friends confess," wailed the *Tribune*, "that he is about defeated on all the things he suggested in his message." On May 3 the Senate demonstrated its control of the situation by voting 27 to 24 to reject the Governor's request for the removal of Otto Kelsey.

The immediate effect of this defeat was a tragedy in the Governor's official family. Through all his darkest hours at the executive chamber Hughes had had the unfailing aid and support of Ernest W. Huffcut, his legal adviser. Huffcut had succeeded Hughes as professor of law at Cornell University in 1893 and moved on to become dean of the law school. Handsome, vigorous and amiable as well as intellectual, the young bachelor was a man of inestimable promise. Governor Higgins had made Huffcut his legal adviser, and Hughes induced the dean to remain with him in the same capacity on extended leave. They had been good friends, and now the bond between them was greatly strengthened as they fought together in a cause that had the undivided loyalty of both.

Huffcut went to the Governor's office on the morning of Friday, May 3, with an armful of bills. He found Hughes dictating a speech to be delivered at Elmira that night. The governor had planned to go directly from Elmira to New York

[15] April 21, 1907.

City, where he was to speak the following night, but when Huffcut said the bills would have to be signed or rejected by Monday night he agreed to return to Albany on the night train.

The dean was dejected because of the Senate's refusal to remove Kelsey. Along with other members of the Governor's staff, he had nervously awaited until 2:00 A.M. that very morning for the Senate to vote. The Governor himself had gone to bed. Being extremely sensitive, Huffcut probably feared that Hughes might be overwhelmed by this defeat.

"Now, Governor," he said, putting his arm around his friend's shoulders as they walked together to the waiting carriage, "don't feel badly about this Kelsey business. It will hurt them more than you. You don't need to worry. Everything will come out all right." [16]

"I'm not disheartened at all," Hughes replied, without a trace of regret in his voice. "I simply showed the people that I was trying to do all I could to reform the Insurance Department. The conduct of that department is now the responsibility of the Senate."

After the speech at Elmira, Hughes took the train for Albany by way of Binghamton. But when the locomotive broke down in the early morning, he gave up trying to get to Albany and wired Huffcut to bring the bills down to the Astor Hotel in New York, where they could work on them together. Instead of Huffcut, an undertaker called on Governor Hughes and his military aide at breakfast that morning. Someone from the Governor's office, he said, had committed suicide on the night boat from Albany. They hastened to the morgue, and there lay Huffcut with a bullet wound in his temple.

Hughes' suffering over the incident was the more acute because Huffcut's action seemed so inexplicable. To be sure, Huffcut had been under severe pressure from a long and exasperating legislative session. But his work had been less exacting than that of Fuller and the Governor himself, and Huffcut had given no indication of undue fatigue. Apparently the Kelsey vote convinced him that he had failed, and the strain was too much for his sensitive and somewhat morbid nature.

Months later the *Ithaca Journal* intimated that Huffcut's death might have been traceable to an interview with the Governor about a legislative blunder.[17] A bill passed by the legislature and signed by the Governor was discovered to have no enacting clause. Someone jumped to the conclusion that Hughes might have reproved his legal aid for failure to note the oversight. Owen L. Potter, who had been assistant to Huffcut, hastened to point out, however, that the bill in question had not been signed until after Huffcut's death and the mistake was not discovered until a week later.[18] The unfortunate dean went to his

---

[16] Author's interview with CEH, April 16, 1946.   [17] Dec. 3, 1907.
[18] *Ithaca Journal* carries Potter's letter dated Dec. 4, 1907, Fuller Collection, Vol. 149.

death without the slightest shadow on his relationship with Hughes. The Governor so highly appraised Huffcut's ability that he had planned to offer him a judgeship.

Nevertheless, the suicide of the Governor's brilliant adviser deepened the gloom that overcast Albany. Hughes had lost the support of the bosses, the legislature, and the White House, and even Fate seemed to have turned her back upon him. The bleak outlook might well have discouraged any lone-handed fighter without a high degree of iron in his will.

Chapter 19

RETAINER FROM THE PEOPLE

NO DOMESTIC issue was more troublesome to the untamed United States of America in 1907 than control of the big public service corporations. Hughes had wrestled with one segment of the problem in the gas and electric-light investigation. On his advice, the state had created in New York City a Commission of Gas and Electricity and, incidentally, Hughes had declined Governor Higgins' offer of its chairmanship. When he was elected governor, he saw that the regulation of utilities would have to be approached on a much broader base. The state had been creating special regulatory bodies for some time, but their jurisdiction was narrow and their powers were meager. The usual outcome was not commission control of the utility but utility control of the commission.

The necessity of prompt as well as comprehensive action was impressed on Hughes when, as governor-elect, he made a firsthand investigation of the "bridge crush." Taking his chance along with thousands of other New Yorkers trying to get across the Brooklyn Bridge in the "rush hour," he was jolted, trodden, and squeezed by a seething mass of men and women fighting for a ride home. He narrowly escaped being pushed into the pathway of the cars. The bridge crush was only a small part of the railway safety problem. The railroads in Greater New York were killing more than 500 persons a year and injuring 2,000. And safety was only one of many neglected phases of utility regulation.

Hughes' broader investigation showed that railroads were practicing "pernicious favoritism"—granting secret rebates and discriminating as to rates and transportation service. "Those who have sought to monopolize trade have thus been enabled to crush competition and grow in wealth and power," he said in his message to the legislature, "by crowding out their rivals who have been deprived of access to markets upon equal terms. These abuses are not to be tolerated." [1] The Board of Railroad Commissioners was an important, machine-controlled body with only the power to make recommendations for enforcement of the law. Its expenses were paid by the railroads as if in cynical recognition of the fact that it was used by them to deceive the people into thinking that regulation existed when it did not.

[1] *Public Papers of Charles E. Hughes, 1907*, p. 29.

In Boston, Hughes' friend Louis Brandeis had successfully concluded a few months earlier a fight for the adjustment of gas rates by a sliding-scale formula.[2] Progressive Mr. Brandeis was still trying to cope with the big public service corporations through specialized commissions and direct action of the legislature. Hughes thought the time for such halfway measures had passed, so far as New York was concerned. He asked that the whole welter of special regulatory bodies be swept away and that two powerful public service commissions be set up in their place—one to regulate transportation and utilities in New York City and adjacent counties and the other to have jurisdiction throughout the remainder of the state. Only strong and expert administrative agencies armed with a mandate from the people could end the era of governmental shadow boxing with gigantic utilities.

Each of the new public service commissions, the Governor said, should have "power to act upon its own initiative as well as upon complaint; to pass upon the issue of stocks and bonds; to examine properties, books and accounts; to require detailed reports in prescribed form; to prescribe reasonable rates; to require adequate and impartial service; to provide for the safety of employees and for the protection of the public; and generally to direct whatever may be necessary or proper to safeguard the public interest and to secure the fulfillment of the public obligations of the corporations under its supervision." [3] The regulatory bodies were to have ample powers of inspection in order to detect abuses before they assumed serious proportions. Their orders were to be enforced through legal action to be brought by themselves and given preference in the courts.

The Governor provided a blueprint for the modern type of public service commission that was to become an increasingly important factor in American life during the next half-century. Wisconsin was pioneering in the same field, and Congress had extended the regulatory power of the Interstate Commerce Commission, but nowhere in America was there a regulatory body of the scope and power that Hughes sought to give his commissions.

The Governor worked with Senator Page and Assemblyman Merritt in preparing the bill, which was introduced on March 6, 1907. He had loyal support, too, from Senators Hinman and Agnew, Assemblyman John Lord O'Brian, and many others. Secretary of State Elihu Root also contributed valuable advice, being especially concerned over the corporations' prevalent practice of issuing watered stock on the basis of mergers.[4]

To facilitate the selection of experts, the bill authorized $10,000 salaries (later raised to $15,000) for the five members of each commission. It gave each commission jurisdiction over railways, pipe lines, tubes, express, gas, and

---

[2] Alpheus Thomas Mason, *Brandeis*, pp. 137–138.
[3] *Public Papers, 1907*, pp. 31–32.   [4] Root to CEH, Dec. 20, 1906.

electric-light companies. It forbade special rates, rebates, free tickets, and unjust discrimination by any device. Fares and rates would have to be posted for the information of the public. The commissions could not authorize the capitalization of franchises, except to the extent that they represented actual payments made to the state or a municipality. Mergers could not be capitalized beyond the amount of the capital stock of the two merged companies. The commissions could quickly abolish discriminatory rates and fix fair ones. Penalties as high as $5,000 could be assessed for each separate day's violation of a commission order, or officers and employees of the offending corporation could be sent to jail. Finally, the commissions would have to keep their offices open from 8:00 A.M. to 11:00 P.M. to hear complaints from the public.

But the commissions could not act arbitrarily. Before filing an order, they would have to give the interested corporation a hearing and make a thorough investigation. The rates they fixed would have to be "fair and reasonable." Hughes looked upon his proposed commissions as ideal agencies that could utilize "special knowledge, flexibility, disinterestedness and sound judgment in applying broad legislative principles that are essential to the protection of the community, and of expanding enterprise."

The Page-Merritt bill, as it became known, commanded enthusiastic support from the press. From the bosses and the corporations seeking to avoid control came a barrage of epithets: "Confiscation . . . violation of vested rights . . . usurpation of power . . . ruination of our prosperity." Never had a bill so stirred up the legislature. The betting odds against it would be one hundred to one, a senator commented, except for one thing—the man behind the bill.[5]

The man behind the bill had concluded that his one chance of getting it enacted lay in mobilizing the people behind it. In two months, early in 1907, he preached his public service commission doctrine at forty dinners and meetings. At first his appeal to the people became a "riotous joke" at Albany. The bosses rubbed their hands in delight and talked of tying ribbons in the Governor's whiskers. As the debate continued, however, they found it increasingly difficult to devise any convincing argument against the bill. The opposition concentrated, therefore, on two objections: first, the power the bill gave the Governor to remove the commissioners, and, second, the limitations it placed upon review of the commissions' orders in the courts.

Hughes had insisted upon giving the Governor power to remove members of the commissions for neglect of duty, inefficiency or malfeasance, without requiring the consent of the Senate.[6] His critics said that this would put the commissions under the Governor's control. It is the duty of the Governor, Hughes replied, to see that the laws are faithfully executed, and the removal of

[5] *New York Press*, March 8, 1907.   [6] CEH, Notes, p. 191.

commissioners who are failing in their assignment is a suitable incident to the discharge of that duty. The inability of the Governor to remove bungling Mr. Kelsey and other timeservers in important administrative posts was a perfect illustration of his point. "It is a great mistake," he said, "to be so intent on preventing bad administration as to make difficult a good one. . . ." [7]

As to judicial review, Hughes drew a fine line of distinction that was profoundly to influence the relationship between administrative bodies and the courts through the following decades. Thirty-three years later Majority Leader Alben W. Barkley of the United States Senate was to insert into the *Congressional Record* Hughes' then famous speech favoring limited judicial review as a guide to Congress in legislating on judicial supervision of administrative agencies.[8] In 1907, however, the corporations had strong backing in insisting that the courts be given "a general review" over all the orders of the commissions. That view was widely accepted at the time. It was championed in the hearings on the bill by a battery of lawyers selected no doubt with the object of impressing the Governor as well as the legislature. There were Joseph H. Choate, Hughes' former mentor and senior associate in various legal battles; Paul D. Cravath, Hughes' former partner; De Lancey Nicoll, a friend of the Governor; and Edward M. Shepard.

Hughes insisted that the commissions should operate without interference from the courts unless they should exceed their statutory authority or issue an unconstitutional order. "In either of these cases," he said, "there should be full judicial review." But the courts should not be asked to make decisions properly within the sphere of the legislature or an administrative body. It was not their province to upset administrative findings supported by evidence and not shown to be arbitrary. "To provide a right of appeal to the courts from every order of the commission," he argued, "not only invites delay and an unnecessary multiplicity of proceedings, but has for its object the substitution of the judgment of the court for the action of the commission. To give the court power to hear such appeals, to take evidence, and to reverse or to modify the orders of the commission comes simply to this: that the court becomes in effect the ruling commission, and the commission created by the Legislature is simply a board to take evidence and make what are, in effect, recommendations." [9] The Governor based his case on the bedrock principle of keeping fact-finding and policy decisions in the commissions and legal and constitutional issues in the courts.

Administrative agencies were then in their infancy, so far as the United States was concerned. But their essential place in modern government was as clear as sunlight to Hughes. It was not difficult to frame legislation establishing general standards, but to translate accepted principles into regulations wisely

[7] CEH, Speech at Glens Falls, April 5, 1907.
[8] *Congressional Record* (appendix) Vol. 85, Pt. 15, p. 2686.
[9] Address at Elmira, May 3, 1907.

adapted to particular cases required an experienced body sitting continuously and removed so far as possible from the blandishments and intrigues of politics. Complaints had to be heard, expert investigations conducted, complex situations deliberately and impartially analyzed, and legislative rules intelligently adapted to a myriad of instances. Only a commission acting under authority appropriately delegated by the legislature could do this job, and only special knowledge, flexibility, disinterestedness, and sound judgment could save the commission from lapsing into a stultifying bureacracy that would not benefit the community but would hurt it.

It was at Elmira in the midst of this fight over the public service commissions that Hughes uttered his most frequently quoted phrase: ". . . the Constitution is what the judges say it is." Through the remainder of his life he was to hear and see this casual phrase, torn from the context of an extemporaneous speech, repeated again and again as if he had, in a moment of candor, exposed the solemn function of judging as a sort of humbuggery. Of course he had done nothing of the sort. "The inference that I was picturing constitutional interpretation by the courts as a matter of judicial caprice," he wrote in his Biographical Notes, ". . . was farthest from my thought. I was not talking flippantly or in disrespect of the courts, but on the contrary with the most profound respect. I was speaking of the essential function of the courts under our system in interpreting and applying constitutional safeguards, and I was emphasizing the importance of maintaining the courts in the highest public esteem as our final judicial arbiters and the inadvisability of needlessly exposing them to criticism and disrespect by throwing upon them the burden of dealing with purely administrative questions." [10]

The inexcusable nature of the distortion to which this segment of his speech has been subjected may be readily seen from the following paragraphs of the text:

I have the highest regard for the courts. My whole life has been spent in work conditioned upon respect for the courts. I reckon him one of the worst enemies of the community who will talk lightly of the dignity of the bench. We are under a Constitution, but the Constitution is what the judges say it is, and the judiciary is the safeguard of our liberty and of our property under the Constitution. I do not want to see any direct assault upon the courts, nor do I want to see any indirect assault upon the courts. And I tell you, ladies and gentlemen, no more insidious assault could be made upon the independence and esteem of the judiciary than to burden it with these questions of administration,—questions which lie close to the public impatience, and in regard to which the people are going to insist on having administration by officers directly accountable to them.

Let us keep the courts for the questions they were intended to consider . . . there will be abundant opportunity for review of everything that should be reviewed.

[10] CEH, Notes, p. 193.

But to say that all these matters of detail which will be brought before the commission,—matters requiring men to give their entire attention to the subject, to get their information in a variety of ways, to have hearings of those interested, and to deal with questions from a practical standpoint,—should, at the option of the corporations, be taken into court, is to make a mockery of your regulation. And, on the other hand, if that policy should succeed, it would swamp your courts with administrative burdens and expose them to the fire of public criticism in connection with matters of this description, from which I hope they will be safeguarded.

The much quoted phrase lacks the deliberate quality usually associated with the Chief-Justice-to-be. But, left in its context, its meaning is unmistakable. So widespread has been the distortion of this phrase, however, that any attempt to restore it to its original meaning suggests Pandora's difficulty in trying to return the ills of life to her box.

The fight for the public service commissions bill took the Governor to many different parts of the state. The joy of combat was aroused in him, and he threw himself into the campaign as if the whole American experiment of government by the people were at stake.

On the fiftieth anniversary of the Buffalo Chamber of Commerce, April 18, 1907, he went to a banquet prepared to eulogize the progress of Buffalo. When the assembled businessmen made it an opposition meeting to the public service commissions bill, however, he put aside his prepared speech and ripped into the contention that the reforms he was championing would wreck legitimate business. The prevailing sentiment of the country, he said, rejoiced in the extension of commerce and the development of industry. It extolled prudence; revered achievement; but it also demanded honesty. "The people . . . have no inclination to hamper industry," he added, "but they are tired of financial jugglery, and they demand proper service."

At Elmira on May 3, Hughes learned from his host, Judge Walter Lloyd Smith, that he was scheduled to speak first at the Chamber of Commerce that night. The privilege of having the last word had been reserved for John B. Stanchfield, prominent up-State lawyer, legislator and former mayor of Elmira. Hughes suspected rigging and asked Judge Smith to have the program altered so that he would speak last. His suspicions were fully confirmed when Stanchfield launched into a slashing attack upon the public service commissions bill, speaking as a citizen "under no retainer from the railroads."

Once more Hughes discarded his prepared speech. "In distinction from my learned friend," he asserted, "I am here under a retainer. I am here retained by the people of the State of New York, to see that justice is done, and with no disposition to injure any investment, but with every desire to give the fullest opportunity to enterprise, and with every purpose to shield and protect every just property interest. I stand for the people of the State of New York against extortion, against favoritism, against financial scandal, and against everything that goes to corrupt our politics by interference with the freedom of our Legislature and administration."

In spite of the country's prosperity, he said, there was a general feeling of discontent. Why? "Will anyone suggest to an intelligent audience that American citizens are in revolt against their own prosperity? What they revolt against," the Governor declared, "is dishonest finance. What they are in rebellion against is favoritism which gives a chance to one man to move his goods and not to another; which gives to one man one set of terms and another set to his rival; which makes one man rich and drives another man into bankruptcy or into combinations with his more successful competitor. It is a revolt against all the influences which have grown out of an unlicensed freedom, and of a failure to recognize that these great privileges, so necessary for public welfare, have been created by the public for the public benefit and not primarily for private advantage."

As he scored point after point, with his profoundly serious and forceful delivery, the applause rose by jumps. The speech attained a power that reverberated throughout the state. Hughes' happy phrase "retained by the people" echoed and reechoed as the battle approached a climax. "People do listen to the fellow," one old-time boss exclaimed with an oath, "and when he sticks his thumbs into his vest pockets and puts his head down, that's the time to watch out!" [11]

The people recognized not only that the Governor was right but also that he was fighting gallantly for their interests without regard for his own political future. A Citizens League was organized to blanket the state with information concerning the Governor's program and the legislative rebellion at Albany. Wave after wave of public sentiment favorable to the Hughes reforms began to roll toward the capital. The Governor's candid communion with the people was bringing results.

After their victory in the Kelsey affair, the legislators rewarded themselves with a week end at home. Instead of congratulations, they encountered a "torrent of reproach." [12] Almost to a man the people said the Governor was right. "When I got home," one senator reported, "the people fairly mobbed me. They took me to task on the street corners and called me up on the telephone in the middle of the night. They said: 'Look here, young man, why aren't you standing with the Governor? Are you tired of political life? You go back to Albany and line up with Hughes, or never dare to ask again for votes in this district.' " [13]

The Capitol was deluged with mail—entreaties, threats, and scathing denun-

[11] Author's interview with John Lord O'Brian, July 25, 1950.
[12] Ida M. Tarbell in *American Magazine*, March, 1908.
[13] *World's Work*, March, 1908, p. 41.

ciations from constituents. The same flood of indignation was reflected in the press. Never within the memory of men had the machine been subjected to such a bombardment from so many sources. Republican bosses who had been laughing at what they called Hughes' "babe-in-the-woods" tactics now turned and ran to cover in almost a panic of submission. Woodruff assembled the Republican State Committee "to demonstrate to the people that the Republican organization is with the Governor." Securing a resolution of unanimous support for the Hughes policies, he rushed to Albany to save the Republican Party from suicide. Senator Raines flip-flopped with astounding dexterity and called a caucus to get his followers on the bandwagon. Speaker Wadsworth also surrendered, and the Assembly passed "the Governor's bill," substantially as it had been introduced, without a dissenting vote. The Senate soon fell into line. Three weeks after Hughes' "appeals to the intellect" began, one journalist observed, "an insolent and hostile legislature was on its knees." [14]

One Assemblyman said that not more than twenty of his colleagues were in favor of allowing the Governor to remove commission members. They voted to give him that power in order to save their necks. Hughes made no bargain with the machine. Armed only with his principles, with public confidence, and the gift of couching his message in terms that galvanized the people, he swept all opposition before him.

Having joined lustily in the fight, the press was delighted by the outcome. "Not since Tilden's day," boasted the *World*, "has New York had a governor who was mentally, morally, professionally and politically capable of carrying out such a policy." [15] James Creelman, writing in *Pearson's Magazine,* pronounced the new Act "the most remarkable and, in its significance, far-reaching law passed by any state in the last quarter of a century, a law that may profoundly affect the whole future of the nation." [16] There was some scattered criticism. But the protests were lost in the avalanche of praise. The Act soon became a model for legislation in other states.

The Governor chose William R. Willcox, former park commissioner and postmaster of New York, to be chairman of the Public Service Commission's metropolitan branch. Other members were Edward M. Bassett, former Democratic member of Congress and traffic expert; Milo R. Maltbie, economist and expert in the utilities field; William McCarroll, merchant; and John E. Eustis, lawyer and experienced public official. When Dr. Schurman turned down the chairmanship of the up-State commission, Hughes named Frank W. Stevens, former Assistant Secretary of the Treasury in Washington. The other members were James E. Sague, engineer and experienced railroad man; Martin S. Decker, who got his training with the Interstate Commerce Commission;

---

[14] Frank H. Simonds in the *Independent,* June 27, 1907, p. 1495.
[15] June 3, 1907.   [16] September, 1907.

Thomas Mott Osborne, businessman and former mayor of Auburn; and Charles Hallam Keep, who had been Hughes' superintendent of banks. Not one of them was a political hack. Only one, Bassett, was a personal friend of Hughes, and he stood out as the best transportation expert available.

Both commissions began their work in the Hughesian tradition, operating without demagogy or outside control. The corporations as well as the consumers were treated fairly, and the previous haughtiness of the interests melted to a spirit of cooperation. It was the beginning of a revolution in the regulation of utilities. Some of the commissions' rulings met with disapproval, but on the whole they functioned efficiently and held the confidence of the people.

While Hughes was working to get the new regulatory system into operation, the legislature passed a bill limiting passenger fares on the railroads of New York State to two cents a mile. He was well aware of the popularity of this measure and of the railroads' past exploitation. Yet he coolly analyzed the bill and vetoed it. The following year a bill forbidding the collection of fares of more than five cents on street railways operating within the limits of a city was to meet the same fate.

No other governor had rejected a two-cent fare bill when confronted by a *fait accompli*. Support of such measures was regarded as the acid test of a governor's loyalty to the people. But Hughes was convinced that public opinion was wrong in this instance and refused to follow it. His reasoning was impeccable. Passage of the bill had not been preceded by a legislative investigation. He did not contend that the two-cent fare would be unreasonably low; it might be high enough in many cases. But the legislature had not attempted to find a proper balance between consumer and corporate interests. It had substituted "unreason for sound judgment . . . a policy seriously mistaken and pregnant with disaster." The Governor insisted that "injustice on the part of railroad corporations toward the public does not justify injustice on the part of the State toward the railroad corporations." [17]

There was, moreover, a better way. The Public Service Commissions now had ample powers to conduct investigations and fix rates in a scientific manner. The Governor insisted that they be allowed an opportunity to do their job free from capricious restrictions.

The two-cent-fare veto brought widespread criticism from those who put immediate relief above principle. But it was hailed by thoughtful commentators for its "statesmanlike quality" and its "soberness and wisdom." Out in Wisconsin Senator Hudnall lauded the courage of the New York Governor and, using Hughes' arguments, defeated a similar two-cent-fare bill that was up before the legislature.[18]

The success of this refreshing renaissance of principle in government brought

[17] *Public Papers, 1907*, p. 89.   [18] *New York Times*, June 16, 1907.

Hughes to nationwide attention. He had suddenly become a giant in public affairs. "In six months," wrote Frank H. Simonds, "the quiet corporation attorney, lacking in political training, destitute of even rudimentary partisan experience, has subjugated a state machine, overthrown a legislative cabal and secured for the people of New York the passage of more progressive legislation than the legislative mills of Albany have ground out in a decade." [19]

More than thirty years later an able and progressive member of the 1907 Assembly, John Lord O'Brian, would still be deeply impressed by the Governor's performance. He wrote:

It is impossible to reproduce for the present generation the aggressive personality, the seemingly inexhaustible energy, the unrelenting insistence of Governor Hughes. It is equally impossible for those who were not eye witnesses to appreciate the dramatic qualities which characterized his efforts, or the overpowering quality of his arguments during those stormy years. . . . Without creating a political faction of his own, he brought to New York State an entirely new kind of political leadership, the effects of which still remain potent. His genius for evoking by personal persuasion the support of popular opinion was as unique as it was successful. The numerous statutes enacted on his insistence present, in themselves, a remarkable record of achievement. But over and above these reforms, it was the force of the man's personality, his genius for masterly exposition and the great confidence of the public in his personal integrity which brought to him the support of the electorate and challenged the attention of the Nation at large.[20]

[19] The *Independent,* June 27, 1907, Vol. 62, p. 1495.
[20] *American Bar Association Journal,* July, 1941, p. 413.

Chapter 20

CRUSADER FOR DEMOCRACY

NOWHERE was Hughes' independence more evident than in the wielding of his veto power. In his first year at Albany he vetoed 297 bills and various items in six appropriation measures. His secretary also estimated that 200 bills were withdrawn because of the Governor's opposition. His firm belief that "our government is one of principle and not of favor" appears to have resulted in the greatest slaughter of special legislation since the days of Cleveland.

One popular measure that went down was a bill to equalize the pay of men and women holding the same positions in the New York City school system. Hughes rejected it because it applied to New York City alone and was an invasion of the powers of the local Board of Education. Another bill designed to force a three-platoon system upon the New York police was vetoed as an encroachment upon home-rule powers. In many instances the Governor wielded his veto to impress upon the legislature the desirability of establishing broad general policies instead of making the law a "patchwork of favoritism."

With the aid of Assemblyman "Al" Smith, Hughes induced the legislature to enact a "clean elections" bill limiting the amounts that candidates for various positions could spend in their campaigns and requiring strict accounting for such expenditures. The Governor's proposed recount of the votes in the McClellan-Hearst mayoralty contest was approved, but the Court of Appeals held the act to be unconstitutional, and a court proceeding under the old law was necessary to lift the cloud of doubt that had hung over McClellan's title and given Hearst a disguise of martyrdom.

Hughes had to call the legislature back into extraordinary session in 1907 to bring about the enactment of a fair bill reapportioning seats in the Senate and Assembly. Subdued by his appeals to the people, the lawmakers also granted the Governor sweeping new power to investigate the organization and conduct of the executive departments and the militia. In one respect this victory seemed to be an extra dividend from his work as a professor of law. At Cornell a student by the name of Sherman Moreland had faithfully stoked Professor Hughes' furnace. Now leader of the Assembly, Moreland was once more disposed to stoke the Hughes furnace. It was he who, at the Governor's request, put through the executive investigations bill, which resulted in numerous probes and enabled Hughes to tie his administration together more securely.

Alert and dynamic though he was, Hughes was caught off guard by the financial panic of 1907. Having transferred Superintendent of Banks Charles H. Keep to the new up-State Public Service Commission, he found it difficult to get the type of man he wanted at the head of the Banking Department for the $7,000 salary the position paid. The post remained vacant for three months. Meanwhile panic was brewing in Wall Street and along with it dissatisfaction over this neglect of the Banking Department. At last Hughes gave the post to Luther Mott of Oswego, son of a Republican state committeeman. Bankers raised their eyebrows in surprise if not dismay. While he was an amiable fellow and had been well recommended, young Mott was inexperienced and proved utterly unequal to the task of nursing the New York banking system through the convulsions that were beginning to shake it.

Within a fortnight Mott went to pieces under the strain. Hughes quickly recognized his mistake and told Mott that he would have to resign.[1] Meanwhile the Governor asked A. Barton Hepburn of the New York Clearing House Committee to name the ablest banker in the state who could be drafted to take over the Banking Department. Hepburn suggested Clark Williams, and under the pressure of the panic Hughes induced Williams to leave the vice presidency of the Columbia Trust Company for this trouble-shooting role at Albany at a small fraction of the salary he had been drawing. Williams took office on October 23, the day after the Knickerbocker Trust Company, with assets of more than $68,000,000, closed its doors following a frantic run by depositors.

A strong and alert banking department might have averted the crisis or at least mitigated its effects. Undoubtedly the Governor had not lived up to his reputation for forehand action. But he quickly recovered his fumble, and induced the banks to cooperate in averting further disaster. Then he named an unpaid commission consisting of Hepburn and five other leading bankers to investigate the causes of the panic and suggest how the state banking laws should be changed to avoid similar emergencies in the future. On the basis of the experts' findings he sponsored bills enlarging the powers of the superintendent of banks, curbing speculation, protecting depositors, and subjecting trust companies that were doing a banking business to the regulations applicable to banks.

The Governor named another group of experts headed by Horace White to delve into the whole broad question of speculation in a free economy and the proper relation of the state to it. While the committee's report was largely devoted to explanation of the economic function performed by the stock and

[1] Author's interview with CEH, Oct. 29, 1947.

commodity markets, it urged that promoters be punished for false statements about securities offered for sale to the public. This idea was to find expression in the federal Securities and Exchange Act a quarter of a century later.

Labor legislation became a specialty of the Hughes régime. John Williams, a practical carpenter, was made state labor commissioner and given the assignment of rescuing the Labor Department from the grip of machine politics. With his aid, Hughes put through a safety measure for railway engineers and firemen, a prohibition against working train-service men more than sixteen consecutive hours, and an eight-hour-day law for railway telegraph and telephone operators and signalmen. Child-labor laws were strengthened and extended, and the working hours of women were limited. Inspection of factories, mines, and tunnels was tightened up; new safeguards to health were established; employees' rights in the courts were more clearly defined, and all New York children were guaranteed an education, with special emphasis on industrial training.

Alarmed by the terrible waste of life and limb in industrial accidents, Hughes named a committee under the chairmanship of Senator Wainwright to devise a new approach to the problem. Industrial America was killing and injuring more workmen in proportion to the number employed than any other country in the world. And the cost of these tragedies was falling largely on the families of the unfortunate workmen themselves. Employers thus had no economic incentive to make their mines, factories, and railroads safe. When the committee brought in its report, the Governor secured the enactment of the first workmen's compensation laws in the United States. One of these provided for an elective compensation plan; the other made compensation for injuries compulsory in certain hazardous industries.

Part of this good work was undone when the New York Court of Appeals upset the compulsory statute as a violation of due process of law.[2] In 1913, however, New York corrected its Court of Appeals by constitutional amendment. That broke the backbone of resistance to industrial insurance. By 1916 thirty-two states had workmen's compensation laws—a belated but nonetheless significant tribute to Hughes' pioneering in this field.

By the end of his second term Hughes' name was on fifty-six statutes for the benefit of labor, "including many of the best labor laws ever enacted in this or any other state." "Now, that Gov. Hughes has retired from politics . . ." commented the *Legislative News,* union labor organ in New York, "the fact can be acknowledged, without hurting anybody's political corns, that he was the greatest friend of labor laws that ever occupied the Governor's chair at Albany."[3]

[2] *Ives* v. *South Buffalo Ry. Co.,* 201 N.Y. 271, 317.
[3] *Legislative News,* October, 1910.

New social legislation and improved state service were largely responsible for the increase in New York State expenditures from $26,978,928 in 1906 to $39,601,224 in 1910. Using his item veto, the Governor stripped appropriation bills of graft and waste but encouraged spending for what he regarded as essential institutions and public functions.

The conservation of forests, water, and natural scenery was a vital concern of the Hughes régime. The guiding principle that the Governor laid down was that "these resources should be preserved and held for the benefit of all the people and should not be surrendered to private interests." [4]

Disregarding the Governor's advice, the legislature granted a charter to the Long Sault Development Company authorizing the construction of dams in a section of the St. Lawrence River, with perpetual rights to the water power thus created. The lawmakers asked nothing in return for this favor. Donation of public rights for private benefit was still the order of the day. But Hughes rebelled. When the innocent-looking bill reached his desk, he sent for Superintendent of Public Works Stevens and asked him to determine how much power the project would generate, what return it would give the company, and what would be a fair amount for the company to pay the state for the rights granted in the charter. Stevens secured the aid of one of the best engineers in the country. When their report reached the Governor, he called in the sponsors of the charter bill and told them it would have to be rewritten so as to require an immediate payment to the state of $100,000 and annual rental charges thereafter. At last an effective blow had been struck at the profligate policy of giving away the state's natural resources. Although the Long Sault charter was later repealed because the company claimed the rights it had obtained were perpetual, the importance of the precedent it had set remained.

President Roosevelt gave the conservation movement great impetus in May, 1908, by assembling a conference of governors at the White House. One of the highlights of the gathering was a speech by Governor Hughes in which he declared that New York was allowing 550,000 horse power of energy worth $6,600,000 to run to waste each year because the state had failed to develop a comprehensive plan for its utilization. Experts were then at work on the problem, but it was not until 1910 that sufficient data had been assembled to permit the formulation of an intelligent water power policy looking toward systematic development of New York's larger rivers.

On the basis of the Water Supply Commission's reports Hughes asked the legislature to accept the following principles as a guide to future action: (1) River flow should be regulated and water power developed "to the fullest extent that may be practicable." (2) Only the state should build and own regulatory or power-generating reservoirs on streams originating in or flow-

4 *Public Papers, 1907*, p. 37.

ing through public parks or state reservations. (3) Hydroelectric power projects should be undertaken by the state "whenever such action appears to be feasible and for the general interest." (4) Power so developed should be made available on "equitable terms and conditions." (5) Rigid scrutiny should be provided to see that the public interest in the state forest preserves would not be jeopardized by water-power projects.[5]

Hughes had no opportunity to carry this forward-looking policy into effect. But it may well have influenced a young legislator who was just then entering the New York Senate and who would later have much to do with the public development of water-power resources both at Albany and Washington—Franklin D. Roosevelt. In his last years at Albany, Hughes also pleaded for larger purchases of land in the areas of the Adirondack and Catskill Parks. And a gift to the state of ten thousand acres of land in the Hudson highlands of Orange and Rockland Counties by Mrs. E. H. Harriman (in addition to large monetary gifts from Mrs. Harriman, John D. Rockefeller, J. Pierpont Morgan and others) made it possible for Hughes to send to the legislature a $5,000,000 project for extension of Palisades Park. This was one aspect of his work as governor that brought much satisfaction.

Hughes took advantage of the summer, when the legislature was not in session, to visit the state institutions and county fairs and to talk with the people. Everywhere he was greeted enthusiastically; the fairs especially gave him rousing receptions. His finger was close to the public pulse. The result was to solidify his strength at the grass roots in preparation for the new tests that awaited him at Albany.

Wherever he went he preached the doctrine of good government or his philosophy of the good life. A powerful current of optimism ran through all his speeches. At no time did he yield to the "destroying cancer of cynicism." To him the United States was a land of unparalleled prosperity and future promise. No country had ever enjoyed a "larger degree of equal rights and equal opportunities." To be sure, rapacity and corruption had attained unconscionable proportions, but this could be attributed in part to the newness of the country—to the rawness resulting from sudden exploitation of a rich continent. More important was the fact that the people were rising to curb rapacity.

Young America was also confidently moving toward a larger degree of stability. "By stability," he said, "is not meant fixity of things or relations, but steadiness. It may be steadiness in motion. Paradoxical as it may seem, human society cannot be stable unless it is progressive. That is because growth and progress are the law of our nature." [6] In his lectures at Yale University he

<hr>

[5] *Public Papers, 1910,* pp. 22–25.
[6] *Addresses 1906–1916,* p. 247. Copyright, 1916, by G. P. Putnam's Sons.

added: "The peril of this nation is not in any foreign foe! We, the people, are its power, its peril, and its hope." [7]

"Under certain forms of government," he said, "stability has been maintained by force exercised for the benefit of a privileged few. . . . In a democracy stability depends upon the reign of reason, and it is the fact that we are a common-sense people that gives us assurance for the future. Reason demands the facts . . . not scrappy sensationalism or distorted emphasis" and open conduct of public affairs that will give the people "the truth, the whole truth and nothing but the truth in regard to matters that concern them."

Good administration, he contended, required a concentration of executive powers in the hands of the governor. Hughes was not, however, reaching out promiscuously for more power. When county delegations came to him and urged that the state take over local functions because of the difficulty of getting local boards to act, he would reply: "My friends, that means that you have no confidence in free institutions . . . the first principle of administration is to keep things in connection with local government locally administered so far as possible. . . . It is the greatest mistake in the world to run to Albany to hold the men whom you elect accountable for the discharge of their duties when you can tend to the matter at home." [8]

Nor was he jealous of the Federal Government's expanding powers. The people had many interests beyond the reach of state authority. The future distribution of governmental powers would be determined, he said, "not by sentiment nor by repetition of arguments regarding the original sovereignty of the states, but will result from considerations of paramount public advantage. If it should appear that the powers of the States are inadequate to deal with a subject hitherto retained in their keeping, and that the interests of the people as a whole imperatively demand the assumption of a power by the Federal Government, the people will provide the assumption of that power." [9]

"The people . . . have reached the conclusion," he added on Washington's birthday at the University of Michigan, "that there should be no limit to the exercise of federal power in connection with interstate commerce short of absolutely securing the people in the freedom of that commerce, and of putting an end to the discrimination and unlawful preferences which have afflicted interstate commerce in the past." It is interesting to note that this concept as to the breadth of the power of Congress to control business reaching across state lines—a concept that was later to be written into many of Hughes' opinions as a judge—was well rooted in his mind even while he was wrestling with state problems and might have been assumed to be partial to states' rights. His sojourn at Albany had not upset his objectivity.

[7] *Conditions of Progress in Democratic Government*, p. 8.
[8] *Addresses 1906–1916*, pp. 219–221.   [9] New York *Sun*, Feb. 13, 1907.

Apostle of hard work though he was, Hughes took delight in spreading "the gospel of play." "The successful worker," he said, "must have the spirit of play in his heart, and the successful man is only a boy with a man's experience. He must have the zest, the devotion, the spirit of comradeship, the capacity for self-forgetfulness, the boy's wholesome outlook upon life, if he is to do a man's work in the world." [10] His address on "Why We Want Playgrounds" was reprinted many times and thirty-nine years after the speech was made the National Recreation Association was still expressing its sense of indebtedness to Hughes.

In lifting up the people, he discarded racial distinctions. The Negro, he said,

is entitled to the advantages of training and education. He is entitled, under the stimulus of free institutions, to an opportunity to prove by his works what is in him and to make his contribution, according to his talent and aptitude, to the sum of our productive labors and of our national life; and he is entitled to the rewards which his character and industry may deserve. There is no color line in good work, whether of hand or brain. . . . It has well been said that whatever problem the progress of the Negro may present, it is not comparable with that which will be presented by stagnation or retrogression. In this land the door of opportunity must be wide open to our citizens. We want neither slaves nor serfs, nor any body of citizens permanently below the standards which must be maintained for the preservation of the Republic. We cannot maintain our democratic ideals as to one set of our people and ignore them as to others. [11]

Democracy, he thought, should secure to every man an opportunity "to make the most of himself." But it also demanded that "no man should construe his opportunity to mean license to exploit his fellow men and unjustly profit himself at the expense of their equal chance. The cry 'Every man for himself' is out of date," the Governor exclaimed. "The demand of the future will be 'Every man for the people!' " [12]

"If the term Bolshevik had been invented then," said Oswald Garrison Villard some years later, "the business community would have applied it to Charles E. Hughes." [13] Yet there was nothing revolutionary in his program. "It is not our part to plan an ambitious scheme for the reconstruction of society," he said. "Our immediate duty is more practical than that. It is to obtain from our existing institutions that full measure of freedom of political action and of equality of opportunity which they were intended and are able to confer." [14]

What Hughes preached night after night and week after week was the more

[10] Address to the Recreation Congress, 1908.
[11] Speech in behalf of Tuskegee Institute, Jan. 17, 1908.
[12] *Addresses 1906–1916*, p. 270.
[13] *Prophets True and False*, p. 38. Copyright, 1928, by Alfred A. Knopf, Inc.
[14] *Utica Press*, Dec. 14, 1906.

effective because he practiced it by day. He became not merely the evangelist of democracy but also the practitioner who employed its principles to produce far-reaching social improvements. Aware of the unrest that permeated the nation, he held unwaveringly to the conviction that that unrest could be cured by courageous leadership and faithful application of the representative principle. Ida M. Tarbell caught the gist of what he was trying to do when she wrote: "Charles E. Hughes is engaged in a passionate effort to vindicate the American system of government." [15]

[15] *American Magazine,* March, 1908, p. 464.

Chapter 21

MAN BEHIND THE WHISKERS

INSIDE the Executive Mansion the Hughes household was managed primarily for the Governor's convenience. Antoinette Carter Hughes presided there with the same natural poise that had always endeared her to husband, children, friends, and servants. But there was a new light in her eye. Her unwavering faith in her husband had been vindicated. He was well launched upon what she knew in her bones would be a great career. Within her own realm of activity she bent every effort to smoothing his way.

No craving for the spotlight actuated her avid interest in his career. She was the antithesis of a social climber. In 1906 she had refused to let her picture be published until after the election, and she assumed her new station as the first lady of New York without a trace of hauteur. Her freedom from pretense even went to the extreme of admitting that she was forty-two. But her ambition to see her husband succeed in whatever he undertook was boundless. She never permitted the children to break in on him or create a disturbance when he was at work. Knowing his excitable nature and his keen sensitivity to his surroundings, she shielded him in a hundred ways without any suggestion from him and in many instances without his knowledge.

The family routine was a reflection of the Hugheses' orderly habits and their love of privacy. Breakfast was always served at precisely the same hour with all members of the family present. Mrs. Hughes invariably came down-stairs dressed as if she were going out for the day. The Governor, too, was always fully dressed for the office before he left his room. At bedtime a cordial "Good night" went the rounds, and when their door was closed it remained closed for the night. None of the children thought of intruding or even knocking until father and mother appeared the next morning.

Yet there was neither stiffness nor stuffiness in their family relationships. Both parents set great store upon their offspring. Mrs. Hughes had come to Albany, as she had gone to Ithaca, expecting a baby. On August 19, 1907, she had the distinction of bringing into the world the first child (Elizabeth) ever born in the Executive Mansion. The event seemed to demonstrate the primacy of her conjugal and maternal interests. She was immensely pleased to be the mother of four children. Young Charlie would be a junior when he returned to Brown University in the fall. Helen and Catherine ("Caca" within the family after her baby sister began to talk) were going to the Albany Girls Academy. The Hugheses were so sufficient unto themselves and so wrapped up in their own activities that they felt little need for intimate friendships outside the family circle.

The comfortable old Executive Mansion on Eagle Street often resounded with merriment. Sometimes, to be sure, Hughes would come home with a Sisyphean burden on his mind and sit through a meal scarcely uttering a word. Sometimes he would unloose a flow of serious talk as if to relieve accumulated pressures. But more often his humor would bubble up through whatever responsibility he carried. One story that brought gales of laughter was a garbled newspaper account of a speech the Governor had made during one of his fights with the bosses. He had characterized them as "petty satraps" but was solemnly quoted as calling them "petty rat traps."

In the bosom of the family he remained a persistent funmaker. He had a habit of winking at his daughters with a meaningful twinkle in his eye and of waving at them with a congenial wagging of the fingers. His reputation for austerity in official life did not restrain him from causing a riot at home by mimicking a cat, lion, or monkey. A stern and uncompromising governor he might be, but to his children he was still a warm, human, and companionable father and the funniest man they had ever known.[1] A visitor privileged to look in upon his antics would have accepted quite literally a comment he once made to a group of school children to the effect that "while men grow to look old . . . every man is a boy in his heart, and he finds it difficult as he grows older to understand why other people do not take him that way." [2]

Contributing also to the homely atmosphere of the Mansion was Mrs. Hughes' canary and the children's mongrel bull terrier named Petie. Hughes had a fondness for animals and was even tolerant of the duck that had been given to the children when they visited the Home for Incurables. Cats won his special favor, and it was not unusual for him to sit down to read with a kitten on his shoulder.

Except during brief vacations, the Governor had no time to take the children on fun-seeking expeditions, as he had done in New York. Their principal playmates were the orphans of St. Joseph's Catholic Home, which adjoined the back yard of the Executive Mansion. Mrs. Hughes had groups of these children over several times a year for games, cake, and ice cream.

In spite of their self-sufficiency, the Hugheses did not neglect the social amenities. Mrs. Hughes readily adjusted her thinking from the small and simple dinner parties that she had given in New York and Ithaca to the large

[1] Author's interview with Catherine Hughes Waddell, June 16, 1948.
[2] Washington's birthday speech in Chicago, 1908.

official receptions that were expected of her in Albany. Her first step was to replenish her wardrobe. She loved beautiful clothes and had always dressed well but in keeping with the needs of the occasion. Now she felt that some elegant gowns would be appropriate and did not hesitate to buy them. Hughes watched approvingly the transformation that was effected by her bright red dress, her canary yellow dress, and the others. But he could not refrain from teasing. "Now, my dear," he would say, "what you need is jewels."

Even during her pregnancy Mrs. Hughes gave two large receptions, in honor of the legislators and the judges, sending out more than 2,500 invitations for each. After her child was born, she made a practice of receiving the ladies of Albany almost every week during the social season. These were memorable occasions. The tall, slender hostess, looking beautiful in her new canary yellow or bright red dress, won the hearts of her guests by cordial greetings, by her intriguing combination of vivacity and dignity, and by her democratic practice of widely distributing the honor of acting as co-hostess. Music by the National Guard band ensconced on the stairway added an official touch. But a homelike atmosphere prevailed when the infant Elizabeth was brought down and invariably screamed instead of cooing for the guests. Helen and Catherine played a part no less domestic but much less conspicuous. It was their task to keep Petie, the bull terrier, in a back room and prevent him from barking, which seemed to necessitate continuous throwing of horse chestnuts for him to chase around the room.

The Hugheses frequently accepted dinner invitations and returned the compliments with dinners at the Executive Mansion. Mrs. Hughes was "queenly and gracious" on such occasions but left most of the talking to others. Seldom did she enter a discussion of public affairs even with her husband. Usually the Governor dominated the conversation regardless of who the guests might be. His dynamism, his impressive manner of speaking, and his good memory combined to give him the center of the stage.

In their four years at Albany the Governor and Mrs. Hughes met and worked with all kinds of people. In many instances there came to be a mutual exchange of high regard and affection. Yet these relations stopped short of intimate friendship. Mrs. Hughes' natural reserve kept friendships on an impersonal basis. She would freeze up in a moment if she thought a visitor was trying to pry into her personal affairs. As for the Governor, personal friendships were less important to him than his work, which absorbed most of the time that other men gave to casual friendly intercourse. And he felt no need to seek personal understanding, sympathy, or solace outside his home. If the events of the day caused him to boil inside, the woman he loved was at hand to soothe his troubled spirit. Sometimes, to be sure, she chided him for trying to do too much, saying that he carried the burdens of office along with him.

But she never nagged him and never sought to restrain him from doing anything she knew he wished to do or believed it his duty to do.

To the bosses, Hughes was still a formidable figure, and many were afraid of him. His extraordinary self-containment and the absence of political intermediaries in the executive chamber encouraged the belief that he was cold and aloof. To the Albany crowd he was "Charles the Baptist" or "Whiskers" —but only behind his back. His secretary confirmed the fact that no one ever slapped the Governor on the shoulder and called him "Charlie." Among those who worked with him, however, he inspired an astonishing degree of loyalty that cannot be explained as devotion to the principles he espoused. One editor concluded that, so far from being an icicle, Hughes had become "a remarkable example of the live, glowing wire." [3]

Traveling from western New York one night with Colonel Treadwell and John Palmer Gavit, the Governor discovered that only one berth had been reserved on the sleeper for his party. Gavit and Treadwell insisted that he should take it. His rest, they said, was of public importance. Hughes laughed and insisted on sharing the inconvenience. Through most of the night they exchanged stories and, according to Gavit, had "a jolly time." It was after this experience that Gavit described Hughes as "phenomenally clear-headed, single-minded . . . inconceivably industrious, absolutely fearless . . . but humanly approachable and friendly, good natured, reasonable, jovial—and on the level with his job." [4]

The Governor took a party of Civil War Veterans and state officials to Gettysburg in September, 1907, to dedicate the Greene Monument on Culp's Hill. General Alexander S. Webb, who had commanded the New York troops at the Bloody Angle, and General Sickles, who had lost a leg at Gettysburg, gave them a memorable account of the battle that saved the Union. In the evening, as Hughes' brilliantly lighted car lay in the railroad yards, he entertained a group of his guests with stories. When he repeated the tale of his son's eerie ascent of the Strasbourg cathedral spire, he danced about, gesticulating excitedly, throwing all his energy into the drama of the story. Then suddenly he caught a glimpse of the large crowd of spectators who had gathered outside to see the show, although they could hear nothing of what he was saying. For a moment Hughes had the look of a dignitary who had been caught clowning, but he joined in the general laughter at his expense.

"That comes of drinking three cups of tea at dinner," he said. "I shall never again be able to tell that story without chills of the spine." [5]

At the Jamestown Exposition of 1907, Governor Hughes first met the man whom he was later to challenge for leadership of the nation. Woodrow Wilson

---

[3] *Kansas City Times,* Oct. 28, 1908.
[4] New York *Evening Post,* June 10, 1916.   [5] *Ibid.*

was then the suave, learned, and conservative president of Princeton University. He had been invited, along with the Governor of New York, to address the descendants of the signers of the Declaration of Independence on July 4. Both were breakfast guests of Henry St. George Tucker in Norfolk before going to the exposition grounds. Later they accompanied General Frederick Grant to Old Point Comfort, reviewed the fleet, and watched the fireworks. It was a full day they spent together as members of an eminent group of officials and dignitaries. Hughes found Mr. Wilson "a most charming conversationalist" and reported that he had "a thoroughly enjoyable time." [6]

Wilson's enjoyment of the occasion seems to have been less pronounced, at least when the formal speaking began. On several visits to New York, Wilson had spoken disparagingly of Hughes' reforms. The courts, he insisted, could do more purifying than the "new instrumentalities [Hughes' regulatory commissions] now being unthinkingly elaborated." His scorn for regulatory commissions was as well defined as his contempt for Bryanism and for Theodore Roosevelt's assault on big business. At Jamestown, after listening to Hughes' speech, Wilson altered the entire plan of his own address. [7]

Intellectual fencing gave way to less weighty matters, however, at the Tucker house. One of Mr. Wilson's sallies brought an expression of surprise from a guest who said she thought the president of Princeton had to be a clergyman. Wilson replied that others had had that erroneous notion and that the university, he feared, had lost a large gift because he had given some offense in repeating a favorite limerick in the presence of an old Presbyterian lady. The amused guests demanded the limerick, and Wilson responded as follows:

> There was a young monk of Siberia
> Whose life grew drearier and drearier,
>   So he burst from his cell
>   With a hell of a yell
> And eloped with the Mother Superior.

In later years, when the once conservative university president surprised the country with the liberal measures he promoted as Governor of New Jersey, Hughes thought Mr. Wilson's limerick might be taken, in a figurative sense, to be autobiographical. [8]

Hughes' yearning for the wilds had to be restrained in the years of his governorship. The family remained in the Executive Mansion all summer in 1907, when daughter Elizabeth was born, and the Governor had only a few days of fishing and tramping with his son in the Adirondack woods, using a forester's camp for their headquarters. In the following two summers the family took

[6] CEH, Notes, p. 201.   [7] New York *World*, Jan. 6, 1908.
[8] CEH, Notes, pp. 201–202.

a cottage at Saranac Inn, which became in effect a summer executive office. Hughes spent most of his time there dictating letters, making appointments, granting extraditions, ordering investigations, and replying to appeals for aid.

In the summer of 1908 he broke away for a brief walking trip with his son and the latter's college chum. From Lake Placid they tramped through the Indian Pass to the Tawahus Club, fished in Lake Colden, and climbed to the top of Mount Marcy. At forty-six he still had an urge to climb every mountain in sight. At the summit they encountered a party of young people, and one of the girls pampered the Governor with a generous offering of huckleberries. In return he gave the party a beefsteak and some tea. At the great campaign meeting in Madison Square Garden that fall, as Hughes was being ushered through the crowd to the speaker's stand, a young woman thrust out her hand and gave him a card. While waiting for the audience to quiet down, he read the card: "Good luck! We ate your steak and drank your health in the tea." [9]

The Governor found some opportunities for reading. While waiting for the balky legislature to act on his measures in 1907, he read six of Dumas' swashbuckling novels. "If the session keeps up much longer," he told one interviewer, "I'll have to begin on Gaboriau." Sometimes he read Ibsen and Henry James. But Ibsen tried to make life too dismal, and Hughes was never persuaded that life was as complex as "Henry James has almost persuaded us that it is." [10] Hardy distorted his characters. Shaw was not to be taken seriously. As an escape from tension, Hughes came to like "blood-and-thunder romance" better than any other type of literature. There is nothing like a good thriller or detective story for a weary brain and a tired back, he said, nothing like it in the world.

His work habits were even more extreme than they had been in his practice of law. He arrived at the executive chamber as soon as the mail was ready. His office received from forty to four hundred letters a day. Usually he ate lunch at his desk in the Capitol—merely a sandwich, an apple, and tea. While eating he listened to complaints or advice from visitors and then resumed his work until six or seven in the evening. When he carried work home —a frequent occurrence—it was not unusual for him to keep at it until midnight or even 2:00 A.M.

There was neither showmanship nor masochism in this performance. Hughes felt that he must handle every problem that called for exercise of the gubernatorial judgment, and he had to have the facts to go on. "No duty was ever too small to receive the closest attention," his secretary tells us, and no obligation was ever so great as to cause him to shrink from its performance.[11] "His

[9] CEH, Notes, p. 205.   [10] *Current Literature*, February, 1906, pp. 207–210.
[11] MS by Robert H. Fuller, Hughes Papers, Library of Congress.

work literally takes possession of him," said Dr. Schurman. "It is consequently impossible for him to do anything he undertakes in a half-hearted or slipshod manner." [12]

New challenges repeatedly reenergized his powers. So far as it was humanly possible, Hughes insisted on finding not merely an answer to each problem but the right answer. Every issue had to be weighed with the deliberation of a judge; then the Governor sat in judgment on his decisions. He had a rare ability to survey even his own work and conclusions with objectivity.

Given his generous measure of common sense, his methods narrowed the margin in which errors were likely to be made. And he had learned as a young man to correct his discoverable errors promptly instead of capitalizing them as precedents for future action. In New York and over an expanding area beyond, therefore, few were disposed to challenge Frederick Boyd Stevenson when he declared, "Hughes is unlike any other man who ever held public office." [13]

[12] Introduction to Hughes' *Addresses 1906–1916*, p. lv.
[13] *Harper's Weekly*, May 9, 1908.

Chapter 22

FIGHT WITH THE GAMBLERS

THE NEW YORK legislature reassembled in January, 1908, with blood in its eye. Now fully conscious of the Governor's power, the lawmakers were nevertheless emboldened by the prospect that his stay in Albany might be short. It seemed improbable that he would seek renomination or that the organization would ever renominate him if he did. Stiff opposition to his policies thus appeared to be a fair gamble.

As for the Governor, he drove straight ahead toward the reforms he believed to be necessary and desirable. He asked for new banking laws; for extension of the public service commissions law to cover telephone and telegraph companies; for a simplified ballot; for a direct-primaries act; for classification of salaries in the state institutions; for several labor and conservation measures and a pure food law. It was a sweeping program that was about as palatable to the Old Guard as earthworm soup.

Nor was the Governor willing to let sleeping dogs lie. After the Senate had refused to remove Otto Kelsey in 1907, charges were filed against him and Hughes appointed Matthew C. Fleming, his assistant in the insurance investigation, to look into the affairs of the Insurance Department. Fleming brought in a report that showed some improvement but also continuation of gross irregularities and inefficiency in Kelsey's organization. Hughes sent the report to the Senate in February along with a stiff message again demanding the removal of Kelsey. "The work of the department," he insisted, "had been a travesty on State supervision." [1] Two weeks later the Senate lashed out with a negative reply—thirty votes to nineteen.

In areas where the Senate's voice was not controlling, the Governor's housecleaning was going forward. Charges of gross negligence had been brought in 1907 against John F. Ahearn, president of the Borough of Manhattan. There was no showing that Ahearn was personally corrupt. The question was whether the Governor could remove a local official for shocking neglect of the streets and flagrant mismanagement of the borough's affairs. Seeing that the case would become a precedent, Hughes presided in person at a hearing, took voluminous evidence, and listened to legal arguments. Ahearn said he wished to thank the Governor for his fair examination regardless of what his decision

[1] *Public Papers, 1908*, p. 179.

might be. But neither his courtesy nor his honesty saved him. Hughes sustained the right of the Governor to act in such cases, and, finding the charges of inexcusable dereliction proved, he removed the borough president.

Similarly he removed Louis F. Haffen, president of the Borough of the Bronx, and Joseph Bermel, president of the Borough of Queens, resigned when summoned by the Governor to face his accusers. Charges were brought against numerous other local officials, including William Travers Jerome, district attorney for New York County. In each case Hughes ordered a thorough investigation and let the evidence dictate his action. Jerome and many others survived this scrutiny, but enough official heads toppled to indicate that New York was an unsafe place for faithlessness and inefficiency in office—enough also to keep the bosses in a state of continuous irritation.

The most dramatic fight of the year came over enforcement of the constitutional mandate against gambling. Hughes gave this issue only casual attention in his message. Following his suggestion, Senator Agnew and Assemblyman Hart introduced a bill for repeal of the Percy-Gray law, under which race-track gambling flourished, but the Governor did not then see it as a cause of major combat. He was not opposed to horse racing and did not take a puritanical attitude toward betting. It was only when bookmaking at the races loomed up as a crass and deliberate violation of the state constitution and when torrential opposition to any change in that special license swept in upon Albany that Hughes' fighting blood was aroused. Then the gray shading disappeared; it became a struggle between right and wrong with Hughes passionately determined to win.

Heavy pressure came from both sides. As letters from the people poured into the executive office, the Governor was made poignantly aware of the relation of gambling to poverty and crime. The politically powerful agricultural societies got little comfort, therefore, when they sent a delegation to the Governor to complain that the Agnew-Hart bill would deprive them of certain benefits obtained from the race tracks. Hughes told them that they knew in their hearts he was right. "The test of respect for law," he said, "is where . . . it is upheld in its majesty even though it hurts."

As the contest began to warm up, the Governor's life was threatened. This was followed by threats to kidnap his baby daughter. Another letter reported that the gambling lobby was preparing to hand out $200,000 in bribes to legislators in order to defeat the bill. The furious Assembly passed a resolution requesting that this letter and any similar communications received by the Governor be turned over to it. Hughes refused to comply. Transmission of the letter could serve no purpose, he said, except, perhaps, to expose the author to revenge.

Opponents of the bill had hoped to place him in the position of antagonizing the Assembly by seeming to endorse the bribery charge. Instead of falling into their trap, Hughes declared, probably with tongue in cheek, that he had "implicit confidence" that the legislature would do its duty—that it would "purge our State of this source of misery and vice which exists only because the will of the people, flatly declared in the fundamental law, has not been carried into effect." [2]

Because of indifferent application of the old laws against gambling the people had written into the constitution of 1894, as amended in 1895, an absolute prohibition against "any lottery, the sale of lottery tickets, pool-selling, bookmaking or any other kind of gambling." They had directed the legislature, using the word "shall," to pass appropriate legislation to effectuate this policy. The legislature had pretended to do so in the Percy-Gray Act, but actually it provided that if no token of racetrack wagers were delivered the only penalty for such gambling would be a civil suit for recovery of losses. This made a mockery of the constitution.

"We either have constitutional government or we do not have it," the Governor told an audience of businessmen. ". . . If it is an easy thing to override the Constitution in order to protect gamblers, some day it will be an easy thing to override the Constitution in its protection of property." [3]

The Agnew-Hart bill passed the Assembly by an overwhelming vote but provoked a hurricane of opposition in the Senate. What at first had appeared to be a majority for the bill began to fade before the onslaught of the racing interests. Bitterness permeated the debate. Mrs. Hughes, who had been listening in the Senate gallery, left before the acrimony reached a climax. Senator Grady, hatchetman in the Hearst-Murphy deal of 1906, assailed the Governor as "a whited sepulchre," and others accused him of deceiving the people. "The name of Governor Hughes will be remembered as a synonym for honesty," Senator Armstrong retorted prophetically, "long after the name of every man occupying a seat in this chamber has been forgotten." [4]

Lobbyists swarmed through the corridors. The press accused them of using money lavishly. Fake letters purporting to be from constituents cluttered the mail of senators. One legislator's investigation showed only four out of one hundred letters written to him in opposition to the bill were genuine.

Boss Barnes tried openly to subvert the legislative will. Both Barnes and Senator Grattan of Albany had assured Senator Agnew that Grattan would vote for the bill. Then Barnes changed his mind, summoned Grattan out of a committee meeting, and brutally ordered him to vote the other way. When Senator Agnew protested and told Barnes that an open switch would disgrace him before the community, Barnes replied that his antagonism toward Hughes

[2] *Ibid.,* p. 39.
[3] Speech to Northside Board of Trade, Bronx, New York, March 5, 1908.
[4] *New York Times,* April 9, 1908.

overcame every other consideration.[5] Grattan's humiliating conformity to his master's demands was openly flaunted in brazen defiance of Hughes' own scrupulous methods.

Senator Knapp also switched his vote overnight, and only the alertness of the sergeant at arms of the Senate saved the antigambling forces from losing Senator Fancher at the crucial moment. The night before the vote was to be taken, Fancher was lured to a residence in Albany by a telephone message to the effect that some friends had a little surprise in store for him. What the surprise turned out to be was not disclosed, but the senator was found asleep at the rendezvous at noon the next day with his watch turned back to indicate that it was only nine o'clock. Located by tracing the telephone number that had been left for him the previous day, he reached the Senate in time to vote but could not stem the tide. The Agnew-Hart bill went down by a tie vote of twenty-five to twenty-five.

On April 23 the legislature adjourned in open defiance of the Governor. Once more a wave of anger swept over the state, leaving a heavy deposit of letters in Hughes' office. The press, even the Hearst papers, gave him strong encouragement to continue the fight. Indignation meetings were held all over the state. Churches turned out dozens of resolutions. The City Club of New York, the International Reform Bureau, the Brooklyn League, and a special Anti-Race-Track-Gambling Committee joined in the crusade. Aid came also from such men as Haley Fiske, Henry L. Stimson, Horace White, Andrew Carnegie, Jacob Gould Schurman, Seth Low, Judge Thompkins, Oswald Garrison Villard, Spencer Trask, Charles S. Whitman, Louis Wiley of the *New York Times*, former Ambassador Stewart L. Woodford, and Edward B. Whitney. Some felt that Hughes' fight was "toughening the moral fiber of the whole country." A. B. Humphrey wired: "Looks like you are deserted by everybody except God Almighty and The People." [6]

One of the Governor's strong supporters, Thomas P. Peters, editor of the Brooklyn *Daily Times*, tried to induce him not to risk calling a special session. Another defeat, he feared, would seriously jeopardize Hughes' chance for renomination.[7] Some of his ablest political associates gave similar advice. But the Governor had the bit between his teeth. Two days after the Senate had defeated the Agnew-Hart bill, he ordered a special election in the Niagara-Orleans district where the death of Senator Stanislaus P. Franchot had left a vacancy. On the very day of the legislature's adjournment he signed a proclamation calling it back into extraordinary session on May 11, the day before the special election was to be held.

Throughout the long fight Hughes kept up a drumfire of speeches. The

[5] Agnew to James Fenimore Cooper, April 22, 1908, Agnew Papers, New York Public Library.
[6] April 24, 1908.   [7] Peters to CEH, April 22, 1908.

racing interests attempted to seize the initiative by denouncing him for trying to coerce the legislature. "Since when," he retorted, "did those who profit by gambling privileges become the guardians of the honor and independence of the Legislature? . . . I have used no weapon but that of reason. I have exercised no prerogative but that of recommendation and argument." [8] If there were any coercion in what he had done, it was the coercion of presenting to New York citizens a cogent array of facts which influenced their judgment and stirred their conscience.

Hughes bore down with special relish on Boss Barnes' perversion of representative government. "What a humiliation it is for a community," he exclaimed, "and what an abuse of leadership, when any man is able to say that he assumes responsibility for the vote of a Senator . . . no party leader has a right to assume the role of dictator, or so to violate the manhood of elected officials as to parade them before the people as subject to his domination." [9] Nothing less than representative government was on trial, and Hughes insisted that it be vindicated.

Then, taking his political life in his hands, the Governor went on a stumping tour of the Niagara-Orleans district in behalf of William C. Wallace, whose sole distinction was his pro-Hughes stand in the antigambling fight. The racing interests flushed the district with campaign money in behalf of the Democratic candidate, and some votes were bought on election day in spite of the private detectives hired to check corruption.[10] Hughes had no campaign fund, and the Republican machine men either went fishing or remained on the sidelines to sneer at "Charles the Evangelist."

Hughes told the voters that when his recommendations were challenged he felt it his duty to lay his case before the people, thus placing the responsibility for the outcome where it belonged. That deference to the people's judgment brought thundering applause and a sense of close identification with the cause. Humble men became warriors against corruption and lawlessness. "Leave your farms and your work shops on Tuesday," the Governor specifically charged them, "and remember that the people throughout the state are watching you, to see whether my confidence in the people and their sobriety, and their strength of character in such an emergency, has been misplaced." [11] To another group his plea was even more direct—"Rise in your might." [12]

So it went at Medina, Lockport, Holley, Albion, Middleport, Niagara Falls, and North Tonawanda. The indignant evangelist of the new democracy fought against seemingly hopeless odds with a sense of complete dedication. The struggle against race-track gambling was almost lost to sight in the larger cru-

[8] Speech to Ulster County Republican Club, March 20, 1908.
[9] Speech at Albany Mass Meeting, April 26, 1908.
[10] Report of detectives in Agnew Papers.
[11] Speech at Medina, May 8, 1908. [12] Speech at Tonawanda, May 9, 1908.

sade for uncorrupted government. "The history of politics," the Governor admonished the voters, "has been the history of men struggling for freedom and for individual rights against all sorts of special privileges. Tyranny and despotism have had their day, and in one place after another have finally been overthrown because they have represented the interests . . . and the will of the few against the interests and the inalienable rights of the many." [13] His faith in another uprising through the ballot box seemed implicit. And it was justified, even though Wallace won by a very slender margin.

Back in Albany, Hughes came down upon the legislature with a series of demands in addition to enactment of the Agnew-Hart bill. Three days later the Senate met for its crucial vote. Tension had been heightened by the fact that even Hughes' dramatic victory in Niagara-Orleans carried no assurance of a majority for the bill. Senator Otto G. Foelker of Brooklyn had undergone an appendectomy on May 10, and for several weeks his condition had been critical. On June 9 the Albany flier had stopped at Staatsburg at the Governor's order and brought Foelker to the capital looking very pale under his black derby. Groaning at every step, he declared that he would vote tomorrow on the antigambling bill "if there is breath in my body." But no one knew how he would vote. In the previous test he had stood with the Governor, but race-track money had been flowing freely and Foelker was reported to have given promises to both sides.

As the final debate crackled in the tense atmosphere of the Senate Chamber, legislators shifted in their seats and asked one another if Foelker could make it to the floor. Just before the roll call on a motion to recommit the bill to the committee where it originated they had their answer. Leaning heavily upon his physician and Canon Chase, Foelker entered the chamber. Advocates of the bill cheered gleefully. The voting went forward. Foelker sat nervously waiting. His lips twitched convulsively and his hands dropped into his lap; he was bewildered by the nature of the motion. "What is it?" he asked, and being uncertain, refrained from voting when his name was called.[14] Other Senators continued to vote. A tremor of excitement ran through the chamber. It was one of the most dramatic moments that the legislature had ever experienced. Catching the import of the recommittal motion, Foelker at last voted No, sank back into his seat, and looked as if he would collapse.

The sick Senator had to remain in the chamber for the final vote on the bill. Senator Cohalan tried to extend the debate, apparently in the hope of driving his ailing colleague back to his bed. But Majority Leader Raines, who in this fight was with the Governor, intervened as a matter of "humane duty," and Foelker was able to cast the winning vote.

Senator "Long Pat" McCarren gulped and then resumed chewing his tooth-

From the New York *World*, May 14, 1908.

STILL "ANIMATED"

(Here Hughes is pictured sweeping into the Senate the vote needed to win his fight against race-track gambling.)

pick, his eyes blazing with fury. The lobbyists were dumfounded. Hilarious supporters of the bill went cheering through the city. Hughes was elated. His smile created a great unconformity between his upper and lower whiskers. "I am deeply gratified," he said simply. "It is a victory for law and order, the importance of which cannot be overestimated." Foelker's courage, he added, merits the same praise that we give "to distinguished service on the battle field." [15]

A fresh current of admiration for the Governor swept over the state. The New York *Evening Mail* commented:

While the legislative record completed today embodies the policies and evidences of the triumph of Charles E. Hughes, it is not in the measures themselves that the greatest achievement is to be found. That lies in the demonstration that public opinion, when rightly interpreted and courageously expressed, will assert itself and dominate every situation. . . . Government for the people and not for politics was the text of every utterance made by Governor Hughes before he went to Albany, and has been ever since. . . . The house of politics is cleaner than it was thanks to the "animated feather duster." [16]

William Barnes' *Evening Journal* (Albany) characterized the defeat of its publisher as an "absurd blunder" attributable to agitation stirred up by sensational newspapers and "public officers who aim at cheap notoriety." But it was a voice in the wilderness. The *Daily Tribune* summed up the predominant feeling: ". . . the victory in the anti-gambling fight will only serve to intensify the public unwillingness to see him [Hughes] retire."

Once more Hughes' victory had been achieved without intrigue, alliances, threats, or use of patronage. The bosses accused him of destroying his party, and some of them were saying that, for their own preservation, they would have to destroy him. So far as their political future was concerned, they had good reason for complaint. Five of the eight Republican Senators who voted against the Agnew-Hart bill were defeated when they sought renomination. But the party was notably strengthened. What the Governor had spoiled was only the old game of using the machine for personal advantages.

The Governor's crusade put out of business many of the New York race tracks that had flourished solely as gambling enterprises, although horse racing continued on a smaller scale. The bookmakers experienced a long period of idleness. The law that the Governor had wrung from an unwilling Senate was to remain on the books until displaced some years later by the pari-mutuel betting system. Within twenty-four months California, Texas, Louisiana, and Georgia paid Hughes the compliment of imitating his anti-race-track-gambling law.

[15] *Ibid.*   [16] June 26, 1908.

Chapter 23

WHITE HOUSE ON THE HORIZON

As SOON as Hughes proved his vote-getting power in New York, in a contest with the most formidable demagogue of the time, men began to talk seriously of electing him President. The key to the whole situation was held by President Roosevelt. Following his election in 1904, T. R. had announced that he would not again be a candidate, but it was clear that, if he held to this decision, he would name his own successor. William Howard Taft, the Secretary of War, appeared to have the inside track, but he was willing to abide by Roosevelt's wishes, and the President's mind remained open. Watching Hughes campaign in New York, they both concluded that he would make an admirable presidential contender, and T. R. told Mrs. Taft that he might feel it his duty to be for Hughes in 1908.[1]

The events of 1907 greatly strengthened Governor Hughes' hold on the public imagination. By comparison, the men who were actively seeking the Presidency seemed to lack spirit and conviction. In his candid discussion of the outlook with Taft in September, 1907, the President admitted that the strongest candidate of all was Governor Hughes.[2]

Many others were saying the same thing publicly. Hughes is "the only man in the party, aside from Roosevelt," said the *St. Louis Mirror*, "who means anything in and of himself. . . . Hughes is the coming man." Returning from the Far West, Oscar King Davis, Washington correspondent for the *New York Times*, reported: "I heard enough Hughes talk in those three months to satisfy me that, if the New York Governor should be the Republican nominee, he would start with a first-class chance of carrying all that part of the country."[3] Most of T. R.'s insurgent friends, including the La Follette group, and the second-string leaders around the President also favored Hughes over Taft.[4] In an open contest there can be little doubt as to who the nominee would have been. In spite of the brevity of his experience in public life, Hughes had the advantage of being personally identified with the fight against exploitation and privilege in which the people were primarily interested.

[1] Henry F. Pringle, *The Life and Times of William Howard Taft*, I, 318.
[2] *Ibid.*, p. 331.
[3] *Released for Publication* (Boston, Houghton Mifflin, 1925), pp. 57–59. Copyright, 1925, by Oscar King Davis.
[4] William Allen White, *Autobiography*, p. 528.

But the decisive factor, it must be remembered, was not Hughes' standing with the people but his standing with President Roosevelt. The Governor had done nothing to encourage the belief that, as President, he would unswervingly walk in T. R.'s footprints. While he had given strong support to the Roosevelt Administration, he had followed his own independent course. As one commentator expressed it, "He would rather be Hughes than President."

Roosevelt's coolness toward the Hughes régime approached frigidity only after the Sanders incident.[5] In removing Sanders from his federal job in Rochester, T. R. was punishing a critic, but he also doubtless sincerely intended to help Hughes in his fight for good government. On his part, Hughes was glad to have the President's aid, even though he deplored the President's use of the patronage club in his behalf. He scrupulously avoided any flaunting of their differences as to methods. But Frank H. Simonds made it his special business to fashion the incident into a red flag and wave it in the President's face from the front page of the anti-Roosevelt *Evening Post*.

Simonds was a brilliant journalist whose facile stories about the new régime created the impression that, of all the Albany correspondents, he was "the closest to Hughes." Actually he was no more intimate with the Governor than were Louis Howe, John Palmer Gavit, Louis Seibold, and several others. Hughes did not play favorites. But Simonds' alertness in picking up information and his shrewdness in forecasting what was going to happen led many to believe that he had an inside track, which irked the other reporters.

On March 29, 1907, a correspondent brought a copy of the *Evening Post* into the Governor's press conference determined to have a showdown. "Governor Hughes will veto the public utilities bill if the corporations succeed in inserting the broad court-review feature," said a front-page Albany dispatch. "He will then call an extra session of the Legislature. . . . This is the programme that the Governor's friends are confidently predicting." Had the Governor, the correspondent asked, given this advance information to Simonds?

Much as he admired Simonds' ability and appreciated his friendly dispatches, Hughes concluded that this story went too far in presuming to speak for him. A careful reader would see that Simonds was relying upon "the Governor's friends," but the casual reader would assume that he was echoing the Governor's own words. The forecast was erroneous, and Hughes felt that the net effect was to put him in a false light before the other reporters and the public. "No statement has been made with my authority," he said. "No one is in a position to predict what course I shall take. . . . when there is occasion to state my attitude with regard to public questions I shall state it myself." [6]

Simonds left the executive chamber deeply offended and did not return for a long time. But he continued to write as if he were the Governor's alter ego.

[5] See pages 196–197.   [6] New York *Tribune*, March 30, 1907.

The Sanders affair gave him a unique opportunity for revenge, and he made the most of it. In two special articles, he wrote that the descent of T. R.'s "big stick" in New York "had made Hughes, in the minds of the politicians, a Roosevelt governor." For that reason the support of the President had "not been welcomed entirely." Simonds intimated that the Governor would have preferred "to win alone"—that he resented "playing 'second fiddle' to Roosevelt." Working both sides of the street, Simonds then pictured Roosevelt as trying to edge himself under the umbrella of Hughes' popularity. "The truth, of course, was that the President desired to punish James W. Wadsworth, Sr., and in order to make a neat cover for this, he announced that it was an action to aid Hughes. It is entirely possible," Simonds continued, "that the governor will repudiate this assistance given through federal patronage." [7]

Roosevelt read this posturization of the Governor as a self-seeking egotist and this assault upon his own motives as if the words had come straight from Hughes' mouth. The dispatch had all the earmarks of a spite story planted by an official speaking off the record. The President did not know that Simonds was no longer seeing Hughes. His anger was kindled, as indicated by a subsequent letter to Taft in which he referred to Hughes as "a thoroly selfish and cold blooded creature." ". . . when I strove to help him," T. R. complained, "he started the entire mugwump press cackling with glee about the way in which he had repudiated my help . . . and relied purely on the people." [8]

After this incident there was no probability of Hughes being chosen as Roosevelt's successor. Hughes didn't "play the game." He was not a Roosevelt man in the sense of subordinating his judgment or his individuality to that of the famous Rough Rider. Roosevelt's dislike for Hughes was apparently communicated to Taft. Since Hughes was the only rival who offered any real challenge to Taft's nomination, the White House circle assigned itself the task of eclipsing his popularity.

Only a determined and spectacular campaign by a new leader of commanding popular strength could have overcome this handicap, and Hughes would not lift a finger in his own behalf. There had been high expectation that he might declare himself a receptive candidate when he addressed the Republican Club dinner in New York on October 18, 1907. Instead, he declared: "I do not seek any public office. . . . To me public office means a burden of responsibility . . . it is far from being an object of ambition."

There was no posing about this seeming indifference to the glittering prize of American politics. Hughes had not been touched by the power complex that afflicts so many politicians. While he would meet the responsibilities of the White House unflinchingly if they should fall to his lot, he did not wish

[7] *Evening Post*, April 22 and 23, 1907.
[8] T. R. to Taft, Aug. 14, 1908, Roosevelt Papers.

them and would not reach out for them. Nomination for the Presidency, he said—laying down a rule that would guide him in 1916 as well as 1908—is an honor that no citizen should either seek or decline.

There was another restraining factor. "I thought," he admitted many years later, "that the position of a successor to Theodore Roosevelt would not be an attractive one. I was sure that, although out of office, he would still desire to have a dominating influence and that he would have a large following which would make the way of his successor hard. Nor did I think that, with his temperament and enjoyment of the strenuous life and especially of political activity, he would long be content to remain out of office. In all probability he would be at least a receptive candidate four years later." [9]

Hughes' high regard for Taft relieved him of any sense of duty in connection with the nomination. Throughout the period when he was being hailed as "the next President," he stood ready to support the Secretary of War—"a most worthy selection." In part this deference to Taft seemed to reflect Hughes' native humility. He was slow in learning to appreciate his own ability. For the first forty-three years of his life he had worked prodigiously without any public recognition. Then suddenly he had risen to the pinnacle of public acclaim in New York. That was difficult enough to swallow. Now the clamor for his advancement to the Presidency of the United States seemed strangely unreal. When his own family began discussing the prospect for his nomination, he dismissed it with a wave of the hand and a flat declaration that "it wouldn't ever happen."

"Oh, yes, it will," Mrs. Hughes contradicted, "you're a man of destiny, my dear." [10]

Hughes was finally persuaded to make a public statement of his views on national issues. People who were promoting his nomination had a right to know what he stood for. When the Republican Club of New York formally made him its candidate, he agreed to address the club on January 31. Meanwhile the New York County Republican Committee passed a Hughes-for-President resolution in spite of much maneuvering and delay tactics on the part of the President's supporters.

Hughes' "announcement" speech was widely heralded. The newspapers gave him an impressive build-up as the only rival to Taft. Might he not sweep the country with an unanswerable speech, as he had often swept New York, and upset the scheme to give Taft the nomination on a silver platter? Roosevelt, who had thrown all his energy into the fight for Taft, decided to take no chances.

What the people saw when they scanned their newspapers the morning after Hughes' speech were blazing headlines of a very different sort: "ROOSE-

[9] CEH, Notes, p. 195.   [10] Author's interview with CEH, Jr., July 8, 1948.

"SO LONG, CHARLIE! WE'D LIKE TO SEE YOU GO!"

(This cartoon was mailed to Governor Hughes during the preconvention fight for the Republican presidential nomination in 1908, with the above comment penciled in.)

VELT'S ONSLAUGHT . . ." "BIG MEN ROASTED . . ." "HOTTEST MESSAGE EVER SENT TO CONGRESS . . ." "MESSAGE DAZES." The President had sent to Congress "the most provocatively sensational utterance" of his career, with careful timing so as to smother the Hughes speech.

Most newspapers that had reserved front-page space for the so-called "Hughes platform" had to use it for the verbal explosion in Washington. "Hughes' temperate, sane, well-thought-out discourse could no more compete for public attention with Roosevelt's effulgence," as Mark Sullivan wrote, "than a crystal spring with a volcanic eruption." [11] Hughes had argued persuasively for effective regulation instead of government ownership of the railroads, for an expert commission to prepare the ground for an equitable revision of tariff rates, for a modified employers' liability law, for improvement of the Sherman Antitrust Law, and for progressive and orderly government. "The battle for free institutions," he had said, "has been a struggle against special privilege." He had had only praise for the Roosevelt Administration and had made no direct bid for the nomination. "I ask no favor and I make no claim," he had said. "I desire that the party shall act for its best interests." T. R. did not know the nature of Hughes' speech when he threw out his trip line, but there can be no doubt as to what his intention was. Newspaper men asked him if his outburst had been maliciously timed, and he replied, "If Hughes is going to play the game, he must learn the tricks."

Hughes' good will toward Taft remained unimpaired. Both candidates were speakers at the annual dinner of the Friendly Sons of Saint Patrick on March 17. In the course of a glowing eulogy of everything Irish, Taft claimed to have visited historic Blarney Castle near Cork and to have "kissed the stone with all its mellifluous consequences." When it came Hughes' turn to bid for Irish favor, he said that he did not doubt Mr. Taft had given a "veracious chronicle" of his experience, but it would have been a joy to have taken a picture of the Secretary "pressing his ruby lips to the famous stone." [12] Gazing on Taft's enormous hulk and knowing full well the inaccessibility of the Blarney stone, the Friendly Sons howled with delight. (The next day a cartoonist pictured Taft being hoisted by a derrick to reach the stone.) To prove his own standing in that genial company, Hughes then trotted out his Irish great-great-grandfather, Michael Connelly. But he also warmly complimented Taft.

When Woodruff wrote to ask his pleasure as to the selection of delegates to the national convention, Hughes said no pressure should be exerted in his behalf and asked for a "free expression" of Republican voters' wishes through their own representatives in the state convention. [13] Part of the delegation

[11] *Our Times* (New York, Scribner's, 1932), IV, 297–304. Copyright, 1932, by Charles Scribner's Sons.
[12] New York *Herald,* March 18, 1908.   [13] CEH to Woodruff, April 4, 1908.

finally chosen was sincerely devoted to Hughes; others merely hoped to get him out of Albany. The Barnes outfit left for Chicago singing, "Goodbye, Charlie, we'll be glad to see you go." The Governor himself was still unconcerned. He went so far as publicly to repudiate the announcement that Hughes headquarters had been opened in Chicago to secure his nomination.

Before the convention opened on June 16, the nomination of Taft was a certainty. Being eager to capture the vice-presidential nomination and feeling inhibited so long as the New York delegation was holding out against Taft for first place, Herbert Parsons asked Hughes to release the delegation from its instructions to vote for him. Hughes replied that he had had nothing to do with instructing the delegates in the first place and therefore had no right to release them. Barnes was furious. Overriding his instructions, he voted for Taft, taking nine New York delegates with him. "This is the end of Hughes," he railed. That defection left Hughes third on the list of candidates, with one vote less than Senator Philander C. Knox's 68 and wholly out of range of the 702 votes that nominated Taft on the first ballot.

At two o'clock on the morning of June 19, Governor Hughes was awakened to receive the following telegram from Elbert F. Baldwin, one of Roosevelt's friends on the staff of the *Outlook:*

The Republican Presidential nominee asks me to telegraph you that he considers you far and away the strongest man for the Vice Presidency if you can be induced to take the nomination. He, the party, and thousands irrespective of politics call for you. As he and the President said to me tonight, no other candidate could add such moral strength to the ticket. Mr. Taft earnestly urges you to stand with him on that ticket, assured of hearty Washington and general support. As your admirer, as Roosevelt's and Taft's friend, I implore you to recognize that Republican success or failure may hang upon your decision, for the Democratic ticket is to be unexpectedly strong.

Hughes could see no challenge whatever in the Vice Presidency and felt that, without a compelling reason, he could not afford to make the financial sacrifice it would entail. His reply was a courteous but unequivocal No, and the nomination went to another New Yorker, James S. Sherman.

The hard-fighting Governor of New York ended his first cool and hesitant flirtation with the presidential bee without rancor or regret. It was to have a more dramatic sequel in 1916. Yet he never lost the conviction that shaped his action in 1908—the conviction that to be fit for high office a man must be willing to forgo it or to leave it at any time.

Chapter 24

SECOND GUBERNATORIAL CAMPAIGN

GOVERNOR Hughes was not inclined to seek a second term because his two years at Albany had left him nervously worn and $20,000 poorer than he had been in 1906. Now a family of eight (the Governor's parents were living with him), the Hugheses had found it impossible to maintain the Executive Mansion and finance the large receptions and dinners it was customary to give on the Governor's $10,000 salary and the meager additional allowances. The $100,-000 fortune that he had accumulated from his law practice was thus undergoing what seemed to be a most imprudent shrinkage.

The drain upon his savings was especially heavy because, on his numerous forays to arouse public opinion, he paid his own way and that of his military secretary as well as the fees of the stenographers who took down his speeches for the press. Only if he traveled strictly on state business did he send in an expense voucher. One day Comptroller Martin H. Glynn, a Democrat, brought into the Governor's office a handful of vouchers indicating that Theodore Roosevelt had charged to the state the entire cost of his travels as governor. "It is absurd," he said, "for you to finance so many of your activities when your whole time is devoted to state business." But Hughes continued to draw upon his own resources for every outlay that was not directly essential to his official duties.

The only public intimation of the Governor's intention was his offhand remark to the National Guard Association early in 1908 that he was making his "second and farewell appearance as commander-in-chief." At that time he hoped that his reform program would be fully enacted at the 1908 legislative session. As the revolt against his policies spread, however, it became apparent that he could not retire without appearing to forsake much of what he stood for.

While the Governor was debating with himself what course to take, Dean Hutchins of the Law School of the University of Michigan (his old associate at Cornell) paid him a visit to ask if he would entertain an offer of the presidency of the university. Hughes had stirred the hearts of the students, faculty, and trustees when he delivered a Washington's birthday address at Ann Arbor in 1907 and was entertained at luncheon by President James B. Angell, who was now about to retire. While still sensitive to the lure of campus life, the

JUST A WHISPER

(Cartoonist Bradley's comment on the reluctance of the New York Republican organization to renominate Governor Hughes in 1908.)

Governor declined because of his feeling that he should take advantage of the great opportunity awaiting him at the bar.

As the weeks passed, his supporters clamored for a fresh subordination of his personal preference to his public duty. "The plain people understand you, love you and are for you," Stewart L. Woodford had written him. "If the people want you for governor again in order to force this reform [the direct primary], I do not see how you can consistently refuse." [1] Similar urgings came through the mails, in speeches, and direct conversation. The Governor saw that he could not relinquish his post without leaving his faithful followers in the lurch. On July 24 he announced that, "upon further reflection," he had decided to accept a renomination, if tendered, in spite of the "entirely personal reasons" that had previously inclined him against it. "But it is my desire," he added, "that the will of the party to which I belong should be freely expressed and that it shall take such action as shall be most closely in accord with public sentiment." [2]

To the Republican leaders, who had been smirking over the prospect of recapturing the governorship, Hughes' announcement was vinegar and hemlock. To President Roosevelt it brought a new dilemma. His dislike for Hughes had not evaporated with the nomination of Taft. The White House was now deluged, moreover, with predictions of Republican defeat in New York if T. R. should permit the renomination of Hughes. The bosses were moving heaven and earth to save themselves from two more years of frustration. Barnes wrote to Secretary Root on August 14 that under no circumstances would the Albany delegates vote for Hughes. Roosevelt, as he wrote to Taft on August 3, was at his "wit's end as to whether it is absolutely necessary to nominate Hughes or whether it would be suicidal to do so." [3]

Taft probably did more than anyone else to soften Roosevelt's attitude. Hughes must be renominated in spite of the Old Guard, he replied, because of the strength he would add to the national campaign, especially in the West. T. R. was inclined to agree, but he was still worried. "There are any number of thoroughly good people," he wrote to Taft on August 12, "who violently object to his [Hughes'] nomination, and we may get beaten out of our boots with him." Relying on his distorted view of the Sanders incident, he conjured up fears that Hughes might accept a nomination dictated from the White House and then repudiate his (T. R.'s) interference.

In his letters to Woodruff, T. R. also accused Hughes of "wantonly and needlessly" insulting the party workers and of allying himself with "some peculiarly malevolent and underhanded enemies of the party." But having aired his ill-founded resentment, Roosevelt bowed to expediency. Frank H. Hitch-

---

[1] Woodford to CEH, March 28, 1908.   [2] *New York Times*, July 25, 1908.
[3] Taft Papers, Library of Congress.

cock, chairman of the national committee, had returned from the West with the conviction that Republican chances would be seriously jeopardized in that area by any sacrifice of Hughes at the behest of the bosses. After a series of conferences at Oyster Bay, T. R. concluded that it would be safer to dragoon the politicians than to antagonize the rank and file. He explained his position in a letter to Taft:

Hughes is not a man I care for; he is not a man whose actions have really tended to the uplifting of political life; but he is financially an entirely honest man and one of much ability, and I am concerned that while to nominate him will do harm, not to nominate him will do more harm because I am convinced that the bulk of the Republicans, including the best men in the party outside the active organization, are for him.[4]

The only real complaint against the Governor was that he had refused to play the politicians' game. The fact is he did not know how to play politics, and he would probably have been beaten if he had tried. Roosevelt's irritation over Hughes' inability to get along with the bosses seems especially strange in the light of his own tirades against the bosses when they opposed him in 1912.

Hughes' reaction to the claim that he was not a good Republican was given pointed emphasis one day when he visited a mental hospital accompanied by a committee of the legislature. An inmate accosted him and inquired, "Are you Governor Hughes?" When Hughes assented, the inmate said, "I don't know whether you're a Republican or not."

"Did you hear that, Governor?" exclaimed Senator Raines, chuckling with delight.

"Yes," Hughes replied. "He's insane."

Taft was so confident that Hughes was an asset to the Republican Party that, even before Hughes announced his decision to run again, he asked the Governor to open the national campaign with a speech at Youngstown, Ohio. It will be "perhaps the greatest meeting of the campaign," Taft said. "I don't know anybody whose words will have more weight than yours." [5] Hughes sensed the compliment and readily acquiesced. It was the first bid for his aid in a national campaign.

Youngstown did its utmost to make this opening rally for Taft impressive. On the morning of September 5 Hughes joined Senator Beveridge, Governor Andrew L. Harris of Ohio, and other notables in reviewing a parade of 15,000 workingmen. It seemed endless. Noon passed and the reviewers got nothing but coffee for lunch. As soon as the last marcher had gone by, they hastened to Wick Park where a large crowd was waiting to hear the oratory. The chairman

---

[4] Roosevelt Papers.   [5] Taft to CEH, July 16, 1908.

spoke for forty minutes and Governor Harris for an hour. Hughes had been scheduled to speak next but he agreed to exchange places with Senator Beveridge when the Senator explained that Mrs. Beveridge was about to give birth to a baby. The Senator's concern over the forthcoming event was not sufficient, however, to end his peroration on the tariff before 5:30 P.M. Hughes felt that the situation was hopeless.

"I have a dry speech consisting only of reasoning," he told James R. Garfield. "The people are so tired they will probably walk out. I suggest that you call it off."

"You don't know Western reserve," Garfield replied. He insisted that the meeting go forward, and the audience vindicated his judgment by listening courteously. Hughes turned his devastating power of analysis upon Taft's opponent, William Jennings Bryan. Recognizing Bryan as an eloquent critic, he nevertheless insisted that if all the schemes the Commoner had advocated in the previous twelve years had been enacted "we should have been overwhelmed with disaster." Bryan's plan to curb the trusts by forbidding any corporation to control more than 50 per cent of the total amount of "any product consumed in the United States" came under an especially withering examination. What was the meaning of that elusive phrase "any product consumed in the United States"? Would it exclude patented articles which the Government had given the owners exclusive rights to manufacture and sell? "When . . . we consider these . . . remedies that are proposed for the trusts," Hughes declared, "we find ourselves journeying in a land of dreams. Again the magician of 1896 waves his wand. . . ."

At the dinner given that evening by James G. Butler in honor of Governor Hughes, there were no repercussions from the speech. No one congratulated him; no one thanked him; no one even mentioned it. The thin-skinned Governor felt depressed. Like Lincoln after Gettysburg, he went home fearful that he had fumbled a great opportunity.

The following day, however, it appeared that the weary Youngstowners who heard the speech were the only ones who had missed its significance. Encomiums for the Governor's "sanctified common sense" all but dripped from the press. "What a masterly speech Hughes made when he opened the campaign in Ohio," exclaimed Roosevelt. "How he cut into Bryan! It is far the best thing yet done in this campaign." [6] Two days later T. R. advised Taft to paraphrase the Hughes speech in his own campaign addresses. Republican headquarters sent out more copies of the Youngstown speech than of any other except Taft's acceptance speech.

Throughout the remainder of his campaign Bryan refrained from pressing the portion of his platform that Hughes had riddled. Taft's speeches and Roose-

[6] T. R. to John A. Sleicher, Sept. 19, 1908, Hughes Papers.

velt's statements drew the Commoner's fire, but he attempted no reply to Hughes. Mark Sullivan credited Hughes with "crumpling" Bryan's campaign in a single speech.[7] Henry L. Stoddard reported that, after the Hughes speech, "the election, though six weeks distant, was only a matter of totalling the vote against Bryan." [8]

So far as Hughes' political fortunes were concerned, the chief importance of the Youngstown speech was its impact on the Old Guard in New York. It blasted the hope of Barnes and his associates that they might be able to unite upon a candidate whom the administration in Washington would have to accept. Root and former Governor Black declined to be used against Hughes, and the bosses were no more successful in their overtures to Joseph H. Choate, Ambassador Horace Porter, and Seth Low. Choate had been asked to be permanent chairman of the convention, but when he let it be known that he was an ardent Hughes man, the organization decided that it needed a chairman more familiar with parliamentary law than the president of the last constitutional convention.

As the convention met at Saratoga on September 14, the only anti-Hughes candidates who had shown any strength whatever were Speaker Wadsworth, with 122 delegates, and William Berri, who had most of the Kings delegation. Wadsworth refused to release his delegates to any compromise candidate. The frustrated bosses went into a huddle and made another appeal to Root. Root repeated that the defeat of Hughes would be a critical blow to the national ticket and produced a statement from the President saying that "while he had no intention of dictating, yet to all his friends who have spoken to him on the matter he has said in the strongest possible terms that he favored the renomination of Governor Hughes." [9]

Hughes himself remained completely aloof from the convention. There were no Hughes headquarters at Saratoga, no organization representing him, no one authorized to speak for him or to promise any favor in return for support. No delegate had been importuned by him. There was no picture of him in the convention hall. When Secretary Root mentioned the Governor's name in his keynote speech, the galleries cheered and shouted but the delegates sat stonily silent. The phrase "Nobody wants Hughes but the people" was eloquently descriptive of the situation.

The final postmidnight conference of the Old Guard hatched a scheme to nominate David Jayne Hill, the American Ambassador to Germany, without his knowledge, so that if he should refuse to run after the convention adjourned the leaders would be free to fill the vacancy as they pleased. Root appears to

---

[7] Mark Sullivan, *Our Times*, IV, 306.

[8] *As I Knew Them* (New York, Harper, 1927), p. 280. Copyright, 1927, by Harper & Brothers.

[9] New York *World*, Sept. 15, 1908.

have broken up this midsummer night's dream by bringing the wrath of T. R. and Taft upon the hapless Woodruff.

Barnes shook his clenched fists and worked himself into a "frenzy of rage" as he denounced Hughes in the process of seconding Wadsworth's nomination. The main speech for Hughes was "chanted" by Senator Page in a monotonous fashion, but Assemblyman John Lord O'Brian and William A. Prendergast cut loose with seconding speeches that raised the rafters. The first ballot gave Hughes 827 votes to 151 for Wadsworth and 31 for former Congressman John K. Stewart. Barnes swallowed his anger and moved to make the nomination unanimous.

Roosevelt wrote to Taft that he had used every ounce of power he possessed to bring about Hughes' renomination. Root, too, concluded that, without the President's help, Hughes would have had no more than 200 votes in the convention. Certainly the President's influence was effectively used in the Governor's behalf, but the underlying fact was that the bosses could choose only between the renomination of Hughes and a still more costly defeat. Actually the bewhiskered executive at Albany had won his own fight simply by being Hughes. "The renomination of Governor Hughes," boasted the Nation, "must be reckoned as one of the most significant political events in the last quarter century. It is a sheer triumph of naked principle, and as such it must mightily strengthen the forces of good government." [10]

Hughes' campaign was a whirlwind affair beginning with his acceptance speech in Brooklyn on September 26. The Old Guard had given him a platform of generalities and weasel words which approved no more of his achievements than was necessary and, without directly saying so, attempted to close the door against the simplified ballot and primary nominations. But Hughes was his own platform. The question before the voters was simply whether or not his administration should be returned to power.

The Democrats had favored him with a weak opponent in the person of Lewis Stuyvesant Chanler. As lieutenant governor from 1906 to 1908, Chanler had proved to be an amiable fellow who worked in harmony with Hughes and often expressed admiration for him. Selected by his party to oppose the Governor, Chanler found himself in an embarrassing position. His struggle to differentiate himself from Hughes and take advantage of the Republican schism led to the inference that he accepted boss rule. Indeed, he was indebted to Bosses Murphy and Conners for his nomination. Chanler's assault on "government by commission" won applause in some quarters, but it brought him into direct collision with Hughes' most successful reform. Trying to back away from that unpopular stand, Chanler urged retention of the Public Service Commissions with election of their members—an artful way of destroying

[10] Sept. 17, 1908.

them. Trying to lure the race-track interests, Chanler also accused the Hughes administration of invading "personal liberty," and a Personal Liberty League spent a good deal of money conjuring up bogies. But this sham issue fell flat when Chanler was finally badgered into saying that he did not favor repeal of Hughes' anti-race-track-gambling law.

The campaign in New York had scarcely begun when Republican national headquarters once more importuned Hughes to make a Western tour. His New York followers were indignant. Because of the combination of interests opposing him and the disaffection among the Old Guard, the need of his campaign talents was greater at home than in the West. After continued urging, however, Hughes promised to make eight speeches on condition that they be indoors, that they be limited to two a day, with no speaking at night. The G.O.P. managers agreed, but as soon as he got on the road he found himself speaking outdoors and indoors, twenty times a day through Nebraska, Kansas, and Illinois.

One incident during this trip always stood out in Hughes' memory "as an illustration of the friendliness and generosity of the American people which even the bitter contests of political campaigns cannot wholly obscure." He tells the story in his Notes:

One evening, shortly before my train arrived at Hastings, Nebraska, there was a severe storm which tore down the tent in which I was to speak. The only hall in the town at that time was taken and already filled by the Democrats who were awaiting the arrival of their speaker. We concluded that we could not have a meeting, but a committee of the Democrats came to the train and invited me to speak at their hall. Their orator's train was an hour or so late. They made the condition that I should appear on the platform alone, without any Republican associates, as their invitation was a courtesy extended to me as Governor of New York,—but I was at liberty to speak as I pleased.

A straggling lot of Republicans followed me to the hall and crowded in as best they could. To the amazement of the Democratic audience I appeared on the platform, introduced myself, thanked the Democratic committee for its courtesy and said that they would not have any respect for me if I did not make the speech I had intended to make at Hastings. I then launched out as usual. The audience gave me a rousing welcome and the hall rang with their applause as I extolled the American spirit of fair play and concluded with a number of questions for the Democratic orator to answer on his arrival, which was shortly after I left.

The tour heightened disappointment among the Hughes men outside New York that he was not the presidential candidate. "If the Chicago convention were to do its work over, in the light of recent events," said the *Cleveland Plain Dealer* on October 25, "there would be but one name considered, that of Hughes."

Roosevelt was delighted with the response to this trip and swallowed enough of his pique to tell the Governor so.

Permit me to congratulate you [he wrote on October 14] upon the admirable campaign work that you have been doing. I think it has been of the greatest service in the West; and what is more, I think it has been of great service in New York, not only to Taft but in the State campaign, to have had you do just what you did in the West. I have kept in the closest touch possible with the different organization men, and I believe now that you will have their hearty and undivided support. I was amused the other day to find that one of the leaders, who had originally been very much opposed to your renomination, was now your enthusiastic backer, having been completely converted by your speeches in the West. . . .[11]

On his return to New York, however, Hughes was confronted by a forecast in the *World* that he would be beaten by 200,000 votes. Wall Street feared a stock market investigation and sought emancipation of the public utilities from the Public Service Commissions. Traveling men were irate over his veto of the two-cent-fare bill. Firemen similarly resented his veto of an unsound insurance bill that would have given them certain benefits. The Prohibition State Committee also fought him on the ground that he was a drinking man, opposed prohibition of the liquor traffic, and had been a director in a liquor-selling company. This brought great amusement in Albany, where the take-it-straight men joked about the Governor's occasional highballs made with one tablespoonful of whisky. As for his directorship in a liquor company, it referred to a title he had once assumed for a few months in connection with the reorganization of an ale-bottling business for which he was counsel. Malicious anti-Hughes propaganda was likewise disseminated among insurance men and other factions supposedly hurt by legislation the Governor had sponsored.

Hughes had only two and a half weeks, after he returned from the West, to answer his opponents. Almost every moment of it he turned to good advantage. Racing from one meeting to another, he sometimes continued to speak until after midnight. His audiences, ranging from up-State businessmen or farmers to Italians, Jews, or Negroes in New York City, were asked to restrain their applause to save his tired voice and conserve the precious moments. Sometimes he talked humorously and sometimes with the deepest seriousness, but always there was keen sensitivity to the wants and aspirations of the people coupled with an appeal to their powers of reason as stalwart citizens. After the meeting at Long Island City, the crowd went "almost wild" in efforts to reach him and shake his hand or even touch him as he passed.[12]

Chanler helped his opponent by asking him ten questions that were supposed to be embarrassing. Newspapers carrying the questions were distributed on the Governor's train at six o'clock the next morning at Rouses Point. Hughes

[11] Hughes Papers.   [12] Henry P. Huling to Robert H. Fuller, Oct. 28, 1908.

called a stenographer and dictated frank, crisp, and satisfying answers to every question. By the time the train reached Malone, he had a typewritten copy of his replies, all numbered and tagged, ready for each of the reporters. In his speech at Malone he threw Chanler's questions back at him with such fervor that one observer thought the townsfolk would "tear the opera house down." Then he asked Chanler some questions that the latter could not answer without spilling some of the water he was trying to carry on both shoulders. The press repeatedly challenged him to be as candid as Hughes had been until he was finally forced to attempt some answers which proved to be pallid and equivocal.

By the end of the campaign Hughes and Roosevelt were almost chummy again. After Hughes had reported on his "hot fight" and warmly thanked T. R. for his help, the President wrote on October 20:

That is such an extremely nice letter of yours that I can not forbear taking up your time by a line of acknowledgment. I have, naturally, the keenest sympathy for you in this campaign, because of the very fact you point out; that is, the two-fold type of attack made upon you: the attack upon you because you stood for the corporations where they were right or where improper measures were aimed at them, and the attack upon you because you have declined to sanction abuses in their management or to refrain from trying to better their management. . . .

Now one word. You say that your feeling is that "if the Republican support is energetic I shall unquestionably be elected." Is there any way that I can help in this matter of the Republican support? Pray let me know if you think that there is.

Taft, by the way, mentioned to me his great sense of obligation to you for your part in the campaign and his purpose to lay all possible emphasis upon the need for electing you, when he makes his speeches in New York.[13]

Hughes replied on October 25:

The week has been very successful, and unless I am very much mistaken it has been the decisive week in the campaign. Chanler's questions were a stupid blunder, of which we lost no time in taking advantage. It seems to me that his candidacy is hopelessly weak; it is evasive, shifting, and stands for nothing whatever. It promises nothing to the radicals and it offers no assurance, in any promise of steadiness or of convictions, to the conservatives. His effort has been simply to capitalize in his favor the various elements of opposition. . . .

I have been very much gratified by the assurances of Republican support that I have received and the many evidences of loyal party activity. . . . The situation is apparently much better than it was two years ago. . . . I have no complaints to make with regard to anybody, anywhere,—for I do not make them unless I have the facts—and I haven't the facts.

The entire Republican ticket was elected, including Horace White as lieutenant governor and Samuel Koenig as secretary of state. Both houses of the

[13] Hughes Papers.

legislature remained strongly Republican. Hughes was cut heavily in New York and Buffalo, where the sporting element was strong, but he finished with a vote of 804,651, which gave him a plurality of 69,462 or 11,565 more than his margin over Hearst. His campaign had cost him $369 as against Chanler's $7,305. "With this expression of the confidence of the people," he said, "I shall devote myself with renewed zeal to their service." [14] Once more he faced the people with no political debts to pay and without having compromised any principle for which he stood.

To Roosevelt's bubbling congratulations, the Governor replied:

I warmly appreciate your kind letter. It was a good fight; and I enjoyed it thoroughly. More than anything else, I enjoyed stumping through the Middle West and the opportunity of speaking for Mr. Taft, whose splendid victory over Mr. Bryan is a tonic to the entire country.

We had a desperate time in New York, and when I consider the variety of influences, powerful and unscrupulous, that were working against me, I confess that I marvel at the result; though all along I felt, for some reason, a strong confidence that we should be successful. These are good Republican days, and I rejoice with you and must congratulate you upon the course of events.[15]

The Governor's enviable position appealed so strongly to the retiring President that he appended the following wistful and prophetic paragraph to a letter thanking Hughes for a trivial favor:

"Good luck to you! I believe and hope that you have a long career in public life ahead of you. As I shall soon leave public life, and in all human probability permanently, I feel a real interest in a man who is in the middle of his career." [16]

[14] New York *World*, Nov. 4, 1908.   [15] CEH to T. R., Nov. 7, 1908.
[16] T. R. to CEH, Dec. 7, 1908.

Chapter 25

THE GOVERNOR'S CONSCIENCE

CEREMONY, drama, and nerve-fraying toil were copiously mingled in Hughes' last years at Albany. The new cordiality between him and Theodore Roosevelt brought him prominently into the Washington scene as the old administration gave way to the new early in 1909. With Mrs. Hughes, he was a guest at the last state dinner given by T. R. on January 28 in honor of Chief Justice Fuller and other members of the Supreme Court. When the men went into the breakfast room to smoke, the President turned his back upon the long-haired Chief Justice and talked exclusively to the Governor about New York until Hughes felt embarrassed by such discourtesy to the guest of honor.

On February 22 the Governor was again in Washington to address the convocation of the George Washington University and receive an LL.D. degree, and on March 2 he and Mrs. Hughes attended the dinner party given by Oscar Straus, the Secretary of Commerce and Labor, in honor of President Roosevelt. Once more there was animated conversation between the President, sitting on Mrs. Straus' right, and the Governor, sitting on her left.

"Well, Mr. President," Hughes consoled the great man who was giving up the big game in America for comparatively dull hunting abroad, "when you come back from Africa we'll all be down on the shore to greet you."

"Will you? Will you?" he exclaimed as if a little incredulous.

That evening in the smoking room the retiring President told the story of his political life—a long and interesting tale that was not inappropriate to the occasion. Hughes saw the President again the next day at the White House levee and was greeted effusively amid a huge crowd. Then—on March 4—came Taft's inauguration.

The Capital awoke almost smothered by snow, with a furious blizzard howling through the streets. Frigid temperatures seemed to augment the coolness between Taft and Roosevelt as they took their last ride together down Pennsylvania Avenue. The inaugural ceremony was held in the Senate Chamber and T. R. hastened to his train to avoid playing second fiddle to Taft in the traditional return to the White House. A new chapter in American history thus began. Its first colorful event was the struggle of the inaugural parade down the Avenue from the Capitol to the White House in heroic defiance of the elements. Governor Hughes, who rode at the head of the New York troops, gives the following account of the incident:

Immediately after the ceremony . . . I went to a designated place southeast of the Capitol where Squadron A of the New York Cavalry was stationed. We waited for over an hour before we could take our position in the inaugural parade. The horses were very restive as the icicles dropped from the trees upon their backs. As customary, I wore a silk hat and a frock coat,—with my Marshal's scarf, and thinking an overcoat too clumsy I had protected myself with a chamois vest. But my hands inside my gloves were very cold and I had to dig them into the horse's flesh to keep them from freezing. As we came down the hill from the Capitol our horses almost slid on the icy street. My horse had always been in the ranks, and it was with difficulty that he could be persuaded to take his place at the head of the procession. But with the cheers of the crowd as we came to the large stands, he seemed to realize that this was his day and he went along at the head, proudly arching his neck and acting his part as a well trained horse of the Commander in Chief should. I made my bows with all the grace I could command and managed to get through without mishap. I dismounted at 19th Street and Pennsylvania Avenue, Northwest, (where the parade broke up) with a keen sense of relief. The storm was so severe that the Seventh Regiment of New York failed to get to Washington in time and President Taft gave it a special review on the next morning, asking me to join him.[1]

Other accounts of the impression the Governor made, riding with uncovered head, are less modest. The *Washington Post* reported that he aroused "the wildest enthusiasm." [2] According to Senator Davenport, a continuous roar of applause . . . greeted him from one end of the avenue to the other." [3] Hughes returned to Albany with a devoted friend in the White House and a gratifying sense of public appreciation for his work.

June, 1909, brought the Alaska-Yukon-Pacific Exposition in Seattle. The New York legislature had voted funds for a special train to ensure the attendance of a large delegation from that state. Hughes vetoed the bill and went to the exposition himself, taking only his military aide and paying the expenses from his own pocket. Once more he was lionized.

After delivering his speech on "New York Day" to an audience of ten thousand people, Hughes felt the joyous release of a schoolboy on a holiday. He had already traveled through Yellowstone National Park in a special relay of buckboards. From Seattle he took a boat to Vancouver, then spent a day at Banff and a day or two at Lake Louise. Still eager to climb every peak he saw, he induced Colonel Treadwell to accompany him to the top of Sulphur Mountain. It was not a severe climb, compared to what he had done in the Alps, but stiff enough to be exhilarating.

[1] CEH, Notes, pp. 202–203.   [2] March 5, 1909.
[3] New York *Tribune*, April 2, 1909.

Other events interrupted the grinding routine of the governorship. A telephone call from Brown University brought the alarming news that son Charles, who was nearing the end of his senior year, had suddenly been stricken by cerebrospinal meningitis after a night of toil on an essay. Mrs. Hughes caught the first train to Providence while the Governor continued to labor over his thirty-day bills in a state of high nervous tension. Young Charlie had the good fortune to fall into the hands of the only doctor in New England who was skilled in administering Dr. Simon Flexner's serum for meningitis and was soon on the road to complete recovery. Incidentally, his paper won first prize. He was following in the Hughesian tradition.

Only a few weeks later, in June, 1909, the Governor's father suffered a stroke while preaching in New York. The Reverend Mr. Hughes had retired from active service as a pastor in 1901, but the spirit still burned within him and he had continued to preach in a number of pulpits in the vicinity of New York. In 1908, while his son was bearing down on the corruptionists at Albany, he was demanding from the pulpit that the New York police stop Gertrude Hoffman's "indecent and demoralizing" Salome dance at Hammerstein's. When his stroke put an end to his preaching, he and Mrs. Hughes went to Albany to spend the remainder of their days with their son. On December 15, 1909, David Charles Hughes died at the Executive Mansion at the age of seventy-seven.

Governor Hughes was still fighting doggedly for some of his reforms. His bill for the regulation of telephone and telegraph companies had been voted down again in April, 1909, and it was not until the following year, after an investigation of the subject by a legislative committee, that a satisfactory measure was finally passed.

Early in 1910 Hughes created a stir by opposing ratification of the proposed Sixteenth Amendment. The Supreme Court had struck down the federal income tax law of 1894, and Congress in turn was trying to strike down the court's decision by changing the Constitution. Governor Hughes felt that the aim was good, but the instrument fashioned to effect it was inept. It would give Congress power to tax incomes *"from whatever source derived."* These comprehensive words, if given their natural meaning, he argued in a strong message to the New York legislature, "would include not only incomes from ordinary real or personal property, but also incomes derived from State and municipal securities." They would enable Congress to limit the borrowing power of the states and "make the performance of the functions of local government a matter of Federal grace." [4]

Hughes did not quibble about the income tax; he favored it and was certain that an amendment making it legal could be drafted without danger of crip-

[4] *Public Papers, 1910,* p. 74.

pling of the states. To be sure, Senator Root and others argued that the amendment then awaiting ratification would merely remove the necessity of apportioning income taxes among the states according to population and would not permit federal taxation of state or local bonds. The other interpretation, however, was clearly permissible. Hughes insisted that the amendment should be stripped of its ambiguity. His influence caused rejection of the amendment in New York, but other states supplied the requisite number of ratifications. When the scope of the amendment was tested in the Supreme Court, Chief Justice White chose the Root interpretation and Hughes, then an Associate Justice, assented. In his Chief Justiceship he treated the issue as closed by White's opinion, but many of the states are still fearful that federal taxation of income from state and municipal bonds may impair the federal system.

Nerve-racking pardon cases weighed heavily upon the Governor's conscience. The law gave him power to commute sentences as well as to pardon convicts, which meant that pleas came up to him in behalf of every person convicted of murder. The first time that a human life hung upon his word he listened to pleas on behalf of the two condemned boys, read the record of their trial with the utmost care, and scrutinized the jury's findings. At the end of his ordeal he came out of his office, white and haggard, and said that he could find no reason to interfere with the judgment of the court. "It was the hardest work I ever did," he confessed to a reporter.[5]

This was typical. Hughes would move heaven and earth to make sure that justice was being done. But he resolutely refused to take over the function of the court or to substitute his own personal caprice for the orderly operation of the law. "I have no right to pardon a man," he would say, "in order to make certain people happy or because I might feel particularly good-natured at the time."

The case of Chester Gillette, out of which Theodore Dreiser was later to fashion *An American Tragedy*, was an acid test of the Governor's sense of justice. Gillette was convicted of drowning the girl to whom he had been engaged by tipping over their canoe out on a lake. His sensational trial rocked the state. The Court of Appeals upheld the judgment of the lower court even though the evidence against the young factory worker was wholly circumstantial. Hughes reviewed the case and declined to interfere. The frantic supporters of Gillette then besieged the Governor for a reprieve in order to permit the presentation of new evidence, but the new evidence proved to be worthless.

Gillette came from a good family, and his mother proved to be one of his strongest defenders. "I'm not going to appeal to sympathy," she said when

[5] Ida M. Tarbell in *American Magazine*, March, 1908, pp. 451–464.

she called on Governor Hughes. "I understand your position. But Chester is not guilty, and I want to prove it." [6] For two hours she reviewed the facts and the trial as if she had been the lawyer in the case.

The Governor promised to read the three volumes of testimony once more. The effect was to buttress his conviction of the young man's guilt. Gillette had insisted that the girl's death was the result of an accident. But the boat had been found bottom side up with her coat lying on top. The totality of the evidence pointed to foul play. Hughes felt certain of his ground. Yet a life was at stake and his conclusion could be wrong. With the execution set for Monday morning, the Governor heard a final plea for Gillette on Saturday. On Sunday, after a terrible day of soul searching, he walked to his office and said the execution would be carried out. About ten o'clock that evening his secretary called to say that Gillette had confessed to his religious adviser.

The Farmer case added physical peril to mental anguish. Farmer and his wife killed an old lady who lived next door, hid the body in a trunk, moved into the old lady's house, forged a deed in favor of themselves, and told inquirers that she had gone to visit friends in the West. The trunk was found, with its gruesome and incriminating evidence, in their possession. Both were convicted. At her separate trial Mrs. Farmer appeared oblivious to what was taking place. Later she gave birth to a child in prison, and these facts were used to whip up a tornado of sentiment against her execution.

Because Hughes did not respond to the clamor, Hearst's *Evening Journal* launched an execrable attack upon him. In an editorial reminiscent of the slander that led to McKinley's assassination, the *Journal* said that if Hughes should permit this woman to be murdered, he would be a legal murderer himself and would get what was coming to him. As this calumny reverberated through the state, Police Commissioner William Bingham warned the Governor of his danger and sent him a special guard. District Attorney Jerome of New York telephoned to say that he was going after Hearst for criminal libel. "Hearst is simply trying to stir up a sensation," Hughes replied. "If you prosecute him, you will keep the sensation alive for a year. The best thing to do is to let it die."

The Governor himself was worried about Mrs. Farmer's apparent stolidity at the trial. He asked for the prison physician's reports, and was sent a large box containing hundreds of little slips of paper. His tedious task of examining these slips one night at the Executive Mansion seemed to be futile until he discovered a sealed envelope containing pieces of rough brown wrapping paper covered with scribbling. Investigation proved the writing to be Mrs. Farmer's. She had recorded the whole story of the trial. She knew the witnesses and had carefully analyzed the testimony. Hughes felt that the assumption of her de-

[6] Beerits' Memorandum, VI, 28.

fenders that she might have been insane at the time of the trial was completely undermined.[7] He permitted the execution to be carried out.

Still more disturbing to the Governor's peace of mind was the stench of corruption that continued to hang over Albany. For many years the legislature had been the venal tool of unscrupulous bosses and corporate interests. Hughes had cleaned out the executive departments and broken the control of legislation by the corruptionists. But the "Black Horse Cavalry," as the newspapers called the combination of exploiters representing both parties in the legislature, was far from being subdued.

The struggle between these forces and the Governor dramatically erupted again with the death of John Raines, the Senate majority leader, on December 16, 1909. To succeed Raines the Old Guard chose Jotham P. Allds, who had been a youngster in Hamilton when Hughes was attending Madison (now Colgate) University. Their personal relations had always been pleasant, but Allds had faithfully served Platt and Odell when he was a member of the Assembly. The elevation of this slow, ponderous, and unprincipled politician to the Senate leadership could be regarded only as betokening last-ditch resistance to the Hughes reforms.

While the caucus was nominating Allds, seven disgusted Senators met separately in protest, and Senator Benn Conger informed his colleagues that he had personal knowledge that Allds had accepted a bribe.[8] Josiah T. Newcomb repeated the story to Oswald Garrison Villard of the New York *Evening Post*. Allds tried to suppress the story, then begged for mercy and threatened a libel suit. When the *Evening Post* printed the story [9] nevertheless, and Conger himself unfolded the sordid details, the state was shaken as if by a delayed-action bomb. Allds demanded an investigation which only confirmed the charges. Several years before the advent of the Hughes régime the American Bridge Company, fighting to defeat a bill that would have upset its monopoly, had sent Hiram T. Moe to Albany with $6,500 in a satchel. In addition to the $1,000 paid to Allds,[10] the testimony showed that $4,000 had gone to Assemblyman Jean L. Burnett, presumably for division among several legislators, and $1,000 to the late Speaker Nixon. Although still asserting his innocence, Allds resigned before the Senate found him guilty by a vote of 40 to 9.

President Taft and Governor Hughes met at the Republican Club dinner in New York on February 13 and surveyed this grim political mess. Both threw their influence on the side of complete exposure of the corruptionists. "This is not the time to retire in dismay from any disclosure," the Governor declared two days later. "The party . . . needs to purge itself of evil." [11] Hughes

[7] *Ibid.*, p. 31.   [8] Burton J. Hendrick in *McClure's Magazine*, September, 1910.
[9] *Evening Post*, Jan. 18, 1910.   [10] New York *Evening Post*, Feb. 11, 1910.
[11] Buffalo *Commercial*, Feb. 12, 1910.

sought an investigation broad enough, as Senator Hinman put it, to uncover "all the crawling things which have been leaving their trails of slime in the legislative halls at Albany." But the Old Guard, with its back to the wall, doggedly fought off every effort to turn the light upon a broader area of its machinations.

The obvious answer to Allds' disgrace was to select the Governor's most conspicuous friend in the Senate, Harvey D. Hinman, as majority leader. Senator Root came out strongly for the nomination of Hinman "as the only course which will . . . correctly exhibit the real relation of the party as a whole to the principles and policies for which Governor Hughes stands and will rightly represent the wishes of the voters of the party." [12] Hughes publicly announced his agreement with this view. So much was at stake that he could no longer remain entirely aloof from the organization of the legislature, as he had done in 1907. But Hinman, sponsor of the direct-primaries bill, was anathema to the bosses. Woodruff and Barnes rallied their forces and elected Senator George H. Cobb as both floor leader and president pro tempore.

As the fight went on, other scandals came to light. In a special message to the legislature on April 11, Hughes asked for an investigation that would be "immediate, impartial, thorough and unsparing." [13] "You know that for years," he said in a public address a few days later, "we have not had decent government in this state but government that has been disreputable and indecent. I am convinced that the time has come when this must stop. The people are aroused. They will stand for nothing less than honest and fair dealing in the public service. Rip the cover off. Let in the light. Get the hooks out of the state departments. For years votes have been shamelessly bought and sold at the Capitol. Send one of the bribe-takers properly branded through the state so that he may be scorned by all honest men and it will have an inestimable effect for good and wholesome things in the service of the state and of the people." [14]

The legislature authorized a limited and restricted inquiry as if it were afraid of what might be turned up. Hope of securing a more thorough exposé was one of the Governor's chief reasons for calling a special session in June, 1910, when he also pressed his primary reform bill for the last time. But his efforts were futile.

This blind repudiation of his leadership quickened his yearning to shake the dust of politics from his feet. For some months his disgust had been mounting. In a postscript to a letter that he wrote to his father and mother on April 11, 1909, his feelings were laid bare:

[12] *New York Journal,* March 11, 1910.   [13] *Public Papers, 1910,* p. 97.
[14] *New York Times,* April 14, 1910.

Your words are encouraging—and certainly I feel the need of inspiration. It seems at times so hard that I have to bear this burden. You have no idea how I dislike public life—and what one can do seems so little. Well, it will be only for a few months longer. My only desire is to do all that I can to make things wholesome—it isn't much—but life is merely doing what you do with all your might. And so, I try to take things philosophically and while my life is far from what I should like to have it, I am not downcast—but rather the more determined, on this my 47th birthday, to make the most of the rest of it.

Chapter 26

FAREWELL TO POLITICS

TWO YEARS of breaking lances with the Republican bosses taught Governor Hughes one paramount lesson: New York would have to improve its governmental machinery if the will of the people were to be translated into workable public programs. In his first term he had struck chiefly at evils produced by the boss system. In his second term he was to strike more directly at organizational defects that made it possible for the czars of politics to use government as a means of powering the chariot of special privilege.

The Empire State boasted of its democracy. Yet it permitted self-appointed satraps to name the candidates for whom the people might vote. It used ballots so lengthy and so baffling as to defeat the central purpose of taking a popular canvass. It maintained an executive branch in which powers were so carelessly diffused that the ship of state seemed to be guided by a dozen different tillers, which caused it to creak and wobble instead of steering a straight course to the desired port.

After his reelection, Hughes seized the first opportunity—his inaugural address—to lay the case for more responsive and more efficient government before the people. The President of the United States, he pointed out, had a Cabinet of his own choice whose members directed the great Executive departments. The Governor of New York had no such opportunity to prove himself. The state comptroller, treasurer, attorney general, and engineer were elected. Sometimes, as in Hughes' first term, these officials were of a different party from that of the governor. Many of the administrators appointed by the governor held their offices for terms longer than his. In most instances they could be removed only with the consent of the Senate.

What Hughes asked of the lawmakers was not a Utopia but feasible, concrete improvements for which the need could be readily demonstrated. One was abolition of the Senate's power to block removal of incompetent administrative officials. The second was a simplified form of ballot. The third was a system of direct nominations that would enable the people to choose their party nominees.

He had already made extensive progress in getting control of his own official family. Investigations under the Moreland Act had helped to ferret out sloth and corruption. After the election of 1908, even Otto Kelsey gave way to the buffetings of public opinion and resigned as superintendent of insurance. The Governor was so swept off his feet that he made a hasty and ill-advised nomination and then withdrew the appointee's name before charges that were bruited about in the corridors of the Senate could be aired on the floor.[1] Having recovered his own fumble, he sent in the name of William H. Hotchkiss of Buffalo, and a new era of thorough and strict regulation of the insurance companies began.

With the aid of Clark Williams, who had become state comptroller in 1909, Hughes initiated a systematic study that led to the establishment of an executive budget in New York. Departmental requests for funds had previously been sent to the legislature in haphazard isolation. Hughes and Williams whipped together an experimental budget in 1910, and at Hughes' request the legislature enacted the rudiments of a budget-making system, although a good many years were to elapse before the executive budget would be fully established at either Albany or Washington.

The fight for ballot reform and direct primary elections had really begun with Hughes' first message in 1907, but the climax came in his second term. He pounced with special vehemence on the monstrosity that passed as a ballot in New York City elections. It was about four feet wide and had nineteen columns for city candidates. The names of some candidates appeared four, five, and even eight times in separate columns. "The use . . . of such an unwieldy ballot with its absurd duplications, in the most important municipal election held in this country," the Governor said indignantly, "is such a serious reflection upon our capacity to devise suitable election methods that we should hasten, out of very shame, to make needed correction." [2]

His attitude toward the direct primary underwent a progressive stiffening as the legislature persistently resisted his appeals. Hughes had no faith in the wide-open primaries that were being used in the West. To avoid similarly disappointing results, New York would have to feel its way cautiously. The Republican organization of Kings County had committed itself to direct primary nominations, and Hughes thought it would be a good idea to let that local group experiment with a permissive form of the primary. When the fight waxed hot, however, this permissive feature became the focal point of attack. Woodruff succeeded in beating the bill on the ground that its application would not be general, but as soon as the Governor suggested a general primary system Woodruff turned his full fury against that also.

In deference to public opinion, the lawmakers finally passed bills with some primary trappings but actually designed further to entrench the party machines. Hughes vetoed these and renewed his pleas for genuine primaries. After his

---

[1] Author's interview with Harvey D. Hinman, Aug. 15, 1948.
[2] *Public Papers, 1910*, p. 30.

reelection in 1908, he made a compulsory direct-nominations bill the leading item in his reform program, frankly describing his fight as "a late phase of the long struggle against the control of the powers of government by selfish interests." [3] The convention method of choosing candidates perpetuated the power of the bosses and the interests that financed them. Delegates to such conventions were "mere pieces on the political chess board." Only by drastic action could the rank and file make their influence felt under such a system. "All that is worst in our public life," the Governor declared, "finds its readiest means of access to power through the control of the nominating machinery of the parties."

What he recommended was a system of direct nominations for all elective offices, excepting presidential electors. As the debate proceeded, however, some of his ideas underwent further evolution. There was no point in taking power from unscrupulous bosses and handing it to unprincipled demagogues. The party would have to be preserved as a center of cohesiveness in government, while being brought under popular control. "Those who would use the direct primary to destroy party organization," he once said, "not only fail in their purpose, but they simply embarrass the efforts of those who are endeavoring to secure clean, wholesome and effective group action for political purposes."

In his fully matured plan, therefore, Hughes struck at the root of the evil by trying to democratize the parties themselves. The people should be able to throw out faithless party leaders as well as faithless public officials. The Hughes plan called for division of the state into small primary districts. The voters of each party in these districts would elect a committeeman. Within each Assembly district the committeemen would meet to select their candidates for assemblyman. Larger groups of the same committeemen would meet in the Senate districts to choose their senatorial candidates. The party committee of each Assembly district would name one of its members to represent it in a statewide committee for selection of candidates for governor and other statewide offices and formulation of a party platform.

Here was a bold scheme to retain the advantages of party leadership and at the same time require party chieftains to seek election on the same ticket with the men whose nomination they advocated. The voting for such leaders would be strictly a party affair. Hughes thought it was absurd to let Democrats vote in Republican primaries and Republicans in Democratic primaries. That confused party responsibility instead of sharpening it.

With party leaders answerable to the rank and file, Hughes believed that most of the defects in the direct primaries then in use could be corrected. High-caliber men who would not go out and campaign for a nomination on

[3] *Public Papers, 1909*, p. 36.

their own initiative could be drafted as the candidates of the party committee. Tickets could be made up with some balance as to geography and representation of various groups within the party. No doubt these tickets would be accepted nine times out of ten. But the Hughes plan left the door open for rebellious party members to enter their own candidates in the primaries by petition if the leaders should botch their opportunity.

Under this system a legislator who had refused to bow to the special interests could not be thrown out for his independence (as he often was under the old system) if his constituents were willing to fight for him. The grip of the bosses could be broken. The plan had its origin in Hughes' own experience. Twice the people had given him a vote of confidence but in each case they had an opportunity to vote for the man of their choice chiefly because Theodore Roosevelt and Elihu Root had overridden the bosses who held the nominating power. Hughes had set his mind firmly against a third term, but he was loath to leave Albany with the boss system still entrenched.

Barnes, Woodruff, and Wadsworth ridiculed the Hughes plan as legalized bossism. Raines and Barnes pleaded with Elihu Root, whom the legislature had just elected to the United States Senate, to come out with a statement that would kill the primaries bill. Divide and rule was their strategy. Root candidly replied at the annual dinner of Barnes' Albany machine. "I count him [Hughes]," he told the hostile Barnes men, "as I count all lovers of their country and their party to be for party organization." As questioning "ohs" resounded through the hall, Root let loose another challenge: "The wide popularity of Governor Hughes, not only with the State of New York, but in the West, is based on the presumption that he has jumped on the politicians." The grand old statesman brought his speech to a climax with a full endorsement of what Hughes was trying to do.

Reason and argument had no more chance in that sea of skepticism, however, than a fisherman on the back of a whale. The legislative correspondents at Albany correctly diagnosed the situation when they gave their annual dinner in the spring of 1909. Across the room was hung a huge banner bearing the words, "CHARLIE, QUIT DREAMING." When Hughes arose to respond to the newsmen's bantering, he said, "I may be a dreamer, but I'm not a quitter." Then he launched into his dream of what New York might be and what its public-spirited citizens and the legislators sitting before him might accomplish by working together in the public interest. His idealism won hearty applause but few legislative votes.

Once more Hughes carried his fight to the people. "I know of no better way of insuring the people against exploitation from corrupt political methods," he told a Rochester audience on the night of April 8, "than by making political managers account directly to the voters of their party and giving to the voters the right of final decision by direct vote upon the candidates that are presented. It is not loyalty to party spirit which occasions the trouble, but loyalty to special interests, which seem to control the party and utilize the party machinery." [4]

That very night the Assembly riddled his primaries bill by a vote of 112 to 28. Against these odds it was futile to call a special session. Governor Hughes awaited the convening of the legislature in January, 1910, to renew the fight. The Hinman-Greene bill was reintroduced with improvements but without change in principle. This time the bosses came forward with a bill of their own resulting from a legislative inquiry into the primary laws of other states. While it incorporated some of the Hinman-Greene provisions, it denied the voters any chance of passing upon party nominees. The *New York Press* accurately characterized it as "a fake bill designed to preserve the power of the bosses." [5]

Barnes also pressed his fight against the Governor personally. Both were guests at the legislative correspondents' dinner on April 7. When the good-natured journalistic ribbing of the distinguished guests was concluded, the Albany boss, fortified by intoxicants, launched into a tirade of abuse against reformers in general and Hughes in particular. It was the most caustic assault upon himself to which Hughes had ever listened or ever would listen. Anger may have burned within him as he arose to reply, but what came to the surface was only an unruffled flow of words that laid bare the sordid triangle of bossism, corruption, and exploitation of which Barnes was the central figure. "Look into each other's eyes," the Governor cried, "and know the truth." Seldom has the despicable business of perverting a government and plundering a people been more skillfully stripped to the core. To those who listened, Hughes seemed to become the embodiment of eloquence, sincerity, and power.[6]

The crowd gave way to delirium. Men stood on their chairs and shouted themselves hoarse. Bosslets and toadying politicians joined in the impulsive demonstration, as if in unavoidable admiration for a man who could shrink the big boss to peanut size without resorting to rancor or distortion of fact. As soon as the excitement subsided, however, they hastened down to the bar and cursed themselves for having lost control of their emotions.

Senator George H. Cobb attempted to save the day for the reformers by drafting a compromise bill applying the Hinman-Greene provisions only to congressmen, members of the legislature, and county officers. Hughes stood ready to approve it as half a loaf, and the Senate passed it by thirty-four to thirteen. Once more, however, the Assembly turned it down and passed its

[4] New York *Tribune*, April 9, 1909.   [5] March 17, 1910.
[6] Author's interviews with John Lord O'Brian and Harvey D. Hinman, eyewitnesses.

own "fake" primaries bill. Without waiting for the official copy to reach his desk, the Governor announced he would veto it.

Hughes decided to try once more. His influence as Governor had gone into partial eclipse because of his impending resignation, but the outlook was not hopeless. The country was bestirring itself to welcome back its hero fresh from new conquests in Africa and Europe—Theodore Roosevelt. Six days before the special session convened T. R. wrote Hughes from aboard ship on the Atlantic:

Are you going to be in New York any time during the next month or two? If so, would you care to come out and spend the night with me, or come out and take lunch with me—whichever you choose? Now, my dear Governor, I know how busy you are, and this may be utterly inconvenient, and if so you must not think of coming; but it would be a very great pleasure to see you and talk over many things with you. If you would prefer, I would gladly meet you in New York, and we could lunch together, but of course it would be a pleasure to me to have you in my house.[7]

Two days later the former President landed in New York amid great popular acclaim and ceremony. The Governor had no part in these events; nor was he able immediately to accept T. R.'s invitation. The delay in their meeting unloosed fresh rumors of coolness between the two men, and Hughes sought in his letter of June 25, 1910, to dispel any misunderstanding:

I beg you not to believe the stories which the mischief makers are endeavoring to circulate, and which here and there find some reflection in the press. I have said nothing directly or indirectly save that I was very glad to receive your invitation and accepted it with pleasure,—the date of the visit yet to be fixed.

In truth, the work has been so insistent—not only days, but night after night until the morning hours—during the past month that I have about reached my limit and am nearly exhausted. I shall not finish the 30-day bills until Sunday night, and I must be in Cambridge Wednesday morning. Not a line of my Phi Beta Kappa address has yet been written.

I am sure you will understand all this, but I do not wish you to have the faintest doubt as to my attitude. I am looking forward with much pleasure to seeing you in Cambridge, and I shall be glad to visit you at Oyster Bay when we are able to fix a mutually convenient date.

Roosevelt replied on June 27:

Indeed, I shall pay no heed whatever to those stories. I believe that you are backed up by the best people of this State, and one of my main reasons for desiring to see you is to tell you so.

Meanwhile William M. Chadbourne had dropped in at the Governor's office to say that he thought Roosevelt would lend his aid to a compromise primaries

[7] T. R. to CEH, June 14, 1910.

bill. Chadbourne undertook to sound out T. R. with respect to the Cobb bill. But the answer came straight from Roosevelt himself when he encountered Hughes in the Yard of Harvard University on commencement morning, June 29. It was their first meeting since the inauguration of Taft sixteen months before. The atmosphere was heavy with speculation as to what the return of T. R. would mean as to both the Hughes policies in Albany and the Taft policies in Washington. Instinctively the other men in the parties fell back and left the two giants of New York politics together under the Harvard elms. The conversation soon turned to the situation at Albany and the fight for direct nominations.

"I don't wish to say anything about this matter," the former President said.

"Colonel," Hughes admonished, "silence means opposition." The Hearst press had been saying that the bill would be beaten because of Roosevelt's disapproval.

"Opposition!" T. R. exclaimed. "Silence means opposition! I'll speak." [8]

The marshal of the parade broke up the conversation by asking the two distinguished visitors to move into the hall. They sat together on the platform and during intervals in the ceremony Hughes whispered to T. R. a more detailed explanation of what he was trying to do at Albany. On the other side of Roosevelt sat Senator Henry Cabot Lodge. His opposition to any participation by the former President in the New York fight resulted in a whispered debate between the Senator and Governor across T. R.'s chest.

At noon Roosevelt presided over the alumni luncheon. "Our Governor has a very persuasive way with him," he said. "I had intended to keep absolutely clear from any kind of public or political question after coming home, and I could carry out my resolution all right until I met the Governor this morning, and he then explained to me that I had come back to live in New York now: that I had to help him out, and after a very brief conversation I put up my hands and agreed to help him." [9]

Roosevelt agreed to accept the Cobb bill, with an amendment excluding candidates for city office so as not to interfere with municipal fusion campaigns, and telegraphed his endorsement to Senator Davenport. President Taft also lent his aid. Big names were not enough, however, to turn the tide of revolt at Albany. The antiprimary forces condemned Roosevelt's intervention in the same terms the Governor had used to condemn the interference of the bosses. There was a difference, of course: neither Roosevelt nor Hughes used the patronage club or any of the forces of invisible government. Their appeal was to public opinion. Nevertheless, the Senate rejected the amended Cobb bill by one vote, and the irate Assembly brought up the old bill and scuttled it again in a petty display of resentment.

[8] Beerits' Memorandum, VI, 18.   [9] Outlook, July 9, 1910.

Governor Hughes thus lost one of the hardest battles of his career. Yet he had given the state and nation, as Burton J. Hendrick pointed out, a "clearly outlined picture of what the old party system means." [10] He had shown the people in unmistakable terms what they must do to bring government under their control. It is true that his plan had the defects of its virtues: it presupposed an alert and intelligent citizenry, which does not always exist. It called for unselfish leaders of the type of Hughes himself, who are difficult to find. In a more friendly climate, however, his direct-nominations plan might well have become the pattern for a great rejuvenation of popular government through the two-party system. New York was ultimately to acquire a primary system less bold in scope and design. A shorter ballot, too, was to be achieved along with reorganization of the executive branch and strengthening of the governor's powers. As several of Hughes' successors fought for these reforms, they realized that their tasks had been made easier by his vigorous spadework.

In those gloomy days of 1910, however, recriminations multiplied. T. R.'s friends were piqued because he had been led into a losing fight. His foes were disgruntled because, having dipped his toe into the hot water of the primaries contest, Roosevelt plunged headlong into the New York political caldron. If Hughes had left the colonel alone, some conservatives were wont to lament, the whole catastrophic split between Roosevelt and Taft might have been avoided. What naïveté! Once back in his native habitat, T. R. could no more avoid politicking than the sun can avoid radiating heat. While still in Europe, he had written Lodge that he was aware of Taft's mistakes and implied that he would have "to plunge into this caldron of politics." [11] Hughes merely offered the colonel a convenient springboard.

Professor George Edwin Mowry goes so far as to accuse Hughes of drawing Roosevelt into the fight and then, belatedly accepting a seat on the Supreme Court, withdrawing himself from the political arena. "The air around Oyster Bay must have been electric," he writes, "after that incident." [12] The facts are that Hughes had accepted the Supreme Court nomination two months before he ever talked with Roosevelt on the primaries bill. So far from being deceived about it, T. R. wrote to Lodge before sailing for home, "Hughes' nomination is excellent." [13]

The air at Oyster Bay may have been electric, but if so it was from the intensity of discussion when the retired President and the retiring Governor met there in July, 1910, for their long postponed visit. Hughes was accom-

[10] *McClure's Magazine*, September, 1910.

[11] *Selections from the Correspondence of Theodore Roosevelt and Henry Cabot Lodge* (New York, Scribner's, 1925), II, 380. Copyright, 1925, by Charles Scribner's Sons.

[12] *Theodore Roosevelt and the Progressive Movement* (Madison, University of Wisconsin Press, 1946), p. 136. Copyright, 1946, by University of Wisconsin Press.

[13] *Selections from the Correspondence of Theodore Roosevelt and Henry Cabot Lodge*, p. 380.

panied by Chairman Willcox of the Public Service Commission and Frederick M. Crossett, his new military secretary. Colonel Roosevelt greeted him effusively. After dinner the two hitched their chairs close together at one end of the capacious veranda, far from the other guests, and plunged into a prolonged discussion of the state of affairs at Albany. From time to time the colonel strode with quick steps up and down the veranda. Then he would resume his seat beside the Governor, talking even more earnestly than before. T. R. seemed to be wholly in sympathy with the Hughes program. Once more they were drawn together in a common cause.

Later that evening the colonel took his guests to his library and humorously described his hobnobbing with foreign potentates on his trip abroad. Speaking of his interview with the Kaiser, he pointed to an enormous but unlovely vase that had been given him and snapped in his inimitable manner, "A bit of German crockery; I will send it to the Germanic Museum at Harvard." Then he brought out a folio on art, with a full-page inscription written in English by the Kaiser, who seemed to regard himself as the highest authority on that subject. T. R. read the inscription with great gusto and observed with a chuckle, as he got to the "Wilhelm I.R." signature, "Slightly ungrammatical." The one gift from the Kaiser that he really prized was a copy of the *Nibelungenlied*. "The Kaiser showed it to me," the irrepressible colonel boasted, "and said something which I at once interpreted as an offer and immediately accepted." [14]

For some months Taft, too, had interested himself in the Republican schism at Albany. His first effort had been to keep Hughes in the saddle as a means of averting disaster. Taft had come to have an unbounded admiration for the Governor in spite of his fear that Hughes might be his rival for the presidential nomination in 1912. "If I am defeated for the next nomination," he had told Captain Butt, "I think it will be by Hughes. And I don't think he will allow his name to be used unless he really feels that I have no chance to win. . . . But I always think of Hughes as President." [15]

In March, Taft went to Albany. The Governor met the presidential party at the station and took Taft to the Executive Mansion with a cavalry escort. Both were speakers at the Tuberculosis Congress before going to the University Club banquet at the Ten Eyck Hotel. Back at the Mansion, they talked politics until two o'clock in the morning, Hughes presenting a full-scale sketch of the debauchery and reaction in the legislature. Taft responded that it was the Governor's duty to run again. Root shared that feeling, he said. The entire hope of the party rested on Hughes.

"I do not dare to run the chance of breaking down mentally," Hughes re-

[14] CEH, Notes, p. 204.
[15] *Taft and Roosevelt: the Intimate Letters of Archie Butt* (New York, Doubleday, 1924), I, 223. Copyright, 1924, by Doubleday, Page & Co.

plied, citing warnings from his doctor. "I must get out and make my family safe while I am able." [16]

Taft spent all day Sunday with the Hugheses, and they had a delightful time together. Baby Elizabeth, having been coached on how to behave in the company of the President, created a riot of laughter when she sat on his ample lap as long as she could stand it, then ran to her mother and exclaimed, "Oh, what a big man!" The Hugheses gave a luncheon for the President at which the guests included the governor general of Canada (Lord Grey), President Nichols of Dartmouth College, former Governor David R. Francis, and Mayor McEwan. They took Taft to church, went driving in the afternoon, and arranged a press conference for him at the Executive Mansion.

"I don't know the man I admire more than Hughes," said Taft to Captain Butt two days after they had left Albany. "If ever I have the chance I shall offer him the Chief Justiceship." [17]

A week later the death of Justice David J. Brewer gave the President a seat on the Supreme Court to fill and he decided not to wait for a vacancy in the Chief Justiceship to get Hughes on the bench. Albany was dumfounded by Hughes' acceptance. The bosses rejoiced, and the Governor's political supporters put on sackcloth and ashes. They realized that his administration, like Samson, had been suddenly shorn of its power. Their hopes of rescuing the Republican Party in New York from its corrupt machine control were utterly shattered. Wails of despair crept into dozens of the congratulatory letters that were showered upon the Governor. Even more general was a profound sense of regret that he had turned his back upon his bright prospect of being elected to the Presidency.

"If your confirmation were submitted to the country," wrote former Governor Black, "I think it would fail, for I believe the sentiment is strong, widespread and active in favor of a career for you more public and conspicuous than that you have chosen." "I cannot but feel," declared E. J. Ridgway, "that the Nation is paying a frightful price for your peace." The most pointed comment of all was the friendly and prophetic warning from Nathaniel Myers, New York lawyer. "If an exigency shall arise and you shall be needed," he wrote, "the People will pull you off the Bench for the higher position." [18]

Hughes had little sympathy with these lamentations. Undoubtedly he could have had a third term as governor. Then he would have been, in 1912, the logical man to have saved the Republican Party from its tragic split between Taft and Roosevelt. But he had had enough of politics. The law was calling him back. He regarded the work of the Supreme Court as of the highest importance and of course he realized his own peculiar fitness for public service

---

[16] *Ibid.,* p. 309.   [17] *Ibid.,* p. 310.
[18] These letters and comments are in the Hughes Papers.

of that type. "I had no right to refuse," he wrote to Ridgway. "A refusal on the ground that some time or other I might be a candidate for the Presidency, particularly in view of the record of the disappointed ambition of so many historic worthies, would have been absurd." [19]

The chorus of regrets was significant chiefly as a measure of the impression Hughes had made upon public opinion in his four years at Albany. He had infused new vigor and new meaning into democratic government. He had taught the people how to use new instruments for their protection and advancement of their interests. The example he set for integrity, efficiency, and judicious use of power had never been surpassed. The *World* unhesitatingly singled him out as the one New York governor who had "done the most toward purifying the State government and re-establishing rule of the people." [20] "This new breath of life which he breathed into our political methods," wrote the *Evening Post*, "came largely from his steadfast reliance upon reason and justice. No public man ever treated a democracy more consistently as a fairminded court that could be prevailed upon to see where the weight of argument lies and what is the right thing to do. . . . We gratefully acknowledge that he has ennobled our public life and quickened our hope in democracy." [21]

In the years that followed, governors in New York and elsewhere paid him the great compliment of emulating his methods. Henry L. Stimson ran as the Republican candidate for Governor of New York in 1910, supporting all the Hughes issues, but could not overcome public disgust with the machine. A few years later, Governor Martin H. Glynn, a Democrat, who had been comptroller during the first Hughes administration, announced publicly that he intended "to follow Hughes' footsteps" in dealing with the legislature.[22] Woodrow Wilson won the governorship of New Jersey in 1910 after a campaign in which he promised to do in that state what Hughes had done in New York.

Time further magnified Governor Hughes' achievements. After a quarter of a century had passed, Russell McInnes of the legislative committee of the New York Citizens' Union analyzed the records of all the New York governors from Hughes to Franklin D. Roosevelt to determine how successful they had been in getting their recommendations adopted by the legislature. Of all the recommendations made by governors from 1907 through 1931, 43.6 per cent had been adopted. Popular and strong though he was, Governor Alfred E. Smith had a batting average of only 33.5 per cent. "And Governor Hughes, who was the most successful of the governors during these twenty-five years," wrote McInnes, "had 56.5 per cent of his recommendations adopted by the legislature." [23]

[19] CEH to E. J. Ridgway, April 27, 1910. [20] April 26, 1910.
[21] New York *Evening Post*, Oct. 6, 1910. [22] Utica *Daily Press*, Nov. 13, 1913.
[23] *National Municipal Review*, May, 1934.

On his last day at Albany, Oct. 6, 1910, the Governor cheered his melancholy staff with a gay stag dinner. Mrs. Hughes had already gone to Washington to get their new household in order. In the course of the evening the staff presented him with a large loving cup filled with champagne. When the wine was gone and the regret-tinged hilarity was at an end, Hughes took his hat and bag and walked out of the Executive Mansion never to return. His carriage whisked him to the station and the train carried him, in a contemplative mood, to a new life that was to be totally different from anything he had known before.

The fighting Governor

By L. E. Shattuck, 1908

On top of Mount Marcy

By L. E. Shattuck, 1908

*Helping daughter Catherine
sail her boat*

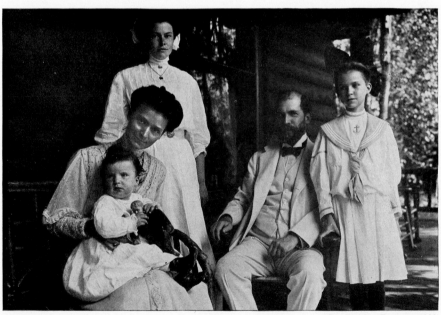

By Waldon Fawcett, 1908

*Governor and Mrs. Hughes and their daughters at their
summer cottage on Upper Saranac Lake*

Chapter 27

ASCENDING THE SUPREME BENCH

THE SUPREME COURT in the first year of the Taft Administration was in a sorry plight. Four of its members, including Chief Justice Melville W. Fuller, were aged and slow, and Justice Moody was ill from overwork. Its calendar was overloaded with stale cases. The President was irate over the unwillingness of "those old fools," as he called them, to retire. "It is an outrage," he wrote to Senator Lodge, "that the four men on the bench who are over seventy should continue there and thus throw the work and responsibility on the other five." [1]

Taft's eagerness to get vigorous new blood on the court impelled him toward Hughes as soon as he learned that the Governor was determined to get out of politics. "I know the reasons that suggest themselves against your acceptance and I do not minimize them," he wrote in offering Hughes the place vacated by Justice Brewer. "I believe as strongly as possible that you are likely to be nominated and elected President some time in the future unless you go upon the Bench or make such associations at the Bar as to prevent." [2] But the court needed Hughes, the President argued, to add strength to its membership and to buttress public confidence in its work. Taft strained himself to overcome the objection that he feared would arise in the Governor's mind. It would not be necessary, he wrote, for Hughes to resign the governorship until October, leaving only two and a half months of his term. The court position was for life. While the salary was then $12,500, Taft said that in all probability it would be increased to $17,500 at the next session of Congress—an overly optimistic prediction, for the increase would be to $14,500.

Then Taft openly dangled the most powerful judicial position in the world before the Governor. "The Chief Justiceship," he wrote, "is soon likely to be vacant and I should never regard the practice of never promoting Associate Justices as one to be followed. Though, of course, this suggestion is only that by accepting the present position you do not bar yourself from the other, should it fall vacant in my term. . . ."

In a postscript he added:

Don't misunderstand me as to the Chief Justiceship. I mean that if that office were now open, I should offer it to you and it is probable that if it were to become

[1] From *The Life and Times of William Howard Taft,* by Henry F. Pringle, I, 530. Copyright, 1939, by Henry F. Pringle and reprinted by permission of Rinehart & Co., Publishers.
[2] Taft to CEH, April 22, 1910.

vacant during my term, I should promote you to it; but, of course, conditions change, so that it would not be right for me to say by way of promise what I would do in the future. Nor, on the other hand, would I have you think that your declination now would prevent my offering you the higher place, should conditions remain as they are.

Hughes was not swayed by this talk about a position that was not yet open. By nature he always avoided counting his chickens before they were hatched. The reasoning that led him to accept the Associate Justiceship is clearly evident in his reply to Taft on April 24:

MY DEAR MR. PRESIDENT,

A careful consideration of the questions raised by your offer to nominate me for the Supreme Court to succeed Mr. Justice Brewer has convinced me that I should accept it. The honor of this appointment, great as it would be in any case, is especially enhanced in my estimation because it comes from you,—in view of your distinguished judicial career and your intimate knowledge of the requirements of the office. So far as my personal inclinations are concerned, they lie in the direction of judicial work. My training and professional interest have been such that I should undertake this work with a personal satisfaction which no other line of effort could command in the same degree. No one could have a more profound sense of the vast responsibilities of the Supreme Court than I have, and while this makes me realize the more keenly my shortcomings, it also disposes me to welcome the opportunity to devote my life to such important service. Against such a life-work, to meet the conditions of which an adjustment could be made, I should not for a moment set any prospect of money-making at the bar.

I trust that I should be able, however, to withstand any personal inclination and not permit it to control my decision, if it were opposed to the obligations of public duty. This is the only question which has occasioned any difficulty. But reflection has re-assured me upon this point. There is no definite sphere of public usefulness, other than the place you offer, which would be open to me at the close of this year and my circumstances would permit me to accept. The opportunities of the future are conjectural. The alternative of your proposal is private practice. Undoubtedly this would permit public service in many ways, but there would also be the exacting demands of active work at the bar. Against this division of effort, and its doubtful fruition, I should have on the bench a definite field of usefulness in the discharge of a function of national government of the gravest consequence to our people and to the future of our institutions.

The question seems to me to be really,—What right have I to refuse this opportunity of public service which is now presented by you and upon what ground could I justify myself in turning aside from such a plain path of usefulness?

I confess that I know of none unless it be found in my present obligations as Governor of this State. But you point out that I need not qualify as Justice of the Supreme Court or resign as Governor until the second week of October. . . . I should regard a refusal to take up at your request this life-work solely because I should have to leave my office here in October instead of remaining until the close of December as based on ground too trivial to be just to you or worthy of myself. . . .

Your expressions regarding the Chief Justiceship are understood and most warmly appreciated. You properly reserve entire freedom with respect to this and I accept the offer you now make without wishing you to feel committed in the slightest degree. Should the vacancy occur during your term I, in common with all our citizens, should desire you to act freely and without embarrassment in accordance with your best judgment at that time.

Assuring you of my esteem and warm personal regard, and expressing again my deep sense of the confidence you repose and the responsibility it involves, I am

Very sincerely yours,

CHARLES E. HUGHES

Had he chosen to return to private practice, Hughes could have earned from $100,000 to $400,000 a year, as indicated by the fact that his fees did reach the latter maximum after he had left the bench. He was well aware of the financial sacrifice he was making. But what was wealth compared to the satisfaction of a judicial career? Were not the courts in the truest sense "the expert agencies of democracy"—the democracy that he cherished? "I am very glad," he wrote to his son, "that you are so entirely satisfied with the decision I have made. . . . We shall have to live within rather narrow bounds; but we can stand that. My only desire is to be able worthily to perform the duties of the office. And I confess that the congratulations and friendly comments that have been coming in have made me feel very humble and have deepened my sense of responsibility." [3]

The President fairly beamed with delight over Hughes' acceptance.

"Yes, Archie," he told Captain Butt, "that is a great appointment. How do you think it will be taken?"

"It will be a monument to your administration," Butt said. "There was every political reason why you should not have made it, and apparently every reason why he should not have accepted it."

"Yes," Taft answered reflectively, "such an appointment makes politics look petty." [4]

The Senate was equally pleased. On May 2, 1910, it confirmed the Hughes nomination in a five-minute executive session without a negative vote being cast. Senator Chauncey Depew, who had been besmirched by the insurance investigation, nevertheless took the lead in pressing the nomination through.

Considering the President's feeling of virtue in making this appointment, it is difficult to account for his next move. En route to Albany by train, he asked Hughes to join him at Pittsfield. His purpose was to induce the Governor, who had not yet taken his seat on the bench, to make a campaign speech in Ohio. When Taft came to the point of voicing his request, however, he couched it as if he were only feebly echoing a suggestion from other sources.

[3] May 2, 1910.
[4] *Taft and Roosevelt: the Intimate Letters of Archie Butt,* I, 336–337.

Hughes immediately said that he thought it would be highly improper for him to make any campaign speeches even in his own state, and the embarrassed Chief Executive dropped the matter.

Mr. Justice Hughes met with his brethren of the bench for the first time on October 10, 1910, only four days after he had resigned as governor. All the Justices greeted him warmly as they assembled in the robing room. Every one of them was pleased to have him added to the court.[5] Hughes donned his flowing black robe, which seemed a little out of place on so active a man, and took the oath of allegiance. Then followed the awe-inspiring procession across the corridor and through the courtroom—the old Senate Chamber in the Capitol where the court had sat since the days of Taney. First in the line was Harlan of Kentucky, huge of frame, shaggy, with heavy brows half covering his eyes. Then came White of Louisiana, with his plump, kindly face looking grave; McKenna of California, with a neat fringe of whiskers on his squarish chin; Holmes, looking at once wise and frisky behind his long white mustache; William R. Day of Ohio, keen but frail; and Horace H. Lurton of Tennessee. Hughes, with his graying beard, thinning hair, firm step, and serious demeanor, looked every inch a judge before he ever ascended the bench. At the end of the line came the retired Justice Brown.

Every seat in the historic, half-circular courtroom was taken. The Cabinet was represented by Attorney General Wickersham and Secretary Nagel. Antoinette Carter Hughes had been waiting for half an hour for the ceremony to begin. Beside her sat her daughter Catherine and the new Justice's mother. Their eyes fastened upon Harlan as he announced the appointment and confirmation of Charles E. Hughes to take the place of Justice Brewer and directed Clerk McKenney to read the new member's commission. "The court extends a cordial welcome," Harlan said.

At the clerk's desk Hughes took the oath of office in a voice that was vibrant with conviction: "I, Charles E. Hughes, do solemnly swear that I will administer justice without respect to persons, and do equal right to the poor and to the rich. . . ." "So help me God," said the clerk at the end. Hughes repeated, "So help me God."

The marshal escorted Hughes to his seat, but not at the extreme left of the Chief Justice where a newcomer customarily sits. Because of the vacancy on the court, he went at once to the seat at the extreme right of the bench. Here Oliver Wendell Holmes shook his hand, and the brief induction ceremony was at an end. While Harlan paid a brief tribute to Chief Justice Fuller prior to adjournment of the court in his honor, Holmes beckoned to Hughes to move up and take the vacant seat of the ill Justice Moody which separated them. The new member knew enough of the traditions of the court not to make such

[5] Judge Peter B. McLennan to CEH, June 14, 1910, quoting Justice Harlan.

a *faux pas.* "I tremble to think," he once said, "what might have happened if I had been innocent enough to follow Justice Holmes' kindly but rather thoughtless suggestion. The other Justices would have regarded me as a fresh and bumptious newcomer, and even the Chief Justices in their marble busts might have raised their eyebrows." [6]

Everything about the court seemed compact and conservative. Its atmosphere was satisfyingly rich in dignity and tradition. Hughes was conscious of the lingering influence of Marshall, Story, Field, Curtis, Bradley, and Miller. Great minds had been at work in the court for more than a century. One could not study their lives and decisions without gaining confidence in their sincerity and independence. Truly they had created a noble institution. De Tocqueville had rightly called it "the head of all known tribunals."

Yet in its physical facilities the court was astonishingly barren. In the absence of a dining hall the Justices lunched together, when the court was in session, in their robing room. Below was the judges' conference room and library, small and cluttered, where they assembled about a table to make their momentous decisions. During the long conferences the room became overheated and stuffy because some of the nine objected to having windows open.

The snug courtroom itself was so poorly ventilated as to be a source of friction. Within their own restricted circle the judges passed down a story of how Justice Gray, a large and full-blooded man, insisted on keeping a window open behind the screen. One day frail Justice Brown, feeling the draft, asked a page to close the window. Justice Gray, overheated, arose from the bench and went behind the screen to confirm his suspicions. "What damn' fool told you to close that window?" he asked the frightened page. "Mr. Justice Brown," the page admitted. "I thought so," sputtered Gray as he stormed back to the bench.

Even less commodious was the clerk's office. Lawyers who wished to smoke or chat while waiting for their cases to be called had to crowd into the entrance room of this office or stand in the corridor outside the courtroom. Probably no high court in the country had fewer conveniences. Yet most of the Justices were loath to leave the Capitol. President Taft was eager to initiate the construction of a Supreme Court building, but the Chief Justice threw cold water on the idea. He feared that the public might lose interest in the court if it sat outside the Capitol—a fantastic notion in view of the thousands of visitors to the white marble temple of justice that has housed the court since the thirties.

At that time none of the Justices had an office at the Capitol. Writing their opinions and doing their research at home, they had to provide working space for themselves and secretaries. The Government supplied furniture for their

[6] CEH, Notes, p. 209.

home offices and lent each member of the court a working library. Hughes found it difficult to rent a house in Washington with space enough to accommodate a family of seven (his mother was still living with him) and afford the necessary office space. At first he leased the house at 2401 Massachusetts Avenue, Northwest, and fitted up an office in the basement. That proved to be unsatisfactory, and he decided to put what was left of his savings into a permanent home. "At a very low price" he purchased a lot on the northwest corner of Sixteenth and V streets, Northwest, from former Senator John B. Henderson. It was then a very quiet and pleasant neighborhood, with no buildings at all on the east side of Sixteenth Street between Meridian Hill and U Street. Here in 1911 the Hugheses built a commodious four-story brick house in which they expected to live for the remainder of their days.

The clerical help provided was meager. Each Justice had only $2,000 a year to pay a secretary. Hughes hired a young lawyer to do this work—three of them served him in succession while he was Associate Justice—but, hating to write in longhand, he kept the young man busy with dictation and did most of his own research. The question of securing more help was occasionally discussed, but some of the Justices feared that if they had law clerks the public might suppose that the clerks were writing their opinions.

Hughes was shocked by the work load that loomed up ahead of him in his very first week on the bench. As he listened to the arguments, he thought he could be ready to make his decisions within a month or so. To his consternation he learned that he would be expected to vote in the Saturday conference on all the cases heard during the week. And they were important Government cases that had been advanced to the beginning of the session because the court was so far in arrears in its calendar. This demand upon his legal judgment sent him delving into the law books far into the night hours in spite of his weariness from a summer of toil at Albany.

Soon he was able to keep up with the work of the court, but he was not content merely to analyze each case as it came along and wait for experience on the bench to fill the gaps in his knowledge. Nothing less than a comprehensive view of the jurisprudence of the court would satisfy him. That could come only from intensive outside reading; so his night work continued far beyond the period of his initial "boning up" on litigation immediately at hand.

Justice Hughes was keenly aware of the difference between the outlook and training of the advocate and of the judge. "The advocate," he said, "is looking for something to support a particular argument and too often seizes upon any sentence in an opinion which he thinks will help him win his case." The jurist must study the whole range and scope of the law. "He learns the points of view of the Justices and to read their reasoning and various *dicta* in that light. Not infrequently a sentence or phrase, or even a paragraph, will get into a majority opinion which really does not have majority support and the effect of which one or more of the majority may be desirous of destroying as soon as they get a chance. A new Justice is not at ease in his seat until he has made a thorough study of lines of cases, so that when a case is argued he at once recognizes, or by looking at a key case brings back to his memory, the jurisprudence of the Court upon the general subject and can address his mind to the particular variant now presented. That is the explanation of the ability of experienced Justices to dispose rapidly of their work, and also of the difficulties the new Justice encounters in going over ground which is more familiar to his seniors on the bench." [7] By his intense application Hughes shortened his novitiate and was soon taking some of the court's most difficult assignments.

At first the atmosphere of the court was less agreeable than he had expected it to be. His only acquaintance among the Justices when he came to Washington was John Marshall Harlan, who had occasionally written to him at Albany. On one of the Governor's visits to Washington in 1909, the giant Justice had also driven him about the city and introduced him to Justice Brown at the latter's reception. Now on the bench together, Harlan was like a father to the new member.

Among some of the older judges, however, Harlan generated unmistakable friction. Harlan and White, both powerful men in the court, had apparently disliked each other since their first dramatic meeting in the spring of 1877. The story came out one day as the Justices lunched together in the robing room. President Hayes had sent a commission to Louisiana to bring about a settlement of local controversies. White, as spokesman for a Louisiana delegation, met the commission and freely described conditions within the state. When he finished speaking, a huge man wearing a buff-colored vest came over to him and said, "Well, you are damned frank." It was Harlan.

The stalwart Harlan, who seemed to embody the strength and dignity of the old court and who was somewhat overbearing in spite of his warm heart, also found much about Holmes that set him on edge. Holmes' opinions abounded in "obscure phrases" and his constitutional views were "unsound." The philosophic judge from Boston reciprocated in kind. He liked to refer to Harlan as the last of the tobacco-spitting judges and insisted that the old man's opinions were verbose and demagogical. While each respected the soldierly qualities of the other, the clash of their personalities often enlivened the judicial conference. Harlan would tartly challenge Holmes' conclusions, and the latter, always urbane, would refer to Harlan as "my lion-hearted friend." [8]

Those trying first months were further complicated by the fact that, with Justice Moody still sick, the court was sitting with only seven members and no

[7] *Ibid.*, pp. 211–212.   [8] *Ibid.*, p. 216.

Chief Justice. Fuller had died in July, 1910, and Taft was still giving "prayerful consideration" to the naming of a successor. Various lawyers and newspapers had suggested Hughes for the post immediately after Fuller's death, and it seemed to be generally assumed that Hughes would be the President's choice, even though nothing was known of his letter to Hughes on April 22. Taft had seemed to confirm this impression when he told Justice Moody that he wished to appoint "someone young and vigorous enough to go into the question of methods in equity cases, and if possible revise the entire procedure of this country and put it more in line with that of Great Britain." [9] Hughes admirably met these qualifications. At forty-eight he was nine years younger than any man then on the supreme bench. Vigor was his dominant characteristic. While the President procrastinated, however, Hughes had taken his seat as Associate Justice.

The age factor turned the President definitely against Elihu Root, who was sixty-five, and he exploded when word reached the White House that Justice Harlan, then seventy-seven, thought he should receive the appointment "as a final ornament to his judicial career." Attorney General Wickersham was delegated to ask the preference of the Justices, other than Hughes, and came back with the reply that Associate Justice White was the court's first choice.[10] But White was the same age as Root. The President continued to survey every possibility to make certain that Hughes was the best choice.

Beneath the smooth dignity of the court it was evident that the vacant Chief Justiceship was causing no little irritation. Harlan was obviously hungry for the honor. He thought the President could reasonably reward him for long service rendered and then, after a comparatively brief period, make Hughes his successor. White felt just as strongly that he was entitled to the place. With Harlan presiding as senior Associate Justice, White had little to say in conference and his usually amiable disposition seemed to have passed under a cloud. Throughout the fall he was offish and disgruntled.[11]

Hughes, too, was irritated by the President's indecision. The way in which the press was bruiting his name in connection with the Chief Justiceship made his position in the court very difficult. He quickly sensed that the brethren were allergic to inexperienced men in the presiding chair. The appointment of Chief Justice Waite directly from the bar, without any experience in court work and without any great prestige in the profession, had created resentment on the bench. Fuller, too, had become Chief Justice with little knowledge of how the court operated. The standing of Hughes in the legal profession in 1910 was much higher than that of either Waite or Fuller had been at the time of their appointments. His investigative work had given him a national reputation; his governorship had lifted him into the realm of high officialdom; and many

---

[9] Butt, *op. cit.*, I, 438–439.   [10] Pringle, *op. cit.*, p. 534.   [11] CEH, Notes, p. 216.

regarded him as presidential timber. Still, judicial work was new to him, and he feared that he would have a difficult time of it if he should be placed over the wise old men then on the bench. Cool reason told him that the President, now that he actually faced the awesome business of naming a Chief Justice, might regard him as too young and inexperienced.

Nor did Hughes think that the President was in any way committed to him. His irritation was solely a product of the embarrassment the President was causing him by his failure to make up his mind. "I thought," he said years later, "that if the President was not going to appoint me he should say so frankly and proceed promptly to appoint someone else . . . it is a mistake for the President to delay making judicial appointments." [12]

As the weeks passed, the public assumption that Hughes would be promoted seemed to be confirmed. "Hughes to Head Court," declared a headline in the *Washington Post* of November 11. On the same day a dispatch to the New York *Sun* asserted that Hughes was still the President's choice for Chief Justice in spite of objections from two members of his Cabinet who thought the former Governor was too uncompromising and from businessmen who feared that he was "a little too progressive." Those objections had been offset by impressive endorsements, including a letter of glowing praise from Francis Lynde Stetson, a Democrat who was president of the New York Bar Association and one of the country's foremost lawyers.

"I should bet," wrote Justice Holmes to his friend Pollock, "that he will appoint Hughes, who has given up a chance of being Republican nominee for the Presidency. . . ." [13] Justice Lurton, a close friend of Taft's since they had sat together on the circuit bench in Cincinnati, intimated to Hughes as he drove him home from the court one crisp December afternoon that he had recently seen the President. "I really think," he said, "you are going to be our Chief Justice." [14] A few days later Justice Day, another of Taft's close judicial friends, told Hughes that he understood that all question as to his elevation had been removed.

On Saturday, December 10, Taft called in the White House reporters and told them that he had made his decision as to the Chief Justiceship and that the nomination would go to the Senate on Monday or Tuesday. Still the finger of destiny seemed to point at Hughes. Toward evening of the next day, Sunday, came a telephone call from the White House.[15] "Would Mr. Justice Hughes please come over to see the President!" The cautious judge suppressed a surge of excitement. He would take nothing for granted. Yet here was a

---

[12] *Ibid.*, p. 217.
[13] Reprinted by permission of the publishers from *Holmes Pollock Letters: The Correspondence of Mr. Justice Holmes and Sir Frederick Pollock, 1874–1932,* edited by Mark DeWolfe Howe, I, 170, Harvard University Press, 1941.
[14] Beerits' Memorandum, VI, 42.   [15] CEH, Notes, p. 217.

summons. It linked itself with Taft's letter, with the reports in the press and the tidings from Lurton and Day. He hastened to dress for the interview.

The telephone tinkled again. Once more it was the White House. "Please cancel the appointment with the President!" Less than half an hour had passed since the appointment had been made. The next morning Hughes read in the newspapers that the nomination of Edward Douglas White to be Chief Justice would be sent to the Senate at noon.

Why and when did Taft change his mind? The answer has never been clarified. In their many associations thereafter Taft offered Hughes no explanation for passing him over or for cancellation of his White House appointment that Sunday evening. What we do know, however, suggests that the President did not change his mind in the brief interval between the telephone calls to Hughes. On the previous Saturday night, while dressing for the Gridiron dinner, Taft had told Archie Butt that he had got the Supreme Court off his mind. His chief concern then was how he was going to break the news to the friend who had been his first choice and was being shunted aside.

The switch appears to have come after a delegation of six members of the Senate Judiciary Committee had called on the President. Not one of the Senators attacked Hughes; his position as Associate Justice was unassailable. But as a lawyer he had never argued a case before the Supreme Court, and he had sat on its bench only two months. The older and more experienced Justices, the Senators said, would not care to be presided over by the junior member who had just been admitted to their fraternity.[16] Taft, a former judge himself, saw the point (as Hughes had done) and decided to enshrine experience instead of vigor in the highest judicial post. There are also indications that White's sponsors convinced the President that selection of Hughes would arouse the ire of Roosevelt.

"Hughes is young enough to wait," the President said, "and if he makes good on the bench I may yet be able to appoint him." [17]

Official and journalistic Washington almost gasped with surprise, although some rumors that a change was in the making had leaked out. Hughes himself was the soul of equanimity. "An admirable appointment," he said. "I hold Mr. Justice White in the highest esteem and his appointment is in every way fitting." [18]

When the uncertainty was over, Hughes was genuinely glad that he had not been chosen.[19] Devoid of any hunger for power, he was fully content to serve under Chief Justice White. Within the bosom of the court White expressed his humility in accepting his new assignment, and Hughes responded

---

[16] Stephen Bonsal in *New York Times*, Jan. 17, 1921, on authority of a Senator who was present.
[17] Butt, *op. cit.*, I, 567.   [18] *New York Times*, Dec. 13, 1910.
[19] Author's interview with CEH, April 30, 1946.

with a warm tribute to the new chief without the slightest trace of resentment. In the tradition that is handed down from judge to judge, this feat of unselfishness has few equals.

From the hindsight of four decades, it would have been no mistake for Taft to have carried out his original intention. Hughes would have found it rough going for a time, but he would soon have been master of the situation, and the tenure of his Chief Justiceship would have rivaled Marshall's and Taney's. His executive ability and his keen legal mind were ultimately to give him power within the court that Chief Justice White never succeeded in attaining.

It is interesting to contemplate the changes in history resulting from Taft's vacillation. Had Hughes become Chief Justice in 1910, he would not likely have resigned to run for the Presidency in 1916, and he would not have arrested the naval armament race in 1922 as Secretary of State. From 1910 to 1930 he would probably have led the court in more sweeping and successful adaptations of the law to our changing industrial civilization than either the White court or the Taft court achieved. And of course Taft would never have realized his great ambition to be Chief Justice. Taft privately lamented in 1910 the irony of fate that forced him to give to another the one position in all the world that he coveted for himself. We may reasonably assume that the possibility of cutting off his last chance to be Chief Justice by naming a man as young and hardy as Hughes flickered through the President's mind. But it must have been a remote factor. In any event, the President was right in saying that Hughes was young enough to wait. Yes, he would still be young enough in a distant day to take the Chief Justiceship from Taft's own dying grasp.

Chapter 28

WHITE, HOLMES, AND HUGHES

THREE strong men emerged in the "new court" of 1911. As Chief Justice, Edward D. White held the spotlight at the time, although his renown would ultimately appear dim beside either Hughes' or Holmes'. White was a Louisiana sugar planter who had been successively rebel soldier, Democratic politician, state judge, and United States Senator before ascending the supreme bench. A powerful man, full of integrity and jealous of the good reputation of the court, he presided over it with extraordinary relish.

White underwent a happy transformation as soon as he moved his chair beneath the bronzed eagle. The gloom and offishness that had afflicted him while the leadership of the court was in doubt now gave way to graciousness and solicitude.[1] He radiated friendliness among all the brethren, and the court entered upon one of its most remarkable eras of good feeling. White was so eager to meet every requirement of his new office that he even dropped the undignified habit of breaking up five-cent cigars and chewing the pieces.

Despite his buoyancy and good humor, the new Chief Justice found his duties a heavy burden. His eyes were beginning to fail; he had to rely increasingly upon his memory of the oral arguments. The judges said he played by ear. To buttress his health he took up walking and was often to be seen trudging homeward in earnest conversation with Holmes or Van Devanter, stopping every few blocks to rest his feet. As the years passed, his ailments degenerated into disabilities, but he continued his work with determination, fidelity, and a keen sense of justice.

White came to rely upon Hughes for counsel in numerous matters before the court. Walking from his home in Rhode Island Avenue, he frequently dropped in at the Hughes home without prior announcement. "Green," he would say to Hughes' secretary, "is the great man in? I'm in trouble. I want to talk with him." [2]

Hughes, for his part, became very devoted to the Chief Justice and many confidences passed between them. His affection for the older man never wavered even though he deplored White's lack of mastery as a judicial helmsman. Sometimes the Chief Justice would bring to conference cases on which he could

[1] CEH, Notes, p. 218.
[2] Author's interview with Laurence H. Green, Nov. 14, 1948.

reach no decision. "Here is a difficult case," he would say with a gesture of despair. "God help us!" [3] In presenting cases to the conference he was seldom clear and concise. He would permit the other judges to ramble far from the points at issue. This inefficient manner of directing a court that seldom came within 150 cases of finishing its work at the end of the term became irksome to the industrious junior member. Hughes made a practice of going to the Saturday conference armed with compact notes and prepared to render a clear-cut decision in every case. When it came his turn to speak, he went straight to the point, analyzed the issues down to the bare bones, and then briefly stated his conclusions. It was the same method he had always used. His effi-ciency, industry, and keen perception enabled him to cut through many a fog-bound argument. But the operations of the court as an institution re-flected the less systematic habits of the Chief Justice.

In spite of the rambling and windy arguments, Justice Harlan thought the court was much too serene. The massive, organ-voiced Kentuckian had swal-lowed whatever disappointment he may have felt at not being appointed Chief Justice and continued his work with little apparent abatement of his vigor. But, having written 316 dissenting opinions in his thirty-four years on the bench, he complained to Hughes that there was too little division in the court. As if to demonstrate his point, he brought his service to a conclusion with a tirade against the Standard Oil decision that almost rattled the benches in the staid old courtroom. His tongue loosened by whisky, he bellowed bitter invectives that caused his brethren to blush with shame. "It was not a swan song, but the roar of an angry lion." [4] Hughes was strongly tempted to reply, but he held his tongue. A few days after the next term opened in October, 1911, Harlan was dead.

Joseph McKenna moved up to the seat of the senior Justice. Friendly and deferential, he had little to say in conference. For a Californian he seemed unusually hesitant about expressing a definite view and often withheld his vote until he could "see the opinion."

Both Lurton and Day had sat with Taft in the Sixth Circuit Court of Appeals, which their brethren accordingly called "the learned Sixth." Because of their close friendship, they were often thought of as a team, but they were a study in contrasts. Lurton, with his walrus mustache, was a typical judge of the old school—solid, experienced, deliberate, and conservative. Day's deli-cate physique was most aptly described by Justice Holmes when he referred to one of Day's husky sons as "a block off the old chip." But Day was men-tally vigorous, clear-thinking, precise, and witty. Proud of his service as Secretary of State under President McKinley, he never failed to give each Justice a carnation to wear on the anniversary of McKinley's birth.

[3] Author's interview with CEH, May 15, 1946.   [4] CEH, Notes, p. 219.

When Congress passed a special law to let Justice Moody retire, Taft nominated Willis Van Devanter of Wyoming, a former assistant attorney general and federal circuit judge. The vacancy left by the promotion of Justice White went to Joseph R. Lamar, formerly of the Supreme Court of Georgia. Lamar won the esteem of his brethren by his gentleness as well as his ability. Van Devanter brought from the West not only judicial experience and an intimate familiarity with the public land laws but also remarkable perspicacity and common sense. "His careful and elaborate statements in conference, with his accurate review of authorities," Hughes commented, "were of the greatest value." His advice was widely sought; Chief Justice White leaned upon him, as Taft was later to do. In those days Van Devanter was by no means an ultraconservative, as indicated by his opinion upholding the right of Congress to regulate virtually every phase of the relationship between the railroads and their employees.[5] His chief difficulty was what Justice Sutherland was later to call "pen paralysis." In conference his statements were so lucid and complete that, had they been recorded, they might have served, with a little editing, as good opinions. But when he sat down to write, the words would not flow. Procrastination in getting out his opinions thus became a habit—a habit that time was to magnify into a real handicap.

To succeed Justice Harlan, Taft appointed Mahlon Pitney, who had been a member of Congress and of the Supreme Court of New Jersey. Pitney's clean-shaven face was a mirror of the sincerity and strength of mind that were to win him the high regard of his brethren. The judges appointed by Taft were now in the majority. On the whole, they were much younger than the men they had replaced. It was indeed a "new court"—and much of its attention was centered on new legal problems.

In point of time and age Holmes belonged to the "old court," but in judicial philosophy and buoyancy of spirit he was often ahead of the new Justices. Of all the judges Hughes came to know intimately, Holmes was the most fascinating personality. It was not that Holmes was a more admirable character than any other. Rather, it was his rare combination of qualities—his intellectual power and literary skill, his freshness of view and inimitable way of expressing it, his enthusiasm and cheerful skepticism, his abundant vitality and gaiety of spirit. The man radiated a constant charm.[6] From beginning to end Hughes' relationship with him was of the happiest sort.

Holmes appears to have enjoyed their association no less than did Hughes. "I shall miss him consumedly," Holmes would write to Pollock on Hughes' resignation from the court in 1916, "for he is not only a good fellow, experi-

[5] *Second Employers' Liability Cases*, 223 U.S. 1.
[6] CEH, Notes, p. 221.

enced and wise, but funny, and with doubts that open vistas through the wall of a nonconformist conscience." [7]

Indicative of the occasional notes that passed between them is the following undated letter in the Holmes Papers:

DEAR JUDGE—
Many thanks for your kind note. I was nearly knocked out and it is very refreshing to be fanned and sponged off. I am more pleased than I can tell you that you approve.

Sincerely
HUGHES

The Magnificent Yankee was interesting even in his method of work. He was the only member of the court who attempted to make comprehensive notes during the oral arguments—a formidable task. Though he greatly admired Holmes, Hughes did not try to imitate this note-taking feat. Apparently he did not think it was necessary. Hughes' amazing memory enabled him to keep in mind the intricate details of many cases. Walking home together after arguments, the two Justices often talked law, and Hughes noted on several occasions when he referred to a troublesome point in a case argued a few days before that Holmes would ask, "Have we that point before us?" Hughes would then recite enough details to bring the issue back to his colleague's mind. In conference, with his sheaf of notes, however, Holmes was armed cap-a-pie.

As soon as Holmes had a case worked out to his satisfaction, he would relax completely. Even on the bench he would snatch a little sleep after lunch while resting his head in his hands over his desk as if in deep study. On one occasion he awoke from such a nap and found a prosy lawyer still droning on with a repetitious argument. "Jesus Christ!" he muttered loud enough to be heard out in the courtroom, and went to sleep again.

Once an opinion was assigned to him, Holmes was miserable until he had finished it. Such assignments were usually made on Sunday, following the Saturday conference. As each Justice completed his opinion, he had it printed and circulated the proof sheets among his brethren for approval or dissent. Holmes worked with such intensity that he would often have his proof sheets ready to distribute three days after getting an assignment. While most of the Justices were laboring on their opinions during the recesses, Holmes was thus free after a few days to indulge his passion for philosophy, social theory, and fiction.

Holmes was not then as popular with the bar as he later became. His

[7] Reprinted by permission of the publishers from *Holmes Pollock Letters: The Correspondence of Mr. Justice Holmes and Sir Frederick Pollock, 1874–1932*, edited by Mark DeWolfe Howe, I, 237, Harvard University Press, 1941.

opinions, always written in his own hand, were short and pungent but sometimes lacking in body and clarity. Chief Justice White occasionally showed Hughes letters from lawyers complaining that Holmes did not adequately spell out the position the court had taken and that his language was frequently vague. Hughes thought it was amusing to have the Chief Justice, who was none too clear in his own style, refer to Holmes' "obscurities." [8]

White was not alone, however, in squirming over Holmes' expansive generalities. Fearful of hidden implications, the brethren frequently insisted on stripping Holmes' opinions of their more fanciful images and seemingly reckless phrases. The good-natured Yankee would agree, reporting at conference that he had the concurrence of his brethren but the "fizz" had been taken out of his opinion. When he wrote to Pollock about drafting opinions some years later, it was not merely the loss of "fizz" about which he complained. "The boys," he said, "generally cut one of the genitals out of mine." [9]

If Holmes liked an opinion written by some other Justice, he would inscribe a gay comment or a bit of verse on the proof sheets. On a Hughes opinion holding that corporate books and papers in possession of an officer may be subpoenaed despite the provisions of the Fifth Amendment as to self-incrimination,[10] Holmes penned, "Yes—twice if I can get in two votes." Another Hughes opinion upholding a West Virginia law imposing heavier criminal penalties on second offenders [11] won the Holmesian accolade, "Clear as a bell and sound as a nut—Yes."

Hughes appears to have fended off a dissent by Holmes in *Peabody* v. *United States*.[12] His opinion held, for an ultimately unanimous court, that the mere location of a battery of guns which had not been fired for more than eight years, and which the Government had no intention of firing, except in case of war, was not an appropriation for military purposes of the land within their firing range. Holmes wrote on the proof sheets:

> How sweet a countenance tyranny endues
> What reverend accents and what tender Hu(gh)es
> Such seeming modesty and justice blent
> Smile at the futile claims of long dissent.
> So I expect to shut up.
>
> O. W. H.

Hughes was inclined to return the compliment when Holmes wrote an opinion for the court construing the Opium Registration Act of 1914 solely as a revenue measure.[13] "I am not convinced that this could not be worked out the other way—as I voted," he penciled on Holmes' proof sheet. "But I am not

8 CEH, Notes, p. 224. 9 *Holmes Pollock Letters*, I, 258.
10 *Wilson* v. *United States*, 221 U.S. 361. 11 *Graham* v. *West Virginia*, 224 U.S. 616.
12 231 U.S. 530. 13 *U.S.* v. *Jin Fuey Moy*, 241 U.S. 394.

disposed to dissent alone. For the present, I sit mute and sorrowful." When Pitney dissented, however, Hughes joined him.

The fascinating candor that Holmes brought to his daily task stood out in his comment on a Hughes opinion involving the effect of a writ of error in a criminal case.[14] "Yes, with humility," he wrote. "I now see what you have been about when I was giving parties their constitutional right to jaw while I slept." Another Hughes opinion [15] brought from his jovial Boston friend this idyllic assent: "Wee—Mussoo—I float in a fairy bark to the bight and serenely anchor there with you." [16]

The New York jurist could not match Holmes' sparkle and incisiveness, but his proof-sheet comments had a charm and spontaneity of their own. On one Holmes opinion he inscribed: "This is as beautiful as an impressionist picture which it requires a wide knowledge of art fully to appreciate. I compliment myself by expressing admiration." Sometimes his *entre nous* comments took on a decidedly unjudicial tone, as when he jotted on Holmes' opinion in *International Harvester Company* v. *Kentucky:* "Yes. Fine! I think this will hold 'em for a while." [17]

When the two went separate ways in a decision, the one in the majority would say to the other, with a twinkle, "You were in the wrong, as usual." Sometimes they even indulged in pig Latin together. Holmes also spiced the conversation at the court with downright vulgar talk. He would "run the full gamut of pungent utterance," enlivening many a legal argument with unprintable phrases. His descriptions were as fresh and down to earth as Dickens'. The huge men on the court he called "mastiffs." Lawyers he divided into three categories: the ordinary run of legal minds were "kitchen-knives"; the sharper ones, "razors"; and the top men of the bar, "stings."

The Oliver Wendell Holmes whom the judges knew had little in common with the humanitarian crusader of the same name who has so often been extolled in print. Holmes' brethren knew that he didn't care a straw for the "social" or "progressive" legislation that he was said to be heroically defending. What he did believe in profoundly was the constitutional right of legislatures to experiment. "In my epitaph," he humorously remarked to Hughes, "they ought to say: 'Here lies the supple tool of power.' " [18] Soon after Hughes' arrival from Albany, he fell into a discussion with Holmes of certain labor laws and spoke of the need for impartial and efficient administration to fulfill their promise. "I don't care anything about these fool statutes," the Yankee jurist replied, "unless they go to the nape of the neck."

Strength was what Holmes really prized and respected—the survival of the fittest. Even ruthless men of power won his admiration. Empire builders

[14] *U.S.* v. *Mayer*, 235 U.S. 55.   [15] *New York* v. *Becker*, 241 U.S. 556.
[16] These comments are in the Hughes Papers.   [17] Oliver Wendell Holmes Papers.
[18] CEH, Notes, p. 226.

such as Hill, Rockefeller, and Harriman might be "malefactors of great wealth" to Roosevelt, but Holmes thought "they should have statues erected to them." His brethren who listened to his candid glorification of power were not surprised when, in his will, he ignored all the "causes" and left the residue of his estate to the United States Government.

The first major opinion Hughes wrote for the court in January, 1911, brought him into friendly collision with the Great Dissenter.[19] The case was brought by Lonzo Bailey, an Alabama Negro, who had been sentenced to 136 days of hard prison labor under the Alabama peonage law. Once before, in 1908, Bailey had appealed to the Supreme Court, and Holmes had written the opinion saying that the constitutional issue had been raised prematurely. Over the dissents of Harlan and Day, the court had sent the case back to Alabama for trial. When it reached the supreme bench a second time, Hughes emerged in conference as the ablest champion of the view that the Alabama law was unconstitutional. Chief Justice White asked Hughes to write the opinion, and Holmes and Lurton dissented.

Bailey had contracted to work on a farm for a year at $12 a month. After about thirty days he quit and did not return the $15 that had been advanced to him. Under Alabama law this sort of conduct was a crime if done with fraudulent intent, and failure of the employee to perform the work or to refund the money advanced was considered prima-facie evidence of his intent to defraud. Alabama's rules of evidence did not permit a man caught in this net of circumstances to testify belatedly that his intentions had been good.

"We cannot escape the conclusion," Justice Hughes wrote, "that, although the statute in terms is to punish fraud, still its natural and inevitable effect is to expose to conviction for crime those who simply fail or refuse to perform contracts for personal service in liquidation of a debt. . . ." Thus judged by its effect rather than its pretense, the statute was a violation of the Thirteenth Amendment. In an almost passionate rejection of the idea that that amendment prohibited only slavery, Hughes asserted:

It was a charter of universal civil freedom for all persons, of whatever race, colour or estate, under the flag. . . . The plain intention was to abolish slavery of whatever name and form and all its badges and incidents; to render impossible any state of bondage; to make labour free, by prohibiting that control by which the personal service of one man is disposed of or coerced for another's benefit which is the essence of involuntary servitude. . . .

Without imputing any actual motive to oppress, we must consider the natural operation of the statute here in question, and it is apparent that it furnishes a convenient instrument for the coercion which the Constitution and the act of Congress forbid; an instrument of compulsion peculiarly effective as against the poor and the ignorant, its most likely victims. There is no more important concern than to

[19] *Bailey* v. *Alabama*, 219 U.S. 219.

safeguard the freedom of labour upon which alone can enduring prosperity be based. The provisions designed to secure it would soon become a barren form if it were possible to establish a statutory presumption of this sort and hold over the heads of the labourers the threat of punishment for crime, under the name of fraud but merely upon evidence of failure to work out their debts.

On finishing his opinion, Hughes went over to Chief Justice White's home and read it to him. White was delighted. "Cannot be improved on," he later penciled on the proof sheets. "Clear, convincing and in my opinion unanswerable." "I am with you 'through & through,'" said a note from Harlan. "Count me that way."

Holmes' dissent took strange refuge in mere legalism as if, to borrow Max Lerner's conclusion, he were leaning backward to get away from a "humanitarian" opinion.[20] "If it is a perfectly fair and proper contract," he wrote, "I can see no reason why the State should not throw its weight on the side of performance." Holmes' brethren were well aware of his scorn for any deviation from the result he thought the law required because that result might be "unjust" to the individuals concerned. It was "the stinking sense of justice," he used to say, that bedeviled a proper administration of the law.[21] In *Bailey v. Alabama,* however, he slipped into a superficial regard for procedural law that he himself would lay great store upon in later cases. Hughes' complete triumph over the Magnificent Yankee in this instance was further confirmed many years later when a unanimous court [22] followed the tightly reasoned and forceful opinion that had kept farm-hand Bailey out of jail.

In several other civil rights cases these two leading liberals of the 1911 court stood side by side against a majority of their brethren. Hughes' first dissenting vote after he ascended the bench had been cast in company with Harlan and Holmes in behalf of the emancipation of women in the District of Columbia.[23] In *Frank v. Mangum,* [24] Hughes worked with Holmes on his dissenting opinion, and in circulating it Holmes wrote a note saying, "I think it would be fairer to say (if you agree) that you and I think the judgment should be reversed and to put *we* for I all through." The opinion came down that way after Hughes had replied, "I shall be proud to be associated with you in this opinion." [25]

Both the dissenters believed that Frank was being sent to his death without a fair trial. Georgia had convicted this young New Yorker of murdering a girl who had worked in the pencil factory of which he had been manager. His trial had been conducted in an atmosphere of intense anti-Semitism plus Southern antagonism against "foreigners" from New York. An angry mob had packed

[20] *The Mind and Faith of Justice Holmes* (Boston, Little, Brown, 1943), p. 338.
[21] CEH, Notes, p. 227.   [22] *Taylor v. Georgia,* 315 U.S. 25, 29.
[23] *Thompson v. Thompson,* 218 U.S. 611.   [24] 237 U.S. 309.
[25] Holmes Papers.

the courtroom and jammed the street outside. The clapping of hands and the stamping of feet in the courtroom had not been controlled. The judge had suggested to Frank's lawyer that there would be "probable danger of violence" if the jury should bring in an acquittal or be in disagreement, and Frank had been kept out of the room when the verdict was announced. It had brought such a roar of applause and such prolonged disturbance that the judge had great difficulty in polling the jury.

In the face of this psychological coercion, which had brought the case to national attention, Georgia's highest court had taken evidence and given no weight to Frank's charge of "mob influence" on the jury. On that basis the United States District Court had denied Frank's petition for a writ of habeas corpus. A majority in the Supreme Court was willing to let it go at that. Holmes and Hughes insisted that the federal courts had a duty to inquire into the facts to determine for themselves whether "the trial was dominated by a hostile mob and was nothing but an empty form."

"This is not a matter for polite presumptions," they asserted; "we must look facts in the face . . . we think the presumption overwhelming that the jury responded to the passions of the mob . . . it is our duty . . . to declare lynch law as little valid when practised by a regularly drawn jury as when administered by one elected by a mob intent on death."

Frank never got a fair trial. Hoodlums took him from a prison farm and lynched him. But the dissenting judges' appeal to "the brooding spirit of the law" was successful. Eight years later, after Hughes had left the bench, Holmes reiterated the doctrine they had worked out together, and this time he spoke for a majority of the court.[26]

The liberals of the court prevailed when Arizona's antialien statute was challenged.[27] That law, requiring employers to hire not less than 80 per cent native or naturalized citizens, caused a restaurant owner in Bisbee, Arizona, to discharge an immigrant named Raich, who carried his demand for "equal protection of the laws" all the way to the Supreme Court. It was not unnatural that Justice Hughes should have been asked to write the opinion. As Governor of New York, he had worked conscientiously to improve the conditions under which immigrants were living, and a commission which he had appointed in 1908 had given New York a leading position in the "Americanization" movement. It was with much satisfaction, therefore, that he expounded the rights of aliens under the Constitution.

Writing for the entire court, except Woodrow Wilson's new appointee, James C. McReynolds, Hughes declared that in spite of the breadth of the states' power to make reasonable classifications in legislating to promote the public health, safety, and morals they could not "deny to lawful inhabitants,

---

[26] *Moore* v. *Dempsey,* 261 U.S. 86.   [27] *Truax* v. *Raich,* 239 U.S. 33.

because of their race or nationality, the ordinary means of earning a livelihood." He continued:

It requires no argument to show that the right to work for a living in the common occupations of the community is of the very essence of the personal freedom and opportunity that it was the purpose of the [Fourteenth] Amendment to secure. If this could be refused solely upon the ground of race or nationality, the prohibition of the denial to any person of the equal protection of the laws would be a barren form of words.

Congress, having full authority over immigration, had invited Raich to these shores. Arizona could not nullify the invitation by threatening him with pauperization.

More liberal opinions came from the court in this period than the country had witnessed in many years. It outlawed the "Grandfather Clause" by which various Southern states had disfranchised the Negro.[28] In another case Hughes took occasion to sound a warning against the denial of equal travel facilities to colored passengers. Five Negroes of Oklahoma had petitioned a federal court to restrain the railroads from complying with that state's "Separate-Coach Law." A unanimous court concluded that there was no ground on which the judiciary could hold up the operations of this statute providing for separate coaches and waiting rooms for the white and Negro races with accommodations "equal in all points of comfort and convenience." [29] It had been well settled that "equal" but "separate" accommodations met the requirements of the Fourteenth Amendment. In writing the opinion, however, Hughes singled out for condemnation a weasel-worded proviso in the Oklahoma law intended to authorize the hauling of dining cars, sleeping cars, and chair cars exclusively for the white race.

The lower court had approved the legislature's deft phrasing, and it appears to have found some support on the high bench. Holmes sent Hughes a memorandum on the point, but Hughes flatly rejected the idea that equality could be found in providing sleepers for white men and forcing colored men to sit up all night until the railroad could make a "black sleeping car" pay. "I don't see that it is a case calling for 'logical exactness' in enforcing equal rights," he replied to Holmes, "but rather as it seems to me it is a bald, wholly unjustified discrimination against a passenger solely on account of race." [30] In his opinion Hughes virtually invited Negroes to bring their complaints to the federal courts if they were in fact denied equality. Holmes, White, Lamar, and McReynolds concurred only "in the result."

Holmes won a short-lived victory over his whiskered friend in *United States*

[28] *Quinn* v. *U.S.*, 238 U.S. 347.
[29] *McCabe* v. *Atchison T. & S.F. Ry. Co.*, 235 U.S. 151
[30] CEH to Holmes, Nov. 29, 1914, Holmes Papers.

v. *Johnson.*[31] The question was what Congress had meant when it prohibited the "mis-branding" of drugs in the Food and Drug Act of 1906. Johnson was charged with delivering for shipment in interstate commerce a worthless fluid called "Cancerine" and tablets of inert matter which together were sold as "Dr. Johnson's Mild Combination Treatment for Cancer." Holmes contended that, as Congress had meant to penalize only misstatements of fact, quacks could be prosecuted for misrepresenting the quality, strength, or ingredients of their nostrums, but not for saying what they would cure, for that was a matter of opinion. This time Holmes carried a majority of the court with him, and Hughes wrote his first dissenting opinion with the concurrence of Harlan and Day.

Hughes conceded that the medical profession was in disagreement as to the curative properties of numerous medicines. But this case concerned worthless stuff about which there was no controversy whatever. To create the impression in a label that it was a cure for cancer was not merely an expression of judgment but also a "downright falsehood." Hughes argued persuasively that Congress must have aimed at false statements of *fact* as to the curative properties of a drug as well as false statements as to what the drug contained. Nor was there any question as to the power of Congress to give its statute this broader meaning. "Why should not worthless stuff, purveyed under false labels as cures, be made contraband of interstate commerce as well as lottery tickets?"

While Holmes carried the court, Hughes carried the country. The following year Congress passed the so-called "Sherley Amendment" in order to give the Food and Drug Act precisely the meaning that the dissenting Justices had attributed to it. In 1916, when a case involving the misbranding of another worthless concoction reached the high bench, a unanimous court, with Justice Hughes as spokesman, upheld the seizure of the drugs and confirmed the constitutionality of the Sherley Amendment.[32] The shrewd, lanky jurist from Massachusetts did not again challenge his keen-witted colleague from New York in a Food and Drug Act case, although Hughes wrote many opinions in this field.

In *Slocum* v. *New York Life Insurance Company,*[33] Hughes and Holmes were together again (joined also by Pitney and Lurton), with Hughes writing a fiery dissent in spite of Holmes' eminence in the common law with which the opinion dealt. Slocum's heirs had sued in a federal court in Pennsylvania on a life-insurance policy that had expired four days before he died. After a jury had heard the evidence, the company's request for a directed verdict had been denied, and the jury had awarded the plaintiff $18,224. The Circuit Court

[31] 221 U.S. 488.   [32] *Eckman's Alternative* v. *U.S.,* 239 U.S. 510.
[33] 228 U.S. 364.

of Appeals found that, under the evidence, no such verdict could be legally sustained. Acting under a practical reform adopted by the Pennsylvania state courts, the Circuit Court granted a motion for denial of judgment. In the Supreme Court a bare majority said that the Court of Appeals had properly reversed the judgment but that the case would have to go back for a new trial. The decision meant in effect that the suit should be tried over again even though there was no possibility of winning it.

Hughes thought the majority was grafting onto the Constitution wholly unwarranted impediments to simplified legal procedure. There had been no invasion of the province of the jury. "Whether there was any evidence for the jury," he insisted, "was a question of law." It had not been converted into a question of fact by the trial court's error. The avoidance of futile retrials commended itself to both bench and bar. Hughes' long and vigorous opinion bristled with impatience over the court's superficial legalism. "Excellent," Holmes penciled on the proof sheets, "I am with you *totis viribus*." As in *Frank* v. *Mangum* and *Coppage* v. *Kansas*, this dissent too was to become the accepted statement of the law.

In spite of the far-reaching influence of their joint dissents, Hughes never shared Holmes' reputation as the Great Dissenter. To him the minority opinion was a device to be used with the utmost restraint. It was "an appeal to the brooding spirit of the law, to the intelligence of a future day, when a later decision may possibly correct the error into which the dissenting judge believes the court to have been betrayed." [34] Where unanimity could not be obtained without a sacrifice of conviction, he thought dissents should be openly expressed; for in the long run it was the character and independence of the judges that sustained the court in public confidence. But the right of dissenting ought never to be used, he felt, merely for self-expression. On many occasions he dissented "without memorandum" or joined in another Justice's minority opinion to save the court from becoming a Babel.

When he wrote for the court, Hughes had a genius for warding off possible dissents by other judges. In his hands an opinion never became a stump speech, a personal essay, or a vehicle for display of his learning. Hughes stated the law, as the court had agreed upon it, in the simplest, most direct and forceful language at his command. Writing as a member of a judicial team and never as a lone ego craving self-expression, he left dissenters little ground on which to stand. In the 150 cases in which he spoke for the court while he was Associate Justice, dissents are recorded in only nine instances and only three of these had the adherence of more than one Justice.[35]

Probably because of their differences, Hughes and Holmes learned much from each other. Holmes was the embodiment of law in the grand manner. To live in his presence was a rich experience—an experience that undoubtedly intensified Hughes' intellectual curiosity and broadened his judicial perspective. And it would be difficult to believe that as wise and genial a man as Holmes did not profit from his numerous brushes with the dynamic intellect of the younger man, as in *Bailey* v. *Alabama* and *United States* v. *Johnson*. For in the memorable cases in which they differed it has been Hughes' viewpoint which has thus far weathered the test of time.

Chapter 29

A FLAT "NO" IN 1912

THE QUIET life of study and contemplation that Hughes had sought without success at Ithaca again eluded him in Washington. Days were crowded with sessions of court, conferences, and toil over opinions, nights with social activities and reading of law.

The "new court" was in the midst of Washington's social whirl. Hostesses swamped Justice and Mrs. Hughes with invitations, as they did the Holmeses and other couples in the judicial hierarchy. Because of the pressure of his work, Hughes tried to limit his social engagements to two nights a week, but when invitations had been accepted on this basis far in advance along came others that could scarcely be declined. Seeking balm for his troubles, President Taft began to favor private hostesses with his ample presence. As he was known to be very fond of Hughes, the latter was repeatedly asked "to meet the President," and in the etiquette of the Capital such invitations were obligatory. Justices of the Supreme Court were also expected to attend all the receptions at the White House. Hughes could enjoy a good dinner and the conversation that went with it as much as any man in Washington, but this multiplicity of parties became a real burden. His best defense, he discovered, was to break away about ten o'clock and return to his library for three or four hours of reading before going to bed.

Hughes had come to Washington weary from overwork, for he had spent all the summer of 1910 reviewing hundreds of applications for pardons and clearing his gubernatorial desk to avoid leaving an accumulation of work for his successor. As a result, he had entered upon his engrossing judicial work nervously worn and lacking his usual zest and vigor.

Worried over her husband's health, Mrs. Hughes bought an electric automobile, with the object of giving him needed relaxation. Several of the Justices had electric cars, which were more common than gasoline-driven vehicles. Only McKenna drove a "gas" car, and Harlan and Holmes still preferred their horses. At the end of the day Antoinette Hughes would call for the weary judge in her new contraption, and they would go for a brief drive together before dinner.

As he fought off fatigue and toiled to extend his grasp of the court's jurisprudence, Hughes looked forward eagerly to the long summer vacation of

1911. In March of that year, however, Taft induced Congress to create a commission to determine the cost of handling second-class mail. One of the three commission members, under the resolution, had to be a Justice of the Supreme Court. Taft informed Hughes that this provision had been inserted for the special purpose of drawing upon his investigative skill. Hughes strongly resisted. Aside from his hangover of weariness, he did not believe that the vital work of judges should be interrupted by administrative assignments. But Taft was insistent; the Justice finally bowed to what seemed to be the inevitable.

His associates in the undertaking were President Lowell of Harvard University and Harry A. Wheeler, Chicago businessman. Taft had assured them that the task would not be difficult—that all the necessary calculations had been made by the Post Office Department. But those calculations were sharply challenged, and the commission had to spend most of the summer of 1911 in public hearings, taking technical evidence on which to make its own calculations. Hughes caught a severe cold and suffered much from lumbago. Still the work went on. Through the fall he had to meet his judicial obligations in addition to poring over postal figures late into the night hours. Holmes thoughtfully offered to relieve his hard-pressed friend by taking some of his cases, but Hughes rebuffed him as if the offer reflected upon his capacity.

The commission's report, finally completed in February, 1912, recognized the desirability of keeping second-class postal rates low so as to encourage the dissemination of news and current literature. It recommended, however, "a moderate increase"—from one to two cents a pound—as a means of relieving the burden on the Post Office without seriously impeding newspaper and magazine circulation. Taft sent the report to Congress with his blessing, but nothing came of it. Because of Hughes' extraordinary efforts, the President ordered that he be paid $2,000 more than the other members of the commission. He refused to accept it, and the President modified the order accordingly.[1]

Looking back upon this disagreeable experience and other demands upon Justices of the Supreme Court for service on administrative commissions, Hughes' opposition to the practice hardened into a firm conviction. While he recognized that, because of their aloofness from politics, judges may often render unique service in an administrative inquiry, this fact was outweighed in his mind by the effects upon the courts. The work of the Supreme Court is so important and so heavy that no outside demand can be made upon its members without seriously impairing the judicial system. If nonjudicial work takes a judge from the bench, moreover, the court may be left evenly divided on some cases. "Again," Hughes wrote in his Notes, "these administrative commissions bring the Justice into a realm of controversy with which he should not be associated. It is best for the Court and the country that the Justices should

[1] Taft to CEH, March 11, 1912.

strictly limit themselves to their judicial work, and that the dignity, esteem, and indeed the aloofness, which attach to them by virtue of their high office as the final interpreters of legislation and constitutional provisions, should be jealously safeguarded."

Except for his one deviation under pressure and his presidency of the board of Garfield Memorial Hospital, Hughes gave himself up wholly to his judicial task. In his office he worked with speed that amazed his secretary, Laurence H. Green. His eye was trained to take in a whole paragraph at a glance, and his photographic mind stored information with almost the accuracy of a microfilm. Green would spend hours running down cases with some bearing on a point at issue. With only the sweep of his eye across a few pages, Hughes would select some of these for citation and discard others.

When he dictated an opinion, he would stride up and down the bare floor as if to get the vigor of physical motion into his words. Often his mind worked on two different aspects of the case at the same time, and Green found it difficult to relegate each sentence to its proper place. In spite of his intensity, the judge's courteous manner never wavered. Sometimes he was positively deferential to his secretary, although he occasionally snorted over an incompetent brief submitted to the court. Shiftlessness and bungling always irritated him. "Green," he would say with a deep awareness of the spotlight of history on the court, "we are building either monuments or tombstones to ourselves." [2]

When he had a baffling decision to make, he would fret and stew over it as if it were a child with an undiagnosable ailment. "I can't see my way out of this one," he would say to Mrs. Hughes at the end of a troubled day.

"You always say that," she would reply with an implication of unlimited confidence in his ability to work it out.

"This time it is different," he would lament.[3]

His worry would intensify his concentration until the light would somehow break through. Then his gloom would pass as quickly as the darkness of an eclipse. His triumph over the intricacies of the law would be written all over his whiskered face. "It's all right now," he would say to Mrs. Hughes, giving her a hearty slap on the back. Or his exuberance might send him to the piano to pound out his one rollicking piece.

Out on the street, when he sought to recharge his dynamo by vigorous walking, a troublesome case was likely to pursue him. If his mind happened to be free on these excursions, he would chatter volubly and gaily to his companion—usually one of his daughters. But if a legal dilemma closed in on him, he would walk in unbroken contemplation. Elizabeth became so accustomed

[2] Author's interview with Laurence H. Green, Nov. 14, 1948.
[3] Author's interview with Catherine Hughes Waddell, July 1, 1948.

to walking silently by her father's side that one day years later when she happened to meet Chief Justice Taft on Connecticut Avenue and walked a short distance with him in animated conversation, she blurted out, "You don't have to talk to me if you don't want to." Taft chuckled with delight when he related the incident to Mrs. Hughes.

The family life was still geared to Hughes' convenience, the more so because he had to work at home. Catherine, who was budding into young womanhood, chafed a little under her mother's restrictions against bringing home crowds of young people who might interrupt the writing of an important opinion. But there were compensations during vacation time. Once the second-class mail investigation was out of the way, delightful summers were in store for the whole family, including grandma, the servants, and the canary bird. A Justice's salary could not be stretched to cover a trip to the Alps, but the Hugheses found delightful retreats in the Adirondacks and Maine. It was nearly always a lake in the mountains rather than the seashore that attracted them. Hughes loved to row as well as to climb. Taking a large boat with two sets of oars, he would assail the water with short impetuous strokes, Helen and Catherine taking turns at trying to keep pace with him. Invariably he played with the same vigor and spurts of energy that marked his work. Even choppy waters did not deter him. Considering the fact that neither he nor Mrs. Hughes could swim, their habit of rowing in all kinds of weather seems strangely out of harmony with his cautious nature. The only explanation one can find is that he was so fond of gliding over a blue mountain lake that he disregarded the risk of an upset during a storm.

Grandma Hughes was no longer with them after December, 1914. That rigid disciplinarian had lived long enough to see her only son and best pupil become famous, though not in the ministry as she had hoped. At eighty-four she died in quiet defiance of the doctor who had said she would never make old bones.

It was during the period of his Associate Justiceship that Hughes began strictly to adhere to a time schedule. His working habits had always been systematic. Now even greater regularity was feasible, and, finding that this increased his capacity, he adhered closely to his routine. His children said they could set the clock by the time he came down to breakfast. As this habit grew upon him, he took his walk, ate his meals, and began his work at precisely the same moment every day. It was not a matter of being a slave to the clock, he insisted, but of taking full advantage of precious moments.

Still feeling as if he were carrying a ball and chain, he also resurveyed his personal habits. Since the insurance investigation he had often sought relaxation in a highball before going to bed. Concluding that a man ought to run on his own steam, he gave up this habit and restricted his indulgence to an occasional light drink at social functions. In the spring of 1914 he began also to look with increasing suspicion upon his cigars.

Hughes had smoked continuously since his admission to the bar, save for a few months in 1895. Being high-strung and inclined to tenseness, he thought smoking helped to maintain his poise. Under pressure at Albany he smoked excessively, in Washington more moderately. His physician advised him that complete abandonment of smoking might be a severe shock to his system, but he felt in his bones that it would be good for him. As he sat smoking with the men at a dinner party one night, he said to himself, "I think I won't smoke any more for a little while." He never smoked again.

The decision brought a transformation in his working habits and apparently in his health. "After breakfast," he said, "instead of sitting with my cigar and morning paper, I started out for a walk of half an hour. I soon found that I came back full of ideas and eager to get to my desk. In the evening, instead of indulging in a last cigar in the late hours, I went to bed. Instead of working late at night, I found that I was at my best in the morning. This gave me confidence, and when I was dealing with difficult problems I would say—'It will all clear up in the morning.' And so generally it did. While I suppose that the final result was no better than in my smoking days, I worked more rapidly, with less friction, and with a much greater sense of *bien être*. . . . Giving up smoking improved my health and increased my efficiency at least twenty-five percent." [4] To his last days Hughes clung steadfastly to the belief that abandonment of his cigars had not only given him new energy and freed him from excessive nervousness but also prolonged his life.

Justice Hughes' conduct completely dispelled any idea that he might keep one foot in the political arena, as Chief Justice Chase and several other members of the court had done. He went out of his way to break off all political ties. In Albany newspaper men had trooped to his door and had seldom left without a story. In Washington he avoided any contact with the press. His rigid adherence to the judicial tradition of aloofness gave rise once more to newspaper stories about his "austerity," a characterization that had been generally abandoned during his governorship.

His invitations to speak in public were multiplied by reason of the fact that he succeeded Justice Brewer, the court's most inveterate speechmaker. Several organizations that had been accustomed to paying Mr. Justice Brewer up to $500 for his speeches sought a similar arrangement with Hughes, without success. He no longer felt free to discuss public affairs, and he never accepted money for making a speech.

[4] CEH, Notes, p. 228.

A few invitations he found it impossible to decline. At a heart-warming dinner given him by the Lotos Club in New York on November 19, 1910, he spoke "under limitations wholly unfamiliar" and centered his brief comments on the theme, "Justice must ever be the chief concern of democracy." Occasionally he addressed legal groups, and he delivered the historical address at the sesquicentennial of Brown University in October, 1914. In this new life, however, his task was, as he told the Lotos Club, "to hear appeals and not to make them." Not for a moment did he forget it.

The rumble of impending battle between Taft and Roosevelt could be heard throughout the land by the end of 1911. Hughes watched the widening of the breach between his two friends with a feeling of deep regret but absolute detachment. From time to time it was suggested that only the nomination of Hughes could save the Republican Party from disaster. The unhappy Taft would have gladly withdrawn in Hughes' favor if he had seen any opportunity of doing so. As early as 1910 he had said that he would favor Hughes if party success seemed to demand someone stronger than himself. "If I could nominate . . . Hughes by a withdrawal it would give me great pleasure to bring it about," he wrote to Hilles just before the 1912 convention. "My chief purpose in staying in is to defeat Mr. Roosevelt, whose nomination . . . would be a great danger and menace to the country." [5]

Holmes thought in April that a certain reserve in Hughes' speech left "possibilities open." His surmise was high and wide. Hughes remained silent because he feared that any statement on his part would be regarded as presumptuous. As the Republican delegates assembled in Chicago, however, ominous rumors reached Camp Abenaki on Lake Placid, where the Hugheses were spending the summer. A prolonged fight between Taft and Roosevelt, it was said, would probably swing a majority of the delegates to Justice Hughes in order to avert calamity. New York leaders sent Judge William H. Wadhams to urge Hughes to permit use of his name. The Justice emphatically refused. [6] Later he issued a public statement through Rabbi Stephen S. Wise outlining his reasons for turning down any conceivable nomination before it could be made. If men were to step from the bench to elective office, he said, Supreme Court decisions might be rendered for their political effect and certainly they would be subjected to partisan criticism. The independence of the judiciary would be weakened along with the nation's confidence in its courts. When the rabbi asked him point-blank whether an extraordinary crisis might "make it your duty to accept the nomination for President," Hughes unhesitatingly replied, ". . . no man is as essential to his country's well being as is the unstained integrity of the courts." [7]

[5] Henry F. Pringle, *The Life and Times of William Howard Taft*, II, 794.
[6] Judge Wadhams to author, May 20, 1949.　　　[7] *New York Times*, June 21, 1912.

He also wrote to Root, chairman of the Republican National Convention:

I am informed that, notwithstanding my published statement, efforts are being made to bring about my nomination. It should be understood, not only that this use of my name is unauthorized, but that, whatever the result, my decision will not be changed. The highest service that I can render in this difficult situation is to do all in my power to have it firmly established that a Justice of the Supreme Court is not available for political candidacy. The Supreme Court must be kept out of politics. I must add, to avoid all possible misunderstanding, that, even if nominated, I should decline.[8]

"I am clearly of the opinion you took a wise and patriotic course," Root replied after the convention was over. "It seems to me that keeping the Supreme Court out of politics is more important than the Presidency." [9] If T. R. had stayed in the convention and a deadlock had developed, Root nevertheless concluded, only a strong expression of Hughes' reasons for declining would have prevented his nomination. William Barnes, the New York boss, three times urged Senator Borah to let his name be used as a running mate for Hughes on a compromise ticket.[10] "If Mr. Hughes had been nominated for President instead of Mr. Taft," commented the New York *World* during the course of the campaign, "there would be no Roosevelt third term candidacy, no Progressive party, no wreck of the Republican organization, no certainty of Republican defeat." [11]

The Republican schism brought Woodrow Wilson to power in March, 1913, without disturbing the equilibrium of the Supreme Court. Hughes occasionally met the new President at official receptions, thus renewing the friendly relationship begun at Jamestown in 1907. Cordial letters passed between them at the time of the first Mrs. Wilson's death and later when the President married again. In November, 1913, the President's daughter Jessie married Francis B. Sayre, who had been a close friend of Charles E. Hughes, Jr., at Harvard Law School, from which both had been graduated in 1912. Young Sayre stayed at the Hughes home for a few days before the wedding. After the honeymoon a White House luncheon was given for the young couple at which the Hugheses were guests. As the President and the Justice sat together after lunch, only one ripple disturbed the placid flow of their chat. Hughes made some joking remark about William Jennings Bryan, who, as a bungling Secretary of State, was giving the President some of his most difficult problems. Wilson stiffened and said in all seriousness, "I have the highest respect for Mr. Bryan." [12]

Nothing in their friendly differences suggested a feud or even any deep-seated antagonism between Wilson and Hughes. On the contrary, Wilson's

[8] CEH to Root, June 21, 1912.   [9] Root to CEH, June 30, 1912.
[10] Claudius O. Johnson, *Borah of Idaho*, p. 139.
[11] New York *World*, Sept. 24, 1912.   [12] Author's interview with CEH, Jan. 7, 1946.

growing liberalism since he had entered public life had given them much in common. He often spoke to his secretary, Joseph P. Tumulty, "in warm and generous terms of the work of Mr. Hughes as Governor of New York, which he admired because of its progressive, liberal character." [13] Wilson also recognized that the idea of a presidential nomination "was not even remotely in the thoughts of the then Justice of the Supreme Court." [14] Little did either realize, as they sat together on that pleasant afternoon, that they would fight each other for the Presidency two and a half years later.

[13] Joseph P. Tumulty, *Woodrow Wilson As I Know Him* (New York, Doubleday, 1921), p. 192. Copyright, 1921, by Doubleday, Page & Co.
[14] *Ibid.*

Taft begs to be commanded in the 1916 campaign

Candidate for President

*On the Campaign Special
en route to California*

*All campaigns are alike. In a copper
mine at Butte*

Chapter 30

WELLSPRING OF FEDERAL POWER

HUGHES' greatest contribution to judicial thinking in this period came in the adaptation of law to the control of national economic policy. The whole country was wrestling with the question of whether the big utility corporations could be effectively regulated in the public interest. At Albany, Hughes had met the problem as a policy maker. Now he encountered it again in the judicial sphere. The question before the court was whether it could fit broader use of the national and state police powers into the constitutional concept of limited government operating according to law.

Congress was relying primarily upon its power over interstate commerce to check the abuses of the new industrial age. It was "cementing the union" with new controls over transportation, trusts, adulteration of foods, meat inspection, and various types of criminal activity. Hughes joined with his brethren in a broad interpretation of the commerce clause which gave vitality to the Pure Food and Drug Act [1] and later to the Mann Act forbidding the transportation of women and girls across state lines for purposes of prostitution.[2] "Congress is not to be denied the exercise of its constitutional authority over interstate commerce, and its power to adopt not only means necessary but convenient to its exercise," he pointedly declared in another case, "because these means may have the quality of police regulations." [3] His most notable commerce-clause opinions, however, were primarily concerned with the regulation of railroad rates.

Armed with new powers under the Hepburn Act of 1906 and the Mann-Elkins Act of 1910, the Interstate Commerce Commission was clamping national regulations upon exploiting carriers. The states, too, were laying down new rules and rates for railroads operating within their borders. Regulation from both these sources was meeting stubborn resistance on the part of the carriers in the courts. State control over rates was denounced as being not only confiscatory but also beyond the power of the states because it impinged upon instrumentalities used in interstate commerce. Conversely, the efforts to make fair and effective national regulations were condemned as an invasion of rights reserved to the states. It was the problem of many governments in

[1] *Hipolite Egg Co.* v. *U.S.*, 220 U.S. 45.   [2] *Hoke* v. *U.S.*, 227 U.S. 308.
[3] *Eckman's Alternative* v. *U.S.*, 239 U.S. 510.

one nation dealing with different portions of unified economic organisms. How could these conflicting regulatory systems be reconciled? How could the overworked Supreme Court possibly hear and decide all the complicated rate cases, with their voluminous records, that were piling up on its calendar? To many it seemed that the decisive challenge to the whole idea of regulating the railroads had come. If the railroads could entangle the Supreme Court in the intricacies of rate making under the constitutional guarantee of property rights or in the rivalries of national and state regulatory agencies, the experiment in rate control for the public benefit could be expected to collapse.

The problem came to a head in the *Minnesota Rate Cases* [4] argued April 9 to 12, 1912. Pierce Butler, later to become a member of the court, put in a 900-page brief for the railroads. Twenty-one states intervened because the lower court's decision threatened to destroy their rate controls. The immediate question was the validity of an order by Minnesota's Warehouse Commission fixing rail rates within that state. Behind it loomed the greatest constitutional issue of the first half of the twentieth century—the relative power of Congress and the states to control the national economy.

In the judicial conference the case proved so complicated and baffling that the judges decided to postpone voting on it. There was a multitude of decisions bearing on different facets of the question, and it seemed impossible to reduce them to an orderly system.[5] Some of the brethren were in doubt as to whether an opinion could be written that would properly guide regulatory commissions and courts through the morass of conflicting claims and rights. At the end of the conference Chief Justice White, conscious of the importance of the outcome both to the country and to the court, decided to dump the whole problem into the lap of the court's most vigorous and perhaps most experienced member in this field—Justice Hughes. In effect he asked Hughes to see if he could work out to the court's satisfaction a comprehensive judicial doctrine on railroad rate control.

Hughes toiled over this case through the summer recess of 1912 and on through the fall and spring, although he also wrote twenty-one other opinions for the court and an important dissent in this period. As soon as he had finished the first section of his opinion dealing with the interstate commerce issue, he took it to the Chief Justice. After reading the proof sheets, White ambled over to the Hughes home in a state of high animation. For Hughes had thoughtfully weighed every national and state claim to power over transportation and come out with a statesmanlike apportionment that would have done credit to John Marshall himself. He had written:

The power of Congress to regulate commerce among the several States is supreme and plenary. . . . The conviction of its necessity sprang from the disastrous experi-

[4] 230 U.S. 352.   [5] Justice Lamar to CEH, June 3, 1913.

ences under the Confederation when the States vied in discriminatory measures against each other. In order to end these evils, the grant in the Constitution conferred upon Congress an authority at all times adequate to secure the freedom of interstate commercial intercourse from State control and to provide effective regulation of that intercourse as the National interest may demand. . . . There is no room in our scheme of government for the assertion of State power in hostility to the authorized exercise of Federal power. The authority of Congress extends to every part of interstate commerce, and to every instrumentality or agency by which it is carried on; and the full control by Congress of the subjects committed to its regulation is not to be denied or thwarted by the commingling of interstate and intrastate operations.

Here was a doctrine pregnant with future possibilities. The fact that local transactions became interwoven with commerce extending across state lines did not give supremacy to state regulations. Nor did it create a no-man's land in which governmental power was paralyzed. Rather it swept those local transactions within the reach of congressional power to any extent necessary for effective regulation of interstate commerce. "This conclusion necessarily results," Hughes asserted, "from the supremacy of the National power within its appointed sphere." Congress, he added, "must be the judge of the necessity of Federal action."

The court decided, however, that the wide range of local activities affecting interstate commerce in some degree but not requiring uniform treatment could be regulated by the states until Congress saw fit to exercise its overriding authority. The states could not prohibit legitimate articles of commerce from moving across their boundaries. They could not discriminate against the products or the corporations of their sister states or fix interstate rates. But a state could govern its internal commerce and "adopt protective measures of a reasonable character in the interest of the health, safety, morals and welfare of its people, although interstate commerce may incidentally or indirectly be involved."

These state powers were not to be stricken down in the absence of conflict with valid federal legislation simply because Congress might at some later date occupy the field. ". . . our system of government," the opinion asserted, "is a practical adjustment by which the National authority as conferred by the Constitution is maintained in its full scope without unnecessary loss of local efficiency."

Turning to the troublesome question of fixing the value of property for rate-making purposes, Hughes struck a blow at inflated valuations.[6] The ascertainment of "fair value," he said, "is not controlled by artificial rules." "It is not a matter of formulas, but there must be a reasonable judgment having its basis in a proper consideration of all relevant facts." The cost-of-reproduction

[6] 230 U.S. 450–454.

method could be used when reasonably applied and when such costs could be accurately determined. Current value, because of price changes and growth of the country, might be more or less than the amount of the original investment. It was the property actually used in service to the public, Hughes pointed out, not the original cost of it, of which the owner could not be deprived without due process of law.

But in this case the railroads had tried to apply the cost-of-reproduction formula to their lands. The result was to give them a speculative "railway value" that "would make the public use destructive of the public right." The court refused to countenance such "conjectural values" and said that railway yards, terminals, and rights-of-way should not be valued at more than "the fair average of the normal market value of land in the vicinity having a similar character." As for plants and equipment, Hughes insisted that proper allowance be made for depreciation through use.

The great decision was handed down on June 9, 1913. In spite of White's unusual procedure in asking Hughes to write the opinion before a vote was taken, there was no dissent, although McKenna concurred only in the result because he found the hundred-page decision too long to read. Mrs. Hughes went to court for the occasion and dutifully listened as the reading went on and on. Justice Day scribbled a note and sent it to her:

"Your husband has done a great work this day—the effects of which will be beneficially felt for generations to come."

Lurton, too, sent down his penciled congratulations: "The subject is not interesting to you and is very complex. But I want to say to you what I have already said to Judge Hughes that his opinion now being delivered is as able and important as any opinion from this Bench since the foundation of this court."

Hughes was apologetic for the length of the opinion, but he had no need to be. With its sweeping survey of what the court had previously said on this subject and its cogent adjustment of constitutional doctrine to twentieth century economics, the opinion was to become a sort of Bible for the court. Holmes heartily endorsed it. Lamar was certain that the opinion "will be a landmark in the history of the court." Pitney scrawled on the proof sheets: "To my mind, they [these 'admirable' opinions] far outclass any of the previous opinions of the Court upon subjects of this character." Even more glowing was the comment of Chief Justice White: "Yes. Admirably well done. The country and Court owe you a debt they would have to go into bankruptcy if called upon to pay." [7]

Former President Taft, now dean of the Yale Law School, sent his comment by letter: "I write to thank you as a struggling teacher of constitutional law

[7] CEH's private papers.

for the benefit you have conferred on my newest profession by your opinion in the Minnesota Rate Cases. . . ."

About a year later the profluent doctrine of the *Minnesota Rate Cases* was directly invoked to upset discriminatory state railway rates. Again Hughes wrote the opinion of the court.[8] The Interstate Commerce Commission had found that the Houston and Texas Railway was charging much lower rates from Dallas to other cities in Texas than from Shreveport, Louisiana, to Texas cities over like distances. It was a clear case of favoritism for traffic within Texas as against interstate commerce, but the railroads argued that the ICC could not touch rates effective only within one state.

Hughes thoroughly shattered that argument with the plenitude of the commerce power. He did not believe in stretching the commerce clause, but he did believe in applying it in the light of current economic facts. "By virtue of the comprehensive terms of the grant," he said, "the authority of Congress is at all times adequate to meet the varying exigencies that arise and to protect the national interest by securing the freedom of interstate commercial intercourse from local control. . . ." Congress was free to regulate local operations "having such a close and substantial relation to interstate traffic that the control is essential or appropriate to the security of that traffic, to the efficiency of the interstate service, and to the maintenance of conditions under which interstate commerce may be conducted upon fair terms and without molestation or hindrance." The effect of intermingling transactions in which both the nation and the states had legitimate interests, he said, reechoing his opinion in the *Minnesota Rate Cases*, was to give Congress the dominant voice:

It is immaterial, so far as the protecting power of Congress is concerned, that the discrimination arises from intrastate rates as compared with interstate rates. The use of the instrument of interstate commerce in a discriminatory manner so as to inflict injury upon that commerce, or some part thereof, furnishes abundant ground for Federal intervention.

In the former cases the court had upheld the state in the use of its rate-making power because the effect on interstate traffic had been incidental, and there was no conflict with national authority. In the *Shreveport Case* it upset the state rates and gave effect to the ICC order because a direct injury had been inflicted on interstate commerce in violation of an Act of Congress. Never before had the commerce power been given such broad scope. This "charter of a vitalised nationalism," as Judge Ransom called the two opinions,[9] would echo down through the decades and come to the fore again in an hour of great peril for the Supreme Court.

[8] *Shreveport Case*, 234 U.S. 342.
[9] William L. Ransom, *Charles E. Hughes* (New York, Dutton, 1916), p. 19. Copyright, 1916, by E. P. Dutton & Co.

"I heartily agree with this admirable opinion," was Holmes' comment on the "Shreveport" proof sheets.

"Yes," White assented. "Clear, powerful, and sound to the core."

"This had to be," wrote Day. "You have written a clear and convincing opinion which all may comprehend."

"I voted to reverse," Lamar admitted, "but my views are much shaken by your opinion. The conclusion is so desirable and the reasons for unanimity so great that, unless others do, I shall not dissent." [10]

Lamar's conversion held even though Lurton and Pitney did dissent.

Hughes also spoke for the court [11] in upholding an ICC limitation of working hours for railway employees. "The length of hours of service," he said, "has direct relation to the efficiency of human agencies upon which protection of life and property necessarily depends." Here again the national power was not to be defeated by any commingling of interstate and intrastate activities.

In *Philadelphia Company* v. *Stimson* [12] a unanimous court, with Hughes as spokesman, upheld the right of the Secretary of War to fix harbor lines on navigable streams. The company claimed that construction of the Davis Island Dam in the Ohio River near Pittsburgh had flooded part of its land on Brunot's Island and deprived it of rights granted by the State of Pennsylvania. But the court held that federal control over this "highway of commerce" could not be fettered by any state action or minimized by changes in the course of the river. The public right of navigation follows the stream, Hughes said, and the authority of Congress goes with it.

Hughes joined with his brethren in upholding President Taft's order withdrawing from public entry extensive public lands on which oil had been discovered.[13] He refused to interfere with the findings of immigration authorities as to the citizenship of a person seeking entry to the United States.[14] And he gave free rein to the new administrative agencies so long as they did not overstep their authority or encroach upon the constitutional rights of the individual.

Hughes was not, however, an extreme nationalist. "An over-centralized government," he said, "would break down of its own weight." What he contended for and what he found in the Constitution was ample power both for the national and for state governments to carry out their functions in a changing world, with no stultifying vacuum between them. His routine practice was to explore every possibility of upholding a public policy. He had a passion for making government successful so long as it did not encroach upon the basic rights of the individual. The intensity of that passion may be noted in his numerous opinions upholding the police powers of the states.

---

[10] CEH's private papers.   [11] *Balt. & Ohio R.R. Co.* v. *ICC*, 221 U.S. 612.
[12] 223 U.S. 605.   [13] *U.S.* v. *Midwest Oil Co.*, 236 U.S. 459.
[14] *Tang Tun* v. *Edsell*, 223 U.S. 673.

The Fourteenth Amendment, he said, was not designed to fasten the states in an archaic strait jacket. Its sponsors had not attempted "to make improvement or rational experimentation impossible." Rather, the amendment sought "to preserve and enforce the primary and fundamental conceptions of justice which demand proper notice and opportunity to be heard before a competent tribunal in advance of condemnation, immunity from the confiscation of property, and, with respect to every department of government, freedom from the exercise of purely arbitrary power." [15]

What chiefly distinguished Hughes as well as Holmes from a majority of their brethren was their freedom from cliché thinking in regard to the rights thus protected. Whenever a person or a corporation claimed to have been deprived "of life, liberty or property, without due process of law," the Holmes-Hughes team brushed away slogans and looked at the substance of the rights granted against the background of modern society. This did not imply any carte blanche for the states. Their power was limited, and those limits could not be overstepped by the simple expedient of declaring legislatively that whatever the state wished to do was in accord with due process. Conformity to "due process" was a test for the courts to make, and the courts could not escape that obligation because "due process" was a vague and elastic concept. Hughes was keenly sensitive to the purpose of the Constitution-makers when they used these words of "indefinite content." "They wanted protection against tyranny," he said, "wherever and however it might hit." [16]

Holmes invoked the due-process clause against state legislation deemed to be utterly unreasonable and arbitrary in *Chicago, Milwaukee & St. Paul Railway Company* v. *Polt*.[17] The following year the court upset a North Dakota statute which had fixed intrastate rates on coal so low as to require its transportation at cost or below.[18] Holmes wholeheartedly approved Hughes' opinion in this case, inscribing a big "A1 (first class)" beside his initials on the proof sheets. White thought the opinion was "masterful and could not be better." "Admirable," commented Lamar in giving his assent. "The argument is irresistible. I take it all, especially the clear statement of the underlying principles."

Hughes had written, ". . . broad as is the power of the regulation, the State does not enjoy the freedom of an owner." The state could prevent extortion, require equal treatment of shippers, and promote safety, good order, and convenience on railroads operating in its territory. But even the public interest could not be invoked to force a carrier to haul commodities with no profit to itself. Nor could the state disguise the actual cost of carrying coal by shifting

---

[15] Address to New York Bar Association, January 14, 1916.
[16] *The Supreme Court of the United States* (New York, Columbia University Press, 1928), p. 186. Copyright, 1928, by the Columbia University Press.
[17] 232 U.S. 165. [18] *Northern Pacific Railway Co.* v. *North Dakota*, 236 U.S. 595.

all the expense for maintenance of roadbeds upon the carriage of wheat or other commodities.

With the demands of "due process" satisfied, however, Hughes saw the states possessed of a wide range of police power. He had joined with Holmes in asserting that the police power extends to all the great public needs. The court, with his assent, upheld a Kansas statute regulating fire-insurance rates.[19] He wrote for the court in sustaining, in the absence of a conflicting congressional Act, a California pilotage law affecting interstate and foreign commerce.[20] Likewise, he found nothing in the Constitution to prevent Indiana from regulating "concentrated commercial food" for livestock.[21]

Franchise rights were a subject of much controversy in the court, with Hughes repeatedly contending for the right of states and municipalities to alter or revoke such privileges. When a majority, including Holmes, agreed with a telephone company that the franchise granted it by the City of Owensboro was perpetual and could not be revoked, Hughes strongly dissented along with Day, McKenna, and Pitney.[22] Only Pitney stood with Hughes in protest when the court held that South Bend could regulate the use of a railway franchise but could not withdraw it.[23]

The hot controversy of the day was over the extent to which "freedom of contract" restrained the states from passing social legislation. Hughes made his position unmistakably clear in the McGuire case.[24] Various railroads had set up "relief funds" to which both the companies and employees contributed and from which workers injured in the course of their employment were paid benefits. Employees participating in these relief plans had to sign contracts limiting their common-law right to recover damages for injuries. Iowa outlawed such contracts and the Supreme Court upheld the statute. Hughes' opinion was emphatic in declaring that private companies and individuals could not upset a public policy within the power of the legislature by making contracts in conflict with that policy. He said:

Freedom of contract is a qualified and not an absolute right. There is no absolute freedom to do as one wills or to contract as one chooses. The guaranty of liberty does not withdraw from legislative supervision that wide department of activity which consists of the making of contracts, or deny to government the power to provide restrictive safeguards. Liberty implies the absence of arbitrary restraint, not immunity from reasonable regulations and prohibitions imposed in the interests of the community. . . .

The right to make contracts is subject to the exercise of the powers granted to

---

[19] *German Alliance Insurance Co.* v. *Lewis*, 233 U.S. 387.
[20] *Anderson* v. *Pac. Coast S.S. Co.*, 225 U.S. 187.
[21] *Savage* v. *Jones*, 225 U.S. 501.   [22] 230 U.S. 58.
[23] *Grand Trunk Western R.R. Co.* v. *South Bend*, 227 U.S. 544.
[24] *Chicago, B. & Q. Ry. Co.* v. *McGuire*, 219 U.S. 549.

Congress for the suitable conduct of matters of national concern, as for example the regulation of commerce with foreign nations and among the several States. . . .

It is subject also, in the field of State action, to the essential authority of government to maintain peace and security and to enact laws for the promotion of the health, safety, morals and welfare of those subject to its jurisdiction.

Hughes reiterated a well established doctrine that the court would not interfere with legislative acts having a "reasonable relation to an object within governmental authority." It was concerned with the power invoked, not with the policy effected. Whether an act was wise or unwise, whether it was economically sound or the best means of achieving the desired result was not a question for the courts. "In dealing with the relation of employer and employed," he said, "the legislature has necessarily a wide field of discretion in order that there may be suitable protection of health and safety, and that peace and good order may be promoted through regulations designed to insure wholesome conditions of work and freedom from oppression."

In a later case [25] Hughes applied the same principle in declaring that the federal Employers Liability Act superseded "relief funds" set up through contracts between railroads and their employees. Here was the bedrock on which his famous opinion in the *Gold Clause Cases* would be based many years later.

When the question of the so-called "yellow dog" contract came before the court in *Coppage* v. *Kansas*,[26] a majority of the brethren veered away from the sound principle of the McGuire case. Only Holmes, Hughes, and Day held the fort of liberal thinking. The court had previously upset a federal statute making it a crime for an interstate carrier to discharge an employee because of his membership in a labor union.[27] Now it was a question of whether a Kansas law forbidding an employer to require of his employees a pledge that they would not join a labor organization could be reconciled with the Constitution. To the majority it was simply a matter of constitutional "freedom of contract." Labor was essentially a commodity about which every man had the right to contract. A law interfering with complete freedom in this field was a "substantial impairment of liberty." Consequently, the statute was at war with the Fourteenth Amendment.

The dissenters looked much deeper into the actualities about which Kansas had legislated. Holmes wrote what was to become a famous opinion pleading for the right of the state "to establish the equality of position between the parties in which liberty of contract begins." Hughes concurred in the longer dissent of Justice Day. "The preservation of the police power of the States . . . ," Day asserted, "is of the utmost importance. . . . The law should be as zealous

[25] *Phil., Balt. & Wash. R.R. Co.* v. *Schubert*, 224 U.S. 603.
[26] 236 U.S. 1.   [27] *Adair* v. *U.S.*, 208 U.S. 161.

to protect the constitutional liberty of the employee as it is to guard that of the employer."

Thirteen state laws restraining use of the "yellow dog" contract went down because the court closed its eyes to a teeming industrial civilization and held fast to an outmoded slogan. Holmes tilted at this strait-jacket thinking because he believed in the right of the legislature to experiment. Hughes shared that view, but, having intimately felt the pulse of the people, he was also warmly devoted to the democratic ideas of fair play, justice, and reasonable use of public power for advancement of the general welfare. When these aims could be attained within a broad concept of the constitutional framework, he was loath to accept any tradition-crusted dogma that might stand in the way. The Constitution was made for the people and not the people for the Constitution.

In upholding the Illinois child-labor law, Hughes said frankly that "freedom of contract" could be a trap for helpless persons in need of the protection of the police power.[28] Two other Hughes opinions gave new underpinning for the right of the states to limit the working hours of women. In *Miller* v. *Wilson* [29] the court sustained the conviction of a hotel proprietor for working a chamber-maid nine hours a day, finding no infirmity in California's eight-hour day for women in various industries. California was also free, Hughes wrote in the other case,[30] to apply its eight-hour regulations to some groups of women and not to others, such as graduate nurses. Both cases had been argued by Louis D. Brandeis. They loosened the judicial joints a trifle more than they had been loosened in *Muller* v. *Oregon* [31] a few years before.

The case of the paper-box factory girl was more difficult. It came up to the supreme bench for argument on December 16 and 17, 1914, with Brandeis again pleading for a broad interpretation of the police power. This time it was an Oregon law prescribing minimum wages for women in industry that was challenged; similar laws in Colorado, Minnesota, Utah, Washington, Wisconsin, and California were hanging in the balance. The question was whether the Oregon Industrial Welfare Commission could compel Frank C. Stettler to add sixty-four cents a week to the meager wage that he had been paying Elmira Simpson for working in his box factory. The Oregon Supreme Court had unanimously upheld this minimum-wage law. But the company's attorneys brought to Washington, D.C., vehement arguments to the effect that the regulation of wages, regardless of the employee's efficiency and other sources of income and of the employers' ability to pay the fixed rate, was a deprivation of property without due process of law and an encroachment upon the "freedom of contract" guaranteed by the Fourteenth Amendment. Exercise of the police power, counsel said, had never been invoked and could not be invoked

---

[28] *Sturges* v. *Beauchamp,* 231 U.S. 320.   [29] 236 U.S. 373.
[30] *Bosley* v. *McLaughlin,* 236 U.S. 385.   [31] 208 U.S. 412.

to supply an individual's needs which were merely *incidental* to employment. Minimum-wage laws might be ethically right and even economically sound, but they were impossible under our form of government. Brandeis argued masterfully on the consequences of paying women so little that they could dress decently and get enough to eat only at the expense of morality.

All the judges were intensely interested in the case. Chief Justice White asked counsel whether such a regulation would not drive some employers out of business. Holmes probed into the degeneracy of the working classes in England before the factory acts curbed absolute "freedom of contract." Hughes listened quietly until he saw an opportunity to cut to the heart of the issue. Then he leaned forward and questioned former Senator Fulton, who was summing up the case for the company.

"Do you base your argument on the theory of freedom of contract?"

"Yes."

"Then is there not a precedent in the Ohio case in which this court held constitutional the 54-hour [week] for women in industry?"

"No, there is a difference between hours and wages."

"What is it?" Hughes persisted.

"Long hours," the lawyer replied, "break down women so that they become public charges; it is a condition growing *out* of employment. The amount of wages has no relation to health and morals."

"But," Hughes retorted, "suppose it has; suppose this court finds that these evils *are* in consequence of wages paid in employment?" [32]

Here was the crux of the issue. Would the court recognize the grim facts of industrial life or decide the case on the fantastic theory that wages of $6 to $8 a week had no relation to health and morals that need concern the community? In conference Hughes and Holmes stood fast for upholding the Oregon statute. The court was sharply divided. Chief Justice White, who always approached a controversy of this sort after the manner of a skittish horse going up to a brass band, failed to bring the case to a vote. When the court met for the October term in 1915, Justice Lamar was too sick to take his seat. He died in January, 1916, and that appears to have left the court evenly divided. Even after Lamar's successor won confirmation by the Senate following a long fight, he could be of no help in this decision, for he was Mr. Brandeis, who had argued so persuasively for the state. The case was finally reargued in January, 1917, and the judgment of the state court was upheld by a four-to-four decision. [33] Hughes had then left the bench, but he was destined finally to settle the question in *West Coast Hotel* v. *Parrish* [34] on a historic occasion two decades in the future.

[32] Mary Chamberlin in *Survey* magazine, Dec. 26, 1914.
[33] *Stettler* v. *O'Hara*, 243 U.S. 629.   [34] 300 U.S. 379.

In six years on the supreme bench Hughes had attained a judicial stature not often equaled in a similar period. His grasp of the law was comprehensive as well as profound. He had persistently avoided the mental grooves that judges sometimes fall into. Without the slightest hesitation, his decisions followed wherever the facts and a statesmanlike view of the law might point. In one case he carried his objectivity so far as to reverse himself in the midst of an opinion he was writing. Convinced by deeper probing that the vote of the court to which he had assented was wrong, he took the case back to conference, converted his brethren, and wrote the opinion to support a verdict precisely opposite to that previously agreed upon.[35]

In protecting civil liberties, Hughes had been more alert to realities than Holmes. By broadly interpreting the states' police powers, he had sought to make the law the servant and not the master of the people's will. Without jeopardizing federalism, he had taken the lead in forging the commerce clause into a potent tool for congressional control over the national aspects of our economy. One observer concluded that Hughes' opinions ranked "among the most important and able pronouncements upon the principles of constitutional law that have come from the Supreme Court during its entire history." [36] Still young for a Supreme Court Justice, he was well launched upon what promised to be one of the greatest judicial careers in America when fate or the voice of the people intervened.

[35] Author's interview with Laurence H. Green, Nov. 14, 1948.
[36] Arthur M. Allen in the *Columbia Law Review*, Nov. 1916, p. 566.

Chapter 31

THE 1916 NOMINATION

WAR FLAMED across Europe in the summer of 1914 and aroused the whole world from its complacency. Belgium and France were invaded. Slaughter in the trenches and on the high seas mounted to incredible totals. It was as if humanity had suddenly given free play to all its worst passions.

America was bewildered. Men hustled to supply the Allies with wheat, machinery, and guns. In their moral sympathies, too, they were drawn ever closer to the cataclysm, like neighbors to a fire. Yet there was much resistance to proposals to strengthen the country's defenses, and a general determination to keep out of the war. It was a period of intense activity and fantastic illusions.

Against this background, the forthcoming presidential contest of 1916 took on epic proportions. Wilson, it was assumed, would make a strong bid for reelection. But the Republican leaders saw in the world crisis an implied mandate for their party. Had they not elected every President since the Civil War, excepting only Cleveland and Wilson? And was not Wilson's victory in 1912 owing solely to the tempestuous quarrel between Taft and Roosevelt? With Europe tearing itself apart and Wilson talking nonsense about the United States being "too proud to fight," the Republicans felt a powerful urge to take the helm once more. But where was the candidate who could run successfully against the popular Mr. Wilson?

Taft had been buried, politically speaking, in 1912. Roosevelt had left his party and sown a whirlwind of bitterness. Root, too, was involved in the schism. Only Charles E. Hughes had a real chance of harnessing the Elephant and the Bull Moose to a victory chariot.

Talk of Hughes for President thus began more than two years before the nominating conventions assembled. Taft feared that "the Hughes talk is absurd, because Hughes would not permit himself to accept a nomination." [1] While Roosevelt was floundering, he said as early as July, 1915, that the Progressives would support Hughes if he were nominated.[2] More impressive was the increasing stream of letters which advised the hard-working judge that he was the only man who could reunite the Republican Party and shape an adequate foreign policy for the United States in a world at war. "If an exigency shall

[1] Taft to W. L. Fisher, Jan. 3, 1914.   [2] *New York Times*, July 20, 1915.

arise," Nathaniel Myers had prophesied in 1910, ". . . the People will pull you off the Bench. . . ." Now the ferment was beginning to work.

Hughes' reaction was first indifference, then irritation. Since 1910 his mind had been closed to political vistas. The idea of a Supreme Court Justice engaging in politics was abhorrent to him. Like most of the other judges, he had even given up voting because a journey to New York for that purpose took too much time away from the work of the court. On May 20, 1915, he dictated an emphatic reply to a query by former Governor Edward C. Stokes of New Jersey as to whether his flat refusal to run in 1912 still stood:

> It seems to me very clear that, as a member of the Supreme Court, I have no right to be a candidate, either openly or passively. I cannot remain working here and hold an equivocal position before the country. I must, therefore, ask that no steps be taken to bring my name before the convention.[3]

Stokes announced on August 18 that Hughes would refuse to accept the nomination if it were proffered, although the letter did not go that far. It is incontrovertible that Hughes wished to continue the work he was doing. The companionship on the bench was most agreeable. He thrived on the intellectual stimulus of the courtroom and the judicial conference. Aware of his growing contribution to the law of the country he loved, Hughes asked only to be left alone. The picture we get of him, as he walked down Capitol Hill at the close of a day's work, is that of a happy marcher "with chest well out, head held erect, full beard breasting the wind, arms loosely swinging, the face of one who is at peace with the world." [4]

But his friends and admirers would not leave him alone. Politicians repeatedly put his name forward, and the press teemed with speculation as to whether the Republicans would go to the Supreme Court for their candidate. Roosevelt sent William Noble to tell Hughes that Roosevelt considered him "the brainiest man now in public life in the United States" and "the best equipped man" for the Presidency.[5] Hughes was "sane, safe and progressive" and the only man upon whom both the Republican and Progressive parties could unite.

The hard-pressed judge reiterated his desire to stay on the bench, and thereafter refused to make appointments with persons he suspected of wishing to talk politics. After this negative response, T. R. found "a considerable feeling that it is not wise to establish a very bad precedent and take a candidate from the Supreme Court." [6] Hughes' disinterest probably reminded the colonel afresh of how disappointed he had been by Hughes' independent course as Governor of New York.

---

[3] *Ibid.*, June 2, 1916.   [4] *Nation*, Sept. 30, 1915.
[5] Noble to CEH, Jan. 5, 1921, Hughes Papers.
[6] Roosevelt-Lodge *Correspondence* (New York, Scribner's, 1925), II, 468. Copyright, 1925, by Charles Scribner's Sons.

In November, 1915, the men who were trying to "smoke out Hughes" circulated a petition to have his name put on the ballot in Nebraska's presidential preference primary. The Justice sharply declined the nomination,[7] and when this proved ineffective, he threatened court proceedings to get his name off the ballot. The sincerity of his effort to squelch any political movement in his behalf was widely recognized and commended. Yet the press was quick to point out that it did not place Justice Hughes beyond the reach of his party. ". . . no man would be given the Presidency merely because he desired it," commented the *Washington Post*, "and no man can keep himself out of it if the people want him in."

"There is not a flicker of suspicion in anybody's mind," asserted the *Nation* a few months later, "that he has used his judicial office as a steppingstone to political office. . . . It is not Hughes the judge who is discussed as a candidate, but Hughes the fearless investigator, Hughes the Governor who put moral courage into his reforms and gave a fighting edge to his constructive plans, Hughes the campaign speaker of 1908 who deeply impressed himself on the country as a man who carried heavy guns." [8]

The politicians, however, found it difficult to believe that Hughes was sincere in rebuffing their efforts to hand him voluntarily the great prize for which most men were so eager to fight. There seemed to be no end to their "smoke out" efforts. To a letter from Representative C. Bascom Slemp of Virginia, Hughes replied on February 9, 1916:

I am entirely out of politics, and I know nothing whatever of the matters to which you refer. I am totally opposed to the use of my name in connection with the nomination and selection or instruction of any delegates in my interest, either directly or indirectly.[9]

Taft's hopes were dashed. "I am quite sure that Justice Hughes will not be a candidate," he wrote to G. V. Howard. "He is not a man who says a thing without meaning it." [10] Nevertheless, Taft continued to pull every string within his reach to bring about the nomination of the judge he himself had appointed to the supreme bench in spite of Hughes' wishes to remain there. On April 11 he carried his campaign directly to Hughes' chambers with a long and persuasive confidential letter.[11]

MY DEAR JUSTICE HUGHES,

I presume your correspondence in these days is increasing. Perhaps it would be more accurate to say that your correspondents are increasing. I have been moved . . . to write you for several months past but refrained. I do not write now for a

---

[7] *New York Times*, Nov. 17 and 19, 1915.
[8] April 6, 1916, p. 376.   [9] *New York Times*, Feb. 10, 1916.
[10] Henry F. Pringle, *The Life and Times of William Howard Taft*, II, 890.
[11] Taft to CEH, April 11, 1916; Hughes Papers.

reply because I hope you will not send me one. I write to express a view to you contrary to that of Mr. Choate in his letter to the New York Times of yesterday. I believe myself to be as anxious to keep the Supreme Court and Supreme Judges out of politics as any one; but there are few general rules of policy, not involving moral considerations, to which circumstances of the country's need may not justify an exception.

What is the country's great need? It is the restoration of the Republican party to power to do the constructive work needed in carrying out a policy of reasonable preparedness which involves financial and economic preparedness. The Democratic party is what it has always shown itself to be—the organized incapacity of the country. I am no partisan but I cannot escape this conclusion. The Republican party was split in two in 1912. The great body of Progressives have enrolled themselves again in the party. To retain them, however, and to win over the others, we must have a candidate who will not revive the enmities of that internecine struggle and who will because of his record stimulate the enthusiasm of both elements and give them confidence in victory. In looking over the candidates, most Republicans and Progressives in their hearts find you to be the only available man. Bridging the chasm of 1912, they all go back to you as the leader of real progress in New York, and the one acknowledged to be your own master under every environment. Your position in this regard is unique. It appeals to all the voters.

Mr. Root is admirably qualified to be President but he will not be a strong candidate. He will not lead a united party. I admire him as a jurist and a statesman and I love him as a friend; but I state the truth.

Mr. Burton is a statesman of long legislative experience, lacking somewhat in the executive quality of decision, but a man of high ideals, studious habit and real ability. He is not a leader of magnetic qualities, either personal or on the stump. Both he and Root are burdened with association with my fortunes in 1912. I think Burton more available than Root but I fear he would not lead a completely united party.

Assuming that Roosevelt is to be preferred to Wilson and the Democracy—a violent assumption which I do not discuss—he cannot be elected. Many who supported me would support him, but a considerable number—enough to turn the scales in doubtful states—would desert him because they feel, whether justly or not, that he is responsible for the present conditions. Then he is the conspicuous candidate who would drive the Germans to Wilson. . . .

Of the other men named, Fairbanks is the best qualified for the Presidency but he labors under the cloud of staleness and he would not attract the Progressives. I have thought McCall a strong man and a possible successful candidate in the last resort but I fear that the Presidential bee has tested his head with its buzzing and the result has not been reassuring.

Now, my dear Justice, you may not agree with my summary of the candidates. I have reviewed all who call for consideration. But what I have said the great body of the American [people] are thinking, and they are going to manifest their thoughts through the Republican Convention and the delegates. They are going to nominate you unless you announce before the convention acts that you will not accept the nomination under any circumstances. I know that if you followed your preference, you would do that now. I know that you prefer your life on the Bench and that should a Republican come to the Presidency, you would in all probability be put at the head of the Court with the acclaim of the country. I know that you are properly most sensitive in respect to the nonpartisan attitude of the judges of the Court and deeply deprecate making a precedent which might inspire other judges to an ambition which would demoralize them and destroy their usefulness and affect the high position of the Court. But I beg of you to consider that your position in the peculiar situation of affairs is so exceptional that it cannot afford a dangerous precedent. You have been most scrupulous to discourage all effort to nominate you. You have declined to express your opinions on any issue of current importance lest it may be inferred that you are a candidate in any sense. The whole country knows your attitude of antagonism to the canvass of your name but in spite of that, the movement grows and the result will be, I verily believe, your unanimous nomination.

Mr. Roosevelt is thundering. He is a genius. In certain ways he commands my admiration more than he ever did for his genius. His powers over correspondents, due to his marvellous personality. His courage to ignore obstacles and inconsistencies of his own creating and what is more his power to induce others to ignore them are sublime. But I cannot think it on the cards for him to win.

I do not conceal from myself his influence in the Election in uniting the party; but he has put himself in a position which makes it absolutely necessary for him to support you if you are nominated. Moreover, he will, after his disappointment, do so with fervor. He saves his face in supporting you as he does in supporting no one else. He is sincerely opposed to Wilson. He is really anxious to defeat him. He will be sincerely for you.

You will certainly be elected if you accept the nomination and you will reunite the only party from which constructive progress can be expected at a most critical time in the country's history. Your opportunity as President to guide the country through the trials bound to come after the war will be as great as Washington's or Lincoln's. And you are equal to it. Strong men will respond to your call because you are yourself so satisfying in strength and in your political courage and patriotism.

In view of all this, my dear Justice Hughes, I appeal to you not to decide the question until the Convention acts. Then approach its decision, as you will, with a solemn sense of the responsibility on you and with the willingness to make the sacrifice if your duty to accept appears clear.

I have written long and perhaps without the force I would like to give to what I say, but I believe sincerely and deeply all I have written. I think I was discharging a duty to myself in writing you. It cannot hurt, even if it does not help what I urge. It may put something in a light to help.

Sincerely yours,
WM. H. TAFT

I have written without any one's knowledge. I have not copied this letter. I do not expect an answer. Indeed I would rather not have one.

The next day Taft added a few more arguments. If Hughes were nominated, Wilson would of course name his successor to the Supreme Court. But that was no reason for not leaving the court, Taft insisted: ". . . think of the vacancies he is likely to fill if he is to be re-elected. He can almost destroy the court." Roosevelt, should he be reelected, would likely "get us into war," and his appointments to the bench might be "in many ways quite as bad as Brandeis." But even Roosevelt would be less distasteful, Taft wrote, "than . . . Wilson whom I regard as the greatest opportunist and hypocrite ever in the White House. . . . As I conceive it, therefore, the exigency presented to you is whether you will save the party from Roosevelt and the country from Wilson." [12]

Taft visited Washington on May 14, and newspaper gossip said that he called on Hughes. The *Chicago Tribune* and some other papers even claimed that Taft went away with Hughes' assurance that he would accept the nomination.[13] But there was no word of truth in either report. Hughes did not reply to the Taft letters; no emissary passed between them, and they did not meet in 1916 until after the convention.

Meanwhile the snowball of Hughes sentiment was rolling at ever increasing tempo. He was the unmistakable favorite in several polls. Republican leaders of New York came out for him on January 13. Governor Whitman added his endorsement two days later. Colonel George Harvey, the political godfather of Woodrow Wilson, concluded in the *North American Review* that the people wanted Hughes. On May 3 he was singled out as the favorite candidate by the Michigan Republican Convention and on the 16th by the Vermont primaries. The Oregon primaries gave him a landslide on the 20th, and Senator Borah said that Hughes would have carried every state primary if his name had been on the ballots.

More important than any of these events was the work being quietly done by Eugene Meyer and Frank H. Hitchcock, who had managed Taft's successful campaign in 1908. With Meyer's encouragement and financing, Hitchcock had surveyed public opinion in many of the big cities and reported that Republican voters favored Hughes over Roosevelt by a large margin. Hitchcock then began to round up delegates for Hughes. It proved to be an easy task, for politicians are always eager to clamber aboard a band wagon that gives real promise of ending its journey at the White House.

Hughes repudiated this work in his behalf and denied through his secretary that he had had any communication whatever with Hitchcock. The latter was well aware of Hughes' irritation over what he was doing, but that did not stop him. As soon as the convention was over, he wrote to Hughes: "I realize that I must have been acting counter to your wishes in advocating your nomination but I have felt that my activities were justified by the exigencies of the situation. I believed you were the man above all others to reunit [sic] our party and lead it to victory." [14]

Through the last trying months before the convention, Hughes was the pic-

[12] Taft to CEH, April 12, 1916.
[13] Harold L. Ickes, in *American Historical Review*, January, 1941, p. 316.
[14] Hitchcock to CEH, June 12, 1916.

From the New York *World*, June 4, 1916.

HIS NIGHTMARE

ture of a man wrestling with his own conscience. No longer could he blind himself to the power of the movement in his behalf. Yet he continued to hope that it would prove to be only a passing nightmare. Looking out over the war-torn world, he foresaw the next President carrying an unconscionable share of humanity's burdens and going to an early grave. While his fifty-four years had scarcely impaired his vigor, he would not choose such a role for himself. "I seek no new titles," he told Henry L. Stoddard, editor of the New York *Evening Mail*, "and I do not want the work that is before the next president. He may wear a crown, but it will be a crown of thorns." [15]

Hughes remembered also that he had left Albany in a mood of disgust with politics and politicians. The Presidency would take him back to many of the old controversies, to squabbles with the bosses who did not like his ways, and to political jockeying that was distasteful to him. "I do not pretend to be more than reasonably well adapted for the work I am doing," he told Stoddard in a confidential interview at his home, "but I feel that I can say that I am better adapted for it than for the work of the White House. . . . My reluctance to think of the Presidency is not because I regard it as an office below my abilities; but because I think it so great and beyond my abilities. Nor am I afraid to risk the possibility of defeat and thus lose my place on the bench and the Presidency, too. It is no time to consider such things when and if as a citizen you are called to a post of duty."

Stoddard said the nomination lay between Hughes and Roosevelt. "Then I hope T. R. will be named," the Justice replied. "I would not put a straw in his way. He is a wonderful man, and I have long believed that he has struck the dominant note of the country. . . . The newspaper stories that Roosevelt is stronger and I am weaker since he spoke out so boldly from Trinidad please me immensely. They are a ray of hope—a rift in the clouds." [16]

In spite of his strong desire to remain on the bench, Hughes could not bring himself to a flat refusal to run in any circumstances. He had done so in 1912, but no national crisis had then complicated his decision, and the rift in the Republican Party had not yet become an open schism. The question of re-uniting his party was an issue of no minor importance in his mind, for a permanent rupture would have meant an end of the two-party system and might have destroyed the Republican Party as a useful instrument of government.

Hughes felt, moreover, that it was highly desirable for the Republican

[15] *It Costs to Be President* (New York, Harper, 1938), p. 114. Copyright, 1938, by Harper & Brothers.
[16] Stoddard made detailed notes of what had been said as soon as he got back to his hotel room. When he published a summary of those notes in 1938, Hughes saw no reason to question their accuracy, but Stoddard had slipped in one particular when he previously wrote about the Justice's mental ferment in this preconvention period. He had said that the dominant thought in Hughes' mind was to return to the practice of law to rebuild his depleted fortune (*As I Knew Them*, p. 447). Not for a moment did Hughes entertain such an idea. His firm intention was to remain on the bench the remainder of his active life (CEH, Notes, p. 230).

Party to return to power. Wilson's foreign policy had been weak and vacillating. Military preparedness had been "shockingly neglected," and the resulting weakness of the United States in a war-mad world was an invitation to disregard American rights. If these policies based on dangerous illusions and backed only by words were to be changed, the Republicans would have to change them. And if Hughes were the only man who could reunite the party and win the election, as his supporters insisted, then he was the only man who could swing the country away from the perilous course it was pursuing. Duty to country thus merged into concern for the future of the party.

In the face of these considerations personal wishes shrank to minor proportions. As Hughes pondered his dilemma against the onrush of the world crisis, he visualized people coming into the Supreme Court in future years and pointing him out. "There is the man," they would say, "who placed his own comfort and preference for the life of a judge above his duty to the nation." That thought was as abhorrent to him as politicking from the bench.[17] He was torn between a profound desire "to keep the judicial ermine unsullied" and another profound desire "not to fail in meeting what might be a duty to the country." [18]

Nomination for the Presidency, he had said in 1908, should neither be sought nor refused. Now he was told on every hand that, if nominated, it would be his duty to run. The advice of Roosevelt, Taft, and other party leaders was not essentially different from that he got within the court and at home. Justice Van Devanter was one of those who expressed sympathy with Hughes' efforts to prevent political use of his name. "But if they should nominate you nevertheless," Van Devanter added, "I think you could not rightly decline." Chief Justice White, in referring to a newspaper comment, expressed the same opinion.[19]

When the children were present, the Hugheses avoided all mention of the momentous events that were threatening to upset the family routine. But the heart of Antoinette Hughes beat faster with the conviction that she had expressed in 1908. Now it was more than ever apparent that he was "a man of destiny." If the convention should summon him from the bench, she said, he would have no right to refuse. Once when she pressed her point he exclaimed, "When you see me in my coffin, remember that I did not want to take this burden on myself."

At various times while Hughes was undergoing his ordeal he felt the pull of partisan forces trying to keep him on the bench as well as those that were trying to get him off. Vice President Marshall praised him in an address before the Chicago Bar Association for not seeking the presidential nomination. Sev-

[17] Author's interview with CEH, Oct. 24, 1945.
[18] CEH, Notes, p. 231.   [19] *Ibid.*

eral Senators urged him in public speeches to announce a positive refusal to run in any circumstances. The Wilson forces favored Roosevelt as the opposition candidate, believing that he could be easily beaten on the war issue. The President himself indicated that a Roosevelt candidacy would give him no concern, but Hughes, if nominated, would "have to be met." [20]

The safest way of dealing with Hughes, of course, would be to keep him on the bench. Apparently in pursuit of that aim Franklin K. Lane, Secretary of the Interior, took Hughes aside at a dinner party and dropped a hint to the effect that if he stayed on the court he would be appointed Chief Justice.[21] Was Lane merely indulging his fancy? That seemed probable at the time. Hughes dismissed the suggestion as of little significance, but after the election Lane again approached him at a Brown alumni dinner and said, "You know what I told you, and what might have been."

Shortly before the date set for the Republican National Convention, Chief Justice White, looking old and worried, came toddling over to the Hughes home. It was evident that he had not just dropped in to discuss a court problem, as he had often done before. The Chief Justice had something special on his mind. Within a few minutes he came out with it.

"Before you decide on what course you will take," he said with unnatural tensity, "I feel that you should know that I am going to retire and that if you do not resign you will succeed me."

"Why," Hughes exclaimed incredulously, "President Wilson would never appoint me Chief Justice!"

"Well," White answered solemnly, "he wouldn't appoint anyone else, as I happen to know." [22]

Hughes was more deeply perturbed than before. White was a man of integrity and a dear friend. In saying that he was going to retire, the Chief Justice must have spoken with complete candor and sincerity. Could his assurance as to the President's intention in naming his successor be any less forthright and well founded? Hughes concluded that White must have spoken with authority from Wilson.[23] In any event, the suggestion that the President would make him Chief Justice if he did not run against the President had the smell of a deal. The people would so regard it. The Chief Justiceship would become the price of his honor. Hughes recoiled from the suggestion and told the Chief Justice that he intended to follow the lead of his conscience without being influenced by what he had just heard.

The anxiety that pervaded the office of Mr. Justice Hughes was relieved temporarily by a letter from his old friend John Palmer Gavit, then managing

[20] Ray Stannard Baker, *Woodrow Wilson—Life and Letters* (New York, Doubleday, 1937), VI, 267. Copyright, 1937, by Doubleday, Doran & Co.
[21] CEH, Notes, p. 231.   [22] *Ibid.*
[23] Author's interview with CEH, Jan. 7, 1946.

editor of the New York *Evening Post*. Noting that William Jennings Bryan, former Secretary of State, was to report the national conventions for a syndicate of newspapers, Gavit offered a similar commission to Justice Hughes. "Notwithstanding your lack of actual newspaper experience," Gavit wrote, "I am sure your reports of and comments upon these gatherings would be readable. I believe I can guarantee you a position on the first page, next pure reading matter; we might even be able to syndicate your dispatches to our mutual advantage."

Hughes expressed his gratitude for the offer on May 19:

DEAR GAVIT:

I cannot tell you how deeply touched I am by your kind offer. At last my secret ambition is laid bare. For many weary years I have longed to be a newspaper correspondent and say a few things. But my talent for up-to-date, virile, philosophical, prophetical, cinematographical correspondence has been unrecognized, and one exigency after another has compelled me to make other arrangements. I am now under contract for work, relatively unimportant, which, however, will detain me here during the time the Convention is held. I put aside my longing to see a Convention; that is very great, but it is as nothing compared to my wish to write one up and to show the best of newspapers how it may be improved.

                                                        Faithfully,
                                                  CHARLES E. HUGHES [24]

Two days before the convention opened, Hughes was under the embarrassing necessity of having to make a speech. Throughout the period while public opinion in his favor was gathering force, he had avoided any utterance that might spark a political movement. Not a word he had written for the court could be regarded as politically slanted. His address to the New York State Bar Association in January, 1916, which had been arranged a year in advance, was cool, philosophical, and entirely nonpartisan. Thereafter he refrained from making speeches, except to carry out his promise of the previous October to present an American flag to two honor students of the graduating class of National Cathedral School of which his daughter Catherine was a member.

"It is a beautiful prize that I am privileged to give. . . ." he said. "It is the symbol of our national unity, our national endeavor, our national aspiration. . . . It means America first: it means an undivided allegiance. It means America united, strong, and efficient, equal to her tasks. . . . There is not a thread in it but scorns self-indulgence, weakness and rapacity. . . ." [25]

The occasion was entirely unheralded, and what he had to say was precisely what he would have said if his name had never been mentioned for political office. The speech was noticed only because a news-hungry press, which had had no other scrap of information as to what Hughes was thinking, blazoned

[24] New York *Evening Post*, June 10, 1916.   [25] Hughes Papers.

it on the front pages. Through his secretary, he denied that it had any political significance.

News of the great Battle of Jutland and a preparedness parade in Chicago heightened the tension as the conventions opened on June 7. The Republicans were seething with disgust over Wilson's attitude toward the war. The Progressive convention was meeting separately in Chicago at the same time. In the preceding weeks Roosevelt had been contemptuous of Hughes because the latter had neither denounced Wilson nor come out with a clear-cut declaration of where he stood.[26] While trying to find another candidate who would be acceptable both to the Progressives and to the Republicans T. R. was still hoping that the country might be in a "heroic mood" and that the lightning might therefore strike in his direction. Gloom hung over the Bull Moose gathering because most of the delegates knew that the colonel had no chance of reuniting the party.

At the request of the Progressives, "peace committees" were named by both conventions. The Republican conferees—Senators Reed Smoot and William E. Borah, former Senator Murray Crane, Dr. Nicholas Murray Butler, and Congressman A. R. Johnson—were not at first unanimous for Hughes. The Progressives, headed by George W. Perkins and Hiram Johnson, talked only of Roosevelt. The conference broke up in disagreement.

Aside from Hughes, the strongest man before the convention was Elihu Root. But Root was only a halfhearted candidate. Earlier in the year he had said that he was too old to run and that the effort to nominate him was ridiculous. Yet he was so disturbed over Wilson's foreign policy that he apparently began to think his tag of "corporation lawyer" might be overlooked in the kind of campaign that would have to be waged.

The only real groundswell at the convention centered in the name of the silent man still wearing his judicial robe in Washington. Hughes had no headquarters at Chicago, no representative, no badges, buttons, or literature. Yet his name seemed to dominate every discussion of potential nominees. Frank Hitchcock, whose work for Hughes had earned only repudiation, kept repeating that Hughes would be nominated on the third ballot. "Nobody seemed to be for Hughes," he said, "except the people." Joe Mitchell Chapple reported that the undercurrent of demand for Hughes was "unfathomable."

Nominations began on the third day, June 9, in the crowded Coliseum "resplendent with color." Alabama passed, and Arizona yielded to New York so as to give Governor Charles S. Whitman the opportunity of placing Hughes in nomination first. "We bring you today," the Governor said, with typical convention eloquence, "the name of a man trained for the battle for the truth. . . .

[26] T. R. to William Noble, May 2, 1916, Roosevelt Papers.

We have seen him the man of action, the champion of the people, the idol of the electorate, the faithful public servant, the profound thinker on national affairs. . . . I do not speak for any man or for any candidate. I do not claim to represent any man or any candidate. The great State of New York offers you . . . her son—her noblest and best." [27]

An audience that had clung to every word broke into sustained yelling and applause. The New York, Michigan, Maine, Vermont, and Mississippi delegates swarmed into the aisles for a demonstration of astonishing warmth considering the absolute silence of their hero in matters political for six years. Leo Weinburg of Maryland and Charles W. Fulton of Oregon made the seconding speeches.

Roosevelt's nomination by Senator Albert B. Fall brought an eruption in the galleries but also hisses and cries of, "Throw him out." On the first ballot Hughes led with 253½. Senator Weeks had 105; Root, 103; Senator Cummins, 85; Theodore E. Burton, 77½; Lawrence Y. Sherman, 66; Roosevelt, 65. The New York vote was split: Root 43, Hughes 42. The second ballot raised Hughes' vote to 328½. Weeks dropped to sixth place. Root was second with 98½ and Roosevelt fifth with 81. As the convention adjourned for the night, Hughes was still 170 votes short of a majority.

In Washington, Hughes heard the repercussions of these events in a solemn mood. He was still trying to work on cases before the court. Stoddard had called on him again on his way to Chicago, and Hughes had conceded privately that it looked as if the forecasts of his nomination were coming true. But he felt that his position had been made unmistakably clear and held to his resolution not to interfere.

As the convention began to vote, he asked Robert H. Fuller, his secretary and political adviser at Albany, to come to Washington. By that time he had probably made up his mind to accept the nomination, if it should be made without compromising circumstances. But he reserved final judgment. When the convention adjourned after the second ballot, he felt that his maximum strength had probably been reached.

"That settles it," he said to Mrs. Hughes. "I shall not be nominated. I am going to bed." [28] He slept soundly.

The reports that filled the newspapers the next morning made it evident that there had been no foundation for Hughes' impulsive conclusion. The judge was agitated. He took his after-breakfast walk as usual. He tried to work and found it impossible. He talked with Fuller. He strode up and down the room, mulling over and over again the predicament he was in.

[27] *Official Report of Proceedings.*
[28] Edward Marshall in the New York *Sun,* Aug. 20, 1916.

"Green," he exclaimed to his secretary, "if they will only choose some one else at Chicago today and let me go out West with my family this summer, I'll be the happiest man in the world." [29]

While Hughes had been sleeping peacefully, the "peace committees" in Chicago had again sought a compromise. Three of the Republican members were still opposed to Hughes, and the Progressives declined to receive a suggestion that was not unanimous. At 3:00 A.M. the conference adjourned. At 4:00 A.M. Dr. Butler talked with Roosevelt over a private wire to Oyster Bay, suggesting agreement on Root, Knox, or Fairbanks. T. R. himself had suggested Root to William Allen White the day before, although he had previously said the nomination of Root would "cut the throat of the Republican Party from ear to ear." [30] Now he refused to discuss Root and felt that neither Knox nor Fairbanks would do. T. R.'s own suggestions—Leonard Wood and Henry Cabot Lodge—aroused consternation among the Progressives and left the Republicans cold. The politically astute colonel must have known what the reaction would be. In the light of subsequent events it is reasonable to suppose that this was his way of throwing his support to Hughes, although he was still unwilling to say so openly in the face of Hughes' silence on the issues of the day.

Charles J. Bonaparte had carried to Chicago a Roosevelt letter intended to thwart the nomination of Hughes.[31] But its wording was evasive, and Bonaparte concluded that its publication would be futile in the face of the sentiment prevailing at Chicago. Hughes could be stopped only by Roosevelt's unqualified condemnation. T. R. refused to gratify the anti-Hughes men by any such maneuver, so the letter was never used.

When the "peace committees" met again at nine o'clock on Saturday morning, the Republicans were unanimously for Hughes. Hiram Johnson and John Parker had walked out in disgust over Roosevelt's suggestion of Lodge. It was then a foregone conclusion that the Republicans would name Hughes on the next ballot. Before the third roll call began, Weeks and Sherman withdrew, and Medill McCormick switched from Roosevelt to Hughes. Alabama, Arkansas, and California went solidly for Hughes. Burton's, Root's, and Fairbanks' names were withdrawn. When Illinois gave its fifty-eight votes to Hughes, it was clear to everyone that the stampede was in full swing.

As soon as New Jersey boosted the Hughes vote beyond the majority mark, bands broke in upon the roll call with patriotic airs, and a wave of hilarity swept through the Coliseum. Hughes' total ran up to 949½, with only scattering remnants left to other candidates. On motion of Alexander P. Moore the

[29] Author's interview with Laurence H. Green, Nov. 14, 1948.
[30] T. R. to E. C. Stokes, May 10, 1916, Roosevelt Papers.
[31] George Edwin Mowry, *Theodore Roosevelt and the Progressive Movement* (Madison, University of Wisconsin, 1946), p. 353. Copyright, 1946, by the University of Wisconsin.

nomination was made unanimous, while New York led a triumphal procession in which all the delegates joined. The nomination of Charles W. Fairbanks for Vice President completed the work of the convention.

The delegates still did not know whether Hughes would accept or whether if he did, Roosevelt would run against him. William Allen White says it was evident that Perkins and Hitchcock "knew definitely that Hughes would accept the nomination." [32] Others have made similar erroneous surmises. Neither Perkins nor Hitchcock nor anyone else could possibly have known what Hughes would do in the event of his nomination, for he had said nothing on that subject to anyone.[33]

Perkins faced a hostile crowd when he reported to the Progressives on the last meeting of the "peace committees." Protests rang through the hall at his suggestion of Lodge or Hughes as a fusion candidate. Being eager to swing the nomination to Hughes, Perkins tried to induce the convention to suspend deliberations until the Republicans had made their choice. John M. Parker insisted that Roosevelt be nominated. Pandemonium ensued. As soon as word came that the Republican roll call was under way, Raymond Robins, who was presiding, recognized Bainbridge Colby. Perkins leaped to the speaker's stand and began to shout. Apparently he had a letter from Roosevelt declaring that he could not accept the nomination.[34] But his loudest cry was lost in the din. Finally Colby placed T. R.'s name before the convention in less than a hundred words, and he was nominated by acclamation.

It was the Progressives' last act of self-intoxication and was swiftly followed by a hangover of disillusionment. Roosevelt wired his "conditional refusal to run"—conditional because he did not know "the attitude of the Candidate of the Republican Party toward the vital questions of the day." [35] Men who had yelled themselves groggy for T. R. a few hours before now roared with rage, tore Roosevelt pictures or badges from their lapels, and stormed out of the hall muttering "apostate," "running out," and similar expressions of disgust. Along with Roosevelt's subsequent support of Hughes, thus went a legacy of resentment against T. R. that was to cost the candidate dearly in terms of Progressive votes.

Mr. Justice Hughes was lunching with his family in the oak-paneled dining room on the second floor of his Sixteenth Street house (a mile due north of the White House) when the momentous news of his nomination came. A flash from Chicago was telephoned to one of the newsmen who were swarming over the premises or waiting on the street corner outside. Green bounded up the stairs three steps at a time.

Hughes came down immediately. Tears glistened in his eyes. Many of the

[32] White's *Autobiography* (New York, Macmillan, 1946), p. 523. Copyright, 1946, by The Macmillan Company.
[33] CEH, Notes, p. 229.   [34] White, *op. cit.*, p. 526.   [35] Mowry, *op. cit.*, p. 354.

newsmen who had seen him only on the bench realized for the first time that he had a heart-warming smile. All his agitation seemed to be gone now. He was the essence of cordiality as he shook the hands of the reporters, called them "you boys," and beamed for the photographers.

Soon the official telegram of notification arrived from Chicago. The nomination had come without prolonged opposition, without encumbrance or any embarrassing circumstance. No longer was there any doubt in Hughes' mind as to where his duty lay. He shut himself up with Fuller and Green to dictate his resignation and a message of acceptance to the convention. Not a word of his acceptance had been written in advance. His secretary did not know until after the telegram arrived from Chicago what Hughes' reply would be.

Catherine Hughes, seventeen, returned home while the hubbub was at its height, wondering what it was all about. She had been lying under a tree at the Cathedral School watching a tennis match when the principal told her she had better go home. She arrived, tennis racket in hand, wearing sneakers and a white sport dress—the picture of carefree youth—and could not get in. When she succeeded in breaking through the mob and learned what had happened, it was the first word she had heard within the family circle about the prospect of her father being made President.

The news reached Charles Evans Hughes, Jr., at the Citizens' Military Training Camp at Plattsburg where he was a rookie. "Has he accepted?" was the young man's first question.[36] "Son," as Hughes always called him, had captured the highest possible honor at the Harvard Law School, the editorship of the *Harvard Law Review,* at the end of his junior year. He had been secretary to Justice Cardozo of the New York Supreme Court for a brief period and had spent two years practicing in the firm of Cadwalader, Wickersham & Taft. In 1914 he had married Marjorie Bruce Stuart, and their offspring— Charles Evans Hughes 3rd and Henry Stuart Hughes—gave the Republican candidate the benevolent status of grandfather.

The Hugheses' eldest daughter Helen was visiting Vassar College, where she had been graduated in 1914. Perhaps most excited of all the children was eight-year-old Elizabeth. "If father is elected and we live in the White House," she exclaimed, "I can bathe in the fountains!"

The first message that came out of Hughes' besieged office went straight to the White House by messenger. It read:

June 10, 1916

To the President:

I hereby resign the office of Associate Justice of the Supreme Court of the United States.

I am, sir, respectfully yours,

CHARLES EVANS HUGHES

[36] *Washington Post,* June 11, 1916.

By Robert Carter in the New York *Evening Sun*, May 25, 1916.

PATRIOTISM WINS

Wilson was irked by the abruptness of the message. It *was* wanting in finesse, but it could scarcely be regarded as discourteous. Feeling that his resignation to run against the President was no occasion for expression of any regrets or for the conveyance of best wishes, Hughes couched his withdrawal from the Supreme Court in the simplest and most direct language at his command.

The second message to emerge was a lengthy wire to the convention:

I have not desired the nomination. I have wished to remain on the bench. But in this critical period in our national history, I recognize that it is your right to summon and that it is my paramount duty to respond. You speak at a time of national exigency, transcending merely partisan considerations. You voice the demand for a dominant, thoroughgoing Americanism with firm protective upbuilding policies, essential to our peace and security; and to that call, in this crisis, I cannot fail to answer with the pledge of all that is in me to the service of our country. Therefore I accept the nomination.[37]

His statement of aims called for "firm and unflinching maintenance of all the rights of American citizens on land and sea," for industrial, economic, and military preparedness, undivided allegiance to the United States, "wise and practical measures" for the settlement of international disputes, and reunification of the Republican Party. The convention had adopted a strong and liberal platform almost identical in substance with the Progressive platform, and Hughes found it quite acceptable.

Having crossed the Rubicon, Hughes turned to the unjudicial business of greeting hundreds of visitors and reading a deluge of telegrams. A violent storm in the evening failed to dampen the spirits of his callers or to reduce their numbers. Prominent among them were Justice and Mrs. Brandeis, who were happy over the end of their long fight for the Justice's confirmation by the Senate.

The nomination of Hughes marked the first time that any major party had taken a presidential candidate off the supreme bench. Naturally, it set off an eruption. Many well informed people who had applauded Hughes' exemplary conduct in trying to avoid the nomination, and who recognized his obligation to take it when it came, nevertheless thought the Republican Party had made a grave mistake in going to the court for its standard bearer. Chief Justice White told James E. Watson that he looked upon the nomination "as a very great blunder and one from which we will be years in recovering." [38] This criticism was rightly directed at the party rather than at the man who had reluctantly responded to its call. The Chief Justice had previously counseled Hughes that he could not rightly decline if the call came. And after the nomi-

[37] Hughes Papers.
[38] From *As I Knew Them*, by James E. Watson, p. 164, copyright, 1936, used by special permission of the publishers, The Bobbs-Merrill Company, Inc.

nation had been made White (in spite of his Democratic affiliation) quietly favored the election of Hughes.

Holmes thoroughly understood his colleague's sacrifice and had no criticism to make. "It was not preference," he wrote to Pollock, "but simply and solely, as I believe, a sense of duty that led Hughes to accept the nomination." [39] To Hughes the genial jurist wrote:

June 11, 1916

DEAR HUGHES

Your first thought was of duty. I must confess that pretty near the first view here was the loss to the Court and especially to me. I shall miss you very much in every way—so much so that I wish the need of the country could have been postponed until I am out of this business. As it is I shall look back with affectionate regret at the ending of the time during which we sat (and stood) side by side.

O. W. HOLMES [40]

Justice Day wrote:

In your case the office has indeed sought the man, and your own conduct through all the trying months just past has been honorable and dignified, in every way worthy of yourself and the great office you now resign. . . . No man has filled the position more worthily than yourself.

Numerous comments in similar vein came from other judges, both Republicans and Democrats. Hughes was deeply grateful because he felt the judges especially would know his own feelings. "You can well understand the deep regret with which I severed my membership in the Court," he replied to Justice Day. "I don't think I have ever regretted anything more." To Judge Joseph Buffington's congratulations he responded:

I did not want to leave the Bench and I dreaded more than I can tell you the sort of activity in which I am now engaged. If there had been an honorable way out I should have taken that way. But under the conditions that existed I felt that I had no alternative and that I must do my best in the work to which I was summoned. Having decided upon this course I have followed it without allowing myself to indulge in vain regrets, and I have committed myself to the work with earnestness and enthusiasm. [41]

An attempt was made to write into the Democratic platform a condemnation of Justice Hughes for "dragging the Supreme Court into the mire of politics," but Wilson suppressed it. There were two compelling reasons for doing so: first, Wilson knew the charge was not true; second, in 1908 the Democrats had gone to the New York bench for their own candidate, Judge Alton B. Parker.

[39] Reprinted by permission of the publishers from *Holmes Pollock Letters. The Correspondence of Mr. Justice Holmes and Sir Frederick Pollock, 1874–1932*, edited by Mark DeWolfe Howe, I, 237. Harvard University Press, 1941.
[40] Hughes Papers.   [41] *Ibid.*

Taft gurgled with glee over the success of the venture which he had helped to guide. The outcome, he wrote to Hughes, was a "testimonial to your standing as a statesman, citizen, and patriot—unique and unexampled in the history of American politics." [42] Lowell of Harvard was "delighted," and Root said it was the will of the rank and file. "No man in history ever has received such an expression of public confidence," exulted Wickersham, "and no man, I truly believe, ever deserved it more." [43]

Most heart-warming of all were the messages of confidence and affection that flowed in from the boys of Colgate, Brown, Columbia Law School, Cornell, and the New York bar of the nineties. "The biggest thing about it all," wrote Benjamin S. Terry, then head of the history department of the University of Chicago, "is its tribute to the character—the clean and honest spirit that we boys discovered and loved way back in Colgate." "Your whole career as a public man, culminating in the splendid triumph of yesterday," wrote Starr J. Murphy, brother in Delta Upsilon, "is the most inspiring event in American history since the Civil War." These alone were enough to illuminate the path of duty wherever it might lead.

[42] *New York Times,* June 11, 1916.   [43] Hughes Papers.

Chapter 32

THE CALIFORNIA INCIDENT

HUGHES' first move, after the initial excitement of his nomination was over, was to flee from Washington. With swarms of visitors and reporters besieging him at home, there was no opportunity to work or to think. On Sunday night, June 11, he slipped away in company with William R. Willcox, who had come to visit him directly from the Chicago convention, and took a train to New York. Arriving at seven o'clock on Monday morning, he set up campaign headquarters at the Hotel Astor and gathered an ample staff around him.

Selection of a campaign manager was the most pressing business. Hughes returned to Washington on July 16 for a couple of days partly for political conferences on the choice of a manager. Advice flowed in from many sources. Taft proposed that Charles D. Hilles be retained, but he had managed Taft's sterile campaign of 1912. Hitchcock was automatically disqualified in Hughes' mind because his appointment might have suggested (contrary to fact) that his preconvention work had been done with Hughes' consent and approval. Hughes was determined, moreover, to find a manager who would reflect the standards, of careful thinking and unbiased administration which he himself represented. In spite of his loss of contact with politics and politicians, he felt that he could not let the Old Guard name his manager. By a process of elimination the choice thus fell upon Willcox, whom Governor Hughes had named in 1907 as the first head of the Public Service Commission in New York City. Willcox had proved to be an able public servant, but in politics he was a novice who did not speak the language of the professionals. Taft regarded him as a "blunderhead." [1] The Willcox appointment was to prove Candidate Hughes' first major mistake.

It was fitting that Brown University, which he loved so well, should have been first to acclaim the new candidate with genuine campaign fervor. Attending the Brown commencement June 19–21, he was cheered at every step. In a great demonstration he marched with his classmates of 1881, hat in hand and "countenance wreathed in smiles," as the crowds yelled for "Charlie Hughes." At the corner of Waterman and Benefit streets a little boy stepped out from the crowd and worked desperately over his camera trying to snap a picture before the famous whiskers passed. Noticing the youngster's

[1] Henry F. Pringle, *The Life and Times of William Howard Taft*, II, 895.

335

difficulties, Hughes stopped, smiled, and waited until the camera had clicked. The crowd roared its approval. The candidate appeared to be thoroughly enjoying his rebaptism into politics.

Colonel Roosevelt swallowed his pique and on June 28 went to dinner with the man he had called a "bearded iceberg." Shortly after the conventions ended, he had announced that he would strongly support Hughes. In a letter to the Progressive National Committee he had candidly recognized that the hope for a new party was dead and urged his Bull Moose followers "not to sulk because our leadership is rejected." His unqualified endorsement of Hughes was followed by similar action on the part of the Progressive Committee.

Two days after the Hughes-Roosevelt dinner the candidate entertained former President Taft at luncheon at the summer home he had established at Bridgehampton, Long Island. Taft begged to be commanded in the campaign. Theoretically the schism in the Republican Party was thus closed. Three months later Roosevelt and Taft met, stiffly shook hands, and stood in the same line during a Hughes reception at the Union League Club in New York. But that reconciliation was even more superficial than the accord between Roosevelt and Hughes. And it was soon evident that there had been no real meeting of minds between the latter two men. Indeed, their mental processes differed so sharply that even when they started at the same point with the same premises, they were soon following divergent courses.

July was a month of reorientation. In those fleeting thirty-one days Hughes attempted to lift himself out of judicial seclusion into the role of a conquering hero. He talked with hundreds of visitors. He assembled stacks of magazines, newspapers, reports, and the *Congressional Record* and crammed for his campaigning ordeal. He analyzed issues and planned tours. Now that he was in the fight, he intended to win it. But he managed to retain his sense of humor. When a campaign committee, having produced a motion picture of the candidate, gave a private showing for Mr. and Mrs. Hughes at Montclair, he criticized his clothes, his walk, his haircut, and his whiskers. If the Republican candidate for President looks like that, he said, his place is not in the White House but in the morgue. At the conclusion he congratulated the committee and said that it had portrayed his character so perfectly that he had decided to vote for Wilson.[2]

His acceptance speech was delivered on the last day of the month. Every one of the 3,000 seats in Carnegie Hall in New York was taken, and large crowds milled around outside while Hughes responded to Senator Warren G. Harding's notification. It was the hottest day of the year. The sweltering crowd divided its enthusiasm between Hughes and Roosevelt, who was appear-

[2] Everett Colby in *Scribner's*, May, 1928, p. 559.

By Clifford Berryman in the Washington *Evening Star*, July 29, 1916.

THE LIVELY LEADER

ing at a Republican gathering for the first time since he had left the party. Hughes held his audience for an hour and a half, feeling it necessary to clarify his stand on all the issues because of his long absence from the political arena.

This speech fixed the tone of the campaign. Hughes gave it the title "America First and America Efficient," unwittingly taking, in the first part of the title, a slogan that Wilson had often used. In those days "America First" did not carry the blight that the isolationists were to give it prior to World War II. Rather it signified opposition to the divided loyalties of the "hyphenated Americans" who were trying to shape the United States' foreign policy to the interests of their ancestral homelands. The climax came in Hughes' cautious but none the less forthright declaration for an international court and for world organization at the end of the war to bring about disarmament and keep the peace. "Freedom from entanglements with interests and policies that do not concern us" was still desirable, he said.

But there is no national isolation in the world of the Twentieth Century. If at the close of the present war the nations are ready to undertake practicable measures in the common interest in order to secure international justice, we cannot fail to recognize our international duty. The peace of the world is our interest, as well as the interest of others, and in developing the necessary agencies for the prevention of war we shall be glad to have an appropriate share. And our preparedness will have proper relation to this end as well as to our own immediate security.

On the whole it was a disappointing speech. It lacked the fire and the bold strokes that had been associated with the name of Hughes in his governorship days. He had not yet shaken off the excessive caution of his craft. If this is all he has to offer, some friendly critics asked, why did he leave the bench?

Before embarking on his series of tours—one of the most strenuous campaigning ordeals ever undertaken by any candidate—Hughes telegraphed George Sutherland of Utah his endorsement of the proposed woman-suffrage amendment to the Constitution, thus adding a plank that the platform makers at Chicago had ruled out. His first big rally was in Detroit, where he experienced a "wonderful demonstration," addressed 10,000 workmen, and leaped a rail at the baseball park to shake hands with the players and chat with Ty Cobb.

Hughes threw himself into the campaign with every ounce of energy he possessed. The Republican convention had ended on a note of perilous overconfidence, but the candidate took nothing for granted. He and Mrs. Hughes embarked upon a relentless round of interviews, luncheons, speeches, receptions, greetings, and travel with zest that seemed almost unlimited. Chicago, St. Paul, Minneapolis, Grand Forks, Fargo, Helena, Butte, Missoula, Coeur d'Alene, Spokane, Tacoma, Seattle: each step was a milepost in an endurance contest. Crowds began rapping on the door of the candidate's car, appropriately designated the "Constitution," at five o'clock in the morning. "Charlie, come out," they would call. "Come out or we won't vote for you." It was a common experience to receive a telegram saying several thousand insistent persons were waiting at the next station where no stop had been scheduled. Usually he would squeeze another brief talk into his schedule.

At one stop of this sort in North Dakota an impromptu reception was held beside the tracks. While Hughes was talking to a group of farmers about their crops, the train began to move. Mrs. Hughes ran to catch it.

"Wait, Mother!" he called after her with a laugh. "These are pretty good people. Let the train go."

"Gosh!" a farmer remarked. "He ain't so unhuman after all."

It was a favorable omen. The austerity myth, which had been revived in some measure while he was on the bench, was wilting once more. But Hughes had not yet hit his stride. Sometimes he seemed to be groping for issues. With war inflaming the minds of the people, he talked about waste, extravagance, inefficiency, a scientific tariff, and the spoils system. Cautious legal phraseology sometimes dulled the impact of his speeches. His practice of having stenographers, working in relays, take down each unprepared speech as he gave it, so that carbon copies would be promptly available to the press, resulted in excellent local coverage. But the big Eastern papers, lacking a text prepared in advance, gave scant attention to his speeches in the West. Hughes spoke extemporaneously because he had no time to dictate speeches, and the idea of a ghost writer was abhorrent to him.

Mrs. Hughes was always with him. She tried to shield him from visitors when he was worn out, curtailed his talking when his voice was overstrained, and pulled his coattail when she thought he had spoken long enough. She won the heart of everybody. Tall, slight, and dressed with good taste, in spite of the fact that she "traveled in a hat box," she impressed thousands as the ideal companion for a presidential candidate. She met tobacco-stained rural politicians and overly perfumed hostesses without the slightest variation in her tact and good nature. Her manner reflected quiet simplicity. She seemed always to know the right thing to do. The first wife of a presidential candidate to make an extended campaign tour, she infused it with feminine charm and added immeasurably to the sense of high adventure that kept her husband in top fighting form. As she sat at a tiny table in the "Constitution," pouring grape juice for the men of the press, Hughes tenderly waved his hand toward her and exclaimed, "Gentlemen—the greatest asset of the Republican Party." [3]

Donning oilskins, she followed her husband to the bottom of a copper mine in Butte and climbed with him to Bear Lake at an elevation of 10,000 feet in the Rockies. Excepting the rallies for men only, she never missed a meeting

[3] *New York Herald*, Nov. 8, 1916.

on their trips. In Missouri a group of women made arrangements for her special entertainment while the men were attending to the dull business of politics. She insisted, instead, on being driven to the hall where she could watch his performance, and as the audience broke into tumultuous acclaim her eyes were luminous with tears. She kept a diary of their tours which gave almost as much space to their quiet meals together as to their big public receptions.

Long before the campaign special reached California, repercussions from the hot fight between Governor Johnson and the Old Guard were reaching its passengers. Johnson was campaigning for the Republican as well as the Progressive nomination for the United States Senate. With the collapse of the Bull Moose in Chicago, the Old Guard was making a ferocious effort to destroy Johnson and all the forward-looking reforms for which he stood. As a national force the Progressive Party might be dead, but progressivism was still an upsurging movement in California. The din of battle between the Progressives and the Old Guard beat with painful effect upon the harmony program that Hughes was so assiduously promoting.

The proud and vindictive California Governor, who had been Roosevelt's running mate in 1912, had left Chicago in a rage. "I'm too mad to be tired," he had told a friend on the day that T. R. deserted the Progressive cause.[4] Before returning to California, however, he had paid a friendly visit to Hughes at the Hotel Astor and pledged his support.[5] Back in Sacramento, he reiterated his commitment to the Republican-Progressive candidate because, he said, "I believe his record warrants it." [6] About the same time Chester H. Rowell, Progressive national committeeman and a member of the national campaign committee, wired Hughes, "I find Progressive sentiment here overwhelmingly and very cordially for you."

In opening his senatorial campaign on July 8, however, Johnson said that his choice of Hughes was a personal one and that each Progressive was free to "measure the candidates" for himself and make his own decision.[7] On the same day Hughes wired to the Governor at the California Progressive conference, appealing for harmony:

The national aims to which we are devoted are so vitally important that I earnestly hope there may be that strong and effective cooperation which will assure their achievement. I desire a reunited Party as the essential agency of national progress, a Party drawing to itself the liberal sentiment of a quickened nation. . . . We are not divided in our ideals, let us work together to attain them.

In a series of telegrams the leaders of the warring factions were importuned to act jointly in making arrangements for Hughes' tour of California. Rowell

[4] *Washington Post*, June 11, 1916.   [5] Author's interview with CEH, April 9, 1946.
[6] *New York Times*, June 28, 1916.   [7] *San Francisco Examiner*, July 9, 1916.

met with Republican National Committeeman William H. Crocker and State Chairman Francis B. Keesling in response to these requests and tried to reach an agreement as to how the Hughes meetings should be handled. Deeper antagonism seemed to be the only result. Rowell complained to Chairman Willcox on July 19 that the Old Guard was going ahead with the arrangements without consulting him. Then both Crocker and Rowell suggested postponement of the tour until after the primaries had been held.[8]

Compliance with this request might have changed history in many particulars. But at the time it seemed impossible. There were two imperatives of the campaign. One was for Hughes to travel as widely and speak as often as possible to overcome the handicap of his long silence on the bench. The other was to confine his efforts in the final weeks to the big cities of the East where, it was believed, the fight had to be won. Both Hughes and Willcox reasoned that the Western tour would have to be made in August or it could not be made at all. But this decision was reached without any real understanding of the intense hatred between the Johnson and Crocker factions. As a matter of fact, Hughes often missed the significance of political feuds inflamed with malice. Being free from personal bitterness, he found it difficult to comprehend the marriage of hate to politics.

Hughes was eager to meet Johnson in his home state and asked that both Republican and Progressive delegations accompany him on his tour of California. A similar arrangement had worked well in Illinois. Campaign headquarters repeatedly urged the California factions to adhere to the spirit of the Illinois arrangement. But Crocker apparently could not endure the thought of the Progressives getting any advantage out of the presidential candidate's visit. He would not agree to Rowell's suggestion (made without Johnson's knowledge) that Governor Johnson preside at Hughes' San Francisco rally and Willis Booth, Johnson's opponent for the Republican nomination, at the Los Angeles rally, although Hughes and Willcox gave their blessing to this proposal. Crocker countered with a proposal that he preside at San Francisco and Rowell at Los Angeles. Rowell disagreed and renewed his charges that the Progressives were being cold-shouldered. Willcox urged Crocker to take note of the Progressives' grievances and to end the feuding. But the fight continued, with Crocker then insisting that he and Rowell, being national campaign officials, could not interfere in a "state matter," and that all arrangements for Hughes' visit be handled by Keesling's state committee.[9]

All efforts to bridge the gulf were futile. Hughes reviewed the row on a sweltering day in St. Paul, and at the suggestion of Frederick M. Davenport asked that Crocker and Rowell meet the campaign special at Portland, reserv-

[8] Charles W. Farnham's report on the California incident, p. 2; Hughes Papers.
[9] Frederick M. Davenport in *North American Review*, Feb. 17, 1917, p. 203.

ing final arrangements until the whole controversy could be threshed out with the candidate himself. Rowell agreed. Crocker wired that all arrangements had been completed. Finally Crocker suggested that Johnson and Rowell join him in conducting the Hughes party through the state. Rowell said this would be impossible because Johnson's own campaign itinerary had been fixed.[10]

Rowell joined the Hughes party at the Hotel Benson in Portland. After reviewing his efforts to reach an agreement with the Old Guard, he told Hughes that Governor Johnson was very popular in California and was almost certain to win. "For the sake of your own candidacy," he said, "you ought to come out for Johnson. If you do, you'll be elected. If you do not, you may not carry California." [11]

Hughes replied that he could not look at the California situation from the local point of view. To come out for Johnson might help him in California, but it would severely hurt him elsewhere. When he was Governor of New York, he told Rowell, many of the machine leaders accused him of not being a loyal Republican. That feeling had generally subsided with the widespread acceptance of what Hughes stood for. But it would be quickly rekindled if he should throw his support to Johnson in his fight against the old-line Republican candidate in California. "Moreover," Hughes said, "I should be 'yellow'—even dishonest—if I should play favorites in California simply because of Johnson's popularity. I couldn't possibly comply with your request," he told Rowell, "even if it should mean my defeat." [12]

Crocker and Keesling boarded the campaign special at Ashland, Oregon, accompanied by a reception committee of Republicans and Progressives— "tame" Progressives, according to Davenport. A memorandum written by Charles W. Farnham, Hughes' train manager, about five months after the incident reports a series of conferences aboard the train. "There did not appear to be any lack of harmony," he wrote, "and it was agreed Mr. Crocker was to preside at the meeting in San Francisco." [13] Davenport, who was traveling with Hughes as a friend and adviser and a representative of Chairman Willcox, insists that Crocker's arrangements were permitted to stand without any question being raised.[14] This is corroborated by Keesling, who says, "We refrained from referring to the senatorial contest in our conversations with Mr. Hughes." [15] In any event, Hughes did not take command of the situation as he certainly would have done in his governorship days. His mistake was in not softening his necessary rebuff to Rowell by insisting that Johnson preside

[10] Keesling to C. E. Kunze, July 31, 1923; Hughes Papers.
[11] Author's interview with CEH, April 9, 1946.
[12] Id.   [13] Farnham's report, p. 7.
[14] Author's interview with Dr. Davenport, Dec. 20, 1948.
[15] Keesling's monograph, *Hiram Johnson and the Hughes Campaign in California*, p. 36.

at the San Francisco rally. Whether or not Johnson could have complied at that late date, such a friendly gesture—stopping short of endorsement—might have averted the series of unfortunate events that was to follow.

The name of Crocker, an amiable philanthropist of high personal repute, was linked to the odious Southern Pacific machine. What that machine stood for was as repugnant to Hughes as it was to Johnson. But Hughes, fresh from the bench, knew little of California politics. On the night of Friday, August 18, he faced a crowd of 14,000 in the San Francisco Civic Auditorium still hoping that he could ride through California with one foot on the back of the Elephant and the other on the back of the Bull Moose. Rowell was on the rostrum in a silent role. Keesling introduced Crocker. As Crocker concluded his presentation of Hughes, there was a shout from the gallery, "Three cheers for San Francisco's favorite son!" What appeared at the time to be an outburst of public acclaim was later shown to be only a sycophantic gesture from an employee in Crocker's bank.[16]

"Fellow citizens," Hughes began in a voice that was hoarse from too much speaking, "I salute with you San Francisco's favorite son, and express my deep appreciation for his very generous introduction." [17]

"I come as the spokesman of a reunited Republican Party to talk to you of national issues—with local differences I have no concern."

It was a naturally generous response to Crocker's greeting and an accurate statement of Hughes' aloofness from the California imbroglio, but it chilled the powerful Progressives. Later his denunciation of political bosses caused the Old Guard to squirm. The rally ended with cheers but no demonstration. Rowell told the press that "the meeting was a frost," talked of Wilson's popularity in California, and openly accused Hughes of abandoning the Progressives to the wolves.[18] The next morning Rowell quit the Hughes party, saying that his wife was undergoing an operation. "We still hope to carry the state for Hughes," he said, "but we won't get the majority that we expected." [19] No other Progressive leader was assigned to take his place.

Crocker and Keesling were enraged by Rowell's disaffection and declared that they would not permit Johnson to preside at Los Angeles or any Progressives to participate in the other Hughes rallies in California. The city seethed with animosity. Impetuous Progressives were hinting openly that unless they got "substantial recognition" many of their votes would go to Wilson. The reactionaries insisted that any gesture toward Hiram Johnson on Hughes' part would drive them into Wilson's arms. Hughes was caught in the cross fire of hostile forces each of which was more interested in destroying the other than in his election.

[16] Francis V. Keesling to Paul Edwards, Aug. 9, 1945.
[17] *San Francisco Examiner*, Aug. 19, 1916.   [18] *Ibid.*
[19] Davenport in *North American Review*, Feb. 17, 1917.

It was painfully evident that the Old Guard was trying not only to keep Johnson from attending a Hughes rally but also to prevent the two candidates from meeting. Farnham discovered that no meeting had been arranged at Sacramento, the capital, apparently in furtherance of this scheme. He insisted on a rally being held there and tried to communicate directly with Governor Johnson.

Meanwhile another political *faux pas* reached its climax. Keesling had arranged a Saturday luncheon for the visitors at the Commercial Club. One of Hughes' advisers had urged him in Portland to cancel the luncheon because the waiters were preparing to strike. Such a course, Hughes replied, might cause the country to think he lacked courage. His managers then asked the union to postpone its walkout until after the luncheon had been held. The union leaders agreed on condition that the "open shop" sign in the window be removed during the luncheon. The Hughes men appealed to Crocker, Keesling, and other party bigwigs to get the sign temporarily removed, but nothing was done. Served by strikebreakers, the luncheon became a potent source of ill will among union men. Once more Hughes had fallen victim to an extraneous row and to the desensitization of his political acumen.

The campaign party left strife-ridden San Francisco at 8:00 P.M. on Saturday with a feeling of relief. Weary and perturbed, Hughes was especially glad that tomorrow would be a day of rest. He had made it a rule not to speak on Sundays. His anticipation of a pleasant and easy day was heightened when three prominent citizens boarded his train. "We think you should have a rest," they said, "and we're going to give you a real rest in Los Angeles."

There was a lively throng at the Alexandria Hotel, however, and the day began with much handshaking. Two old friends, C. W. Pendleton, Hughes' roommate at Brown, and John Murray Marshall, who induced him to go into law, were among the hosts and well-wishers. Immediately after breakfast Hughes was told that he was expected to attend a meeting of the Temple Baptist Church. He was applauded so enthusiastically when Dr. Len G. Broughton, the pastor, called him "the man of the hour" that he got up and bowed. At the end of the services two thousand persons insisted on shaking his hand.

While Farnham again tried to locate Governor Johnson, the candidate and his wife granted interviews to the press. Then their hosts casually suggested a drive to Pasadena. En route they stopped to see former Senator George F. Edmonds and Mrs. Garfield, widow of the martyred President. In Pasadena they also stopped to greet the children of the Boys' and Girls' Aid Society Home. By strange coincidence the Republican City Committee of Pasadena had arranged a luncheon for two hundred persons at which Mr. and Mrs. Hughes became the honored guests. Calls for a speech were heard, but he insisted that it was not one of his speaking days. Of course he could not refuse to shake the hands of the good people who had come out to greet him. Before the gathering dispersed, Hughes thought the entire population of Pasadena must have pumped his arm.

"Wouldn't you like to visit Long Beach on the way back to your hotel?" his escorts then asked. "It's a lovely drive." The idea of rest seemed to have gone a-glimmering. Hughes consented. Over a rough and dusty road they reached Universal City, a motion-picture center, and stopped to shake hands with the actors and impresarios. It was 5:00 P.M. when the automobiles drew up to the Virginia Hotel in Long Beach.

Ostensibly the guests were taken to the hotel to rest and to get a favored view of the Pacific. But word of their imminent arrival had gone up and down the beach, and 5,000 persons filled the hotel and blocked the entrance to it. The visitors succeeded in getting through the crowd, but the candidate and his wife had spent only a few minutes in their room when the clamor and shouting that came up from the street brought another surrender to the local committee's request that they "shake hands with the crowd." It was dusk when they walked to the parapet for a fleeting glance at the free-rolling Pacific; then the eight-car caravan got under way again.

Back in Los Angeles, they passed a brilliantly lighted building. "We have a wonderful museum here," an escort said with California fervor. "It has a fine collection of saber-tooth tigers and the world's best exhibit of prehistoric animals. We have arranged to have it all lighted so that you can see it now." As they went through the museum, the Hugheses were photographed beside the skeleton of a mastodon estimated to be 30,000 years old and felt a strange affinity to it.

At last they were back at their hotel, dirty, rumpled, and tired. Only a late evening was now left for relaxation. Optimistic Mr. Hughes was beginning to feel gratified that at least he could have a quiet dinner alone with his wife when a delegation called on him and said that the First Methodist Church was having a meeting in his honor, that the elders and congregation were waiting, and that he simply must come. Taking time only to wash, he went to the meeting without any dinner, made a brief speech, and submitted to another handshaking ordeal.

It was after ten o'clock when the exhausted candidate returned to his hotel and found Farnham waiting with a bombshell. While the Hughes party was at Long Beach, Farnham said, Governor Johnson had been there too in the same hotel.

"Why didn't you tell me at the time?" Hughes demanded with undisguised anger.

Farnham replied that he had no knowledge of Johnson's presence in the hotel until a newspaper man had passed the word to him after they had returned to Los Angeles.

"Drive down to Long Beach at once," Hughes ordered. "Explain to Governor Johnson that I did not know he was at the hotel and that I am sorry I did not meet him and ask him to preside at my meeting in Sacramento." [20] Farnham induced Keesling to go with him; Crocker refused.

At midnight on his "day of rest," with the burden of the Virginia Hotel mishap on his mind, Hughes left for San Diego, where he was to address a large crowd at the exposition on Monday.

"If I had known that Johnson was in the hotel," he told Davenport shortly before catching his train, "I would have seen him if I had been obliged to kick the door down." [21]

Governor Johnson had motored into Long Beach from Bakersfield. When he registered, he asked why the lobby was full of people and was told that Hughes was expected to arrive in a few minutes. As Johnson wrote his name, he overheard Frank Roberts, one of his most bitter political enemies, remark, "Wouldn't it be just like the Progressives to horn in on our party." [22] Bristling and resentful, Johnson went to his room, accompanied by E. A. Dickson and Paul Herriott, and remained there while the Hughes party came and went. His irritation was understandable, but he must have known that Roberts had no connection whatever with the Hughes party.

Johnson made no effort to see or greet the candidate whose cause he was espousing. He sent no one to let the Hughes people know he was in the hotel.[23] Several writers who have investigated the incident have concluded that the men around Hughes knew Johnson was in the hotel and deliberately kept the information from him. Keesling insists, however, that no member of the Hughes party, including the Southern California reception committee, had any inkling of the Governor's presence.[24] The hotel manager was a Republican politician who was doubtless eager to keep the candidates apart.

There are various conflicting accounts of what took place at Farnham's and Keesling's interview with Johnson. Some facts, however, can be nailed down. Admitting that he knew Hughes was in the hotel, Johnson said "that the people of . . . California would not wish their governor to break through any cordon surrounding him in order that he might shine in Hughes' reflected light. . . ." [25] Farnham reports Johnson as saying also that he had expected Hughes or Farnham to send for him before leaving the hotel.

[20] Author's interview with CEH, Oct. 24, 1945; CEH, Notes, p. 234.
[21] Author's interview with Dr. Davenport, Dec. 20, 1948.
[22] Keesling's interview with E. A. Dickson, recorded in a monograph by Keesling in 1943–1944, p. 51.
[23] John Murray Marshall, letter in Boston Evening Transcript, Dec. 16, 1916.
[24] Keesling's monograph, p. 51.
[25] Frederick M. Davenport in American Political Science Review, April, 1949, p. 328, quoting Johnson's letter to Rowell.

Farnham repeated what he had said in the beginning—that if Hughes had known of Johnson's presence he would have insisted upon seeing him without standing upon formalities. By any code of etiquette, however, Farnham reminded the Governor, it was his obligation to greet the visiting presidential candidate—not vice versa.

Johnson expressed regret that no meeting had taken place but said it was too late for him to go to Los Angeles or for Mr. Hughes to return to Long Beach. Farnham suggested that the Governor cancel his next speaking engagement so that he and Hughes could review the whole situation on Monday night; also that Johnson preside at the Sacramento rally. Johnson replied that the petty Republican politicians surrounding Hughes were determined to prevent any such meeting. According to Johnson's account, Keesling stalled and would not reply when Farnham asked him if he would object to the Governor's presiding at Sacramento.[26] Keesling says that he told Johnson that "the Republican committeemen had always desired his meeting and accompanying Governor Hughes throughout the state" and that if the presence of any Republican created an impossible situation arrangements could be made for Johnson to "continue with Governor Hughes under congenial conditions." [27] Johnson thought he left the door open to further discussion of the Sacramento meeting, but Farnham interpreted the Governor's remarks about the impossibility of changing his itinerary as a definite rejection.

The train manager's final request was an exchange of friendly telegrams between Johnson and Hughes. Johnson scoffed at the idea of greeting the visiting candidate on the eve of his departure from California. He said the question of telegrams should be taken up with Hughes. Farnham understood Johnson to agree nevertheless to send a telegram that could be read at the Sacramento rally. The conference trailed off into a Johnsonian scorching of Crocker, Keesling, and the Southern Pacific crowd. From the instant Hughes' coming to California was announced, he said, the trip had been used by Crocker and Keesling and those acting with them, not for the benefit of Hughes, but for the promotion of their petty ambitions, "so that the foul regime which had governed California prior to 1911 might again be fastened upon the state."

When the results of this conference were reported to Hughes on Monday morning, he approved an exchange of friendly telegrams, the texts to be agreed upon in advance to avoid any possible embarrassment to Governor Johnson. Farnham telephoned this suggestion to Johnson while Hughes was speaking at San Diego under extra guard because of a threat against his life. Johnson seemed to acquiesce, but when his telegram arrived it was addressed to Farnham rather than to Hughes as follows:

[26] *Ibid.*, p. 329.   [27] Keesling's monograph, 1943–1944, p. 49.

LONG BEACH CALIF. Aug. 21, 1916.

Mr. Charles W. Farnham
Care Governor Charles Evans Hughes
Hotel Alexandria, Los Angeles, Cal.

MY DEAR MR. FARNHAM your early telephone message from San Diego this morning suggesting that I wire Mr. Hughes and that he would respond as well as your suggestion last night that I go to Sacramento and there preside at Mr. Hughes meeting I have thought of most carefully. It goes without saying that I wish and have wished to extend to Mr. Hughes a most cordial and hearty welcome to California and that in view of my advocacy of him I would be very glad to present him to my fellow citizens and to state to them the reasons for my advocacy. Until now it has been rendered impossible for me to do either. The men surrounding Mr. Hughes in California and who have been in charge of his tour are much more interested in my defeat than in Mr. Hughes election and they have made it manifest both publicly and privately that they would vote for Mr. Wilson if the commonest courtesies were exchanged between Mr. Hughes and myself. At this late day when both our itineraries are full and fixed and upon the eve of Mr. Hughes departure from California for me even at your suggestion to wire Mr. Hughes and for him to reply or for me to preside at his Sacramento meeting would be misunderstood and misinterpreted and maliciously distorted. I have just been informed that tonights meeting has been elaborately staged for a Booth demonstration by the very people who protest they wish Mr. Hughes California trip wholly divorced from local candidacies such a thing in my behalf I would not of course tolerate or permit and I do not wish to be open even to the unjust accusation that I have attempted it. With kindest regards to yourself and Mr. Hughes and with best wishes for his success I am very sincerely yours,

HIRAM W. JOHNSON

It was not a greeting but a partisan lament from an official whose inflated sense of dignity had been wounded. In part it was based on misinformation that Johnson could have readily corrected. Instead of being a demonstration for Booth, Johnson's opponent, the Los Angeles meeting was a model of inter-party cooperation. Equal numbers of Republicans and Progressives sat on the platform and united in supporting Hughes' candidacy. It was the kind of meeting that he had planned to have throughout California and would have had, except for the blind stubbornness of Crocker and the irritability of Johnson.

Farnham telephoned Johnson that the telegram was not what he had promised. Once more the Governor agreed to send his greetings and asked what the nature of Hughes' reply would be. Farnham could say only that it would be a proper acknowledgment. Johnson then asked Farnham to readdress the telegram he had sent so that it would go to Hughes and to strike out everything except the greeting.[28] When Farnham declined to tamper with the telegram, Johnson again promised to send a message to be held until he had a satisfactory

[28] Farnham's report, p. 11.

reply from Hughes. It never arrived, and Farnham thereafter got no response to his telephone calls and telegrams to Johnson.

Hughes went on to Sacramento with an appeal for progressive policies but with only Crocker and Keesling accompanying his party. Through a large part of California he was thus presented to the people by political leaders who were about to lose their shirts. Both the candidate and his managers were worried, but Hughes felt that he could neither dismiss the official representatives of the Republican Party nor compel any Progressive to accompany him. He had done everything humanly possible to wipe out any offense that might have resulted from the misadventure at Long Beach, which was no fault of his in the first place. Certainly there is no ground for saying, as careless writers have repeated for more than three decades, that Hughes snubbed Johnson. If there was any snubbing, it was done by Governor Johnson himself. Many Californians were "disgusted and humiliated" [29] by the conduct both of Crocker and of Johnson.

After a great barbecue in Reno and a rally in the Mormon Tabernacle in Salt Lake City, Hughes went on to Estes Park, Colorado, for three days of rest. On the day of his departure Johnson won the Republican as well as the Progressive nomination for senator in California and complete control of the Republican Party in the state. Hughes wired his hearty congratulations, wishing Johnson great success in his campaign for election. "I was very glad to receive your telegram of congratulations," was Johnson's frigid reply, "and I thank you for it." [30] That alone was sufficient notice to Johnson's followers that he was nursing a grievance.

The severest test of the remarriage between the Republicans and Progressives had been bungled. The self-serving tenacity of the Old Guard and the vindictive attitude of Hiram Johnson had cast a shadow over the entire campaign.

[29] J. A. Hayes to CEH, Aug. 21, 1916.   [30] Hughes Papers.

Chapter 33

THE WAR ISSUE

ONLY a few times in our history have the people had an opportunity of choosing between presidential candidates of the caliber of Charles E. Hughes and Woodrow Wilson. Both were men of high integrity and powerful intellect. The parallelism in their careers has often held attention. Both were the sons of clergymen; both had been university professors and progressive governors of their states; both had fought the bosses and the trusts and united divided factions of their parties; both were men of vision and idealism who foresaw that isolation for the United States was nearing an end and that peace and democracy could be made secure only by world organization. Even Roosevelt sometimes spoke of Hughes as "the whiskered Wilson."

In the sphere of domestic policy both candidates talked the language of progressivism and pointed to records of substantial achievement. "I would not be here," Hughes declared again and again, "if I did not think of the Republican Party as a liberal party." His program included control of public utilities, old-age pensions, safeguards for labor, and protective legislation for women and children. But the Wilson Administration could point to a creditable record in domestic reforms, including the Federal Reserve System, the Federal Trade Commission, and the Farm Loan Act, and these accomplishments were much fresher in the public mind than Hughes' fights for the people as Governor of New York.

The general similarity of their aims naturally made the campaign more difficult for Hughes, for Wilson already occupied the Presidency. Hughes' case had to be built, of course, on their differences and contrasts. These were momentous and offered ample scope for a great national debate. But here again Hughes was at a disadvantage because his main reason for challenging the Administration lay in the uncertain and treacherous sphere of foreign policy, and he refused to make foreign-policy commitments that might embarrass him in office. The course of the next administration, he knew, would be determined largely by what happened in Europe and not by any policy devised in advance at the White House. He would not pretend that he could change the inevitable. The result was a campaign devoted for the most part to secondary issues, which keenly disappointed many of his friends.

Willcox's mismanagement of the campaign was another source of much concern. "If the election were held in the next fortnight," Medill McCormick, the Chicago publisher, warned Hughes on the last leg of his Western tour, "Wilson would win." [1] Taft too was alarmed. In Washington Senators Smoot, Weeks, Wadsworth, and Curtis were so concerned over the blunders of Chairman Willcox that they asked Harvey D. Hinman to come to the Capital for a conference. Since their fights together at Albany, Hinman had been known as Hughes' best friend among the politicians. The Senators asked him to go to Hughes and convince him that, in order to win, he would have to name a first-class politician as a back-stage manager for Willcox.

Hinman met Hughes' train at Buffalo and frankly outlined the weaknesses of the campaign up to that point. Hughes listened without comment. Then for ten minutes he gazed out of the window in silence. It was a perfect autumn day that seemed to magnify his troubles by contrast. When he turned to Hinman, he unburdened his heart. The campaign was not going well. The California mishap had complicated the difficulty of uniting the Republicans and Progressives. Willcox had demonstrated far less political gumption than Hughes had attributed to him. Hinman was undoubtedly right in saying that an experienced politician was needed at campaign headquarters.

"But I can't take it up with Willcox," Hughes said.[2]

The upshot of the conference was that Hinman, at Hughes' request, visited Willcox on his farm and tried to make him see the necessity of grass-roots organization and basic campaign strategy. Willcox laughed and said that Hughes was a great candidate, the campaign was going well, and he had no question about the outcome. A sweeping Republican victory in Maine in September tended to confirm this view.

A few weeks on the hustings, moreover, greatly improved Hughes' campaigning technique. His skill in managing an audience was put to an extraordinary test in Nashville on September 4. When Republican State Chairman James Taylor had talked in unflattering terms about the Wilson Administration, pandemonium had broken loose. Judge George N. Tillman had tried to introduce Hughes and had been driven back to his seat by an outburst of hisses and boos. The candidate walked forward smiling and waited patiently for the uproar to subside. When there was a lull, he began speaking in a conversational tone about his delight in visiting Nashville and his gratitude for the many courtesies he had received from the good people there regardless of party affiliations. Men who had been hissing sat back abruptly "as if they had received a slap in the face." [3] Someone laughed. Then came a ripple of applause. Here was the opening Hughes had hoped for. He plunged into the strike issue and won lusty cheers. After that even the hostile part of the

[1] McCormick to CEH, Aug. 25, 1916.
[2] Author's interview with Harvey D. Hinman, Aug. 15, 1948.
[3] *New York Times,* Sept. 5, 1916.

audience listened while he drove home his points with more force and vigor than he had attained in any previous rally. When he talked about Mexico, a man in the top gallery called out, "What would you have done?"

"What would I have done?" he flashed back, shaking his finger at the questioner. "I would have protected the lives of American citizens." [4]

The audience sprang to its feet cheering. Even the *New York Times* dropped its drumfire criticism of Hughes long enough to applaud his skill in turning insult to advantage.

After attending the Republican rally at Lincoln, Nebraska, David Lawrence drew a vivid picture of Hughes on the stump. The candidate stood erect with head uplifted, except when he dropped his chin, with its now short-cropped beard, to emphasize a point. "Nobody shoots out thought after thought, idea after idea, with more marvellous clarity or rapidity than the Republican nominee for the Presidency," Lawrence wrote. "He talks faster than most people think. . . . He is rattling it off at the rate of 200 words per minute . . . when he gets to a climax he is pounding so hard . . . that as he touches top speed and stays there for several sentences at a time, he holds the applause in check until he rounds it off with an epigrammatic phrase, when he finally releases the pent-up enthusiasm of his crowd, and the effect is like a cannon shot. . . . Mr. Hughes reaches over, drinks a glass of water in the interval, steps forward and is ready to go on. There is a rhythm to it all, a grammatical perfection and rhetorical mastery that catches the ear and transfixes the mind." [5]

His seriousness was usually leavened by bits of humor. When Wilson, forgetting his heavy reliance on his unofficial adviser, Edward M. House, said that a return of the Republicans would mean "invisible government," Hughes fired back that he preferred "government through two Houses and not three." While he was often severe in his criticism, he avoided personal enmity and never hit below the belt. "We are all friends," he insisted, "however divided politically."

While Hughes campaigned in the West, Wilson made votes in Washington out of the threatened railroad strike. First, he summoned the disputants to the White House and asked them to arbitrate their differences. The brotherhoods refused and called a strike for September 4. Incredulous when he heard of it, Wilson nevertheless hastened to Congress and asked for immediate enactment of a law giving the brotherhoods most of what they demanded—an eight-hour day with payment of the same wages that had previously been paid for ten hours. With 400,000 labor votes at stake, Congress too gave way and passed the Adamson Eight-Hour Act in time to avert the walkout.

Hughes thought this action was a "shocking abandonment of principle"

[4] Mrs. Hughes' diary.   [5] New York *Evening Post*, Oct. 17, 1916.

and condemned it in many speeches. He favored the eight-hour day, and as Governor of New York he had signed a bill prescribing an eight-hour day for railway telegraphers and signalmen. But he could not tolerate dictation to government. "Labor least of all can afford to surrender the rule of reason," he declared. "We must never permit any of the processes of government to be surrendered to the dictates of any power. That is the path of disaster. . . . I would rather stand on that principle and be defeated than yield one jot or tittle of it to get into office." [6]

Many workingmen applauded this forthright stand. At Terre Haute 400 laborers escorted Hughes and gave him a boisterous reception. It was not the labor vote that would cost him the election.

Preparedness was a hot issue throughout the campaign. "The President has never realized the gravity of our unprepared position . . ." wrote Colonel House in his diary. "If war comes . . . it will be because we are totally un-prepared and Germany feels that we are impotent." [7] "The people here [in Germany]," said James W. Gerard, the American ambassador, "are firmly convinced that we can be slapped, insulted, and murdered with absolute im-punity, and refer to our notes as things worse than waste paper." [8] Yet Wilson had continued a policy of weakness in the face of world upheaval.

When the President gave no support to Secretary of War Lindley M. Gar-rison's proposal to increase the Regular Army to 142,000 and set up a new "continental army" of 400,000 men, Garrison had resigned in protest. During the second year of the World War and the worst year of the difficulties with Mexico, the Administration had added only 227 officers and 1,248 men to the Regular Army. Wilson's biographer, Ray Stannard Baker, concludes that "the programme he approved was at best only a strong gesture." [9]

Hughes bore down heavily on this Wilsonian blind spot. "We have outlived the time," he asserted at San Francisco, "when Americans can go up and down the earth boasting of a free government and of the unparalleled resources of America and win respect for that declaration." [10] We must measure up, he declared, "in efficiency and strength." "Adequate preparedness," he said at Fargo, "is not militarism: it is the essential assurance of security," for "weak-ness breeds insult, insult breeds war: honest, firm, consistent, determined de-fense of rights establishes peace and respect throughout the world." The one hope of keeping out of the European war, he contended, lay in building up our military strength and protecting our rights with courage and firmness.

Probably the severest criticism of the campaign was leveled at Wilson's

[6] New York Times, Sept. 7, 1916.
[7] H. C. F. Bell, Woodrow Wilson and the People (New York, Doubleday, 1945), pp. 190–191. Copyright, 1945, by H. C. F. Bell.
[8] Ibid.
[9] Woodrow Wilson: Life and Letters, VI, 304, New York, Doubleday, 1937.
[10] San Francisco Examiner, Aug. 19, 1916.

Mexican policy. He had used the influence of the United States to drive General Huerta from power while pretending to follow a policy of "watchful waiting." Huerta was an adventurer who had seized the government by force, but he had won recognition from Great Britain, Germany, France, Russia, Spain, and Japan. The Mexicans failed to depose Huerta after the United States had withdrawn its embargo on arms in the hope of aiding the revolutionaries. Wilson then urged an election in Mexico and sent John Lind as his "personal spokesman" to the unrecognized Huerta to demand that Huerta should not be a candidate in that election. Lind told the German minister that "Huerta will be put out if he does not get out." [11]

In April, 1914, moreover, Wilson had ordered Admiral Mayo to "take Vera Cruz." The ostensible purpose was to enforce the admiral's demand for an apology and salute after the Mexicans had seized members of the crew of a United States steamship. Actually, however, this invasion of Mexican territory was ordered in a naïve effort to prevent a German ship from landing a load of munitions for Huerta, and, according to a Cabinet officer, "to show Mexico that we were in earnest in our demand that Huerta should go." Nineteen Americans and over a hundred Mexicans were killed in the fighting that ensued. Huerta got his ammunition through another port. Admiral Mayo did not get the salute and ignominiously withdrew after a short occupation of Vera Cruz. ". . . we intervened," Hughes declared, "but we didn't stay intervened. We had intervention for an ignoble purpose, and a retreat without accomplishing anything, except the destruction of the only government Mexico had." [12]

Hughes' second count against the Mexican policy was its failure to protect American citizens. After Villa's bandits had killed sixteen American mining men on a train and invaded, looted, and burned Columbus, New Mexico, an American military force had penetrated several hundred miles into Mexico without punishing anyone. "We have not helped Mexico," Hughes declared. "She lies prostrate, impoverished, famine-stricken, overwhelmed with the woes and outrages of internecine strife, the helpless victim of a condition of anarchy which the course of the Administration only served to promote. We have made enemies, not friends. Instead of commanding respect and deserving good-will by sincerity, firmness, and consistency, we provoked misapprehension and deep resentment. . . . We have resorted to physical invasion, only to retire without gaining the professed object. It is a record which cannot be examined without a profound sense of humiliation." [13]

The strangest issue of the campaign was the accusation that Hughes was truckling to the German-American vote. Many citizens of German extraction

[11] Lind to Nelson O'Shaughnessy, April 5, 1914; Hughes Papers.
[12] *San Francisco Examiner*, Aug. 19, 1916.   [13] Acceptance speech, p. 6.

in New York had supported him as governor, and their loyalty carried over to 1916. Others rallied to him at first because they thought Wilson was pro-British. Hughes refrained from insulting these people, but there was never the slightest reason to suspect him of sympathy for the hyphenates. "Whether native or naturalized, of whatever race or creed," he had said in his very first political utterance in 1916, "we have but one country, and we do not for an instant tolerate any division of allegiance." That view was often reiterated, and Hughes made it unmistakably plain that, if elected, he would deal more severely with any German invasion of American rights than Wilson had done.

On October 22 the Democratic National Committee released a sensational charge that Hughes had secretly met German-American and Irish-American groups and made "a campaign deal" with them.[14] Four men representing the American Independence Conference had called on Hughes about the middle of September through arrangements made by Charles Beecher Warren. They were Carl E. Schmidt, wealthy Michigan manufacturer; Frank Seiberlich; William R. MacDonald, an organizer of the Embargo Conference; and Jeremiah O'Leary, chairman of the American Truth Society. Directly or indirectly, these latter organizations were getting German financial support. Wilson later rebuked O'Leary and said that he did not want his vote or the vote of anyone like him. At the time of the meeting, however, Hughes knew neither the individuals nor their connections. He listened to their views, as he had done with all other groups that came to see him, and reiterated his own determination, if he should be elected, to give protection to American lives, property, and commerce. Nothing that was said gave the slightest ground for suspicion of intrigue or an improper bid for votes.

News of the "sensation" reached Hughes at the Montclair Hotel in New Jersey where he was dining with Willcox, Colonel Harvey, Travis H. Whitney, and several others. Immediately he dictated a reply setting forth the facts and declaring, "I have said nothing in private that I have not said in public." Two days later, in speaking at Schuetzen Park in Queens to an audience largely of German ancestry, he said emphatically that he did not want the vote of anyone "who would not instantly champion the rights and interests of our country against any country on earth."[15]

Undoubtedly Hughes would have won votes by making this emphatic statement earlier in the campaign. But the absurdity of the charge against him two weeks before election day is magnified by the historic fact that the German vote went largely to Wilson. Josephus Daniels, who was Secretary of the Navy, noted that after T. R. began his bellicose speeches for Hughes "the trend of the German vote from Ohio to the Pacific set in toward Wilson."[16]

[14] *New York Times*, Oct. 23, 1916.   [15] *Ibid.*, Oct. 25, 1916.
[16] *The Wilson Era: Years of Peace—1910–1917* (Chapel Hill, University of North Carolina Press, 1944), p. 466. Copyright, 1944, by the University of North Carolina.

The war issue overshadowed everything else. Hughes played it down because he was confident that he would be elected and was determined to remain free to deal with any emergency in accord with his best judgment when all the facts and circumstances could be known. In sharp contrast, the Wilson forces pitched their entire campaign to the key, "He kept us out of war." Martin H. Glynn, the temporary chairman of the Democratic National Convention in St. Louis, had reached his climax by citing historic occasions on which American rights had been violated. Each story had ended with the intoxicating declaration, "But we didn't go to war." Then Senator Ollie James, the permanent chairman, had credited Wilson with wringing from Germany an agreement to American demands, "without orphaning a single American child, without widowing a single American mother, without firing a single gun, without the shedding of a single drop of blood." [17] Even Bryan, who had resigned as Secretary of State because Wilson's policy was too "militant" for him, joined in the orgy, and the platform reiterated the kept-us-out-of-war theme.

Knowing how precarious was the peace the United States still enjoyed, Wilson himself avoided this opportunistic and deceitful slogan. "It begins to look as if war with Germany is inevitable," he had told Tumulty as early as June.[18] To a newspaper man he had said, ". . . we ought to be in [the war] now, for the conditions are getting desperate for the Allies, and it is possible we may come in too late." [19] One gets the impression that he had little hope of keeping the United States out of the war even though he had failed to prepare for the inevitable.

In spite of this, the President's followers chanted the "Wilson and Peace" slogan from one end of the country to the other, and for a time they seemed to have some ground for the claim, for Germany had temporarily suspended her attacks upon neutral shipping in the Atlantic. "Gerard's utterances had made it clear," the Kaiser said, "that Wilson was seeking a ladder for re-election. It was better, then, that we should offer him the ladder of peace than the ladder of war, which will eventually fall on our own heads." [20] Undoubtedly the moderate faction in Berlin succeeded in holding the murderous U-boats in leash in part because of the recognized advantage to Germany of keeping Wilson in the White House.

In October, 1916, however, that expedient arrangement began to crack up. Ambassador Gerard returned to the United States with an urgent message from von Jagow, German Secretary of State. Unless Wilson could do something quick for peace, von Jagow had said, "German public sentiment would compel

[17] Baker, op. cit., pp. 250–253.
[18] Joseph P. Tumulty, Woodrow Wilson as I Know Him, p. 159, New York, Doubleday, 1921.
[19] Harold Garnet Black, The True Woodrow Wilson (New York, Revell, 1946), p. 161. Copyright, 1946, Fleming H. Revell Co.
[20] Bell, op. cit., p. 256, quoting Count Bernstorff.

the government to give in to the demands" for resumption of unrestricted sub-marine warfare.[21] Before Gerard got across the Atlantic, it was evident that Wilson could do nothing. Briand and Lloyd George, feeling that Germany was on the ropes, had flatly rejected the idea of a negotiated peace.

Gerard's message became in effect, therefore, a warning that the slaughter of Americans on the high seas was soon to be resumed. His ill tidings were broadcast through the newspapers. Wilson thought it best to delay seeing Gerard until after the election in order to dispel the idea that a new submarine crisis was at hand. Trying to close his eyes to the ugly picture, he declared on October 21, "I am not expecting this country to get into the war." [22] He had previously declared that the Republican alternative to his policy would mean war.

After two weeks of hesitation Wilson saw Gerard and learned the painful truth firsthand. There was also a report from Joseph C. Grew, secretary to the American Embassy in Berlin, that the German Navy had asked the emperor to permit an immediate U-boat campaign. House carried to the President a secret memorandum from the Kaiser predicting that Germany would have to regain her "freedom of action." [23] The sinking of six steamships off the Island of Nantucket a month before the election gave special emphasis to these warnings and greatly alarmed the East. The juggernaut of war was rolling re-lentlessly toward American shores.

Burdened by this ominous knowledge, Wilson let his campaign run its course with increasing frenzy for peace. "He kept us out of war." "You are Working; Not Fighting!" "Alive and Happy;—Not Cannon Fodder!" "Wilson with Peace and Honor?" Or "Hughes with Roosevelt and War?" [24] The wild oratory for a peace that had already vanished was accompanied by a lavish display of posters depicting the carnage of war, with a horrified mother and her children looking on. Underneath the legend proclaimed, "He has protected me and mine."

It is doubtful whether any other presidential campaign has reached com-parable depths of slogan intoxication. Wilson had been hoodwinked by the Germans; and now that his illusions were exploding, his followers were con-tinuing to hoodwink the people for the sake of his reelection. The fact that he was to become a great war President does not minimize the disingenuousness of the means thus used to return him to power.

In contrast, Hughes did not have access to the confidential State Depart-ment reports or to Ambassador Gerard. He did not know that war was imminent. Yet he honestly reminded his audiences that it might be necessary to go to war to protect American rights and interests. He took note of the

[21] Baker, *op. cit.*, VI, 356.   [22] *Ibid.*, p. 360.
[23] *Ibid.*, 361.   [24] *New York Times*, Nov. 4, 1916.

pledge in the Democratic platform of 1912 to protect American citizens in all parts of the world. "That is good doctrine," he said at Seattle, "and I believe in making it real. I do not think that in making it real we should encounter the danger of war. I would not shrink if we did in performing our obvious duty." [25] "We have honest rights," he reiterated at St. Louis, "and, so far as I am concerned, I am not too proud to fight to maintain those rights." [26]

The crowd roared approval in Ogdensburg when he declared, "I do not want to be President of a people that are not ready to give their all for their liberties, their land, their country that they love." [27] He felt that the United States should stand as the champion of international law and human rights. If the country "thought more of dollars than of human lives," he said, it should not turn to him.

At Louisville on October 12 Hughes finally answered the question which the press had been throwing at him ever since the campaign began and which no one had given him a chance to answer in an open rally. As he condemned Wilson's shilly-shallying, Alvin W. Durning of the *Courier-Journal* stood up and asked, "What would you have done when the *Lusitania* was sunk?"

"Put him out!" yelled the audience.

"Please permit the question to be asked," Hughes shouted. "I do not want any one shut off from a courteous question. Go on, sir."

It took half an hour to quiet the crowd so that the question could be answered. At last Hughes made himself heard:

I would have had the State department at the very beginning of the Administration so equipped as to command the respect of the world [applause]; and, next, when I said "strict accountability," every nation would have known that that was meant; and, further, when notice was published with respect to the action threatened, I would have made it known in terms unequivocal and unmistakable that we should not tolerate a continuance of friendly relations . . . if that action were taken; and the *Lusitania* would never have been sunk.[28]

Hughes strongly insisted that he was a man of peace and that his policy of preparedness and firm protection of American lives would keep the country out of war. Possibly he was right. Germany unleashed her U-boats after Wilson's reelection because, as Admiral von Holtzendorff wrote on December 10, "There is reason to hope that . . . the United States will confine itself to the use of big words." [29] But it is more probable that it would have been too late in the winter of 1916–1917 for a policy of firm dealing and preparedness to succeed. Germany had one chance left, and she gambled on success before the befuddled and unarmed giant across the Atlantic could bestir him-

[25] *Ibid.*, Aug. 15, 1916. [26] *Ibid.*, Sept. 3, 1916. [27] *Ibid.*, Oct. 28, 1916.
[28] *Ibid.*, Oct. 13, 1916. [29] *Official German Documents*, II, 1183.

self. The fact remains that Hughes' policy of facing up to the German menace and of preparing to meet the consequences, whatever they might be, was infinitely more realistic than the "Wilson and Peace" slogan, which turned sour two months after the election.

In November, 1916, however, many Americans were intoxicated with the idea that they could reap the fabulous profits of war and let the Europeans do the fighting and dying. With this head-in-the-sand attitude encouraged by a great political party, the people of the West, feeling remote from the war, swarmed into the polls and voted their illusions.

Chapter 34

DEFEAT WITHOUT BITTERNESS

HUGHES closed his campaign at Madison Square Garden in New York, with 62,000 supporters parading and yelling their devotion to himself, Mrs. Hughes, and Theodore Roosevelt. When the cheering finally subsided that Saturday night, the candidate and his wife went to the Hotel Astor to catch up on sleep and await the voice of the people. Both had come through their ordeal in good health and excellent humor.

On election day, November 7, Mrs. Hughes took her three daughters to see *The Music Master*. The candidate had a good sleep. Awaking after dark, he looked out over Times Square, where a huge lighted signboard advertised, "U.S. Tires." "Perhaps they will complete that tomorrow," he joked, "by adding 'of Wilson.'" Many New Yorkers were betting that the people were tired of Wilson, the odds being ten to seven on Hughes.

As the family ate dinner, friends repeatedly burst into their suite to overwhelm them with good news, and an avalanche of favorable bulletins descended upon their table. Robert Fuller said Hughes had carried New York by 100,000. Governor Whitman telephoned his congratulations from Albany. Chester Rowell wired his from California. The *World* and several other New York newspapers conceded Hughes' election. Reporters begged for a statement. "Wait till the Democrats concede my election," Hughes replied; "the newspapers might take it back." [1] It began to appear that the Republican ticket might carry every state outside the solid South. Times Square flashed the news of a great Hughes victory to a crowd estimated at a hundred thousand.

An American flag was flung out from the roof of the Astor with two searchlights playing upon it. Beside it a huge electric sign blazoned "HUGHES" through the night. Delegations from the Republican and Union League clubs importuned the "President-elect" to appear on the balcony and accept the plaudits of the milling multitude below. "If I have been elected President," Hughes replied, "it is because the people of this country think that I'll keep my shirt on in an emergency. I'll start right now by not yielding to this demand when I am not positive that I have been elected." [2]

Meanwhile Mrs. Hughes aroused nine-year-old Elizabeth so that she might share the family's great moment in history. "Elizabeth, you should see this,"

[1] *New York Times*, Nov. 8, 1916.   [2] Berrits' Memorandum, VII, 35.

360

her mother said as they went to the window. The *Times* was flashing the election of Hughes. A sea of humanity below was yelling, "Hughes! Hughes! Hughes!" The child rubbed her eyes and took in the scene with an inner glow of delight.

Excitement was still running high at midnight when Hughes concluded that he preferred sleep to further returns. It has been repeated ten thousand times that he went to bed assuming he was elected, but he did not. Hughes never took for granted anything that was uncertain. Wishful conclusions were utterly contrary to his nature. When he retired that night, his thinking went no further than that his election seemed probable.[3]

Another delightful bit of fiction is the story that a reporter bearing bad news to Hughes' door the next morning was informed by his son that "the President" could not be disturbed and replied, "When he wakes up tell him he's no longer President." Much repetition of this remark does not alter the fact that Charles Evans Hughes, Jr., did not stay at the Astor over election night. After leaving his parents about midnight, young Hughes and his wife spent a couple of hours at Republican headquarters and then returned to their own home in New York. Nor did any other member of the Hughes family talk with a reporter that morning. The story is "such stuff as dreams are made on."

When Hughes awoke about 8:00 A.M., he was still being greeted as President-elect by numerous newspaper editorials filled with gratuitous advice. But the returns then coming in told a different story. While Hughes had swept the East, Wilson had swept the South and West. As the day wore on, the count stood: Wilson, 251 electoral votes; Hughes, 247, with California, Minnesota, North Dakota, and New Mexico still doubtful. Hughes' restrained optimism of the night before quickly vanished, and he prepared to face defeat with good grace.

In the difficult two days that followed, the Hughes family went to the theater twice, drove about the city, received hundreds of friends, and waited for the final returns from California. Hughes' poise and dignity were utterly unshaken. On Wednesday, Chairman Willcox prepared a statement and asked Hughes' permission to release it. Hughes said it would not do and while he was still on the telephone dictated a wholly objective and unemotional statement of the situation as it then stood. It was not until Friday morning that Wilson's victory was confirmed. On Tuesday night the President had been dissuaded by Tumulty from conceding the election of Hughes. Because of the emergency he was prepared, moreover, to turn the Presidency over to Hughes immediately. He had written to Secretary of State Lansing asking him, in the event of Hughes' election, to resign along with Vice President Marshall. Wilson would then appoint Hughes Secretary of State and resign himself so that, under the law

[3] Author's interview with CEH, Jan. 7, 1946.

then in effect, Hughes would succeed him without waiting for the four-month interval separating election day from inauguration day.[4] Hughes never indicated whether or not he would have cooperated in this plan if he had been elected.

With some states going Democratic by only a few hundred votes, Republican cries of "fraud" were heard, but Hughes quickly suppressed them. When all the returns were in two weeks later, he sent his congratulations to Wilson:

Because of the closeness of the vote I have awaited the official count in California and now that it has been virtually completed, permit me to extend to you my congratulations upon your reelection. I desire also to express my best wishes for a most successful administration.[5]

The final electoral vote was 277 to 254, and the popular vote stood: Wilson, 9,129,606; Hughes, 8,538,221. Each candidate received more votes than had ever been cast for a presidential nominee before. Since Hughes got about a million more votes than both Roosevelt and Taft had in 1912, he had succeeded reasonably well in reuniting the rank and file of the Republican and Progressive parties. But California had denied him the 3,775 votes he needed to win, while Hiram Johnson, on the same ticket, was carrying California by nearly 300,000 votes.

The delayed count in California and the closeness of the vote dramatically emphasized the part that state had played in Hughes' defeat. He had lost the Presidency on that "day of rest" in Los Angeles because, through no fault of his own, he had not shaken hands with Johnson. The Senator-elect from California was promptly accused by many Republicans of betraying his party's presidential candidate. The resulting controversy will probably never be finally settled, but a few facts appear to be well established. Johnson and some of his lieutenants continued to speak for Hughes after the Virginia Hotel incident, but the word went around among his followers to vote for Johnson and Wilson.[6] Hughes was severely cut in San Francisco, Sacramento, and Fresno—the Progressive strongholds. Southern California gave him a plurality of more than 40,000 votes. It is clear enough that Johnson's followers were disgruntled.

The initial mistake was Hughes' insistence on making the California tour while the primary fight was in progress, although the situation would have been even more complicated later if Booth had won the Republican nomination, as he came within 15,000 votes of doing. To this must be added Hughes' delay in asking Johnson to preside at one of his rallies and his overly generous words to Crocker. But these errors resulting from lack of familiarity with the California situation would have been erased from the mind of a less vindictive man

[4] Copy of Wilson's letter to Lansing in Hughes Papers.
[5] Ray Stannard Baker, *Woodrow Wilson: Life and Letters,* VI, 300.
[6] John Murray Marshall's letter in Boston *Evening Transcript,* Dec. 16, 1916.

than Hiram Johnson by Hughes' friendly overtures at Los Angeles. After failing to extend a minimum of courtesy to the visiting candidate, Johnson made it impossible to overcome the repercussions from his own aloofness at Long Beach.

Hughes harbored no animosity toward Johnson. Years later when he was Secretary of State one of his subordinates drafted a bristling reply to a query from Senator Johnson. Laughing heartily, Hughes exclaimed, "I may not feel like sending love and kisses to Senator Johnson, but I'm certainly not going to sign a letter of this kind." He ordered the letter to be redrafted to make it a courteous and considerate reply.[7]

More damaging to the Republican cause than the California incident was Willcox's general mismanagement of the campaign. Hughes could have won if he had had a few thousand additional votes in New Mexico, North Dakota, and New Hampshire or in several other states. In congratulating him when it was believed that he had been elected, the *New York Herald* said editorially that he had been "handicapped by bungling campaign management from the start."[8] "Mr. Hughes did better than the Republicans had any excuse for expecting," said the *New York Times*.[9]

Willcox had been quite unaware of the prairie fire of pacifism that was sweeping the West. Only Charles Beecher Warren had sensed it. At his request Hughes had returned to Michigan and, as a result, carried that state. Obviously he should have stayed in the Midwest instead of going to the border states. Hughes always felt that if he had discovered Will Hays in time to have made him campaign manager in 1916, his victory would have been assured.

Another incredible blunder that any experienced manager would have avoided was the women's campaign train sponsored by Mrs. Payne Whitney, Mrs. Cornelius Vanderbilt, Mrs. Mary Harriman Rumsey, Mrs. Elizabeth Stotesbury, and others. Not every woman on the train was the "incarnation of fat dividends," but enough were in that category to make their campaigning a source of irritation instead of good will. The train was promptly dubbed the "Billion Dollar Special." Western women who had the vote especially resented advice on how to use it from voteless Eastern moneybags. This venture may well have cost Hughes more votes than he won by his forthright stand for woman suffrage.

Finally, there was the incubus of Roosevelt's war speeches. Because of the previous split in the party, Roosevelt's good will was indispensable to Hughes. But T. R. campaigned more for war than for the Republican-Progressive ticket. Since it was widely assumed that if Hughes were elected Roosevelt would have a hand in formulating the policies of his administration, this line

[7] Author's interview with Mrs. Ruth B. Shipley, Sept. 9, 1949.
[8] Nov. 8, 1916.   [9] Nov. 11, 1916.

of campaigning gave the Democrats an opportunity to exploit the war issue with devastating effect. A group of New York Democrats who had supported Hughes wired their congratulations to Roosevelt on the election of Wilson to which, they said, "you contributed more than any other person in America. . . . Wilson ought to give you a Cabinet position," the telegram continued, "as you elected him beyond doubt . . . you made Wilson a million votes." [10] Many Progressives also went over to Wilson to punish Roosevelt for his last-minute "betrayal" at Chicago.

Taft was filled with bitter regrets. On November 10 he wrote to Hughes:

MY DEAR GOVERNOR,
  The election seems to be against us. I write to express my profound disappointment at the result and my very great admiration for your bearing in the campaign, for the great speeches you made, for the unstinted energy with which you sacrificed yourself and the marvellous endurance you showed.
  There never was a man in public life whom good luck has aided so much as Woodrow Wilson. Good luck and the most unblushing opportunism brought him his success. It makes one indignant to think how effective was his appeal to the opportunism of Americans. The Kansas farmers' motto was, "I don't care a dern what happens so long as it doesn't happen to me." This prevailed throughout the jack rabbit states. . . .
  I feel myself conscience stricken in that I urged you to the great sacrifice you have made with so disappointing a result. What Wilson will do with the Court now, the Lord only knows. I hope that the brethren on the Bench will stay in the harness as long as possible to prevent any more injury than is inevitable. . . .
  As I look through the States, I find you suffered much from the ill jointed condition of the party. If a candidate for Senator or Governor was a Republican, he gave his first attention to his own election—so too if he was a Progressive. Your interests were not made paramount as they should have been and as they would have been with a solid party. . . .
  Please present my affectionate regard to Mrs. Hughes. . . .
  Tell her that I know there are many worse things than defeat. I have had some experience in this. You have nothing to apologize for. You have nothing to take back. I hope to have the pleasure of talking the whole matter over at no distant day.

With great respect
greater than ever
Sincerely yours

WM. H. TAFT

Hughes was not cast down by his defeat. "I had done my best," he later wrote in his Notes. "While of course I did not enjoy being beaten, the fact that I did not have to assume the tasks of the Presidency in that critical time was an adequate consolation." His buoyancy of spirit is clearly reflected in his reply to Taft:

[10] Hughes Papers.

During the past few days I have been sitting up with the mourners and there has been no opportunity to answer your very kind letter. You must not chide yourself for urging me to make the fight. I had no honorable alternative in view of the action of the convention and I do not think that anyone of common sense has entertained the idea that my acceptance hurt the dignity of the Court. I did not wish to leave the bench, but it was a high privilege to be chosen to lead in the endeavor to establish sounder national policies and to make the Republican party once more an effective instrument of national service. So far as I am personally concerned, I have no complaints and no regrets.

There are some grounds for gratification. The miserable appeal to "Labor" as a class vote succeeded only in part. Its failure, for example, in New York was conspicuous. Apparently, it did succeed in Ohio, but that was an exception. The entire weight of Gompers' influence and the direct appeal of the federation were not sufficient to convince workingmen, as a class. There is hope in that. Then, the division was not along the lines of sympathy with the warring Nations. I am grateful for that also. On the other hand, it is mortifying that the cry of "peace and prosperity" was so potent. I fear that we shall suffer in the coming years through the revelation of our "soft spots." It is hard to understand California and Washington. They have not had the prosperity there that other parts of the country have enjoyed. The bitterness of the factional strife in California passes belief, and I presume it accounts for the result. Of course, I did not snub Johnson. I had no idea that he was in the Long Beach Hotel when I was there. . . . All the facts doubtless will appear in due time. . . .

It was a very difficult campaign—there were so many cross currents. At times, it seemed impossible—even here in the East—to hold together the groups whose support was essential to success. For your own able and untiring efforts I am most grateful. Your article in the "Yale Review" was a most convincing statement. Nothing fairer, more lucid, or more completely unanswerable appeared during the campaign. It seems incredible that the Administration of which such a criticism was possible should have received a vote of confidence. Despite its victory, I trust that the closeness of the vote and the manifest feeling in the most populous states will be heeded, and that hereafter the Administration will represent the Nation more worthily. If the recent contest has this result, it will not have been wholly in vain.

I have been waiting for the official count in California—the vote was so close, I could not do otherwise—to close this chapter, and on January first I shall return to the practice of the law in New York City with a feeling of eagerness for the varied activities which it permits.[11]

For a time Hughes was depressed when people stared at him on the subways or on the streets. But he persistently joked about his defeat in public as well as in private. Speaking to the New England alumni of Brown, he brought roars of laughter with his sallies at his own defeat. "This is a very happy time for me," he said, "for I have the pleasure of resuming entirely human relations." [12]

When Root welcomed him back to the law at a dinner given by the New York Bar Association and said that he was glad to see Hughes but "wished

[11] CEH to Taft, Nov. 20, 1916; Taft Papers.   [12] *Boston Post*, Jan. 24, 1917.

he were somewhere else," the latter blasted all lamentations. "I have no wounds to exhibit," he said. "I shall say nothing of either battle or murder or sudden death. I have no desire to evoke sympathy by any suggestion of misfortune." [13]

As time rolled on he came to view the outcome in 1916 with philosophical satisfaction. When the United States went into the war in spite of the "Wilson and Peace" campaign, political differences were forgotten in that common struggle. Hughes could not help wondering whether the Democrats who had campaigned so vehemently for peace would have joined as wholeheartedly in the war effort if he had been President. Could Wilson have endured defeat and then urged his followers to support the new administration in the war effort without becoming bitter and vindictive? Wondering, Hughes told his friends, "It is better this way."

Again when Wilson went to his grave broken and disillusioned, Hughes expressed a thankfulness that he had escaped the tragic fate that fell to his opponent. "The Presidency in those war years would have killed me as it killed Wilson," he said. In his later life he thus came to look upon his defeat in 1916 as the key to a happy and fruitful future.

[13] *New York Times,* Jan. 23, 1917.

Chapter 35

CIVILIAN WAR WORKER

AFTER RESTING for a few weeks at Lakewood, Hughes embarked upon a new career for the fourth time in a decade. The idea of being President had been completely banished from his mind. He dropped the role of standard-bearer as completely as he had dropped the practice of law when he became governor and politics when he went to the Supreme Court. Now again he was a practicing lawyer. Instead of moping because he had been denied leadership of the nation, he set out to win leadership of the bar.

In order to finance his new venture, Hughes sold his Washington home and some furniture to Senator John W. Weeks, realizing $44,438.13. Aside from this, his assets consisted of $7,500 invested in mortgages. But money was no problem. One organization offered him $50,000 a year, without office expenses, to take charge of its legal work. Frank Munsey offered him an editorial berth on the New York *Sun* with a free hand in making policy. From Cadwalader, Wickersham & Taft came a still more attractive offer of the place in that firm vacated by the death of John L. Cadwalader in 1914. Hughes declined these enticing bids for his services because he wished to regain his position of independent counsel and to have his son, now a thoroughly trained and able lawyer, associated with him. Those objects could best be attained, he thought, by rejoining his old friends and partners, Arthur C. Rounds and George W. Schurman. His firm thus became Hughes, Rounds, Schurman & Dwight.

At once he was swamped with legal business and found it necessary to reject about as many cases as he accepted. As counsel for New York City, he gave an opinion that a proposed agreement between the city and the New York Central Railroad for West Side improvements was legal. He became referee in a suit by the Brooklyn Borough Gas Company to restrain enforcement of the eighty-cent gas law. When Mayor John Purroy Mitchel was cited for contempt by the New York Senate on a charge of having uttered a "false and malicious statement concerning Senator Robert F. Wagner," Hughes went to Albany to defend the mayor. In one of his patriotic outbursts, Mitchel had accused Wagner of being pro-German. There was a lively hearing and a heated argument that ended in the early morning hours with dismissal of the charges.

Relieved of official duties, Hughes also gave an enormous amount of time to civic work. In 1917 he was elected president of the Legal Aid Society, the

Union League Club, the New York State Bar Association, and the St. David's Society. A year later he became president of the Italy-America Society for encouragement of Italy's war effort. He made several speeches for the Red Cross and became chairman of the committee of lawyers conducting a special wartime Red Cross drive. In the field of politics he endorsed the Fusion Committee's renomination of Mayor Mitchel and spoke several times for him; he headed a committee working for the renomination and election of Justices McLaughlin and Cardozo and supported William L. Ransom for district attorney.

The impending involvement of the United States in the war overshadowed everything else in the winter and spring of 1917. Less than three months after his defeat Hughes was urging all Americans to "stand loyally behind the President, without a partisan thought." [1] On March 20, six hundred Republicans met at the Union League Club behind closed doors and virtually declared war on Germany ahead of the government. "Let us not delude ourselves," Hughes pleaded. "Germany is making war upon the United States, making war with a ruthless barbarity. . . . Our citizens have been murdered, are being murdered. Our ships have been sunk. . . . I regard these attacks, the method of their conduct, as an onslaught on liberty and on civilization itself." [2] Roosevelt, Root, and Joseph H. Choate joined in declaring that Germany's illegal attacks should be repelled. The resolution that was passed "begged the President to give the people a chance to defend themselves."

War talk continued when Roosevelt, Root, Robert Bacon, and Hughes foregathered in a café after the meeting. T. R. was bubbling over with fighting zeal and the conviction that he should have a military command abroad. "You must see Wilson," he declared, turning to Root and Hughes, "and get his consent to let me go." His voice deepened with solemnity and emotion. "I must go," he said, "but I will not come back. My sons will go too, and they will not come back." For a moment there was silence out of respect for T. R.'s evident sincerity. Then Root spoke up, with his unfailing humor, "Theodore, if you can make Wilson believe that you will not come back, he will let you go." [3]

Wilson summoned Congress to meet on April 2, and the war resolution was signed four days later. Hughes was delighted to see Wilson's policy transformed from hesitation and weakness to strong prosecution of the war, and he took advantage of every opportunity to throw his support behind the Administration. [4] While he did not speak as the leader of the opposition party, thinking it absurd for a defeated candidate to retain any such prerogative, he threw all the influence of his personality as a private citizen into the war effort.

[1] New York Times, Feb. 2, 1917.   [2] Ibid., March 21, 1917.
[3] CEH, Notes, p. 239.   [4] New York Times, April 13, 26, and May 2.

At the same time he insisted on maintaining the rights of free criticism. Focusing the spotlight upon governmental mistakes was as much a part of the war effort as the making of steel and ships. No democratic leader could ask immunity from it. Much as he deplored politics in wartime, Hughes declared that if he had to choose between partisanship with criticism and the absence of both he would unhesitatingly take the former alternative. His acid test of criticism was its effect on the war effort. If it merely caused embarrassment, the people would have none of it. If it helped, the more of it, the better. For this high-minded attitude, the New York *Sun* dubbed him "the Patriotic Critic."

The country was in an intellectual ferment. Participation in a world war for the first time not only unleashed new powers; it brought also a flood of new problems for the traditionally isolated American Republic. Hughes could no more be impassive in this situation than could a bobolink at the burst of dawn. As his law practice took every moment of his office hours, he and Mrs. Hughes were often up at 5:00 A.M., he to write speeches and she to make coffee and lend moral support to his efforts.

At the first of a series of meetings held by the National Conference on Foreign Relations, he urged a concert of all the great powers after the war, with the United States taking the lead:

If the world is to be made safe for democracy, it must be a world in which the nations recognize and maintain the supremacy of law. . . . If we can see at all into the future we know that it offers no chance for isolation to the United States. We have vast resources and extraordinary privileges and we cannot shirk our duty to mankind. Self-interest as well as a proper sense of obligation demand that we should aid in rearing the structure of international justice, and certainly that we should not make its establishment impossible by holding aloof.[5]

When the American Bar Association met at Saratoga in September, 1917, Hughes blasted the timorous and narrow-visioned groups that were saying America could not fight a modern war without destroying the Constitution. "While we are at war," he declared, "we are not in revolution. . . . The Constitution is as effective today as it ever was and the oath to support it is just as binding. But the framers of the Constitution did not contrive an imposing spectacle of impotency. . . . A nation which could not fight would be powerless to secure 'the Blessings of Liberty to Ourselves and our Posterity.' "

To those who were saying that the draft law which Congress had passed in May was unconstitutional, Hughes replied, "The power vested in Congress is not to raise armies simply by calling for volunteers, but to raise armies by whatever method Congress deems best, and hence must be deemed to embrace

[5] *Proceedings of the Academy of Political Science in the City of New York,* Vol. 7, No. 2, July, 1917, pp. 195–207.

conscription. The power to wage war," he went on, "is the power to wage war successfully." Since nations were fighting with all their economic strength, Congress could also regulate the food supply as well as industrial plants and materials essential to military success. At the same time, he said, the basic rights of the individual remained secure against "unwarrantable attack."

"It has been said that the Constitution marches," Hughes concluded. "That is, there are constantly new applications of unchanged powers, and it is ascertained that in novel and complex situations, the old grants contain, in their general words and true significance, needed and adequate authority. So, also, we have a *fighting* Constitution. We cannot at this time fail to appreciate the wisdom of the fathers, as under this charter . . . the people of the United States fight with the power of unity,—as we fight for the freedom of our children and that hereafter the sword of autocrats may never threaten the world." [6]

Distributed throughout the country, the speech was widely applauded, and its reasoning was reaffirmed by the Supreme Court. Hughes' happy phrase "a *fighting* Constitution" was to be reechoed by the Supreme Court in World War II, and the speech continues to be read as one of the most authoritative and compelling statements on "War Powers Under the Constitution" in our political literature.

On July 26, 1917, Hughes interrupted his strenuous regimen of legal work and speechmaking for a vacation in the White Mountains. The morning after his arrival Governor Whitman notified him of his appointment as chairman of the District Draft Appeals Board for New York City. Without even taking a day to indulge his regrets, he returned to New York and plunged into a most exacting task.

This appeals board consisted of thirty members, including Chief Judge Edgar M. Cullen of the New York Court of Appeals, former Presiding Justice George L. Ingraham of the Appellate Division of the New York Supreme Court, Judge Edwin L. Garvin, who was secretary of the board, George W. Wickersham, Louis Marshall, William N. Dykman, and other distinguished men. Its jurisdiction covered the entire city, with many local draft boards and nearly 600,000 registrants. When Hughes took over, a vast number of appeals were awaiting decision, and there was no organization to handle them. He had the baffling problem of "building a wagon and riding in it at the same time."

Mail poured in upon the board at the rate of 4,000 pieces a day. Crowds of men seeking to have their appeals heard overwhelmed its makeshift quarters in the old New York Post Office Building. The volume of work was staggering. Hughes borrowed a number of trained men from two leading banks and the New York Telephone Company. The board was divided into six subcommittees, each with many clerks and assistants, to which the appeals were

6 Address of Sept. 5, 1917; Hughes Papers.

initially directed. When a subcommittee had about fifty cases ready, it would take the list to Hughes' desk, the committee would gather around, and each appeal for exemption from service would be granted or denied. In this manner the board decided about a thousand cases a day.

Since it might be a question of life or death, Hughes insisted on signing in person the papers of every man who came before the board. There were hundreds of these papers to be signed in quadruplicate every day. While the organization was taking shape, the chairman toiled until midnight or later every night. He and Judge Garvin were "nearly floored by the task." [7] His digestive system refused to function, and for a time it appeared that his health might be seriously impaired. Mrs. Hughes came back from the White Mountains to see that he got proper food, and, as always, her presence brought relief.

Overburdened though he was, Hughes found time to greet his daughter in verse on her nineteenth birthday, August 11, 1917:

> To Catherine—
> My dearest Katrine
> As you are nineteen
> It's time that I write you a letter;
> Enclosed you will find
> Not a piece of my mind
> But a check which no doubt you'll like better.
>
> My advice, it is slight
> For I cannot indite
> Any words which meet the occasion;
> To a wise Sophomore
> It is always a bore
> To be subject to too much dictation.
>
> It will not be amiss
> To send you a kiss*
> And the love which ever grows greater;
> Once more I'm away
> On your happy birthday
> Here's hoping for better luck later.

Many happy returns and every good wish from
                                     FATHER

* Meaning many kisses, but the miserable necessities of rhyme interfere with the expression of my affection.

His son's participation in the war gave him many anxious hours. Young Hughes enlisted as a private in November, 1917, in spite of the fact that, being the father of two children, he was not likely to be drafted. Both he and his

[7] CEH, Notes, p. 241.

To Catherine —   Aug. 11, 1917

My dearest Katrine
As you are nineteen
It's time that I write you a letter
Enclosed you will find
Not a piece of my mind
But a check which no doubt you'll like better.

—

My advice, it is slight —
For I cannot indite —
Any words which meet the occasion
To a wise Sophomore
It is always a bore
To be subject to too much dictation.

—

[not through yet — over]

It will not be amiss
To send you a kiss*
And the love which ever grows greater
Once more I'm away
On your happy birthday
Here's hoping for better luck later.

—

Many happy returns
And every good wish from
Jackie

* Meaning many kisses, but the miserable
necessities of rhyme interfere with the
expression of my affection —

father scorned any suggestion of special privilege for him. He went overseas with the 305th Field Artillery as a regimental sergeant major. Hughes had spoken with the utmost seriousness when he said, "We should spare nothing in prompt and intelligent preparation for the vigorous conduct of the war."

At the Draft Appeals Board he bore his burden patiently. When he was inadvertently kept waiting for an unconscionable period in the outer office of Major Judge Advocate Hugh S. Johnson (later administrator of the NRA), Johnson apologized profusely for wasting the time of so distinguished a citizen.

"There are no distinguished citizens," Hughes replied, "except as they are doing distinguished duty." [8]

During the fall and winter he resumed his speechmaking, but his law practice had gone to pot. Occasionally he took an hour or two off from his unpaid war work for consultation on a case, and once he dashed to Chicago overnight, argued the American Press Association case at a special session of the Circuit Court of Appeals, left Chicago two hours after his arrival, and was back at the Draft Appeals Board the next morning. Many cases that would normally have come to him went to other lawyers, and others piled up to await his resumption of active practice after the war.

Although he had sat on the Supreme Bench for six years, Hughes argued his first case before that court on December 12, 1917.[9] While in Washington he asked for an appointment with the President and found Wilson both courteous and agreeable. That was not surprising, for in spite of their spirited fight in 1916, Hughes had since generously and consistently supported the President. Now he offered to take any wartime assignment in which the President might find his services useful. Five months were to pass, however, before the President would take advantage of the offer.

The spring of 1918 brought a new German offensive, new horrors of gas warfare, and the disastrous treaty of Brest-Litovsk in which Russia's new Bolshevik government made a humiliating peace with an apparently victorious Germany. Root and Hughes had led a mass meeting which rejoiced in "the triumph of democracy in Russia" when the Romanoff dynasty had been overthrown, but the subsequent destruction of the Kerensky régime by Lenin and Trotsky had turned their hopes to ashes. Hughes promptly aired his profound distrust of the new dictatorship of the proletariat, and that distrust was to remain with him to the end of his days.

As if to add to the gloom of the war news from Europe, typewriters began to click and tongues to wag about a scandalous breakdown of the American aircraft program. The most alarming charges were made by Gutzon Borglum, the sculptor. Wilson had authorized Borglum to run down the facts, but he came up with only more fuel to feed the sensation he had created. With the

[8] Johnson's radio address, April 13, 1937.   [9] *Towne* v. *Eisner*, 245 U.S. 418.

nation's resources at its command, he said, the Aircraft Board had not produced a single service or battle plane that could be ordered across the lines. Hundreds of millions of dollars had been squandered, he claimed, and enormous contracts given to men having no connections with aircraft production solely because of their "pull" with Colonel E. A. Deeds.[10]

Wilson repudiated Borglum and appointed a committee to examine his charges. By this time the aircraft program was under attack from many quarters. The Senate Committee on Military Affairs launched an investigation. The press drew pointed contrasts between the War Department's "almost boastful aviation promises" and its meager performance. Wilson ordered a full-fledged inquiry by Attorney General T. W. Gregory and was further criticized for having one segment of his Administration investigate another on the eve of the 1918 congressional campaigns.

The President's deep concern led him at last to appeal to Hughes, apparently at the suggestion of Colonel House. On May 13, 1918, he wrote to his former opponent:

Because of the capital importance of this branch of the military service, I feel that these charges should be thoroughly investigated and with as little delay as possible. . . . I requested the Department of Justice to use every instrumentality at its disposal to investigate these charges, and, with the approval of the Attorney General, I am writing to beg that you will act with him in making this investigation. I feel that this is a matter of the very greatest importance, and I sincerely hope that you will feel that it is possible to contribute your very valuable services in studying and passing upon the questions involved.[11]

"You may be assured," Hughes replied, "that nothing would give me greater pleasure than to render any assistance within my power." [12]

Resigning from the Draft Appeals Board, he wound up his affairs in New York within three days and took the train to Washington. Actually he regarded the aircraft inquiry as a cross that had to be borne. While his appointment was being rumored, several Republican leaders had begged him not to pull Wilson's chestnuts out of the fire. "The country is at war," Hughes had replied. "Our troops at the front are fighting without aircraft." His long experience in investigative work told him that he had been drafted for one of the most unpleasant civilian assignments of the war, but he plunged into it without the slightest hesitation.

At the outset Hughes made certain that he would have a free hand and that the findings of the investigation would be made public.[13] One other condition he laid down was that he should select his own assistant. The young attorney to whom he turned was Meier Steinbrink of Brooklyn, who had been with him in

[10] New York *World*, March 21, 1918.
[12] CEH to Wilson, May 14, 1919.
[11] Wilson to CEH, Hughes Papers.
[13] CEH to T. W. Gregory, May 18, 1918.

the Draft Appeals Board and who later became a justice of the New York Supreme Court.

Arriving in Washington, Hughes almost took the Attorney General's breath away by saying that he would launch the investigation the next morning. The very first witness, Colonel S. E. Wolff, brought in evidence of gross inefficiency. Wolff insisted that he would have to go to Paris to find out the extent of the United States' commitments to supply airplanes to Great Britain and France. Contracts to build planes for our allies had been authorized up to $47,000,000, but from the reports he had been getting Wolff feared that "over commitments" had been made possibly to the extent of $304,000,000.[14] Hughes suggested that the information be obtained by cable. Wolff replied that his cables brought no satisfactory results. Hughes scrutinized the officer's stack of cablegrams signed "Pershing" and agreed that they added up to confusion. When Hughes called Secretary Baker, he knew nothing about the inadequacy of the records or of Wolff's plan to go to Paris for want of an accurate cablegram. But Baker hastened to cable General Pershing, and the information was then forthcoming.[15]

Colonel Wolff also supplied figures showing how much the Army had spent on aircraft up to that time. Nearly five months later, when Wolff brought in more recent figures, Hughes called for a comparison of the two totals, and Wolff could not remember the sum he had named in May. "Wasn't it so and so?" Hughes asked, drawing upon his amazing memory. Steinbrink checked the record and found that his chief was right, down to the last digit.[16]

To avoid embarrassment to the war effort or disclosure of military secrets the hearings were conducted *in camera*. Attorney General Gregory or his assistant, William L. Frierson, later Solicitor General, was always present and kept a close watch on everything Hughes did. The investigator welcomed this precaution as insurance against any charge of improper conduct. Only once, however, did the Attorney General ask a question. There was no interference. Nor was there any consultation between the investigators and the silent watchers as to how the inquiry should be conducted. Week after week the story of an infant industry struggling for mass production under loose and ineffective supervision was unfolded, until 280 witnesses had been examined and 17,000 pages of testimony had been taken. When the investigators moved from Washington to Dayton, Detroit, New Brunswick, and Buffalo, Hughes visited aircraft and "Liberty engine" factories, examined company books and records, and questioned executives without taking them away from their vital work for any length of time.

Because of the quiet nature of the investigation, many defects in the make-

---

[14] *Aircraft Hearings*, I, 1ff., National Archives.   [15] CEH, Notes, pp. 242–243.
[16] Author's interview with Judge Steinbrink, July 24, 1947.

shift aircraft procurement system were corrected without publicity as Hughes brought them to official attention. He was thus successful in greatly stimulating the production of military planes. The exposure of official misconduct was a decidedly secondary aim.

While in Washington, Hughes and Steinbrink lived together in a little house on New Hampshire Avenue. They became good friends and shared all the work, disappointments, and exhilaration of the aircraft inquiry together. Steinbrink was fascinated by Hughes' companionability and his skill in distilling the essence of humor from the miscellany of each day's activities. One summer morning Steinbrink noticed through the open door of Hughes' room a strange shadow moving rhythmically up and down in the light of the rising sun. His curiosity impelled him to investigate. What he found was the supposedly austere gentleman who had missed the Presidency by a hairsbreadth down on the floor doing push-ups.

"Oh, it's you," said Steinbrink. "I couldn't imagine what on earth you were doing."

"Well, what do you think now?" Hughes asked as he continued his daily dozen.

"It looks as if you were sweeping up the floor with your whiskers," Steinbrink ventured. Hughes rolled over on his back and laughed convulsively.

"Steinbrink," he asked in the course of one of their congenial chats, "why does the public continue to regard me as a human icicle?"

"I think there are two reasons," his friend replied with the utmost candor. "First, the public doesn't know you. Second, you wear a full beard. Can you think of any public man with a big, formidable beard who has the reputation of being affable and friendly?"

A few days later Hughes trimmed his beard notably shorter. Al Smith was quick to observe the change when next they met at a Gridiron dinner. "Why, Governor," he exclaimed, "you've bobbed it!"

The most dramatic episodes of the investigation concerned the activities of Colonel Deeds, who had been in charge of the aircraft program as head of the Signal Corps' Equipment Division. Before taking that assignment, Deeds had been associated with H. E. Talbott and Charles F. Kettering in numerous business enterprises at Dayton, Ohio. Just before going to Washington in 1917, he had helped Kettering and Talbott organize the Dayton Wright Airplane Company (although he did not become a stockholder) which was subsequently given highly profitable Government contracts. Borglum had charged Deeds with staggering offenses, and one of Hughes' most important tasks was to sift out the facts regarding the colonel's interests and activities.

At Dayton, Talbott was examined in detail on his relations with Deeds. His memory seemed to be conveniently vague, and there was a good deal of difficulty in nailing down the facts. While Hughes was plying the witness with questions, Steinbrink walked over to the plant's filing room and told a clerk that Mr. Talbott would like to have the confidential file. The clerk yielded it without question, and the attorney, opening it to "Deeds" and "Talbott," found telegrams which established a confidential relationship between the two men after Deeds had taken charge of the aircraft production program for the Army. Confronted by this evidence, Talbott was compelled to shift his testimony from intellectual fencing to pertinent comment on concrete facts.

That evening the investigators shared a good deal of satisfaction as they walked together to their hotel. Steinbrink told the story of how he had obtained the confidential file. "Steinbrink," was Hughes' pithy comment, "Deeds not words!" [17]

It was late in October when the inquiry was completed. Hughes then worked frantically on his report. During the last three days he wrote steadily in longhand, stopping for very little sleep. Steinbrink checked the facts against the exhibits and testimony. On Saturday morning they delivered the report to the Attorney General. Gregory was very pleased with its objectivity and hastened to Hughes' office to tell him so. Frierson had independently written an elaborate report of the inquiry, but Gregory discarded it. "I have $100,000 available to pay for this excellent piece of work," he told Hughes, but the latter would take nothing more than reimbursement for his actual cash outlays. Steinbrink, conferring separately with the Attorney General, also refused compensation.

In sending the Hughes report to the White House with only a brief supplement of his own, Gregory called it "a remarkably accurate statement of substantially all the transactions had since the beginning of the war in the course of the development of the aircraft program." After carefully examining this statement, he informed the President, "I find myself in substantial accord therewith and do not consider it necessary to present to you a somewhat full report which has heretofore been prepared in the Department of Justice. . . . I also find myself in accord with the conclusions presented by Judge Hughes on questions of dishonesty and malversation." [18]

A wave of relief swept over the country when the President released the report on October 31, 1918. Hughes had found incompetence, confusion, a lack of central responsibility in the aircraft program, and some minor violations of law but no thievery or major corruption. That good news coincided with the collapse of the Austro-Hungarian Empire and the seizure of a large slice of Belgian territory from the collapsing German armies. With only a few days remaining before the congressional elections, supporters of the Adminis-

[17] Id.
[18] U.S. Department of Justice—Aircraft Inquiry (Government Printing Office, 1918), p. 2 of supplement.

tration took immediate advantage of the Hughes report to confound the critics who had been making capital out of the Borglum charges.

"Probably there has never been a more searching and thorough investigation under direction of the Government," said the *New York Times*.[19] Wilson put his praise into a brief note:

I write to express to you my sincere thanks for the painstaking and exhaustive examination you personally gave to the aircraft production situation, in cooperation with the Attorney General. I appreciate as much as the Attorney General does the thoroughness of the investigation and feel confident that the results of it put the country in possession of all the pertinent facts.[20]

The significance of the aircraft report was minimized, of course, by the Armistice of November 11. With the war over, the public quickly lost interest in the efficiency of the aviation industry, and the report became a target for those who found its unbiased presentation of facts distasteful. Chief among these were the friends of Colonel Deeds who tried to make it appear that Hughes maligned him by distorting the facts.

Actually Hughes cleared Deeds of the most serious charges that had been made against him. There was no evidence, he reported, that Deeds was pro-German, that he was guilty of major corruption or the violation of any statute. But the report did present evidence of "reprehensible conduct" and recommended disciplinary action through a court-martial. Although Deeds was under military discipline, he had continued to act as confidential adviser to his former business associates. To avoid criticism he had also falsified his report to the Secretary of War as to his stock holdings in companies with which the Aircraft Board might be doing business. And he was held responsible for statements grossly misleading the public as to the progress of the aircraft production program.

Secretary Baker sent the Hughes findings to the Judge Advocate General's office and got back a reply saying that "the report of Judge Hughes . . . clearly indicates conduct calling for his [Deeds'] trial by general court martial." [21] Not satisfied, Baker called in Acting Judge Advocate General S. T. Ansell and indicated that he wished to have additional facts considered. That unusual procedure led to the appointment of a "board of review" for the Deeds case, although boards of review usually hear only appeals from men convicted by courts-martial. The board took statements from Deeds' attorney and two business associates connected with the contracts that had been under scrutiny and exonerated him. A select committee of the House of Representatives found this conduct "astonishing and significant." [22]

---

[19] Nov. 1, 1918.   [20] Wilson to CEH, Nov. 7, 1918.
[21] *Hearings of House Select Committee on Expenditures in the War Department—Aviation*, Serial 2, Vol. 3, p. 2667.
[22] *House of Representatives Report 637*, 66th Congress, 2nd session, p. 19.

Colonel Deeds' biographer, Isaac Marcosson, draws heavily upon this board's findings in attempting to dissipate the uncomplimentary facts disclosed by the Hughes report. He points especially to a telegram from Deeds to the Dayton Wright Airplane Company on August 3, 1917, urging that a sample De Haviland airplane which was being shipped to the Dayton plant be put under guard. The De Haviland 4 had been chosen as the foreign plane most suitable for adaptation to mass production in the United States, and sabotage was feared. The telegram is said to have been opened by a secretary who bruited its contents among employees of the plant. A desire to assure more restricted handling of such messages, says Marcosson, prompted Kettering to wire Deeds on August 4 and ask that all future "confidential telegrams" intended for the Dayton Wright Company be sent directly to Talbott or George B. Smith, who was both Deeds' and Talbott's confidential agent.[23] Deeds telegraphed his agreement.

The Hughes report made no mention of the telegram of August 3, and that fact has led several of his detractors to accuse him of suppressing it. Had he included this telegram in his report, along with the exchange of telegrams between Kettering and Deeds on August 4, it is said, his charge that Deeds was continuing to act as "confidential adviser" to his former business associates would have fallen flat. But that conclusion utterly ignores the testimony that Hughes had taken from Kettering, Talbott, and Deeds themselves. Talbott at first denied that he had had an arrangement for receipt of confidential telegrams, and when Hughes showed him the wire of August 4 he explained it as merely a means of expediting the delivery of telegrams to him.[24] Kettering also examined the August 4 message and said that his purpose in sending it was merely to establish a central delivery point for wires from Deeds. "I do not know," he said, "why we called them confidential telegrams." [25] Deeds said the chief purpose of the arrangement was to get telegrams through "without delay," although he touched upon the security angle. None of the three mentioned the telegram of August 3 that Hughes was later accused of suppressing. Apparently its relation to Kettering's wire of the following day, if it had any, was an afterthought. To accuse the investigator of suppressing a telegram that none of the witnesses concerned seemed to regard as worthy of mention is absurd on its face.

More important is the fact that Hughes' charge of reprehensible conduct rested only slightly on the telegrams of August 4 and very heavily upon Deeds' wire to Talbott on September 16, 1917, as follows:

For your personal information as coming from your local attorney. Judge Advocate General has ruled it legal for Government to select one, contractor one

[23] Isaac F. Marcosson, *Colonel Deeds: Industrial Builder*, pp. 278–280.
[24] *Aircraft Hearings*, X, 596–597, National Archives.   [25] *Ibid.*, p. 714.

and the two a third, as appraisers of market value of plant at expiration of contract. If you care to raise the question the above will be found to be the final ruling.[26]

Hughes insisted at the hearing that the information Deeds was thus passing on to his former associate was "an inside tip."

"It depends," Deeds countered, "upon what sense is implied by the word 'tip.' "

"You said, 'For your personal information as coming from your local attorney!' " Hughes repeated.

"Yes, sir," Deeds admitted.

"That meant that the information you were giving in this telegram should be treated by him as though he had received it from his local attorney, did it not?"

"I imagine it did," Deeds again affirmed. He admitted that he had given inside information and did not wish to be known as the source of it.[27]

"When this last telegram, which puts in a strong light the relations of the parties, was sent, Deeds was an officer in the Army," Hughes wrote in his report. "This highly improper conduct, in holding communication in this manner with his former business associates in a transaction pending between the Dayton Wright Company and the Government Department in Colonel Deeds' charge, demands the attention of the military authorities." [28]

The exonerating board said that Talbott had been holding up a contract until the question of plant depreciation could be settled, that the Judge Advocate General had made an oral ruling to be followed by a written ruling, and that the information which Deeds passed along to Talbott was available to other contractors. The fact remains that Deeds had done precisely what Hughes accused him of. The case against Deeds was based on his own admissions. To say, as Mr. Marcosson does, that "Hughes was out to 'make a case' regardless of how it conflicted with the facts" [29] is to turn away from facts and make words do the ugly duty of smearing.

Hughes also examined in detail the charges that Deeds had violated the criminal statute forbidding any official to represent the Government in the transaction of business with a corporation in which he has a pecuniary interest. He could find no evidence to sustain this charge and frankly said so. But in setting forth the facts he did show the falsity of Deeds' letter of August 28, 1917, to the Aircraft Production Board and the Secretary of War, claiming that he had "made a bona fide transfer to other parties" of all his stocks in the four companies with which he had been associated. Deeds' 17,500 shares of United Motors Corporation stock were transferred on October 13, not in August (and then only to his wife), although Deeds claimed a previous "informal transfer."

[26] *Ibid.*, XXIII, 88ff.   [27] *Ibid.*   [28] *Aircraft Report*, pp. 32–33.
[29] Reprinted by permission of Dodd, Mead & Company from *Colonel Deeds: Inaustrial Builder*, by Isaac F. Marcosson, p. 280. Copyright, 1947, by Dodd, Mead & Company, Inc.

Deeds admitted that he still held his stock in the Domestic Building Company more than a year after he had told Secretary Baker that he had disposed of it.[30] He had merely arranged with Kettering to take this stock off his hands "if it should prove necessary."

Hughes' second count against Colonel Deeds was that he had given representatives of the Committee on Public Information "a false and misleading statement with respect to the progress of aircraft production." The official release of February 21, 1918, for which Deeds was responsible, had boasted:

> The first American built battle planes are today en route to the front in France. This first shipment, though in itself not large, marks the final overcoming of many difficulties met in building up this new and intricate industry.

Actually no planes had at that time been shipped overseas. Only one had been delivered from the factory for the AEF, and it did not leave the United States until a month later. No other shipments were made until April 3.

In his brief supplementary statement Attorney General Gregory found Deeds "guilty of censurable conduct" and underscored Hughes' recommendation of "disciplinary measures." [31] That alone is sufficient to buttress the objectivity of Hughes' findings. It is true that Hughes measured Colonel Deeds by a rigid and unbending concept of public duty. But it was the concept that he had consistently applied to himself and his own associates. Some of the other accusations in his report were petty. Hughes frankly recognized that fact but thought the law should be enforced against even minor infractions as a warning against future laxity. To deride a great investigator because he refused to whitewash deception, falsehood, and clandestine dealings in the public service is like assailing Moses because some people do not live up to the Decalogue.

[30] *Aircraft Hearings*, XXII, 565–571.   [31] *Aircraft Report*, supplement, p. 7.

Chapter 36

CHAMPION OF LIBERTY

HUGHES celebrated the end of the aircraft investigation by plunging into practice once more and making a series of speeches. His long silence during the inquiry had been broken only on such occasions as Bastille Day. Now he felt a release of spirit. As the country reeled with emotion and confusion in its shift from war to peace, his voice was heard and applauded before all sorts of audiences.

On October 29, 1918, he welcomed Governor Whitman and his fellow Republican candidates to the Union League Club. Four days later he breathed a fine idealism into the Madison Square rally of the United War Work Campaign. "I have read your living words and I cannot be silent," wrote one of his admirers. "One sentence especially rings in my ears: 'Democracy is not of the flesh but of the spirit—its forms in themselves are vain, and its meaning and justification must be found in service to mankind.' I thank you for that sentence: it is immortal." [1]

As president of the Legal Aid Society, he attempted to give every man assurance of legal protection of his rights. "There is no more serious menace," he said, "than the discontent which is fostered by a belief that one cannot enforce his legal rights because of poverty. . . . Without opportunity on the part of the poor to obtain expert legal advice, it is idle to talk of equality before the law." [2] His influence was a great stimulus to the movement within the legal profession to offer free service to those unable to pay for it.

Fate seemed to be marking the end of an era by removing some of its most eminent figures. On May 14, 1917, Joseph H. Choate, diplomat and great man of the bar, wrote a note to Hughes, whose early practice he had so much influenced. On the same day came news of his death. Theodore Roosevelt's restless spirit was finally stilled on January 5, 1919. Six months previously Hughes had signed a round robin urging T. R. to become a candidate for Governor of New York. It had then been widely assumed that Roosevelt would be the Republican presidential candidate in 1920. But he was not to enjoy any such revenge against the man in the White House. Hughes delivered the Roosevelt memorial address at the Republican Club in New York on February 9, with a

[1] Mrs. Spencer Trask to CEH, Nov. 5, 1918.
[2] *New York Times,* Aug. 28, 1920.

warm tribute to T. R.'s industry, courage, self-discipline, and democratic instinct.

The former Justice was called upon to honor new leaders no less than to eulogize those who had passed on. At a Lotos Club dinner he joined in lauding the character and achievements of Governor Alfred E. Smith. Some months later he presented the Civic Forum's medal of honor to Herbert Hoover, the wartime food-control wizard who had made a name for himself at home and abroad.

There seemed to be no end to the demand for Hughes' speeches. While he declined at least 95 per cent of the requests made of him, he found himself accepting the colors of a Negro infantry division, condemning the crime of lynching, denouncing the massacre of Jews in Europe, pleading for the rehabilitation of disabled soldiers, weighing the values in education, condemning arbitrary government, and delving into dozens of other subjects of general public interest. Busy as he was at the bar, he gave approximately one-third of his time to speeches and civic work. In 1919 he became president of the New York County Lawyers' Association, head of a commission to study war-risk insurance, president of the National Municipal League, and chairman of various other civic groups.

In the legal sphere it seemed that almost everyone with an intricate or baffling case was beating a path to Hughes' door. Many of his cases were brought to him by other lawyers eager to take advantage of his skill in stripping involved problems to their bare bones and laying the most complicated issues before a court with unfailing clarity. While he rejected numerous cases for want of merit, he never hesitated to take a case in which the odds were against him if he thought the issues were such that they should be presented to the court. In twenty-eight months he argued twenty-five cases in the United States Supreme Court in addition to the numerous cases that took him into the lower federal courts and the state courts. His reputation entitled him to the cream of the legal business, and his energy enabled him to take a thick skimming.

Once he accepted a case, Hughes threw himself into it with the vigor of a dynamo. Every litigant, he used to say, is entitled to have his case handled with all the ability and the resources at his counsel's command. John D. Rockefeller wanted an opinion as to whether he could put anything in his will that would prevent his executors (who would be getting millions anyway) from being allowed their statutory commissions. Hughes assigned the research to a new lawyer in the firm—Oscar R. Ewing. When Ewing reported on every New York case he could find, Hughes said, "Well, that's fine. Now what have you from outside of New York?" Ewing said that, as Rockefeller lived in New York, he had not supposed there would be any interest in decisions from other states. "Why," Hughes came back, "I want the law looked up for every state in the Union."[3]

In an argument he made it his business to know everything that his opponent could say. When he arose to argue, it was always a tour de force. He seemed to lose himself in the intensity of his own effort, but behind each performance was a studied technique designed to get his case so clearly, quickly, and cogently before the court as to forestall any objection to the conclusions he wished to draw before such objection could arise in a judge's mind.

Hughes would come into court with banners flying—with the air of one who had a great cause to defend. The judges were well aware of his forensic power. Judge Cardozo of the New York Court of Appeals once said that he always reserved judgment for twenty-four hours in any case argued by Hughes to avoid being carried away by the force of his personality and intellect.[4]

Yet there was neither arrogance nor overconfidence in Hughes' attitude. He scoffed at the idea that anything was important merely because he said it. Never did he assume that his reputation would make his argument irresistible. On the contrary, he tended to magnify in his own mind the strength of the opposition. And while his poise suggested that he was master of every situation, he always addressed the court with fear and trembling inside. It was not unusual for him to lie awake most of the night worrying about a case he was to present to the Supreme Court the next day. Sometimes he would go before the court feeling almost that he had his life in his hands.[5] But his self-control enabled him to pour his agitation into his argument, with the effect of adding power to reason.

His first big case after the Armistice was a suit against Postmaster General Albert Burleson challenging the Government's seizure of the Atlantic and Pacific cable systems. The President's seizure proclamation was dated November 2, 1918, but the action was not announced until November 21 and the actual seizure was alleged to have taken place five days after the Armistice became effective. Burleson had taken drastic action because of disagreement over cable charges and alleged discrepancies in figures provided by the companies to different governmental agencies. Hughes insisted that the action was "wholly unwarranted and arbitrary" and "beyond valid authorization."

Arguing for nearly three hours before Judge Learned Hand, Hughes rattled off numerous cases with scarcely a glance at the law books before him. Judge Hand ruled against him, and he carried the case to the Supreme Court. While rumors of a decision in his favor were being circulated in the spring of 1919, the cable systems were returned to their owners and the cases became moot.[6]

---

[3] Oscar Ewing to author, March 24, 1950.
[4] Justice Cardozo to Justice Owen J. Roberts to author.
[5] Author's interview with CEH, May 15, 1946.
[6] *Commercial Cable Co.* v. *Burleson*, 250 U.S. 360.

Hughes also challenged the validity of the Food Control Act of 1917 in a series of cases.[7] This statute made it a criminal offense to charge excessive prices for necessaries, without forbidding any specific or definite act and without setting up any ascertainable standard of guilt. Just before Hughes' argument in one of these cases, Judge Augustus N. Hand had fined some people $10,000 for charging too much for potatoes. That was in accord with a ruling of the Circuit Court of Appeals, but Hughes was so persuasive that Judge Hand deferred further decisions under the Act until a case then before the Supreme Court was decided.[8] In the Supreme Court, Hughes argued three cases involving the Act, and the court followed his logic in holding it unconstitutional, although choosing a case which he had not argued—*United States* v. *Cohen Grocery Company*—as the subject of its controlling opinion.

The National Prohibition Cases [9] were a severe test of Hughes' independence at the bar. The State of Rhode Island, with the aid of Root and Guthrie and the opulent backing of the brewing and liquor interests, was challenging the constitutionality of the Eighteenth Amendment. Guthrie urged his friend Hughes to join in a grand assault upon the right of Congress and the states to write "basic changes" or "alterations" such as the Eighteenth Amendment into the Constitution. It was reported that a fee of $500,000 was dangled before the former Justice. Actually no sum was mentioned. The liquor interests made it clear to him that the financial reward would be enormous, but they did not get to the point of discussing terms, for Hughes insisted that what they were trying to do was absurd and refused to have any part in it.[10]

Acceptance of this retainer would also have given him a chance to strike a blow at a policy he distrusted. While he had taken no part in the debate over drying up the flow of liquor by law, he felt from the beginning that national prohibition was both unwise and impracticable. But that was beside the point. Whether they acted wisely or unwisely, the people had an unlimited right to amend their Constitution as they saw fit.

After rejecting the money of the brewers, Hughes filed a brief as *amicus curiae* on behalf of twenty-one state attorneys general in support of the Eighteenth Amendment, for which he received a comparative pittance. Going back to the records of the Constitutional Convention, he showed that the Founding Fathers drew no distinction between "amendments" and "alterations." By Article V they had left the door wide open to any change that experience might prove to be desirable. Should the court limit the nature of changes that could be made, Hughes argued, our political system would be in danger of degenerating into despotism or revolution. The fate of the Eighteenth Amend-

[7] *Tedrow* v. *Lewis,* 255 U.S. 98, etc.
[8] Hughes memorial address by Judge Hand; Dec. 12, 1948.
[9] 253 U.S. 350.
[10] Author's interviews with CEH, Nov. 19, 1946, and June 4, 1947.

ment was insignificant compared to maintenance of this safety valve in the Constitution. The Supreme Court held to this view.

A Hughes opinion prepared for private clients in this period helped to give constitutional footing to the broad social legislation of the thirties and forties. The Supreme Court had not then definitely passed upon the meaning of the clause giving Congress power to "lay and collect Taxes . . . to pay the Debts and provide for the common defence and general Welfare of the United States. . . ." Several bond houses sought Hughes' advice as to whether the Federal Farm Loan Act of 1916 was consistent with this general welfare clause and whether the tax-exempt bonds to be issued under that Act were valid. He wrote an elaborate opinion that was widely used in promoting the sale of these bonds. When their validity was attacked, he was retained by a Federal Land Bank to present to the courts the compelling view he had previously outlined.

The case was tried in the District Court in Kansas City with an eminent array of counsel, including, besides Hughes, William G. McAdoo, who had been Secretary of the Treasury when the bonds were issued, and former Attorney General Wickersham. Hughes challenged Madison's view that the general welfare clause is limited by the Constitution's enumeration of the powers given to Congress. Rather, he found "the most weighty support" for the view taken by Hamilton and Story that Congress could appropriate funds for "the general welfare" beyond the scope of its enumerated powers.

From this premise he concluded that Congress "necessarily has a wide range of discretion" in selecting the objects for which federal funds may be spent and that in these matters the courts have no warrant "to substitute their judgment for that of Congress." The taxing and spending power was not unlimited; it could not, for example, be invoked for "a purpose essentially private." But the agricultural interests of the country, broadly considered, he said, "are of National and not merely of State concern." [11]

In the Supreme Court, Hughes argued the case twice, and the Federal Farm Loan Act was upheld,[12] although on other grounds which he had also advanced —that the land banks were duly created depositaries of public money and purchasers of government bonds. Not until after Hughes had become Chief Justice did the court write the Hamilton-Story view of the general welfare clause into the basic law.

In *New York* v. *New Jersey*,[13] Hughes sought an injunction for his native state to prevent New Jersey and the Passaic Valley Sewerage Commissioners from polluting the Upper Bay of New York Harbor. At one point the argument became an intellectual fencing bout between Hughes and his good friend Justice Pitney of New Jersey, whose interruptions became so frequent as to

[11] Brief in CEH's private papers, p. 28.
[12] *Smith* v. *Kansas City Title & Trust Co.*, 255 U.S. 180.
[13] 256 U.S. 296, 314.

suggest that he was deliberately trying to confuse the attorney and prevent an orderly development of New York's case. When Hughes referred to the law of New Jersey on a certain point, Pitney cut in with, "That is not the law of New Jersey."

"Your honor has the advantage of me," Hughes lashed back at him. "I know the law only as I read it in the statutes or in the decisions of the courts."

Hughes' defense of John L. Lewis and forty-two other officials of the United Mine Workers of America is memorable largely because of his matching of wits with a czar on the bench, Judge A. B. Anderson of the Federal District Court in Indianapolis. The setting for the encounter was perfect. The courtroom was jammed with union officials, attorneys, reporters, and curious bystanders. Knowing Judge Anderson's arrogance and severity, the Indianapolis lawyers were delighted to let Hughes take the lead in the case.

"Your honor," he began, "I have a disagreeable duty to perform, but both justice and a proper administration of the law require me to perform it." He went on to show that Judge Anderson had prejudiced the interests of his clients by laying a false statement before the grand jury which had indicted them. The charge against the union officials was conspiracy with the mine operators to raise the price of coal in violation of the Lever Act. The judge had cited to the grand jury a speech by a congressman quoting John L. Lewis, then acting president of the United Mine Workers, as saying that the operators' association and the union were working together to wipe out competition. Actually, the statement had been made by Thomas L. Lewis, who was not then connected with the union. While Judge Anderson squirmed and spectators struggled to hold their elation in bounds, Hughes bore down heavily on this error. He could conceive, he said, "of no more prejudicial statement which could have been made to the grand jury." [14]

Judge Anderson denied Hughes' plea in abatement, and the argument was then shifted to constitutional grounds. When court adjourned, the judge sent for Hughes, and they chatted pleasantly in his chambers. While the case was not mentioned, Hughes told his clients that it would never be tried, and he was right. Judge Anderson could not face the embarrassment of such a trial.

Later in 1920 Hughes argued the appeal of the United Mine Workers in the first Coronado case.[15] The miners were being sued for treble damages under the antitrust laws in connection with a strike in Arkansas. He admitted that individual miners had destroyed company property, but insisted that the strike had no relation to interstate commerce that would justify action under the Sherman Act. "If whatever may be deemed to have an indirect . . . relationship to, or effect upon, interstate commerce were regarded as being within the

---

[14] *Indianapolis Star*, May 7, 1920.
[15] *United Mine Workers* v. *Coronado Coal Co.*, 259 U.S. 344, 350.

commerce clause," he asserted, "it would be difficult to find any activity of importance in any community that fell without it. Such a construction of the Constitution would destroy the Constitution itself." Speaking for the Supreme Court (after the case had been reargued in 1922 without Hughes' aid but on the basis of his brief), Chief Justice Taft followed this reasoning and complimented counsel for the plaintiffs on the "rare assiduity and ability" with which the case had been prepared.

Possibly the most controversial case of Hughes' entire career at the bar was that of Senator Truman H. Newberry, who had been Roosevelt's Secretary of the Navy. While Newberry was on duty in New York as an officer in the Navy in 1918, a group of Michigan Republicans had secured his nomination for the United States Senate in a primary contest with Henry Ford. In "averting the Ford peril" they had spent about $195,000, although the legal limit on the amount a senatorial candidate might spend in a primary was $3,750. At first charged with bribery and various other acts of corruption, Newberry had succeeded in stripping the case to the question of excessive campaign expenditures. But the trial judge had instructed the jury to find Newberry guilty if he became a candidate or continued as such after learning that more than the amount specified in the statute had been contributed and was being expended in the campaign, even if the candidate himself had made no contribution and had not caused others to contribute and if the expenditures had been made without his participation. It was a direct appeal for a finding of guilt by association.

Hughes had nothing to do with the trial, but he argued Newberry's appeal in the Supreme Court and won a unanimous reversal of the conviction.[16] Meanwhile, however, Newberry's name had become a symbol of vote-buying regardless of the legal merits of his case. The Senate did not seat him until January, 1922, and then by a margin of only five votes. At the same time it condemned the lavish use of money in his behalf as "being contrary to sound public policy, harmful to the honor and dignity of the Senate, and dangerous to the perpetuity of a free government."

When the Reverend Hugh B. MacCauley wrote to Hughes in pursuit of facts about the Newberry case, he responded with too little regard for the circumstance that he had ceased being Newberry's attorney and was then Secretary of State. After reviewing the case, he asserted: "The plain fact is that Senator Newberry was wrongfully and most unjustly convicted and his conviction was set aside. . . . Accordingly, Senator Newberry stood as a Senator duly elected by the people of the State of Michigan and entitled to his seat in the Senate of the United States. . . . There seems to be a general misconception of the nature of the litigation and its results, and Senator Newberry has suffered in consequence a most serious injustice." [17]

The letter fell into the hands of the Republican National Committee and was widely circulated, without Hughes' permission, as an offset to the anti-Newberry campaign. The result was a political tempest in which Hughes was denounced along with his former client. The *World* said the letter was "Mr. Hughes' dirtiest day's work." A "life-long" Republican described himself as

By Rollin Kirby in the New York *World*, 1922.

"SANCTIFIED"

"blushing with shame." Editors wrote of "shock and humiliating disappointment." Congressman Cordell Hull drew a highly inaccurate word picture of the Secretary of State stooping to a whitewash job at the behest of the Republican National Committee. And in the Senate, Joseph T. Robinson shouted that the letter "discredits the reputation for sincerity and fairness which Secretary Hughes long enjoyed." [18]

These barbs literally missed their mark, for shortly after writing the controversial letter Hughes had left for his long-scheduled trip to Brazil. Even after his return, however, the controversy continued. Few people seemed to

[16] *Newberry* v. *U.S.*, 256 U.S. 232.   [17] Associated Press dispatch, Aug. 21, 1922.
[18] *Literary Digest*, Sept. 2, 1922.

understand what Hughes had actually written in his letter. His comment had been confined solely to the nature of the litigation and its results. And this involved, he replied to a stinging editorial in the *World*, "as gross a miscarriage of justice as had ever come under my observation." [19] He also contended that "there is not a line in my letter which has been or can be contravened." [20]

The fact remains that Newberry's election to the Senate was an offense against a basic principle of popular government. In trying to correct a personal injustice, Hughes had ignored a public wrong. Certainly this was a lapse from his customary objectivity. His letter to the Reverend MacCauley is one of the few instances in his long official career in which his defense of a maligned individual was blurred by failure to take account of the public interest.

For the full flower of Hughes' passion for justice we must turn to his voluntary defense of the Socialists ousted from the New York legislature. For months after the close of the war he had watched with deep anxiety the mounting fever of intolerance that swept over America. The Department of Justice was making wholesale arrests without warrant or any process of law, holding men and women incommunicado, searching homes without warrants, seizing property, and shamefully maltreating workmen suspected of radical views. By January, 1920, the raids had reached a shocking peak of hysteria. Then the New York Assembly suddenly decided to suspend its five Socialist members merely because of the unpopularity of their beliefs. That seemed to Hughes a last straw.

The Socialist Party was legally recognized in New York. The five men— Louis Waldman, August Claessens, Samuel A. DeWitt, Samuel Orr, and Charles Solomon—had been duly elected and held proper certificates of election. Two of them had previously served in the Assembly without question. At the beginning of the 1920 session all five had been admitted to full membership and participated in the organization of the Assembly. Then they had been summoned to the bar of the House, lectured by the Speaker, denied their seats pending an investigation, and herded out of the chamber by the sergeant-at-arms.

Hughes' first step was to write a letter to Speaker Sweet protesting this outrageous invasion of the people's right to choose their own representatives:

If there is anything against these men as individuals, if they were deemed to be guilty of criminal offenses, they should have been charged accordingly. But I understand that the action is not directed against these five elected members as individuals but that the proceeding is virtually an attempt to indict a political party and to deny it representation in the Legislature. This is not, in my judgment, American government.

[19] CEH to Walter Lippmann, June 13, 1924.
[20] CEH to William Jillson, Nov. 20, 1922.

Are Socialists unconvicted of crime to be denied the ballot? If Socialists are permitted to vote, are they not permitted to vote for their own candidates? If their candidates are elected and are men against whom, as individuals, charges of disqualifying offenses cannot be laid, are they not entitled to their seats?

I understand that it is said that the Socialists constitute a combination to overthrow the Government. The answer is plain. If public officers or private citizens have any evidence that any individuals, or group of individuals, are plotting revolution and seeking by violent measures to change our Government, let the evidence be laid before the proper authorities and swift action be taken for the protection of the community. . . . But I count it a most serious mistake to proceed, not against individuals charged with violation of law, but against masses of our citizens combined for political action, by denying them the only resource of peaceful government; that is, action by the ballot box and through duly elected representatives in legislative bodies.[21]

His next step was to move, at a special meeting of the Association of the Bar, that that august body defend the maligned Socialists. There followed a classic battle over civil rights, with the eminent and formidable William D. Guthrie contending that no Socialist could conscientiously take the oath of office and Hughes proclaiming the right of the people to elect and seat their legislators regardless of nonconformist beliefs. In the end the Hughes motion carried, and a committee was appointed under his chairmanship to argue the case at Albany. All the members of the committee were opposed to socialism, but they had a profound belief in freedom for minorities.

The committee of lawyers went to Albany to appear before the Assembly's Judiciary Committee that had the Socialist members "on trial." The excited legislators refused to let the lawyers testify, but Hughes filed a brief in behalf of himself, Morgan J. O'Brien, Louis Marshall, Joseph M. Proskauer, and Ogden Mills. The act of the Assembly in depriving its Socialist members of their seats and then putting the burden of proof on them to show that they had a right to be reseated, the lawyers asserted, "is a reversal of the rule applicable to the meanest criminal. . . . This is the first time in American history that one against whom treason and disloyalty are sought to be imputed has been called upon to establish the negative. It reminds one of the English State Trials in the sixteenth and seventeenth centuries. . . . We have passed beyond the stage in political development when heresy-hunting is a permitted sport. . . . If a majority can exclude the whole or a part of the minority because it deems the political views entertained by them hurtful, then free government is at an end." [22]

The legislature not only expelled the five Socialists; it also passed a law out-

[21] Zechariah Chafee, Jr., *Freedom of Speech* (New York, Harcourt, Brace, 1920), p. 337. Copyright, 1920, by Harcourt, Brace & Co.
[22] Hughes' brief, pp. 23–32.

lawing the Socialist Party. "The Assembly was past saving," wrote Zechariah Chafee, Jr., professor of law at Harvard University, an eminent authority on civil liberties, "but the nation was saved. The American people, long be-drugged by propaganda, were shaken out of their nightmare of revolution. . . . A legislature trembling before five men—the long-lost American sense of humor revived and the people began to laugh. That broke the spell. The light of day beat in not only upon the Assembly, but upon the Congress and the Department of Justice. . . . The raids of January 2nd were flood-tide, and with Governor Hughes' letter on the 9th, the ebb set in." [23]

Hughes broadened the scope of his assault on bigotry, witch-hunting, and official lawlessness. At every opportunity he pleaded for a new birth of free-dom. "The most vicious wrong in democracy," he had once said, "is the abuse of power—the betrayal of the people by their own agents." [24] The Adminis-tration had talked of democracy and liberty, he later declared, "but these have been betrayed in its own house. We have been amazed at the abuses scathingly denounced by the Federal Court in Boston. We have burned with shame and indignation as we have read the report of the Committee of Twelve . . . charging and specifying atrocities committed by the American Government on American soil in the course of pretended vindication of American institu-tions by the Department of Justice. No one can be trusted to save democracy by methods which displace liberty and due process in favor of administrative caprice."

Let it be known, he urged, that we shall secure ourselves against the violence of those who would overthrow the government. "But let it also be known, as our surest protection, that with calmness and sanity we propose to maintain the guarantees of free speech, free assembly and the right of representation, and that no one, however poor, friendless or accused, shall be deprived of liberty without due process of law." [25]

Repeatedly he linked freedom with the progressive revision of policies within the constitutional framework, to meet the changing requirements of the times. "The lover of the institutions of liberty," he said, "never stands pat, he is always looking for their more perfect working, for a better adjustment to the great purpose of making life brighter and happier and more secure in all its resources." [26]

Intelligent conduct was always the twin brother of liberty. "Free speech," he said at the semicentennial of Cornell, "is essential to a republic, but free speech without the insistent demand by the community for fair speech is the opportunity of rogues and demagogues." [27] Law, too, had to justify itself by its

[23] Chafee, *op. cit.,* pp. 338–339.   [24] Speech of January 17, 1919.
[25] *New York Times,* Sept. 19, 1920.   [26] Address of June 21, 1920; Hughes Papers.
[27] Address of June 20, 1919; Hughes Papers.

intrinsic merits. "It is true that democracy cannot live without respect for law, but it must be remembered that law in democracy will have only the respect it deserves." [28] Champion of freedom and law though he was, he had only contempt for the prostitution of freedom to mean and unworthy ends and the debasement of law to selfish or arbitrary purposes.

[28] Address of June 21, 1920; Hughes Papers.

Chapter 37

FIGHT OVER THE LEAGUE OF NATIONS

THE MAKING of peace proved more difficult for the United States than the making of war had been. Suddenly catapulted into a new world role, the American people had no clear idea of what their postwar foreign policy should be. There was, however, a strong desire to see the "peace-loving" nations organized into a concert of power that might be able to prevent future wars. Hughes stood out as one of the leading exponents of this view.

Along with Taft and Root, he was prominently mentioned for membership on the Peace Commission. There was a good deal of feeling that Wilson owed him this recognition because of his generous support of the President throughout the war and his herculean work in the aircraft inquiry. Undoubtedly he would have accepted such a call, but Wilson selected a delegation that would readily follow his own wishes. Completely ignoring the Republicans' victory in 1918, which had given them control of Congress and would give them the last word in ratification of the peace treaty, the President named all members of the Peace Commission from his own party, with the exception of Henry White, a professional diplomat.

In February, 1919, the League of Nations Committee of the Peace Conference met in Paris and began work on Mr. Wilson's four drafts of the proposed Covenant. Within a few weeks a preliminary version of the Covenant was released. Hughes read it in his newspaper at the breakfast table with avid interest. When he came to Article X, he knit his brow in disapproval. It carried a commitment "to respect and preserve as against external aggression the territorial integrity and existing political independence of all Members of the League." Reading it to his wife, who sat across the table, he snapped, "The American people will never stand for that." [1]

Before venturing to discuss the proposed Covenant in public, however, he scrutinized it with typical Hughesian thoroughness. "It is a great American question," he told the New York County Bar Association at its victory dinner on March 9, "and whether we are on one side or the other, it has nothing to do with partisanship." [2] The more he thought about Article X, the more convinced he became that it was a grave mistake. Wilson had gone to Paris with a version of Article X that specifically made allowance for territorial adjust-

---

[1] Author's interview with CEH, Nov. 26, 1946.   [2] *New York Times,* March 9, 1919.

ments. The text he brought back had no such flexibility. Hughes told the Union League Club on March 26:

I regard this guaranty as a trouble-breeder and not a peace-maker. . . . its inflexibility should condemn it.

Unless the League is disrupted, the guaranty may be regarded as a permanent one. The guaranty makes no allowance for changes which may be advisable. It ascribes a prescience and soundness of judgment to the present Peace Conference in erecting States and defining boundaries which no body in the history of the world has ever possessed. Even as to the new States, it attempts to make permanent existing conditions, or conditions as arranged at this Conference, in a world of dynamic forces to which no one can set bounds. It gives no fair opportunity for adjustments. It is in the teeth of experience. The limitation of the words "as against external aggression" is a frail reliance; no one can foresee what the merits of particular cases may be. . . .

The guaranty would be unwise even if it could accomplish its apparent purpose. But I also think that it will prove to be illusory. . . .

Certainly, each power will be the judge of what in good faith it should do. In the case of the United States, the guaranty will not be made good except by the action of Congress, and it will be for Congress to decide whether we are bound and what we should undertake. The course of recent debates has sufficiently indicated what the attitude of Congress is likely to be, if the resort to war pursuant to Article X is opposed to the opinion of the country. . . .

I think that it is a fallacy to suppose that helpful cooperation in the future will be assured by the attempted compulsion of an inflexible rule. Rather will such cooperation depend upon the fostering of firm friendships springing from an appreciation of community of ideals, interests and purposes, and such friendships are more likely to be promoted by freedom of conference than by the effort to create hard and fast engagements.

This speech was part of the opening round in the great national fight over the League. Hughes offered seven specific amendments to the Covenant, some of which were similar to changes suggested by Taft, Root, and members of the Senate. Five of these were adopted in part when Wilson returned to Paris, although Hughes regarded the changes made as inadequate. The revised Covenant made provision for a nation to withdraw on two years' notice, instructed the Council not to go into purely domestic questions, and made a gesture toward recognition of the Monroe Doctrine. Taft thought it was acceptable in that form, but Hughes' objection to Article X was too strong to permit him to embrace any league embodying that "trouble-breeder."

With many protests against Article X ringing in his ears, Wilson tried to outmaneuver his opponents by incorporating the League Covenant into the peace treaty.[3] The European statesmen did not want it that way, but Wilson was insistent. At the same time he allowed the principles outlined in his Fourteen

[3] Lothrop Stoddard, *Lonely America*, p. 33.

Points to be dangerously whittled away to secure agreement. In June he returned with his treaty and revised League Covenant, and the historic debate over their approval by the Senate began to rock the country. The hatred of the Irreconcilables for Wilson and his denunciation of them as "a battalion of death" inflamed the contest and made it more a struggle for power than the hammering out of a sensible foreign policy.

This turn of events was very disappointing to Hughes, who was eager to have the United States join the League with reservations. In July he received a letter from Senator Hale saying that the treaty was in danger of being rejected and asking his view as to the validity of interpretative reservations and also what specific reservations should be made. Hughes replied that the Senate could consent to ratification of the treaty with a few clarifying interpretations that would leave its main provisions unimpaired and would not necessitate a resumption of the Peace Conference.[4]

"There is plain need for a league of nations," he advised, "in order to provide for the adequate development of international law, for creating and maintaining organs of international justice and machinery of conciliation and conference, and for giving effect to measures of international cooperation which from time to time may be agreed upon. . . . I perceive no reason why these objects cannot be attained without sacrificing the essential interests of the United States. There is a middle ground between aloofness and injurious commitments."

Hughes suggested four "reservations and understandings" to be made a part of the instrument of ratification. The first would have clarified the right of any member to leave the League on two years' notice, while closing the door to escape from debts or liabilities previously incurred. The second would have made clear that immigration and duties on imports are domestic questions outside the jurisdiction of the League. The third was a much too sweeping declaration that the United States need not "submit its policies regarding questions which it deems to be purely American questions to the League of Nations or any of its agencies. . . ." The fourth would have undercut Article X by declaring that only Congress should determine in each case whether the United States had an obligation under that Article and, if so, how its obligation should be fulfilled.

Hughes thus gave the Republicans a formula with which they could have defeated Wilson's extremism and saved the League at the same time. The *Providence Journal* thought his proposals "must commend themselves to anyone except deaf, dumb and blind admirers of the Administration." [5] But the Irreconcilables were no more open to reason than the President to compromise.

Sponsors of the League insisted that, without any reservations, the United

[4] CEH to Senator Hale, July 24, 1919.   [5] July 30, 1919.

States would have a right to review the advice of the Council as to what means should be used under Article X to protect the territorial integrity and independence of fellow members. Hughes agreed. The right of Congress to declare war, he said, is basic in our constitutional system. His objection was that, by underwriting a blanket guaranty to every member, the United States would expose itself to charges of bad faith. He assumed that Congress would not declare war because of minor boundary changes in Europe or Asia and insisted that we should not pretend to make a far-fetched commitment to defend such boundaries.

In some instances, moreover, Article X pledged League members to the defense of gross injustices. Hughes feared that if China went to war with Japan over the theft of Shantung, to which Wilson had reluctantly acquiesced in the Treaty of Versailles, League members would be bound to support Japan. Sponsors of the League replied that boundary changes could be made under Article XIX. But Article XIX merely provided that the Assembly might "from time to time advise the reconsideration" of treaties "which have become inapplicable, and the consideration of international conditions whose continuance might endanger the peace of the world." At best it offered but a remote possibility of obtaining desirable territorial adjustments in a dynamic world.

What Wilson offered the nation, as Walter Lippmann has pointed out, was "a very bad choice: either to involve itself in every disputed European question or to withdraw from the organization of the general peace of the world." [6] Public sentiment had been favorable toward cooperation to keep the world at peace, but as the great debate rolled on month after month, it became evident that if the showdown came on the more extreme issue, the League would be defeated.

The President decided to stump the country in the hope of arousing the public and forcing the Senate into line. The day before he left, he invited Senator Irvine L. Lenroot of Wisconsin, a mild reservationist, to the White House. The only real obstacle to ratification of the treaty, Lenroot told him, was Article X. If the President "would agree to a reservation relieving the United States from the obligation of that article," Lenroot said, "ratification would be certain" and Mr. Wilson's speaking trip would become unnecessary.[7] Wilson replied that the League would be of no value in maintaining peace without Article X and declined to budge.

After the President was stricken during his tour, the fight continued without his leadership. The treaty went down to defeat in the Senate on November 19, 1919, by the combined votes of the "little group of willful men" and Wilson's

[6] *Washington Post,* April 1, 1943.
[7] Judge Lenroot's article in the Washington *Evening Star,* March 4, 1945.

own supporters. Sick and isolated, the President had instructed his followers to vote against the Covenant because of the reservations that had been attached. Had these Senators ignored the advice or had the advice never been given, says Stephen Bonsal, the Covenant would have been brought "into the haven of ratification" by a vote of 81 to 13.[8] The treaty, with the Lodge amendments attached, was again defeated in March, 1920, and the debate was transferred to the larger forum of national politics.

Hughes again became an active participant. To the Wilsonian argument that Article X was the heart of the Covenant, he replied, "If it is, the covenant has a bad heart." His attitude toward the League has often been described as "legalistic," but that is only because he insisted on calling a spade a spade. Wilson had said that Article X created an "absolutely compelling moral obligation." "What higher obligation can there be than this?"[9] Hughes asked. He was legalistic enough to insist that the United States should not give either legal or "compelling moral" promises which it was not ready to live up to.

Nor was the nature of the issue changed, he insisted, by the facts that the United States would have a representative on the Council and that the Council could act only by unanimous agreement. "Are we to put a representative on the Council," he asked, "for the purpose of welching on our undertaking?"

At no time did he have the slightest sympathy with the Irreconcilables. Their conduct was beyond the pale of reason. Yet he always believed that the direct cause of the United States' failure to enter the League was President Wilson's uncompromising attitude.[10] History has given strong buttressing to that view. Lord Grey, the British ambassador, indicated in a letter published in the *Congressional Record* that even the Lodge reservations would have been acceptable to Great Britain.[11] It was not Europe but Wilson who insisted on Article X. In 1920 Léon Bourgeois, president of the Council, said that "Article X could be eliminated without in any way modifying the effectiveness of the League of Nations."

In the actual operation of the League, moreover, Article X had little significance. Colonel House told Bonsal in 1929 that "by common consent of all who signed it" Article X "has become a dead letter."[12] More important is the fact that when the nations had an opportunity to start afresh on the task of shaping a world organization to keep the peace after World War II, they completely discarded Article X. The Charter of the United Nations contains nothing comparable to it. The wisdom of Hughes and Root prevailed on this

[8] Stephen Bonsal, *Unfinished Business* (New York, Doubleday, 1944), p. 278. Copyright, 1944, by Doubleday, Doran & Co.
[9] Speech at Youngstown, Oct. 30, 1920.   [10] CEH, Notes, p. 259.
[11] Judge Lenroot's article in the Washington *Evening Star,* March 4, 1945.
[12] Bonsal, *op. cit.,* p. 288.

point at San Francisco. "The conference abstained," as John Foster Dulles pointed out, "from seeking to legislate perpetual peace by a single Article sanctifying for all time things as they are." [13] It is interesting to note that two of the other three objections to the Covenant set forth in Hughes' letter to Senator Hale are also fully satisfied in the United Nations Charter.

[13] *Foreign Affairs,* October, 1945, p. 3.

Chapter 38

BACK TO WASHINGTON

THE ROAD to the White House was clear in 1920. Defeated, bitter, and physically broken, Wilson was at the end of his tether. No Democrat of power and imagination had arisen to succeed him, and the country was recoiling from the fetid backwash of the war and European intrigue. It was bound to be a Republican year, and, with Roosevelt in his grave, Hughes stood head and shoulders above any other Republican in presidential stature. The great prize of American politics could have been his for the asking.

To be sure, Hughes had the handicap of his defeat in 1916, but he had lost by a narrow margin under circumstances that now seemed to redound to his favor. Since then he had shaken off the judicial reserve that had blunted the edge of his campaign. His acceptance of defeat with good humor, his war work, his emergence as a leading champion of liberty, and his efforts to secure a League of Nations without Article X made him the logical Republican candidate and the logical successor to Woodrow Wilson. At fifty-eight, he was still young enough to be President. But Hughes had never shared his wife's feeling that he was a "man of destiny"; he was even less interested in being President in 1920 than he had been in 1908 and 1916.

Looking back at his 1916 campaign, he saw it as an ordeal that he was determined not to repeat.[1] His great success at the bar, moreover, had fortified his disinclination to seek any office. There was a strong possibility that his party might override his resistance, as it had done in 1916, but even this prospect was changed by the heavy hand that sorrow laid upon the Hughes family.

Through three decades of married life, Hughes' adventures, triumphs, and disappointments had merged into a happy domestic background. In addition to the felicity between himself and Mrs. Hughes (she still referred to him privately as the dearest husband in the world), his children had been a source of much satisfaction. "No association that you will ever make in life," he told a friend, "will pay you greater dividends than association with your own children." Back from the war, "Son" had become his father's "right bower" in handling their enormous practice. His father spoke of him with a glow of pride. Helen, the eldest daughter, also won an overflowing measure of fatherly

[1] Author's interview with CEH, Nov. 5, 1946.

affection. "A ray of sunshine," he called her, or "just pure gold!" "A rare and joyous spirit," he once said of her, "radiating happiness not only in our home but in all her associations, dedicating her life to good works, she realized my ideal of a beautiful character." [2]

Graduated from Vassar College in 1914, Helen had taken up volunteer work for the YWCA, organizing "Friendship clubs" among high-school girls. Later she became a member of the YWCA War Work Council in Boston. When the influenza epidemic swept the country in the fall of 1918, she taxed her strength in hospital service, contracted the disease, and was then an easy victim of pneumonia. After recuperating at home, she returned to work in April, 1919. In June she attended her fifth class reunion at Vassar and a YWCA conference at Silver Bay, Lake George, having become a member of the YWCA traveling staff. Joining her family at the Lake George cottage they had taken for the summer, she was stricken with a high fever thought at first to be typhoid. About ten days later her doctor discovered that she had an advanced case of tuberculosis.

Hughes suffered the greatest shock of his life. As Governor of New York, he had taken an influential part in the fight against tuberculosis, not dreaming that it might invade his own family. He sent for Dr. Horace J. Howk, an eminent specialist, but all the medical skill that money could buy could not change the outlook. In the autumn they took a house on Warren Street in Glens Falls to avoid moving Helen to New York. Catherine went back to Wellesley. Mrs. Hughes, with her youngest daughter, remained at the Glens Falls house nursing Helen while her strength ebbed away. Burdened with work and sick with grief, Hughes lived alone in the family's New York apartment at 32 East 64th Street. Every Saturday he went to Glens Falls, always returning on Sunday night with his crushing weight of sorrow heavier than before.

In late winter Dr. Howk informed the grief-stricken parents that there was no hope for Helen. The depth of Mrs. Hughes' suffering may well be imagined from the following paragraph of a letter she wrote to her husband on February 10, 1920:

Oh the pathos of it! I have never struggled with myself more desperately than I have this week, with the result that I have kept up through the day, but the nights have been hideous. I thought after all that we went through last summer I was prepared for anything but I was not prepared for the definiteness of Dr. Howk's statements. My imagination ran riot and the many practical matters with their complications nearly drove me mad.

Hughes carried the letter into his son's room at their law offices and wept like a child. It was the first time that Charles Junior had ever seen grief break

[2] CEH, Notes, p. 251.

down his father's self-control. Some weeks later Helen died at the untimely age of twenty-eight.

A beautiful memorial chapel bearing her name was erected at Silver Bay, Lake George, whence she had gone to her last YWCA conference. Through the subsequent decades her father still spoke of her with a quaver in his voice. Her passing "in the fullness of her young womanhood—a victim of devoted services—" still seemed to him "the saddest of life's ironies." [3] It left a wound that never healed.

When friends pressed him to "run again" in 1920, the wound was fresh and painful. In February he asked a group of admirers in Nebraska to withhold his name from the primaries. Will Hays, chairman of the Republican National Committee, put out a feeler to see if Hughes would act as temporary chairman at the national convention and deliver the keynote address. Senator Johnson frowned upon this idea when the National Committee met, but Hughes had previously dismissed the suggestion as soon as it had been made. With no dominant candidate in the race, he was fearful that if he made the kind of speech the situation demanded a draft-Hughes movement might sweep the convention.

Some of the kingmakers were not satisfied. Shortly before the convention opened, a conclave including Senators Lodge, Wadsworth, and Calder met in Washington and decided that, after initial honorary votes had been cast for favorite sons, their influence would be thrown behind the nomination of Hughes. Senator Calder asked Meier Steinbrink to sound out the prospective candidate.

"I'm going to ask you to do me a favor," Steinbrink began when he and Hughes were ensconced in a private dining nook at the Lawyers' Club. "Don't interrupt me until I have finished what is on my mind."

"Steinbrink," Hughes replied solemnly, "there is no subject that you can't talk about with me."

The younger lawyer told his story, concluding, "These Senators want to be able to vote for you as their presidential candidate."

Hughes' eyes filled with tears. "I beg of you to believe me," he said. "Since our daughter died, Mrs. Hughes and I are heartbroken. I don't want to be President of the United States. I request that my name be not even mentioned in the convention." [4]

"Whoever is nominated will be elected," Hughes predicted before the lunch was over, "but in my opinion he will not fill out the term." Doubtless he was thinking about the shattered man in the White House and the accumulation of postwar dilemmas that Wilson would leave to his successor, but the remark was to prove prophetic.

[3] *Ibid.*   [4] Author's interview with Judge Steinbrink, July 24, 1947.

In conformity with Hughes' request his name was kept entirely out of the convention, and the New York vote went to President Butler of Columbia University. The Republican hierarchy in the smoke-filled room at Chicago took a long shot on Warren G. Harding without any advice whatever from the candidate of 1916. When he wired Harding after the convention, it was a routine congratulation from a former candidate who had no thought of ever returning to public life.

"I am just coming to the realization of the responsibilities which I have assumed," Harding replied. ". . . if I were undertaking the task in a reliance upon myself alone, I should not make the venture. . . . I very much wish your cooperation, your counsel, your advice and your assistance." [5] Late in August, when Hughes went to St. Louis to address the American Bar Association, he stopped over at Marion and briefly shared the spotlight of the "front porch" campaign with Al Jolson and the Harding and Coolidge Theatrical League. This was the second time he had met Harding, the first time having been the notification ceremony of 1916.

On leaving Marion the next day, Hughes issued a statement praising Harding and expressing the belief that his election would "afford the surest way of securing our proper relation to international cooperation." [6] The election of Harding, he implied, would mean United States adherence to a world court and the League of Nations without Article X. Harding had approved the statement and was obviously delighted to have Hughes' support. The candidate's pro-League attitude in his talk with Hughes was watered down in some of the speeches that George Harvey was writing for him, but, hoping for the best, Hughes took an active part in the campaign. In any event, the alternative to Harding was James M. Cox, the Democratic nominee, who was committed to Wilson's uncompromising stand. In that course Hughes could see neither reason nor hope. For even if Cox could have swept the country, he would have had no chance of getting the treaty through the Senate without reservations.

In October, Root initiated the statement of thirty-one distinguished Republicans who were eager to see the United States "do her full part in association with other civilized nations to prevent war." Hughes signed it in good faith, along with Hoover, Wickersham, Henry W. Taft, Stimson, Lowell, Butler, and William Allen White. They concluded that the "true course to bring America into an effective league to preserve the peace" was frankly to call upon other nations to agree to changes in Article X. "For this course," they said, "we can look only to the Republican Party and its candidate." [7]

The smashing victory of Harding and Coolidge followed. Wilson had called

[5] Harding to CEH, June 15, 1920. [6] *New York Times*, Aug. 26, 1920.
[7] *Washington Post*, Oct. 15, 1920.

for a solemn referendum on his treaty. Here was the answer. In retrospect it is difficult to tell whether Wilson or Harding was the more bewildered by the avalanche of "noes."

Harding's bewilderment sprang out of his own unfitness to be President and his lack of a national program. Few men seem big enough for the Presidency before they take over the office; Harding seemed only knee-high to it. A small-city editor who had ridden a streak of good fortune to the Senate, the President-elect had hoisted himself chiefly by his knowledge of politics, his affability, his old-fashioned oratory, and his skill in effecting compromises. His dislike for controversy had saved him from making enemies, and his follow-the-leader tactics had aroused among his cronies in the Senate hopes that the Marionite might serve them as a marionette. Senator Brandegee had frankly described Harding as "the best of the second raters." Even that could be said only because his inability to say No had not been tested under the merciless pressures of the Presidency.

Conscious of his own meager knowledge of economics, government, and world affairs, Harding sought to minimize his oppressive burden by assembling a Cabinet of the best minds in the country. At least that was his announced intention, although many posts went to his cronies. One Republican bigwig was so concerned over the prospect of Harding's Cabinet being filled with no-account politicians that he sent Everett Colby to ask Hughes if he would agree with various other high standing men in the party not to accept appointment unless all were invited to serve. Hughes replied, with his customary reluctance to pass judgment on other men, that it was not his business to dictate to the President-elect.[8]

While Harding was in Texas trying to dispel his misgivings in unpresidential hilarity, he asked Hughes to confer with him, after his return to Marion, on "the problem we have to solve in dealing with our new world relationship." [9] Hughes kept an appointment on December 10, expecting only to discuss the legacy of chaos in foreign relations that the old administration was passing on to the new. The outcome of the conference was a request that he head the Harding Cabinet as Secretary of State.

Senator Albert B. Fall once claimed that Harding first offered him the position of Secretary of State. Certainly Fall was seeking that appointment, but Harry Daugherty, who was playing Mark Hanna to Harding's McKinley, scouts the idea that his chief had any serious thought of Fall for the State Department, and Harding told Hughes that he had not offered the position to anyone else. Apparently Harding was sincerely eager to carry out his "best

[8] Everett Colby in *Scribner's*, May, 1928, p. 565.
[9] Harding to CEH, Nov. 13, 1920.

minds" pledge so far as the State Department was concerned. "I have simply got to have Hughes in my Cabinet as Secretary of State," he had told a friend. "There is nobody else who is in the same class with him." [10]

For his part, Hughes found the idea of being Secretary of State very enticing. He promptly accepted the offer, subject only to consultation with his partners. When his final acceptance was given, the President-elect replied: "I am sure the country will be glad, and welcome your return to public service in that capacity. Of course, the proffer itself is the best evidence of my own confidence. . . . The big thing is that you will serve. It strengthens my faith, because I believe in you, and feel that the American people share my high opinion." [11]

Finding it difficult to complete his Cabinet, Harding let two months elapse before publicly announcing Hughes' acceptance. Meanwhile Washington buzzed with rumors coupled with senatorial hostility to the idea that the "whiskered Wilson" might become Secretary of State. Hughes' stand in favor of the League of Nations made him anathema to the Irreconcilables. Other Senators, inebriated with power, openly scorned the liberalism both of Hughes and of Hoover. Harding was urged to place at the head of his Cabinet some "amiable and colorless futility" who would not irritate the Senate. Boies Penrose haughtily asserted that it would make no difference who was Secretary of State; the Senate would control all matters of foreign policy anyway. Others urged the substitution of Root for Hughes. By January the anti-Hughes sentiment in the Foreign Relations Committee was said to have reached the proportions of a "revolt."

Always thin-skinned to criticism, Hughes flinched under this flailing of a decision that had already been made. Harding's procrastination in making the announcement was embarrassing also because the Secretary of State-to-be could give no reason for refusing to take numerous lawsuits that were pressed upon him. But Hughes made no complaint. On the contrary, he was full of deference and good feeling toward his new chief. At Harding's request, he urged Hoover to join the Cabinet. Hughes was no Salmon P. Chase. "I cannot conceive of any greater privilege, or higher duty," he wrote to Harding, "than to serve under your leadership in carrying out a sound Administration policy at this difficult time." [12]

Harding remained unmoved by the senatorial ranting. By letter he asked Hughes to visit him at St. Augustine, Florida, in February for a discussion of top officials in the State Department. Hughes spent most of the morning with the President-elect, and they were still together when Harding held his press conference. "I invited Mr. Hughes here," he said, "in order to offer him for-

[10] Rev. Mr. William F. McDowell to CEH, Sept. 3, 1923.
[11] Harding to CEH, Dec. 22, 1920.   [12] CEH to Harding, Dec. 25, 1920.

By Rollin Kirby in the New York *World*, February 21, 1921.

A MAN'S JOB

mally the portfolio of Secretary of State. I am very happy to say that he has agreed to accept."

The reporters seized upon the opportunity to ask the President-elect what his foreign policy would be. "You must ask Mr. Hughes about that," Harding replied. "That is going to be another policy of the next administration," he added, with a smile tilted at Wilson's domination over foreign affairs. "From the beginning the Secretary of State will speak for the State Department." [13] Obviously pleased by this candid delegation of control over foreign policy into his hands, Hughes would say nothing more than that he had regarded acceptance of Harding's offer as an "imperative obligation."

The President-elect's good will was overflowing, and he seemed to be genuinely desirous of keeping his administration on a high plane. Yet the atmosphere at St. Augustine was far from being auspicious. A horde of politicians and camp followers was hounding him for favors. Knowing her husband's inability to say No, Mrs. Harding told Hughes, "You've got to help Warren resist these demands." [14] But the head of the new Cabinet could not visualize his assignment as that of a special aide to keep the President out of trouble. He was "taking a new case for the people in foreign affairs," and it was obvious from the beginning that this would absorb his entire energy.

The selection of Hughes brought widespread applause and some carping here and there. "If the nation believed that all the Cabinet appointments were to be of similar calibre," asserted the *New York Times*, "it would thank God and take courage." [15] "Mr. Hughes' name is luminous throughout the country," said the Baltimore *Sun*. "No public man has set higher standards of public service," observed the New York *Evening Mail*. "Intelligence, courage, and experience," concluded the *Evening Post,* "predestine Mr. Hughes for a place with the best who have held that office." "Une belle intelligence," wrote Stéphane Lauzanne in *Le Matin* of Paris. "Un homme de droit et de droiture." [16] A digest of fifty-nine editorials, most of them in Democratic papers, showed almost unanimous approval.

In the Senate there was much grumbling but no rebellion. "Hughes won't last thirty days," one Irreconcilable forecast. But Harding's cronies in the Senate were not yet ready to fight. On the day of his inauguration the President presented the names of his Cabinet to the Senate in person, and they were unanimously confirmed. The following day Hughes took the oath of office from Mr. Justice Day in a simple ceremony attended by the retiring Secretary of State, Bainbridge Colby, Undersecretary Norman H. Davis, Undersecretary-to-be Henry P. Fletcher, Mrs. Hughes, Mr. and Mrs. Charles E. Hughes, Jr., and their two children.

[13] *New York Times,* Feb. 20, 1921.   [14] Author's interview with CEH, Nov. 19, 1946.
[15] Feb. 21, 1921.   [16] Clippings in the Hughes Papers, Library of Congress.

The new Secretary established himself in the large rectangular room on the second floor of the bizarre structure just west of the White House then known as the State, War, and Navy Building. It was a pleasant room with south windows affording a view across the Mall to the Washington Monument, with the portraits of many great Americans looking down from the walls, and with a huge mirror crowned by the coat of arms of the United States over the stone-faced fireplace. Here John Hay and Elihu Root had done their most distinguished work. Here also was the spirit of the great Secretaries of State of earlier days—John Quincy Adams and Webster as well as Jefferson, Madison, and Monroe. Hughes found a deep satisfaction in joining the select company of men who have directed the United States' foreign policy. It was good to be back in the public service. He plunged into his work with enthusiasm—in spite of the wound that would never heal.